# "If the Other Guy Isn't Jack Nicholson, I've Got the Part"

# "If the Other Guy Isn't Jack Nicholson, I've Got the Part"

## Hollywood Tales of Big Breaks, Bad Luck, and Box-Office Magic

### RON BASE

CB

CONTEMPORARY
BOOKS

CHICAGO

**Library of Congress Cataloging-in-Publication Data**

Base, Ron.
    "If the other guy isn't Jack Nicholson, I've got the part" :
Hollywood tales of big breaks, bad luck, and box-office magic / Ron
Base.
          p.    cm.
    ISBN 0-8092-3528-5
    1. Motion pictures—United States—Casting.    2. Motion picture
actors and actresses—United States.    I. Title.
PN1995.9.C34B34    1994
791.43′028—dc20                              94-20814
                                                    CIP

Published in Canada with the title *Starring Roles*
by Stoddart Publishing Co. Limited, 1994.

Copyright © 1994 by Marquee Publishing
All rights reserved
Published by Contemporary Books, Inc.
Two Prudential Plaza, Chicago, Illinois 60601-6790
Manufactured in the United States of America
International Standard Book Number: 0-8092-3528-5
10   9   8   7   6   5   4   3   2   1

*There was a boy who grew
up in a small town.
Each night when he went to sleep,
he dreamed of the movies.
He never stopped dreaming.
This book is dedicated to him.*

# ACKNOWLEDGMENTS

T RACKING THE HISTORY OF MOVIE STARDOM THROUGH THE SOUND era proved to be a massive undertaking that included, where possible, firsthand interviews with producers, directors, writers, and stars. It also involved a great amount of research, piecing together existing biography and journalism on the subject to form what is hopefully a unique insight into the dramas surrounding the winning and losing of movie stardom. It could not have been completed without the assistance and advice of a diverse number of people, a great many of whom went to extraordinary lengths to help simply because the subject of the book intrigued them. I was often astonished by the generosity of just about everyone with whom I came in contact. They made the writing of this book an unexpected joy.

Particular mention should be made of the staff at the Margaret Herrick Library of the Academy of Motion Picture Arts and Sciences in Beverly Hills, where the majority of the research for this book was conducted. The most exhaustive collection of books, periodicals, and clippings pertaining to the movies ever put under one roof is gathered here. Everyone was endlessly patient and helpful in the face of my almost daily requests and demands over a two-year period. I would also like to thank Stuart Ng and Ned Comstock at the School of Cinema-Television at the University of Southern California where the Warner Bros. archives are housed. The Warner studio insisted that everything be written down, and thankfully just about everything was, on specially printed memo pads, each page emblazoned with the reminder: "Verbal messages cause misunderstandings and delays." At USC, the voluminous records of a long-gone studio era were cheerfully opened for inspection to an appreciative film buff dazzled by such proximity to movie history. One had the eerie feeling going through these files, complete with handwritten notations in the margins, that Jack Warner had just left the room and would return momentarily. I also made use of the research facilities at the Beverly Hills Library as well as the Metropolitan Toronto Reference Library.

This book could not have been written without the help of freelance journalist Craig Modderno, who did interviews, introduced me around Hollywood, and made available material he had collected over the past 20 years. He also provided endless reminiscences and editorial advice. Likewise, Ray Bennett, one of my oldest and closest friends and a tremendously talented journalist, came to my aid, not only with interviews but also with extensive research. Charles Fleming, formerly a reporter for *Variety* and now a *Newsweek* correspondent, was so extraordinarily kind and generous with his contacts and his knowledge that I hardly know where to begin to thank him.

In New York, journalists Stephen Schaefer and Donald Chase not only did interviews for the book, but also provided endless insights and advice. In Toronto, Jack Gardner made a large number of suggestions that vastly improved the manuscript, while Alexandra Lenhoff, as she has so diligently in the past, managed the production process. David Haslam, my partner and co-author in *The Movies of the Eighties*, not only provided the interim financing and the infrastructure that made this book possible, but combed various archives in search of the photographs that accompany the text. I am particularly indebted to Bill Hanna of Stoddart Publishing of Toronto for his endless enthusiasm. And of course there is Alan Samson of Little, Brown in London, good friend and movie lover extraordinaire, who got me started on this whole subject sitting around his office one afternoon two and a half years ago.

Thanks for their time and their input into the manuscript also go to Tony Bill, Martin Bregman, David Brown, Jerry Bruckheimer, Dick Clayton, Geena Davis, Dick Delson, Al Ebner, Prudence Emery, Robert Evans, Mike Fenton, Albert Finney, Michael J. Fox, Doug Galloway, Carl Gottlieb, Goldie Hawn, Buck Henry, Earle Jolson, Arnold Kopelson, Martin Kove, Paul Lynch, Adrian Lyne, Alan Markfield, Bart and Nancy Mills, Gregory Peck, Zak Penn, Steve Roth, Paul Schiff, Judi Schwam, Arnold Schwarzenegger, Henry Sera, Don Simpson, Joan Singleton, Sylvester Stallone, Venicia Stephenson, Eric Stoltz, Lawrence Turman, Lewis Yablonsky, and Robert Wise.

# CONTENTS

# INTRODUCTION

O
N THE NIGHT OF 9 APRIL 1984 BURT REYNOLDS, THEN THE MOST
popular movie star in the world, sat in his trailer on the set of
*City Heat* watching stardom slip from his grasp. With him was
his *City Heat* co-star Clint Eastwood and his longtime manager,
Dick Clayton. The three men huddled around a television set as, live from the
Dorothy Chandler Pavilion, the 57th annual Academy Awards were presented.
Among the nominees was Jack Nicholson, for his portrayal of the flamboyant
former astronaut Garrett Breedlove in *Terms of Endearment*. Burt Reynolds knew
all about that role. It was a part he was supposed to have played — the part that
James L. Brooks, the director who had fashioned the screenplay from Larry
McMurtry's novel, created with him in mind. The two had worked together in
a dramatic comedy titled *Starting Over* in 1979, one of Reynolds' few critically
applauded movies, and Brooks was anxious to continue the relationship.

"It's not a huge part," Brooks had said to Clayton over the phone two
years earlier, "but I think it's perfect for Burt."

Clayton read the script and liked it tremendously. He urged Reynolds
to do it, believing *Terms* could have the same beneficial effect on his career that
the movie *Deliverance* had had 10 years before. Clayton had known Reynolds
since he was a television actor during the '60s and had fought to establish him
in movies, capitalizing on his relationship with director John Boorman in
order to propel Reynolds into *Deliverance*, the movie that turned him into a
household name. Clayton also pushed hard for his client in *One Flew Over the
Cuckoo's Nest*, and he almost succeeded in getting him the role — but director
Milos Forman could not be dissuaded from his intention to have Jack
Nicholson.

At first, Reynolds was disposed to do *Terms of Endearment*. Then came the curse of movie stardom, the second thought. When you are a star there are many whispers in the dark, and some of those whispers held that a new Blake Edwards movie, *The Man Who Loved Women*, was the preferable script. What was *Terms of Endearment*, after all, but a supporting role? *The Man Who Loved Women* — a ladies' man consigned to the analyst's couch by his obsession with beautiful women — had Oscar written all over it.

Clayton disagreed, and had already telephoned Edwards twice in London to say so. But Reynolds changed his mind. He would not do *Terms* after all. Instead, his star presence would grace *The Man Who Loved Women*. "He wasn't thinking straight," was all Clayton would say much later about the incident. "There is a lot of pressure when you get to be where Burt was. They get scared; they're there, and they got to figure out how to stay there."

And so, as Burt Reynolds sat watching in his trailer that night in April, *Terms of Endearment* won five Academy Awards — Oscars for best picture as well as best director and screenplay. The best actress award went to Shirley MacLaine, and Jack Nicholson was named best supporting actor.

Inside the Dorothy Chandler Pavilion, a half hour into the show, Nicholson rose to accept his award. He wore dark glasses and that cocky smirk that suggested he had successfully hustled the world. "All you rock people down at the Roxy, and up in the Rockies, rock on," Nicholson admonished with a grin. Clayton looked over at Reynolds. He never took his eyes off the set, never blinked. And he never said a word.[a]

*The Man Who Loved Women* was released the same year as *Terms of Endearment*. It was both a critical and commercial flop. Reynolds followed it with *Stroker Ace*, yet another good ol' boy auto-racing movie, the sort of thing on which he had built a worldwide constituency over the past decade.

---

[a] When he would talk about it at all, Reynolds later claimed that the movie he chose over *Terms of Endearment* was *Stroker Ace*. "God no!" says a horrified Dick Clayton when asked about this. "It was bad enough that he did *The Man Who Loved Women* instead." Reynolds told Craig Modderno during an interview with the *Los Angeles Times* 4 January 1987: "When it came time to choose between *Terms* and *Stroker,* I chose the latter because I felt I owed [director] Hal [Needham] more than I did Jim. Nobody told me I probably could have done *Terms* and Universal would have waited until I was finished before making *Stroker.*"

This time, however, the public was not buying. *Stroker Ace* failed badly in the summer of 1984, and almost overnight, Reynolds' awesome box-office clout evaporated.

In retrospect, turning down *Terms of Endearment* all but spelled the end of Reynolds as a movie star. He continued to make pictures, but each seemed worse than the last, and each was ignored by the public. By the 1990s, the actor who had begun the decade as the world's number one box-office star was back where he started: in television. "What happened broke my heart," said Dick Clayton. "He could have had a career like Jack Nicholson's."

But he did not, and therein lies the story of what is to follow. This book is about movie stardom, who got it, and who did not; how it was won, and how it got lost. It is about the manner in which various actors and actresses chose and rejected roles, and how those choices shaped not only their careers, but also the destiny of movies in the sound era.

Film stardom is an incredibly potent and envied force, and the dramas surrounding its arrival — and very often, abrupt departure — can be even more dramatic than the creation of the movies themselves. Accident and stupidity both play large parts, as do greed and cunning, and plain old-fashioned luck. Indeed, it really does help, as most actors will be only too glad to tell you, to be in the right place at the right time. The laws of physics, Greek mythology, and movie stardom are remarkably similar, each action demanding the creation of its own immutable reaction. If George Raft had not turned down every script Warner Bros. offered him, it is doubtful that Humphrey Bogart would have become a star. As for Shirley Temple, had she been allowed to do *The Wizard of Oz*, Judy Garland might have remained a minor player lost in the crowd at MGM's vast stable of beauty and perfection.

Similarly, if Marlon Brando had not come along at precisely the time in the 1950s when the studio system was breaking up and the way was open to a different kind of actor for the first time since the introduction of sound, it is questionable whether James Dean, Paul Newman, or Steve McQueen could ever have become successes. And had the tragic death of James Dean not occurred, Paul Newman might not have amounted to anything in Hollywood. Without Steve McQueen's jealousy of Paul Newman's success, Robert Redford might well have remained a blandly undistinguished leading man. For that matter, if Warren Beatty had not helpfully stepped out of Redford's way on more than one occasion, there would be a much different Sundance Kid and another billionaire in *Indecent Proposal*. Either Geena Davis or Michelle Pfeiffer could have decided to do *Basic Instinct,* and Sharon Stone would have remained a minor B-movie actress with long legs and a tart tongue. Alec Baldwin twice ran afoul of Harrison Ford, and because he did, he remained a respected leading man, but has not become a major box-office star.

Movies are the mythology of the 20th century, their stars the gods we worship. We seldom consider how the gods arrived in the movie heavens, and the gods themselves state over and over to an adoring press only too anxious to reinforce the mythology that they had no wish to be in the firmament, but simply woke one day to find themselves there. And could one god ever be substituted for another? *Impossible.*

Nothing could be further from the truth, of course.

The competition for movie stardom has been marked as much by pathos and heartbreak as fortune and triumph. No one in these pages wanted anything but stardom, despite all the protests you will hear to the contrary. Some were more ambivalent than others, but not much more. The attaining of movie stardom remains such a difficult, soul-rattling pursuit that, above all, the pursuer must be dedicated. What follows will often have little to do with talent, although it has seldom hurt. It has much more to do with the accident of timing and the innate ability to say yes when everyone else around you is yelling no. If there is a moral to this story, it is that the actor who says yes stands a chance of becoming a movie star. The actors who said no find themselves miserably at the sidelines of this book.

The individuals in these pages occasionally had immortality handed to them, and occasionally they took it, albeit grumbling, as did Clark Gable. Sometimes, when the opportunity presented itself, they ruthlessly snatched immortality from someone else the way Al Jolson did it. Every so often, it was simply given away out of laziness or stupidity or a combination of both. George Raft certainly falls into that category, as do Marlon Brando, Burt Reynolds, and John Travolta.

If the fates had conspired differently, some casting choices would have approached a delirious madness. Gary Cooper came much closer to playing Rhett Butler than you would ever think. George Raft was three days away from *The Maltese Falcon*. MGM would have gladly had Rock Hudson as Ben-

Hur. If the producers had had their way, Cary Grant would have been a 60ish James Bond, Burt Reynolds could have played Superman and John Travolta, Rambo, while Sylvester Stallone might have been the Beverly Hills Cop. Luckily, cooler heads prevailed — or sometimes, regrettably, they did not. It is all so subjective, this conjuring of one actor rather than another in a role, but even so, the casting misses sometimes leave you salivating at the thought of what could have been.

Suppose Vivien Leigh had played opposite her lover, Laurence Olivier, in *Wuthering Heights* instead of dull Merle Oberon? Or as the heroine in *Rebecca* rather than the febrile, mannered Joan Fontaine? How much better a movie *West Side Story* might have been with Warren Beatty as Tony, rather than the milquetoast Richard Beymer. What if Sterling Hayden had portrayed Quint in *Jaws* instead of that bombastic chewer of scenery, Robert Shaw? And Steve McQueen would have brought the star presence to Willard in *Apocalypse Now* that Martin Sheen, good as he was, lacked, not to mention what Kurtz would have been like with Jack Nicholson rather than the tubby Brando. Perhaps if the world truly unfolded as it should, there would be two versions of all the great films, so that we could see what Errol Flynn and Bette Davis would have been like in *Gone With the Wind,* or Laurence Olivier and Humphrey Bogart together in *The Bridge on the River Kwai,* or Robert Redford in *The Graduate*. Or perhaps not. Whatever else those movies might have been, they would have been different, and being different might have robbed them of the one thing they all share — greatness.

The fantasy casting choices that can be woven out of these histories are endless. But this, finally, is not a book of fantasy but of choices, and how they were made, and the movie stars we ended up with because of them. None of this has much to do with anything real, of course. The greatest gunfighter on the movie screen was not a gunfighter at all; the men and women who led the charges, saved the day, and lived happily ever after were all pretending. Or were they? That uncertainty, suspended in the darkness, is what captures our imaginations, keeps us coming back to the movies, and somehow believing, against all rational impulse, in movie stars. The triumph of pretending, the sustaining of uncertainty, and the faith in those shifting fluid images erupting out of the darkness inform this book. It is dedicated to the people who brought off those illusions better than anyone else.

# PART I

The Contract Players

# 1

# "GO BACK TO SLEEP, GEORGIE."

*The stolen immortality of George Jessel*

I N 1980, NEAR THE END OF HIS LIFE, HIS HAIRPIECE ILL-FITTING AND funny, his jowls sagging, the bags beneath his eyes deep and abiding, George Jessel was asked in an interview about his old friend and nemesis, Al Jolson. These were the questions Jessel had been asked thousands of times about "Jolie": where he met him (San Francisco in 1912); what he was like (an egomaniac); and where he stood in the show-business pantheon (the greatest entertainer).

Jessel was 82, and on 24 May 1981 he would be dead. He tended to ramble and lose the thread of the interviewer's questions. But like many of the old troupers who had been around forever and done everything, he could still remember all the names and every date. During the questions and answers, Jessel tried to add something that the interviewer might not have known. He tried to talk about *The Jazz Singer*, and how he had originated that role on Broadway, and how Jolson had done it in the movies because Warner Bros. was short of money, and Jolie had lots of it, and was willing to put up some of it. The interviewer listened abstractedly, then slipped to the next question. He couldn't have cared less. The moment passed. Jessel answered all the other inquiries about Jolie by rote. As usual, he did not show how much he hated Jolie — and loved him, too. He said nothing about how Jolie had stolen the role of his life, how it had hurt, and how it gnawed at him for more than 50 years. Jessel knew as soon as it happened that he had lost the most important role of his life and missed his chance at immortality.

The questions now were always about Al Jolson. Jolson was the legend, not Jessel. Jolson was the world's greatest entertainer, not Jessel. The questions had nothing to do with Jessel's long life and career as a singer, vaudeville performer, movie star, producer, and raconteur. Nobody wanted to know about the four wives, the young showgirls who got him into so much trouble. As fascinating as it was, his life had been overshadowed by Al Jolson. Jolie would be remembered as the star of the first talking picture. Jessel would hardly be remembered at all. If he was mentioned, it was in the context of a minor national joke — America's "Toastmaster General," they called him now. A funny old man in a toupee who wore a uniform festooned with medals and told old jokes at testimonial dinners for dying show-biz veterans. It should not have been. It should not have happened the way it did. But the fates somehow conspired against Jessel, and favored Jolson. Jessel could never get over it.

G EORGE JESSEL ORIGINALLY FOUND *THE JAZZ SINGER*. OR PERHAPS IT would be more accurate to say *The Jazz Singer* found him. In the mid-1920s, the two most important Broadway producers were Al Lewis and Max Gordon. They sat down with Jessel in the summer of 1925 to discuss a script titled *Day of Atonement*, written by a young playwright named Samson Raphaelson. Jessel had never actually appeared in a legitimate play, but Lewis thought he might be right for the part of a cantor's son torn between his duty to his Jewish religion and his love of show business.

Jessel immediately identified with the material, although there was certainly no such conflict in his own life. If there had been, show business certainly would have won. His father was a producer, playwright, and manager who had married Jessel's mother, an errand girl 30 years his junior. Jessel's father did not want him to be an actor, but he died when Georgie, as everyone called him, was only 11. Daddy was no sooner in the ground than his son quit school and started to sing at a Harlem picture theater for five dollars a week. He caught the attention of a promoter named Gus Edwards, and soon Jessel was performing with the juvenile Walter Winchell (who would become much better known as a gravel-voiced Broadway newspaper columnist) and Eddie Cantor, a close friend for the span of his life. Jessel later told various stories about how he was able to perform so young. Depending on his mood, he would say that he stole his brother's birth certificate or alternately that he used a midget's birth certificate. In order to add to the impression of maturity, Jessel swaggered around with an unlit cigar.

By the time he met with Al Lewis and Max Gordon about *Day of Atonement*, Jessel, at 27, had gained some renown as a monologuist and vaudeville performer. He was best known for a sentimental bit that featured him talking to his mother on the telephone.

After some discussion about the merits of *Day of Atonement*, Jessel met with the young playwright, Samson Raphaelson, and decided he did not like him. "He didn't want his brainchild touched," Jessel remembered later. Nonetheless, Raphaelson worked with Al Lewis and Jessel, and, after six weeks, they emerged with what was now titled *The Jazz Singer*. In the story, a cantor's son runs away from his strict Jewish upbringing and becomes famous as a blackface singer. At the end of the play, he rejects the glitter of show business and returns to his roots, singing "Kol Nidre" — "Day of Atonement" — as his beloved father lies dying.

The play tried out in Stamford, Connecticut, before moving to New York, where it opened Thursday 9 September 1925. The New York critics hated the play, but the public loved it. On opening night, after the performance, Jessel stepped out to thank the audience. "I'm glad you enjoyed my little play," he said, forgetting that Raphaelson might have had something to do with it. But someone in the audience remembered. A voice called out, "Author! Author!" and everyone took up the chant. Jessel announced that the author could not be located, and the curtain was quickly lowered.

What Jessel did not know — what he may never have known — was that the owner of that voice in the audience was Al Jolson, and he was already plotting how he could get his hands on *The Jazz Singer*.

EDDIE CANTOR HAD BEEN RESPONSIBLE FOR THE FIRST MEETING BETWEEN George Jessel and Al Jolson in San Francisco back in 1912. Jessel forgot many things over the years, but that was a date he *never* forgot. Jolson had been a star for about two years when he arrived at the Orpheum Theater after hearing that this kid named Cantor did a great impression of him. Jessel later claimed Jolson so hated anyone else getting applause that he would turn on the faucet in his dressing room to drown out the sound. However, he was sufficiently impressed with Cantor to take him and his pal Georgie Jessel out to dinner that night. Cantor was a very religious Jewish kid, and insisted on a kosher restaurant. Jolson was glad to oblige.

There is nothing surviving today, not his recordings or early TV appearances, certainly not his movies or even the two films that were made of his life, that provides a contemporary audience with a real sense of just how big a star Al Jolson was in his day. "Jolson was the icon of the first half of the twentieth century," says Doug Galloway, a *Variety* reporter who has spent years studying the life and career of Al Jolson. "He was a superstar at a time when they didn't even know what the word was. Today, he is seen as a caricature, this minstrel in blackface, singing old-fashioned songs. But at the time, he was singing cutting-edge, contemporary music, and no one could touch him."

Jolson was born Asa Yoelson in Srednike, Lithuania, in 1886. In America his father became a cantor in a synagogue, and it was there that Jolson began singing. He went on to work in a circus and began making a name for himself. But it was when he joined the Lou Dockstader Minstrels that his career truly took off. The Dockstader singers, like other minstrel shows, entertained their audiences by sending up the lifestyles, songs, and traditions of the black experience in America. The whole concept of white men performing in blackface seems alien and even repugnant today — witness the controversy in the wake of Ted Danson's appearing in blackface in 1993 at a Friar's Club roast for Whoopi Goldberg. It is now hard to believe that for a hundred years or so, this was a phenomenally popular form of entertainment among working-class audiences who delighted in the sense of superiority that came from making fun of blacks.

Eventually, minstrel shows parodied just about everything: the wealthy Establishment, city folks, political corruption, even America's obsession with westward expansion. Eric Lott, in his book *Love and Theft: Blackface Minstrelsy and the American Working Class*, argues that minstrel shows were the precursor to a variety of entertainment forms, from vaudeville to Elvis Presley when he emerged in the 1950s. Presley was merely another in a long line of white men who successfully exploited African-American culture. It is interesting that Al Jolson and Elvis Presley, two of the most popular performers of the 20th century, essentially attained their immense success after they began to imitate black men.

By the time Jolson joined the Dockstader singers, the tradition of blackface was on the decline, but it was still popular, and it was how Jolson maintained his stardom for most of his career. In vaudeville and then on Broadway, he was never out of blackface.

Even Jessel was willing to concede that there had never been a performer quite like Jolson. Most Jewish players of that time wore beards and dark, ill-fitting suits, and told pity jokes. Not Jolson. He bounced on stage all power and authority with that huge baritone voice. "Like a Georgian prince," is the way Jessel described him. In those days, performers did not use microphones. Jolson did not need one — or a show — or a joke. Jessel remembered how Jolie would switch the punchlines of his jokes around, but the audience would laugh anyway.

"When Jolson was on Broadway, he would stop in the middle of a show, and say, 'Do you want to see the rest of the show or do you want to hear me?'" says Doug Galloway. "And that would be it. He'd just dismiss the cast and do a concert. That was one of the reasons people went to see him. They wanted that to happen."

In an era when movies were still in their infancy and entertainment options were few, Jolson was king. In addition to his live performances, songs such as "My Mammy" and "Rockabye Your Baby" made him America's number one recording artist. For the first time, the public was not buying a record because of the song, but because of the singer. Jolson had conquered everything except movies, and that was about to change.

SAMSON RAPHAELSON WAS A SENIOR AT THE UNIVERSITY OF ILLINOIS THE first time he saw Jolson perform at a theater in nearby Champaign, where he was appearing in one of his most famous revues, *Robinson Crusoe Jr.* Raphaelson heard Jolson perform popular numbers such as "Where the Black-Eyed Susans Grow," "Where Did Robinson Crusoe Go with Friday on Saturday Night," and "Yaaka Hula Hickey Doola." Jolson's exuberant, jazzy delivery transcended the trite silliness of the material he was performing and so impressed Raphaelson that the singer's life became the basis for one of his first short stories, "Day of Atonement," published in *Everybody's* magazine in January of 1922.

A couple of years later, Raphaelson, by this time a reporter at the *New York Times*, was introduced to Jolson at the Palais Royale by a friend, Peewee Byers, who played saxophone with the Paul Whiteman band. Jolson had read "Day of Atonement" and was interested in meeting its youthful author. The singer wanted to adapt the story into the kind of Shubert Winter Garden Theater musical in which he had become so popular. "I'll play in it," Jolson said. "I'll tell you what to do."

As much as he liked Jolson, Raphaelson had other ideas. He wanted to turn his story into a serious play, not a musical vehicle for Al Jolson. "Hell, I used to see those shows," Raphaelson said, "but I wouldn't be caught dead writing one."

Jolson, as evidenced by his appearance at *The Jazz Singer* on opening night, kept a close eye on the project. Jessel appears to have known none of this. He regarded *The Jazz Singer* as very much his child, not surprising since the show became the biggest success of his career. Despite downbeat reviews and predictions that it would not last two weeks, *The Jazz Singer* ran for a year and a half. People came back to see it again and again. Irving Berlin saw it six times. However, there had been no overtures from Hollywood about turning the play into a movie. Jessel suspected its Jewish theme might be too controversial for a mainstream audience.

Hollywood may well have been nervous about *The Jazz Singer*, but Harry Warner loved the show. From his New York offices, Harry oversaw the day-to-day operation of the Warner Bros. studio. The four Warner brothers — Harry, Jack, Sam, and Albert — got their start in the movie business in 1903 operating a nickelodeon in Newcastle, Pennsylvania. By 1923 they were Warner Bros., and by 1925 that included former independents Vitagraph and First National Pictures. Nonetheless, the company was stumbling uncertainly along and chronically short of cash. Something new and dramatic was needed if it was to survive. Even though Harry sneered at the idea, it was increasingly apparent that talking pictures could be the answer to the Warners' problems.

In 1926, Jessel and Jolson, as well as Eddie Cantor, were involved in experimental sound-on-disc recordings for a new company partially owned by Warner Bros. called Vitaphone. The show-business newspaper *Film Daily* commented on both the Jolson and Jessel performances. "They made an instantaneous impression on the audience," the paper said.

There seems to have been little interest in turning Jolson into a movie star, perhaps because the movies were silent, and if there was ever a performer who needed noise in order to survive, it was Jolie. D. W. Griffith had signed him to make a picture called *Mammy's Boy*, but it was never completed. Jessel was easier to deal with. The Warner brothers brought him out to Hollywood to do something called *Private Izzy Murphy,* about a Jewish boy who pretends to be Irish and goes off to World War I to become a hero before confessing his true religion. It was while doing *Izzy Murphy* that Harry Warner suggested to Jessel that it might be possible to do *The Jazz Singer* on film, employing the new Vitaphone sound-on-disc.

Jessel later said he brokered the deal that enabled cash-strapped Warner Bros. to purchase the rights to *The Jazz Singer* for $50,000, although little money changed hands. The purchase price was actually a series of notes payable as far in advance as 1928. A month later Jessel, who had been touring around the country with *The Jazz Singer*, embarked from New York on what promised to be a triumphant return to Hollywood. Mayor Jimmy Walker himself saw Jessel off at the train station. He was on his way west to the movies, fame, and fortune. Nothing could stop him. His future was assured.

Reaching Los Angeles, Jessel and his wife, Florence, checked into a bungalow at the Beverly Hills Hotel. When he awoke in the morning, he said later, he could hear hummingbirds singing. The birds did not sing for long, however. He had already fought with Harry Warner over his contract before leaving New York. Jessel felt that if *The Jazz Singer* was to be done with sound, he should get more money. This did not go down well with the penny-pinching Harry, but Jack Warner assured Jessel that everything would be settled once he got out to Hollywood, and he was relieved when three checks arrived, each for $2,500, the money owed for the short sound films he had done for Vitaphone.

At the Beverly Hills Hotel, amidst the singing birds, the *Jazz Singer* script arrived, and Jessel sat down to read it. "My first look at the scenario threw me into a state of shock, almost apoplexy," he reported.

The ending had been totally reversed. "Instead of the boy leaving the theater and following the tradition of his father by singing in the synagogue, as in the play, the scenario had him return to the Winter Garden Theater as a black-faced comedian with his mother applauding wildly from a boxed seat."

"Black-faced comedian?" That sounded suspiciously like Al Jolson. As he finished the script, Jessel for the first time began to get nervous and suspect that Jolson was at work behind the scenes — and that he was responsible for the changes in the play. It was, after all, the sort of ending that would have been perfect for an Al Jolson musical at the Winter Garden.

That same day, Jessel got a call from New York. The three $2,500 checks Warner Bros. had paid him had all bounced. Jessel was beside himself. He demanded his *Jazz Singer* fee up front, and at the same time, he wanted the studio to make good on the $7,500.

Jessel was still angry when he went to visit Al Jolson, who was appearing in town at the Biltmore Theater. Perhaps he was drawn by his nagging suspicions about *The Jazz Singer*. Over dinner at the Biltmore Rendezvous, Jessel poured out his troubles, but, whatever his misgivings about Jolson, he apparently did not express them. Jolson for his part was sympathetic, although Jessel got the impression — as he always did with the singer — that Jolson couldn't really care less.

By the time the two men finished dinner, it was late. Jolson suggested that Jessel spend the night in his suite, and Jessel agreed. When he awoke early the next morning, he found Jolson getting ready to leave. "Go back to sleep, Georgie," Jolson said with a grin. "I'm going to play golf. I'll see ya later."

Jessel would not see Jolson again for a long time. A few hours after Jolson left, supposedly for the golf course, Jessel picked up the *Los Angeles Times*. There he discovered that his pal had been signed the previous day to star in the Warner Bros. movie of *The Jazz Singer*. All through dinner, while Jessel talked at length, Al Jolson had known that Jessel was not going to be in the picture he had his heart set on doing. But Jolie had not said a word.

THE NIGHT *THE JAZZ SINGER* OPENED AT THE WARNER THEATER IN New York — 6 October 1927 — is set into history. It forever changed movies, and Hollywood, when Jolson said, "Wait a minute, wait a minute. You ain't heard nothing yet, folks! Listen to this!"

Doris Warner Vidor, the wife of director Charles Vidor, was the only member of the Warner family in the audience (the brothers were attending to the funeral arrangements for Sam Warner, who had died the day before the opening). She later remembered the audience applauding each time Jolson sang — unheard of in a movie theater at that time. When Jolson spontaneously uttered the first words ever spoken in a movie, the patrons, she recalled, became hysterical. Jolson was in tears as he took a bow at the conclusion of the movie.

Although sound was not yet synchronized throughout, as it later would be, the moving pictures could talk, and within months the silent cinema was no more. The speed of the revolution was astounding. Every studio in town now rushed to get sound movies into production. *The Jazz Singer* transformed Warner Bros. from a tiny, financially strapped production company into a major Hollywood studio. Jolson was at his peak when *The Jazz Singer* was released, the biggest star on Broadway as well as America's foremost recording star. Now he had also made movie history, and *The Jazz Singer* made him into a legend. He would *forever* be the first actor who ever talked on a movie screen.[1]

The popularity of *The Jazz Singer* almost immediately killed off Jessel's stage version of the show. On the last night, a saddened Jessel stepped out in front of the meager audience and delivered a farewell speech, "berating what had been done to me by Hollywood and Jolie in particular."

Jessel did not speak to Jolson for a year. That he ever spoke to him again was amazing. Jessel was convinced that Jolson had connived behind his back from the beginning to steal *The Jazz Singer* away. The only reason the Warner brothers had even allowed him to come out to Hollywood, he concluded, was because they did not want him to be in New York when those checks bounced.

When Jolson and Jessel finally did confront one another, Jolson said to him, "I had to play the role because it was the story of my life." Jessel, still furious, would not buy that for a moment: "That was as true as Jolie being at the crossing of the Delaware." But it *was* true. As Raphaelson had maintained from the beginning, *The Jazz Singer* was, indeed, the story of Jolson's life.

IN THE END, JOLSON GOT *THE JAZZ SINGER*, IN PART BECAUSE OF HIS tremendous popularity, and in part because he had a lot more money than anyone else. The deal he secretly negotiated with the Warners, even as Jessel headed for Los Angeles by train, called for Jolson in effect to co-finance *The Jazz Singer*'s production. Morris Safier, a Warner relative, got Jolson to agree to put up $80,000 in cash in order to get the film off the ground. All of this was done behind Jessel's back, of course.

Was Jolson capable of such underhandedness? Infinitely, maintained

[1] Samson Raphaelson was not at all impressed with what Hollywood had done to his story. "I had a simple, corny, well-felt little melodrama, and they made an ill-felt, silly, maudlin, badly timed thing of it."

those who knew him over the years. "A cruel and intolerant man," was the way Irving Ceasar, who wrote "Swanee," described him. Jolson's willingness to cheat his friend paid off beyond even his own wildest, most egotistical imaginings. *The Jazz Singer* made him the biggest star in the movies — and the highest paid. His next picture, *The Singing Fool,* was the most popular movie ever made until *Gone With the Wind* came along 11 years later. Audiences loved the sentimentality of *The Jazz Singer*, and so Jolson played on that same soppy, sentimental formula in film after film.

However, the immense popularity borne of *The Jazz Singer* did not last long. As sound pictures became more sophisticated in the 1930s and attracted better actors, Jolson, who unbelievably was still appearing in blackface, refused to change. By the time *Hallelujah I'm a Bum* opened in 1933, audiences were tired of him, and the movie flopped. By 1940, he was finished in films. His wife, Ruby Keeler, a former nightclub dancer and gangster's moll whom he had married in 1928 when she was 19 and he was 42, had become a bigger star, a cornerstone of Warner Bros.' newly acquired prosperity in a series of musicals created by Busby Berkeley and co-starring Dick Powell — beginning with *Forty-Second Street* in 1933.

If the movies no longer desired Jolson as an actor, they could have him as an icon in a pair of biographical pictures, *The Jolson Story* (1946), and its sequel, *Jolson Sings Again* (1949), the only time in screen history that a single performer required two entire movies to contain his exploits. There was, of course, no mention in either installment of George Jessel or the way Jolie had worked to steal *The Jazz Singer*. Both films were hugely successful, and they renewed Jolson's popularity with a whole new audience. Wisely, however, the producers decided to leave Jolson offscreen. His voice was heard on the soundtrack, but Jolie himself was played by actor Larry Parks. Jolson, who still bristled at anyone else getting attention, hated Parks and barely acknowedged his involvement.

I N THE TRIUMPHANT CHAOS AND CONFUSION THAT SWEPT ACROSS HOLLY-wood after the appearance of *The Jazz Singer*, George Jessel was all but forgotten. He still had a contract at Warner Bros. and had completed *Private Izzy Murphy* (1926) as well as a sequel, *Sailor Izzy Murphy* (1927). In the three years he spent in Hollywood, he starred in a half dozen movies, more than

Jolson made in the same period. But none of them had the revolutionary impact of *The Jazz Singer*. While Jolson became the number one movie star in the world, Jessel languished in what were basically low-budget programmers. Jessel, paranoid about Warner Bros. in particular and movies in general, was convinced his pictures were being badly made on purpose. Hurt and bewildered, not only by the movie business but by a star-crossed affair with the actress Constance Talmadge (whom he married in 1932), he retreated to New York.

Despite his bitterness, he found himself back in Los Angeles nearly two decades later, producing movies for Darryl Zanuck at 20th Century–Fox. "Jessel suddenly confounded the wiseacres and bobbed up as one of the very clan he had derided for years," noted his friend, humorist S. J. Perelman. He even found himself apologizing to columnist Hedda Hopper for his previous comments about the business. "Every time a man is hungry, Hedda," he implored, "you must excuse his bitterness." He produced a series of lightweight musical comedies, including *The Dolly Sisters* (1945), *I Wonder Who's Kissing Her Now* (1947), and *Dancing in the Dark* (1949).

There was never any mention of his involvement with *The Jazz Singer*. When he got into the papers, it was usually over trouble with a woman. During his marriage to Constance Talmadge, he declared a number of times his intention to commit suicide. After he divorced Talmadge in 1940, he was briefly attached to a showgirl, a 16-year-old beauty named Lois Andrews whom he married when he was 42. After that came a series of encounters with a succession of actresses, showgirls, and singers, all of them young, all of them announcing at one time or another that they were engaged to him, and all of them ending up fighting either with him or with each other, usually in public.

But his true fame would come not from Hollywood or Broadway or from his encounters with starlets. By 1953, Jessel was renowned as a toastmaster. "Rather than be a star of a television show or a hit on Broadway," wrote Maurice Zolotow in the *Saturday Evening Post*, "Jessel would prefer to be the toastmaster of a convention of potato merchants in Boise, Idaho or deliver the eulogy at the funeral of a great star." At the age of 55, he estimated he had acted as toastmaster over three thousand times. "Jessel's specialty is funerals," said *Time* magazine in 1966. "Nobody in Hollywood gets buried properly unless Georgie is there to coax a few tears of remembrance."

Jolson and Jessel remained awkwardly joined at the hip for 20 years after their clash over *The Jazz Singer*. Even if they had wanted to, they could not escape one another. They had been cut from the same bolt of cloth, held together by their Jewish roots, their show-business backgrounds, and by the curious rituals of recurring celebration in which the performers of their generation constantly participated. Part of a vanishing breed of showman, they were thrown together out of a shared sense both of survival and of reaffirmation, showing up at the same testimonial dinners and charity affairs. If Jolson was honored, Jessel was a guest. If Jessel was the object of a roast, Jolson was present. Always in attendance, either stated or unstated, was the prickly subject of *The Jazz Singer*.

Jessel was a member of the so-called Comedians' Round Table at the Hillcrest Country Club, and Jolson sometimes sat in with the boys. Jessel had to endure a lot of jokes about *The Jazz Singer*. Jolson was not beyond bringing up the subject himself. "And I know he's still mad at me about *The Jazz Singer*," the singer cracked during a 1948 Friar's Club roast in Jessel's honor. "He always imitated me, always stole my women."

The part about imitating him was true. To hear Jessel sing "My Mother's Eyes," a hit song he had in the '20s, is to hear someone trying to sound like Al Jolson (during a radio interview, Jessel once conceded that "everyone has a little Jolson in them" — and among the performers of that era, this certainly was true). Jessel stoically endured all the cracks and the jokes, but they grated. He was torn between a desire to exist in Jolson's aura and an enduring hatred for what Jolie had done to him. (*Time* magazine reported during a 1966 interview that Jessel intensely disliked Jolson — hardly news to anyone who knew them.)

Jolson for his part was decidedly ambivalent about Jessel hanging around. "The only actor he had any respect for was me," Jessel declared at the end of his life. But Earle Jolson, Jolie's fourth wife, said her late husband thought little of Jessel. There exists curious footage of the two men at the Photoplay Gold Medal Awards ceremony in 1947 where *The Jolson Story* was being honored as the year's most popular film. When Jolson makes his appearance, Jessel hurries to his side. Jolson appears uncomfortable and tries to move away. Jessel takes him by the arm and pulls him back. Jolson looks even more uneasy.

At the end of his life, Jolson was wary enough of Jessel and his reputation for speaking at the funerals of the famous that he asked Earle to make sure Jessel did not deliver his eulogy. On the last night of his life, 27 October 1950, Jolson encountered for the last time the man he had robbed of immortality.

That night Jolson and Earle were dining at LaRue, a popular Sunset Blvd. restaurant. Jolson had just returned from Korea where he had been entertaining the troops. In the midst of dinner, Jessel suddenly appeared, walked up to Jolson's table, and incongruously asked him for a dime to buy a newspaper. When he had departed, Jolson turned to his wife and sneered, "When I die he'll bury me, and the next day, he'll ask you for a date."

The following day, Al Jolson, once known as the greatest entertainer who ever lived, was dead of a massive heart attack at the age of 64.

And even though Jolson had expressly demanded otherwise, George Jessel, the friend and enemy who was consigned to a lifetime of living in Jolson's shadow, delivered the funeral oration. It was everything Jolson might have feared: overwritten, dripping with pompous oratory and purplish prose. "A breeze from San Francisco Bay and the life of the greatest minstrel America has ever known is in the balance," was the way Jessel began. "The turn of a card — a telling of a gag — and within a few moments, a wife, a legion of admirers, and a nation are brokenhearted."

He continued: "Those of us who tarry behind are but pale imitations, mere princelings. . . . I am proud to have basked in the sunlight of his greatness, to have been part of his time, and to have only a few days ago — this last Sunday night — hugged him and said, 'Good night Asa, take care of yourself.'"

Jessel did not mention the dime he had borrowed from Jolie. During a lifetime of losing to the great Al Jolson, getting 10 cents out of him on the last night of his life may have been George Jessel's only victory.

# 2

# SOUND, SHIRLEY, JUDY

*And the way to the Yellow Brick Road*

WITHIN A YEAR OF THE 1927 RELEASE OF *THE JAZZ SINGER*, THE new technology of sound overtook the business, forever changing the movies as well as the actors who appeared in them. In 1927, the movie industry in Hollywood employed 42,000 people. Its production facilities were responsible for 82 percent of the movies seen around the world, and foreign revenues accounted for 40 percent of the industry's grosses (during World War II, the figure obviously plummeted, but generally it has changed little in the past 60 years). There were nine major studios: Fox, Metro-Goldwyn-Mayer, Paramount, United Artists, First National, Pathé, Universal, Producers' Distributing Corp., and Warner Bros. In addition, there were 15 smaller companies, including Columbia Pictures. The newly established Central Casting Corporation listed 70 performers as "stars," with 200 categorized as "feature players" and 2,000 lumped together under the catchall "persons regarded as actors."

Those rated as stars made $2,500 a week, while feature players were paid $750. Naturally, the superstars of the era, as they do today, earned much, much more. Emil Jannings, the Swiss-German actor who had arrived in Hollywood in 1927 and despite his immense girth had become a box-office sensation in *The Way of All Flesh* and *The Last Command*, earned $6,000 a week. Also in the $6,000 category was Pola Negri. Born in Poland, she had danced in Russia and become a star in Berlin before arriving in Hollywood to make mostly indifferent films while loving Rudolph Valentino and feuding with Gloria Swanson. As for the Chicago-born Swedish-Italian Swanson, she was the reigning queen of Hollywood, glamor personified for most American women.

In 1926, Swanson turned down $900,000 for three pictures, plus *half* the profits, preferring to produce her own films through United Artists. Tom

Mix, the screen's first bona fide action star (he actually preceded the swash-buckling Douglas Fairbanks), was earning $1 million a year in 1928. Charlie Chaplin was earning $10,000 a week, plus a $150,000 annual bonus, about the same amount as Mary Pickford was receiving, although she was getting a $300,000 bonus. (When Chaplin joined with D. W. Griffith, Douglas Fairbanks, and Mary Pickford in 1919 to form United Artists, the company was privately held, so it was impossible to tell exactly what any of the principals was making, but the sums were astronomical.)

Sound, a phenomenon few in Hollywood had even contemplated, in little more than a year had finished some of its biggest stars. While it has been debated how much effect sound really had on careers, given that a number of performers already were aging, their popularity on the wane, it is hard to ignore the damage that was inflicted on many. At the least, it would be the equivalent today of Tom Cruise, Julia Roberts, Mel Gibson, and Harrison Ford waking up to discover that, because of a technical innovation, their careers were at an end.

Emil Jannings and Pola Negri, hobbled by thick accents, were almost immediately finished. Mary Pickford's popularity had peaked before the advent of sound, although she won an Oscar for her 1929 role in *Coquette*. But her second talking picture, *The Taming of the Shrew* (also 1929, with additional dialogue credited to Sam Taylor), with husband Douglas Fairbanks as costar, virtually finished her career.

Gloria Swanson was never comfortable with sound, and neither was Chaplin. He remained popular, but he was reluctant to deal with dialogue and made fewer and fewer pictures. (The Little Tramp made his final appearance in the 1940 classic *The Great Dictator*.) The end of the silent era finished John Gilbert, second only to Valentino as the great romantic idol of his time. It was not that his voice was so terrible, but sound drew the curtain on the sort of romantic ideal Gilbert personified, and he just was not actor enough to carry off anything else. His despondency over the loss of one of the great star careers in movie history drove him to drink; he died of a heart attack at the age of 41. May McAvoy, now totally forgotten, was very popular in the early 1920s, and even won the heart of poet Carl Sandburg, who called her "a star-eyed goddess." She played Esther in the 1926 version of *Ben-Hur*, and was the love of Al Jolson's life in *The Jazz Singer* — the silent love, it should be added. But the year after the coming of sound, she was gone, washed up in movies because of an alleged lisp, although she always denied that Warner Bros. had dropped her contract because of her voice.

Sound formed a line of demarcation, so much so that the beginnings of movie history and the stars who created it tumbled into the oblivion of silence and were forgotten. A whole generation of fabulously popular stars simply ceased to exist, even though, at first, pictures only included sound sequences rather than full-length stories with dialogue. Audiences, as intrigued as they were with people talking on the screen, tended to laugh at the dialogue. But it was not long before the necessary adjustments were made for this new medium, although they were not always accomplished without trial and error. Dolores Costello would go on to become an effective actress in talking pictures (most notably, Orson Welles' *The Magnificent Ambersons*). But in reviewing her first two sound films in 1928 — *Tenderloin* and *Glorious Betsy* — *Variety* gently pointed out that there seemed to be difficulty getting Costello's facial expressions to match the emotion in her voice. Silent actors had only had to act with their faces; now they had to be aware of their voices as well.

Whatever the problems, technical or otherwise, it was apparent that sound was not a fad but was here to stay. Hollywood, therefore, was in a state of panic, with rumors abounding that the studios would make all actors record their voices, and those recordings would be held on file to be played back before anyone was hired. Trainloads of stage actors, it was said, were headed west from New York. Actually, that rumor was not far wrong. Faced with a new reality, the studios hurriedly concluded that cultured voices were needed, and they could be found only in the East. There was even a brief infatuation with turning movies into filmed stage plays. What with cameras that could hardly be moved and actors who had to stand directly under microphones in order to be properly recorded, this seemed logical. But the motion picture medium could not long remain static, and as soon as the technology improved, it became increasingly apparent that movies required a more naturalistic kind of actor. One had to behave in front of the camera rather than emote. More than just a cultured voice was required. Thus, the movies had to discover a whole new generation of actors who could be transformed into stars to replace those discarded at the end of the silent era, and who could adapt to this rapidly evolving technology.

Previously, an exotically romantic kind of European had dominated movies: from Rudolph Valentino (Italian) to Emil Jannings (Swiss) to Pola

Negri (Polish) to Greta Garbo (Swedish). Although Garbo survived handily, and Hollywood by no means closed the door to foreign stars, particularly beautiful exotic women (Marlene Dietrich arrived in 1930), now the movies required a more natural kind of American performer.

Frank Cooper, a former stunt rider from Montana, had never amounted to much as Gary Cooper in silent pictures. But sound transformed him. His inability to emote hysterically worked exceedingly well in the talkies. Cooper, along with everyone else, soon discovered that the less he said or did on the screen, the more effective it was. Many of the performers drawn to Hollywood with the advent of sound had at least some stage experience, but it tended to be brief. Hollywood was far away from Broadway, and at the beginning of the '30s, that distance prevented people from jumping easily back and forth between the stage and the screen. If you arrived in Los Angeles, it was to stay. The talent scouts who combed Broadway grabbed new talent and shipped it west as soon as possible. Thus, these unique beings who would inhabit an entire era of classic Hollywood movies all seemed to arrive at once. They must have been tripping over each other at the train station in 1930 and 1931.

Joan Crawford, who had actually started in silents, was from San Antonio, Texas, but discovered by MGM scouts in a Broadway chorus line. James Stewart, from Indiana, Pennsylvania, and Henry Fonda, from Grand Island, Nebraska, had barely put a foot on a Broadway stage before heading off to Hollywood. Clark Gable, from Cadiz, Ohio, was with a touring company and had appeared in various Broadway productions, but only for a couple of years before establishing himself permanently in the movie capital. James Cagney, from New York City, actually lasted five years on Broadway before he went to Hollywood. Bette Davis, from Lowell, Massachusetts, had appeared for less than a year on Broadway before Universal signed her to a contract. Humphrey Bogart and Edward G. Robinson had appeared on the New York stage in various roles, Bogart for the better part of a decade, Robinson for 15 years, before they both arrived in Hollywood at about the same time. Spencer Tracy, from Milwaukee, had had to work long and hard to get on Broadway, but almost as soon as he appeared in *The Last Mile*, director John Ford spotted him and sent him to Hollywood for the lead in *Up the River* in 1930. Ginger Rogers, from Independence, Missouri, had managed to appear in two Broadway musicals before Pathé put her under contract. Jean Harlow, from Kansas City, arrived in 1928 with no stage experience whatsoever and became the prototype for a million more blondes who would arrive in town over the years with a lot of hope and no training.

Economics also spurred the anxious embrace of what essentially were a lot of inexpensive young kids. "I was in the last year of my contract at the time," recalled Adolphe Menjou, as the trains deposited new batches of youthful Midwestern faces in downtown Los Angeles. "My salary was $7,500 a week [this was 1929]. I knew that unless I proved I could talk before my contract expired, I would be a dead pigeon." Menjou could talk, and talk well, so he was spared dead pigeon status, but with the United States on the brink of depression, and motion picture attendance down by as much as 50 percent, the loss of a whole generation of expensive movie stars was an unexpected economic windfall. Thus, a combination of technology and bottom-line cost cutting helped induce one of those grand accidents that defies design or premeditation.

No one could have set out to assemble this unique group of faces with voices who had not existed as such a couple of years before, but who in short order would come to be irreplaceable. Often without knowing what they were getting themselves into, they became intrinsic to a new art form as it came into its own, and that somehow endowed them with an energy and promise that survives in those movies to this day. Moreover, color was not perfected until the middle of the decade, and by 1939 only about 20 color films had been produced. These new gods and goddesses were therefore cast in startling black and white images, not quite real, somehow beyond flesh and blood. Viewed in a contemporary context, cast in a silvery glow, they often seem to have drifted down from another world, remote and somehow unreachable. We have never quite recovered from those faces. They continue to haunt our celluloid dreams in a way that subsequent generations of movie stars have never been able to match.

WHETHER OR NOT REALITY TREATED YOU AS A GOD OR A GODDESS depended very much on the earthly studio in which you happened to find yourself. The studios were defined not just by the kind of movies they made, but by the stars who inhabited them. At MGM, Louis B. Mayer thought the public should indeed regard his stars as gods and goddesses, and he treated them accordingly. Over at Paramount, the stars were a little more sophisticated and worldly than they were elsewhere — epitomized by Mae West, W. C. Fields, Jean Arthur, Marlene Dietrich, and, for tough-guy relief, George Raft. Gary Cooper, the quintessential westerner, was present as well, but even he could be gotten into a suit and tie and made to be urban when the need arose. RKO was also known for its urbanity, thanks to Cary Grant, Katharine Hepburn, the Astaire-Rogers musicals, and, briefly, Orson Welles. Columbia Pictures, run by the ogre Harry Cohn, leaned heavily on director Frank Capra's genius, but was movie-star poor and had to rely on imports to provide names for its movies.

In the middle of the decade, Twentieth Century was amalgamated with Fox to form 20th Century–Fox, a studio that had to make do with Will Rogers and Shirley Temple when it came to movie stars. Universal, which in the silent era had been home to Rudolph Valentino and Wallace Beery, now had fallen on hard times and was forced to rely on the charms of Deanna Durbin and Ma and Pa Kettle (Marjorie Main and Percy Kilbride), as well as Boris Karloff and Bela Lugosi — the latter two presiding over its assembly line of horror movies — and later on such exotic adventure stars as Maria Montez and Sabu. Warner Bros. liked to think it had no need of stars, and Errol Flynn was the only player on the lot who actually looked like a movie star. Bette Davis was attractive in a certain light, and Olivia De Havilland was pretty. Otherwise, the likes of Paul Muni, James Cagney, Edward G. Robinson, and Humphrey Bogart had the kind of faces that peered out from dark alleys late at night.

The Hollywood these performers found themselves inhabiting just three years after the introduction of sound was already a factory town, created largely by banking institutions that had rushed to invest in talking pictures. With New York–based financiers in charge, the studios consolidated and sought ways to turn out movies as quickly, efficiently, and inexpensively as possible, and thus the so-called studio system quickly evolved. Movies now were a business enterprise, and their backers kept one eye glued to the bottom line. The stars were important cogs in the machinery — certainly more important than most of the directors, who were hardly thought of at all — but they were cogs nonetheless. Gone were the days when actors such as Tom Mix had control over their own destinies, and there would be no more shenanigans of the Chaplin, Mary Pickford, Douglas Fairbanks type, with actors starting up their own studios. Everyone fit into the system, into the way business was done, so that even the biggest stars were under seven-year contracts that for the most part gave them almost no freedom to pick and choose what they wanted to do. At the end of the decade, Clark Gable was the most popular star in Hollywood, the "King," but, as critic David Thomson pointed out, the king was also a slave. A star who acted up or refused to do as he or she was told was put on suspension, without pay, and the time so spent was added onto the end of the contract.

In such a restrictive atmosphere with actors basically being told how to dress, where to go, what to do, fights over roles frequently erupted, and refusals to do certain movies could affect entire careers. Hedda Hopper reported that MGM contract player Robert Young became a star after Robert Taylor, then one of the major stars on the lot, turned down *Northwest Passage* (1940). Spencer Tracy objected strongly to appearing in *Captains Courageous* (1937), the movie that helped win him an Oscar and propelled him into major stardom. Gary Cooper had to be talked into doing *Sergeant York*, which won *him* an Oscar. Myrna Loy did not like the script for *Reckless,* opposite William Powell, became conveniently ill, and was replaced by Rosalind Russell, whom the movie turned into a star.

But these stories tended to be the exception rather than the rule. Mostly actors were forced to do the roles studios wanted them in, and their fates could rise or fall according to whim. Warner Bros. in 1930 assigned an actor named Eddie Woods to star in a gangster picture titled *The Public Enemy*. After filming was under way, director William Wellman noticed a secondary player named James Cagney in the rushes and thought he would be much more effective in the lead. The next thing, Woods was playing the second lead, and Cagney was the star. That studio-inspired switch, made almost casually and with no fuss, assured Woods of anonymity and James Cagney immortality.

What you thought of this state of affairs depended largely on how you were treated. James Stewart was at MGM where Louis B. Mayer, the boss of the studio, had a high appreciation of talent. Stewart naturally recalled his years there with great affection. "The major studios, such as MGM, were more than just big factories as some critics described them," said Stewart, who had attended Princeton University and planned to become an architect before finding his way to MGM in 1935. "They were institutions of learning as far as we were concerned. . . . When I was under contract at MGM, I remember a period when I was acting in five motion pictures at once. Rather than keeping me sitting around waiting for that really big part to come along, MGM would put me in a small part in a big picture and a big part in a small movie to keep me busy acting and training, so to speak. It was a good system, I thought. We were hired by a major studio, brought up through the ranks, taught how to act, how to dress, how to behave in general, and by the time we achieved stardom, we had pretty well prepared to carry out our responsibilities."

Cagney, at Warner Bros., had quite a different view. "It seemed as if the Warner boys were confusing their actors with their racehorses," James Cagney once noted. "The pace was incredible. I think I did about six pictures in the first forty weeks." George Brent, a rakish Warner contract player, made seven films in 1932 alone. Over at MGM, Gable went home at five every night (a practice he continued to the end of his career), but it was not uncommon for the actors at Warner Bros. to work through the night in order to finish a picture on time. "They get you up before daylight, and work your ass off all day until after sundown," Bogart once complained. "Working in pictures is for the birds."

The Warner Bros. studio in Burbank was like a prison camp — a camp full of rebellious, spirited detainees who took a suspension for misbehavior much the way the characters they played in movies would take a stretch of solitary confinement — with a sneer. It was part of the price of doing business with the brothers Warner.

Jack Warner, who ran the studio with his brother Harry, made no bones about the fact that his favorite actor was not even human, but a dog — Rin Tin Tin. Ironically, the Warner Bros. stars would become the most memorable single fraternity ever to come out of Hollywood, but in the day-to-day life on the lot, stars were considered distinctly secondary to the stories. That attitude was echoed by Darryl F. Zanuck, who started writing scripts for Warner Bros. in 1923 and even wrote for Jack Warner's favorite star, Rin Tin Tin. Zanuck rose from that to become the studio's executive in charge of production but left Warner Bros. in 1933, unable to endure Jack's meanness any longer.

Zanuck, only 31 at the time, was regarded as "the hottest young man" in Hollywood. The same year, he and Joseph M. Schenck established Twentieth Century Pictures with some help from Louis B. Mayer. It was instructive in light of what subsequently happened that Zanuck and Mayer always had an uneasy relationship. The founding of Twentieth Century Pictures had been marked by feuds between the two men. In 1935, the company would merge with the older Fox Pictures to form 20th Century–Fox.

When he arrived at Fox, Zanuck found the studio in a state of panic. Everyone was afraid they were about to lose their jobs, fears that Zanuck soon made reality. He fired employees with abandon, tossed out scripts, and halted movies in mid-production; 20th Century–Fox was going to be his studio and no one else's. At Warner Bros., he had had to operate in the shadow of Jack and Harry Warner. Now there would be no shadow but that cast by Darryl F. Zanuck.

Fox had only two real stars on the lot, Will Rogers, the humorist, and Shirley Temple. But Rogers died in a plane crash the year Zanuck took over, and that left Shirley Temple, a seven-year-old phenomenon.

Shirley Temple had blonde ringlets that every mother in America wanted for her daughter, a round, dimpled face, sparkling blue eyes, and a natural warmth on the screen that even today can work magic. Two hundred and forty million people had seen her movies, more than twice the population of the United States. There were $11 million worth of products on the market bearing her name and likeness, including dolls, dresses, and coloring books. There had never been a star like her, and in terms of her impact on a society that loved and adored her, there has not been anyone like her since. The year before — 1934 — she had become America's most popular box-office star, astoundingly, given her age, appearing in no less than nine movies, including two of her most popular, *Little Miss Marker* and *Bright Eyes*. The success of her pictures was all that kept the newly-formed 20th Century–Fox from going bankrupt.

Zanuck was impressed, but not unduly so. His subsequent actions would betray a man who had never really believed in the power of movie stars. Over at MGM, Louis B. Mayer believed, "Talent was like a precious stone. Like a diamond or a ruby. You take care of it. You put it in a safe, you clean it, polish it, look after it. Who knows the value of a star?"

But Zanuck was a product of the Warner brothers. Stars did not make pictures as far as he was concerned. The pictures made the stars. At Warner Bros., he had missed Clark Gable's appeal entirely. "His ears are too big," he had declared. "He looks like an ape." Zanuck did not spot stars much more accurately when he started to run Fox. He passed on such potential talent as Cary Grant (who went to RKO), Errol Flynn (to Warner Bros.), and Fred Astaire (also to RKO). Zanuck came to do many things well, but creating stars was never one of them. His contract players eventually included Tyrone Power, Loretta Young, Betty Grable, Don Ameche, and Henry Fonda — the weakest lineup of stars at any studio in Hollywood. There was no one on that list who would ever approach the sort of popularity Shirley Temple was enjoying when Zanuck took over Fox.

Various biographers have portrayed Zanuck's relationship with Shirley Temple as warm and even fatherly. Given what he subsequently did to her, it is remarkable that anyone would buy into that description. Certainly the lady herself would have none of it.

"A very few times we had visited him at his beach house so I could play with his three children," Temple recalled much later. "On such occasions, he had always sat studiously apart, showing little interest in talking at length with Mother, and none in speaking with me or getting to know me personally."

That same ambivalence extended to Shirley Temple's movies. There was no discussion of how her career might best be shaped, and no inclination to do anything but constantly repeat the same formula that had been working since 1934. "One way to handle me was to resist change and stay put," Temple said. "My formula was working — perpetual childhood and cheerful resolution to any problems whether divorce, deceit, mayhem, loneliness or war. . . . As long as I was a winner, it was relatively effortless and profitable. Afterward? Forget me."

Despite a few naysayers and Zanuck's passing concern about adolescence, Shirley Temple's popularity was not suffering as 1937 turned into 1938. Over at MGM, that popularity was coveted. The studio was about to start filming an expensive movie fantasy, and they needed a 10-year-old star. Shirley Temple would be perfect — if only the studio could get her.

E XACTLY WHO ORIGINATED THE IDEA OF TURNING *THE WIZARD OF OZ* into a movie remains in dispute. While they were alive both Arthur Freed, the lyricist, and Mervyn LeRoy, the producer and director, insisted on taking credit. Both men said they had read the L. Frank Baum books as boys and fallen in love with them. Whoever was responsible, in the fall of 1937, Louis B. Mayer bought the rights to *The Wizard of Oz* from Samuel Goldwyn, who had been holding onto them for the past five years. Ironically, Fox had reportedly tried at one point to buy the rights from him with the idea of turning *Oz* into a movie for Shirley Temple. Goldwyn had turned the studio down, and held out until Mayer came along with a more tempting offer — $75,000.

From the moment he became involved with *The Wizard of Oz*, Arthur Freed wanted a plain, dumpy teenager from Grand Rapids, Minnesota, named Frances Gumm to play the role of Dorothy. While there are numerous other stories about who actually discovered the young woman who became Judy Garland, Freed wanted all credit. He said that Jack Robbins, the head of MGM's music publishing, called him one day and insisted that he get over to Stage One. When he got there, he found young Frances with her father Frank. He heard her sing "Zing! Went the Strings of My Heart," then, according to his retelling of it, he literally raced around to Mayer's office and dragged the head of MGM back to the stage, whereupon Frances sang a Jewish song, "Eli, Eli," that left Mayer in tears.

A less dramatic version had Mayer's assistant, Ida Koverman, bringing Frances Gumm into his office where he listened to her and was impressed enough to have her come back to Stage One the next day to sing for a group that included Arthur Freed and Jack Robbins. In any event, the 13-year-old was signed to an MGM contract on 27 September 1935, just one of over 100 such players at the time.

The reality of MGM in those days was as close to movie fantasy as any studio in town. Everything about the studio was designed to suggest sleek style and expensive good taste. What set Frances Gumm apart from all this was her absolute plainness. She was the sow's ear in a dream factory that prided itself on beauty and perfection. The newly dubbed Judy Garland was awkward and overweight, and, as Mervyn LeRoy later pointed out, her teeth were "funny." But she had the most incredible voice in the world, and, as Garland herself came to believe, it was the voice that MGM wanted.

Arthur Freed and his music assistant, Roger Edens, quickly became Garland's biggest boosters. If not for them, it is doubtful that she would have survived. Edens, a tall, suave Texan, was particularly taken with Judy and came to act as her mentor both personally and professionally. However, it was Freed who orchestrated the break that got her noticed at MGM. Mayer was organizing a party for Clark Gable's 36th birthday (1 February 1937) and Freed was in charge of the entertainment. He had Garland sing a specially written number entitled "Dear Mr. Gable," that segued into "You Made Me Love You."

Garland's performance of the song literally stopped the show and led to her being shoehorned into *Broadway Melody of 1938*, where she performed the same number. It was her first break after two and a half years at MGM.

At the same time as Garland was struggling to get noticed, Shirley Temple was at the height of her popularity. *Look* magazine called her "the most popular little girl in America." If Garland was nothing like anyone's fantasy of a teenage girl, Temple was still the personification of every mother's perfect daughter. What's more, she was nearer the right age to play Dorothy (who in Baum's book was six years old) than the 16-year-old Garland.

Arthur Freed and Roger Edens, as well as Mervyn LeRoy, were adamant about Judy Garland for Dorothy. "She *looked* more like Dorothy than Shirley Temple did," LeRoy argued. No one else seemed to think so. Mayer was noncommittal, but in New York, Nicholas Schenck, who ran Loew's Inc., MGM's parent company, was definite. *The Wizard of Oz* was to be an expensive gamble for the studio. They needed insurance. They needed a star. They needed Shirley Temple. Mayer put in a call to Darryl Zanuck.

For Zanuck, the call from Mayer was probably just what he was waiting for. Finally, he had something that the quick-tempered and tyrannical Mayer wanted. What he did not seem to understand, however, was that what would be good for MGM would also be good for Shirley Temple — and by extension, for 20th Century–Fox and Darryl F. Zanuck. He had a franchise in Shirley Temple, but it was in need of renewal. Because Zanuck did not care about stars, he could not see the value of putting a star into the kind of picture that would give her career a boost. At the time Mayer approached him, Zanuck, if he thought about it at all, probably thought Temple's career needed no help. Besides, says producer David Brown, who started at Fox in the early 1950s and worked with Zanuck for many years, studios were very reluctant to allow their stars out of their sight. "A studio simply would not want to trade off one of its assets so that a rival studio could benefit," Brown said.

Still, for a moment, it looked as though Mayer might get the star he wanted. Initially, Zanuck suggested that Fox buy *The Wizard of Oz* from MGM and cast Shirley Temple, but Mayer declined that offer. He then played his strength. MGM had lots of stars; 20th Century–Fox had Shirley Temple. Temple wrote in her autobiography, *Child Star*, that Mayer offered both Clark Gable and Jean Harlow in return for her services. Since Harlow had died on 7

June 1937 of cerebral edema at the age of only 26, and Mayer did not purchase the rights to *The Wizard of Oz* from Sam Goldwyn until later that autumn, that seems unlikely.

But it is very likely that Mayer did offer the services of Gable, the most glittering jewel in his crown, and the number two star in the movies after Temple. There were certainly suggestions that, at a later date, the two might co-star in a movie. That got into the papers and prompted a response from Gable. As usual, faced with something that might be good for his career, Gable was hesitant, albeit humorously so. "Sure we have dimples in common," he said, "but she [Shirley] has three strikes on me from the start. I'm big and she's little. I'm dark and she's blonde. And men still prefer little blondes. Then there's the great ear problem. Hers are hidden, mine are naked, free to the wind. They should be hidden, too."

Freed later claimed that MGM went so far as to send Roger Edens over to Fox to audition Shirley. According to Freed, Edens came back and told him, "What can I say, Arthur? Her vocal limitations are insurmountable." That story would seem highly apocryphal. Shirley Temple was the number one box-office star in the world. It is doubtful that she would have had to audition for anything at that point in her career, and it seems even more doubtful that Zanuck would have allowed it. Temple makes no mention of any audition in her autobiography.

In the end, it made little difference what either Freed or Edens thought of her: Darryl Zanuck was not about to let go of his prize. In early 1938, when Mayer probably made his approach, Zanuck was convinced that Shirley Temple "would go on endlessly." He therefore tossed her into yet another vehicle carefully constructed to fulfill her audience's expectations — *Rebecca of Sunnybrook Farm*, a rehash of a movie that previously had been contrived for Mary Pickford in 1917. "Instead of dancing down a yellow brick road to see a wonderful wizard," Temple wrote bitterly, "I would return to retrace the path I had already traveled."

Mayer made one last stab at casting another actress as Dorothy. He went after Deanna Durbin, who briefly had been under contract at MGM before being let go. Universal, the studio for whom she was now working very successfully, would not hear of sending her back to MGM. Mayer was left with little choice but to cast Judy Garland.

"MGM has acquired the screen rights for *The Wizard of Oz* from Samuel Goldwyn, and has assigned Judy Garland to the role of Dorothy," reported *Daily Variety* on 24 February 1938.[2]

The following year, Shirley Temple suffered something she had never suffered before — failure. *Susannah of the Mounties* flopped at the box office. As had been predicted in some quarters, there were now signs that the public was tiring of the same old formula in Temple's films. After being the number one box-office star for four years, Temple suddenly fell to number five.

The apathetic response to *Susannah* was the wake-up call at Fox. Something had to be done about Shirley Temple. Zanuck must have been having regrets about so quickly rejecting *The Wizard of Oz*. There can be no other explanation for mounting such a lavish Technicolor production of a children's fantasy called *The Blue Bird*, when Zanuck had previously had no interest in anything quite so ambitious for his most valuable property. If Shirley Temple had not needed a bridge between childhood and adolescence before, she needed one now — and if it was not to be *The Wizard of Oz*, then the next best thing was to get as close to *Oz* as possible without setting foot on the yellow brick road. That opportunity, Zanuck decided, was afforded by Maurice Maeterlinck's 1908 play about a little girl seeking the bluebird of happiness.

A great deal of expense and care went into this Technicolor concoction, but none of it worked. The finished movie was leaden where *Wizard* had been lighthearted. Moreover, the usually effervescent Temple seemed stiff and charmless. Perhaps no actress could have given charm to a character Temple herself described as a "peevish, greedy, spoiled brat. . . . My goody-goody image was in tatters." So was her box-office invincibility. *The Blue Bird* was a resounding failure. *Time* magazine summed it up succinctly: "*The Blue Bird* laid an egg."[3]

Zanuck, as well as Temple's parents, now found themselves floundering.

---

[2] Buddy Ebsen, who had co-starred with Shirley Temple in *Captain January*, was cast as the Tin Woodman but had to drop out before filming started because of his adverse reaction to the silver body makeup. He was replaced by Jack Haley. Mayer badly wanted W. C. Fields to play the Wizard but balked at paying his $150,000 asking price. Thus, the legendary Fields missed the opportunity to be associated with one of the true classics. Instead, Frank Morgan, a character actor under contract at the studio, was assigned the part and gained a certain immortality.

[3] *The Blue Bird* originally was filmed in 1918. A version filmed in 1976 in Russia by the veteran George Cukor and featuring Elizabeth Taylor was also a flop.

Gertrude and George Temple were torn between putting their little girl into school and keeping her working. There is little doubt they wanted her to keep on making movies, but not so many. Their timing was questionable, however. Temple had now suffered two flops in a row, and the studio was plainly nervous. There was debate over her next movie, whether it should be *Schoolmates* or *Young People*. Finally, after considerable waffling, *Young People* (1940) was settled upon. It was a melodrama about a show-business couple raising an orphaned girl and conflicted about whether or not she should work professionally. At the end, the Temple character opts for early retirement, and thanks the audience for its past loyalty. The band strikes up "Auld Lang Syne" and everyone sings along. "It was," said Shirley Temple, "a shattering piece of symbolism."

That was the last scene she ever appeared in for 20th Century–Fox. On 12 May 1940, Joseph Schenck, the studio's chairman of the board, announced that the most valuable star on the lot was being released from her contract 13 months early. "The 20th Century–Fox studio will note the absence of Shirley Temple with regret," Schenck's announcement coldly read. "However, we are proud to have had the opportunity to present the world the happiness and entertainment she provided. I look forward to Shirley someday winning as great popularity as an actress as she has as a child star." What Schenck seemed to be saying was that Shirley Temple was finished. She had appeared in 22 pictures for the studio, and Fox earned over $30 million in profits. But it made no difference. At the age of 12, Shirley Temple was finished. She was not yet in the seventh grade.

*T*HE *WIZARD OF OZ*, ON THE OTHER HAND, TRANSFORMED JUDY Garland overnight into a star and sent her beyond the yellow brick road on the way to legend. The fact that her sad life often echoed the plaintive lament of little Dorothy singing "Over the Rainbow" helped broaden and sustain that legend. There was a pathos about Judy Garland that Shirley Temple never possessed — the sad, stocky little girl yearning to escape to a better place. Shirley represented sunshine and happiness — indeed, a foil to reality for millions of moviegoers during the Great Depression. But Shirley Temple's own life lacked that dark edge.

Still, her career undoubtedly would have taken a very different turn had she been allowed to star in *The Wizard of Oz*, and the movie might have been even more successful than it was — at least initially. The MGM brass turned out to be right about needing star power to fuel such an expensive enterprise.

The movie opened well, but because its audience consisted largely of children who paid less for theater admission, it did not gross what it might otherwise have. *Wizard* had cost $2,777,000 to produce, and it ended up grossing $3,017,000 when first released — good, but not spectacular considering the movie's high cost. Moreover, when the cost of prints, distribution, and advertising were added in, *The Wizard of Oz* actually lost money. It was not until CBS began showing the movie on television in the 1960s that it became a huge moneymaker for MGM and started to be considered a classic.

Would the movie have fared better if Shirley Temple had starred in it? Given her immense popularity at the time, it is hard to believe that its commercial potential would not have been improved; however, *The Wizard of Oz* would hardly have been the same movie. Even Temple acknowledged that many years later. "Sometimes," she said, "the gods know best."

The gods also play curious tricks. Eight months after leaving 20th Century–Fox, Shirley Temple turned up where she should have been in the first place — at MGM. At the end of 1940, she signed a contract to make movies for the studio. To add to the irony, she found herself seated across from Arthur Freed, the producer who had been so opposed to her doing *The Wizard of Oz*. Freed had a reputation around MGM that had nothing to do with his ability to turn out musicals. "The word was out that he was lecherous," said Mary Ann Nyberg, who became his costume designer in 1949. Still, nothing could have prepared the 12-year-old Temple for what happened next. Freed, without ceremony, stood up and exposed his penis to the little girl who might very well have been Dorothy in the land of Oz.[4]

Temple reacted in much the same way Dorothy did when confronted by the Cowardly Lion — she laughed. This incensed Freed. "Get out," he

---

[4] Movie executives were notorious for the way they carried on with women. Darryl Zanuck literally closed down Fox each afternoon for an hour and a half while he had sex, with a different woman each day. It was known around the studio as the "sex siesta." The French actress Corinne Calvet reported in her autobiography, *Has Corinne Been a Good Girl?*, that Zanuck called her in one day, and exposed himself. What it was about Hollywood executives that inspired them to wave their penises around in their offices before young actresses is a subject yet to be explored.

screamed at her. "Go on, get out!"

At about the same time, Shirley's mother Gertrude was seated in Louis B. Mayer's office. Mayer also had a reputation, and it had nothing to do with running a studio. As Arthur Freed exposed himself to Shirley, it seems that Mayer was making a pass at her mother. Mother and daughter retreated from MGM that afternoon, dazed and shaken, wondering what they had gotten themselves into.

As it turned out, MGM had no more sense of what to do with Shirley Temple than had 20th Century–Fox. She was supposed to make two pictures a year, one of which would be a musical with Mickey Rooney. Instead, she made the kind of predictable little-girl story that had gotten her into trouble at Fox. By May of 1941, the *New York Times* reported from Hollywood that "the town is displaying some amazement over the precipitous fall of Shirley Temple and the brevity of her career with Metro."

Temple continued to make movies through the remainder of the 1940s for various studios as she grew into a young woman. But she was nothing like the box-office attraction she had been, and in 1949 she quietly retired from movies.

A year later, paradoxically, Judy Garland, who as Dorothy got the role that could have saved Temple's career, was finished at MGM. At 28, after too many amphetamines and sleeping pills and suicide attempts, Garland fell from the studio's good graces. Songwriter Harry Warren summed up MGM's attitude succinctly: "She was too much trouble, and too costly."

# 3

## "A FANTASTIC, ARRESTING MASK"
### Raft and Bogart face off

T HE DIFFERENCE BETWEEN HUMPHREY BOGART AND GEORGE RAFT came down to this: Bogey was an actor; Raft was a gangster. Bogart acted tough. Raft was tough. Raft conspired to ensure that no one remembered him. Bogey, the phony tough guy, became legend. What a character Raft was, though, with his pearl-gray hat pulled rakishly down over one eye as he made his entrance into the nightclubs and racetracks and boxing matches he loved to frequent. He stood 5 feet 10 inches tall, with glossy black hair and a ferret-like face that gave no hint of emotion, that hid everything. "A fantastic, arresting mask," Edward G. Robinson once called it. He wore beautifully tailored suits with wide lapels, and pants with creases so sharp you could cut your finger on them. He always wore high-collared shirts, and he popularized the idea of wearing a black shirt with a white tie. He neither drank nor smoked but he made love to as many as three women a day. The women, taking note of the size of his penis, nicknamed him the Black Snake.

He was married only once — in his late 20s — to a woman named Grayce Mulrooney, but claimed he never had sex with her. He had love affairs with Carole Lombard, Marlene Dietrich, and Betty Grable among others. Grable in particular was in love with him and wanted to marry him. But the Black Snake would not divorce the wife he never slept with. He had a certain code about things, and, although it was often elusive and bull-headed, it was his code.

Before he went to Hollywood and became a movie star, George Raft had worked variously as a baseball player, a boxer, and most successfully as a taxi dancer who specialized in the tango. His dancing was admired by such legendary hoofers as Fred Astaire and James Cagney. Everything he did, however, was the backdrop to what he was — a hoodlum. He grew up with gangsters, socialized with them, and, on occasion, ran errands for them. They made him what he was, and in return he remained one of theirs for a lifetime.

In Hollywood, he was always an outsider who never quite seemed to get the drift of the place, never understood the difference between acting and life. Raft thought if he played a certain kind of role in a picture, that was what he was. The men who played gangsters in the movies were actors. George Raft was different. He was a gangster who became an actor. Raft fought a curious lifelong battle with his past, at once rejecting it and embracing it. His biographer, Lewis Yablonsky, reported noticing that paradox early in their relationship. Many times Raft would deny completely his mob connections, and, at other moments, sit and fondly reminisce about the hoods he had known. Because he was a gangster, he did not want to be known as one, and that got in the way of his career. If he had gone along in Hollywood, he might have been legend. But he could not go along, and fought everyone, and he missed out on some of the greatest roles ever offered an actor. No one in the history of movies rejected as many opportunities as did George Raft.

Humphrey Bogart, Raft's nemesis and rival at Warner Bros., grumbled but acquiesced, and by accident as much as anything inherited the parts Raft did not want. Thanks to Raft's obstinacy and plain stupidity, Bogart became the movie icon, his image reproduced on postcards and posters, his movies replayed constantly, his life — although less interesting than Raft's — made the subject of endless biographies. Raft, for his carelessness, was all but forgotten.

James Cagney, an Irish bartender's son from New York's Lower East Side who began in show business as a female impersonator, thought George Raft the toughest guy he ever met in Hollywood. Raft had a quick temper and a propensity for throwing a punch, and he could never quite brush the chip off his shoulder. "Nobody ever gave me anything I didn't fight for," he once said. "Nobody, except Mom."

Humphrey Bogart, in contrast to Raft, was born with a silver spoon in his mouth, the son of a noted Manhattan surgeon — and, as Raft liked to point out somewhat disparagingly, college educated (the Phillips Academy in Andover, Massachusetts, in preparation for medicine at Yale). Edward G. Robinson, whom Raft never liked, grew up on the Lower East Side, like Cagney, but had a good education, planning at one time to be either a lawyer or a rabbi, and had attended the prestigious American Academy of Dramatic Arts on a scholarship.

Raft was none of that. Uneducated, raised in the Hell's Kitchen section of the city, he was part of a poor German immigrant family of 11 kids. In those days, he was known as George Ranft. He had left school at the age of 14, and, although he had no idea what he eventually wanted to do with his life, he was sure of two things: "I did know definitely I wanted people to know my name, and I wanted them to be glad to see me when I came around."

As a kid, he believed the real heroes were the hoodlums he encountered. "When they patted me on the back and said, 'Georgie, you're an okay guy,' it was like an orphan getting the nod from John D. Rockefeller." It was a view that would color his entire life. His boyhood friends included Owney Madden and Ben ("Bugsy") Siegel, who became two of the era's most notorious gangsters and would have a great impact on his career.

In New York, when Raft became a professional dancer, his sleek, saturnine looks were often compared to those of Rudolph Valentino. Then known as Rodolfo Guglielmi (his real name), Valentino had worked with Raft as a dancer. In the early 1920s, Raft was on top of the world. Even Mae West, who was working on Broadway in those days, was impressed. Women were crazy about him and thought him highly erotic. "The tango was his specialty, and he danced it divinely," said actress Joan Bennett. "He was classy, debonair, dapper, extremely well dressed at all times."

But even as he lived the glamorous, sophisticated life of a popular Broadway dancer, Raft could not resist the gangs of New York and liked nothing better than to fill in as a driver aboard one of the cars protecting Owney Madden's Prohibition-era beer trucks.

It was Owney Madden who bankrolled Raft in Hollywood. Madden thought his boyhood friend would make a terrific movie star — the mob's own man in the movies. Raft did not appear to have an overwhelming interest in acting, and it is doubtful he would have amounted to much had the director Howard Hawks not cast him in his 1932 gangster picture, *Scarface*, opposite Paul Muni. Raft played Guino Rinaldo, the loyal gunman who does all the dirty work for "Scarface" Tony Camonte. As Raft himself later acknowledged, there were lots of young, good-looking actors in Hollywood much better trained than he was. But Hawks knew of his mob connections. He had seen Raft at a prizefight and thought he carried a gun for the mob — which Raft always denied. Hawks was intrigued with the idea of having a real live gangster in a movie about gangsters. *Scarface* was a thinly fictionalized version of Al Capone's life, written by Ben Hecht, and since Raft had known Capone in the days when he was still called Al Brown, there were all sorts of questions he could answer about how the gangster dressed and how he walked and talked. Raft was as much a technical advisor as he was an actor.

The character of Guino in the film was a nasty piece of work, redeemed only by his death at the hands of the even more vicious Scarface, angry that his best friend had secretly married his beloved sister. Raft was noticeably edgy on screen. He appeared more alarmed at being in front of a camera than dangerous. No one seemed to notice, however, and there was the wonderful piece of business with Raft as Guino constantly flipping a nickel. It was Hawks' idea, but it became something of a trademark for Raft. *Scarface* overnight turned George Raft into the last thing in the world he had ever expected to be — a movie star.

But if the movie made Raft famous, it also made him uneasy about his image — and his abilities. Raft was not an actor and had no enthusiasm for what it took to learn the craft. When he saw what Muni went through in order to prepare himself for the part of Tony — recording his voice on a dictaphone, then playing it back so that he could add the appropriate gestures — he said he would rather not act at all if he had to go through that sort of thing.

He began to worry that people might actually mistake him for a gangster. Since he was a gangster, it was not something he wanted people to know. He began the process of trying to hide his real self, and that induced the sort of wrong-headed, thoughtless role choices that ultimately destroyed his career and any chance at lasting fame.

By 1937, Raft was making $202,666 a year. He was the third-highest-paid actor in Hollywood. Only Warner Baxter, the original Cisco Kid (who earned $285,384), and Gary Cooper ($265,384) made more money than he did. Despite his success, Raft increasingly was dissatisfied not just with the dialogue, but with the kind of roles he was playing. He wanted badly to be liked, both off screen and on.

"I don't want to confine my work to playing 'heels' because that can break a movie actor, too," he said. "If you're a meany in every role, the people back in Deep Sleep, Wyoming get to think you're really that kind of guy. And they don't want to see you any more." The fact that he could not read or write well — Jack Warner believed he could not read at all — did not help him when it came to judging the sort of material he was playing. His preoccupation with likeable roles and his inability to judge material on its own merits combined to cause his first major career blunder.

T HE PRODUCER SAMUEL GOLDWYN WAS MOUNTING A MOVIE VERSION of the Sidney Kingsley Broadway hit *Dead End*. Goldwyn, in his inimitable way, decided to smooth out the play's sharp edges — "cut off its balls" was the way Lillian Hellman, who adapted the screenplay, later described it. The story dealt with the confrontation between the rich and the poor, but Goldwyn demanded that the focus be shifted around to fall on one of his favorite players, Joel McCrea. He portrayed the poor but honest white-bread hero in love with Sylvia Sidney, their affair conducted against the backdrop of a dead-end street on the East River, where a large modern apartment building loomed over everything. By far the most interesting character in the movie was Baby Face Martin, a psychopathic gangster who returns to his old haunts for a visit. Goldwyn and director William Wyler wanted James Cagney, but Cagney — as was his wont in those days — was involved in a legal squabble with Warner Bros., and Goldwyn was advised to stay away. Goldwyn next turned to George Raft. When he read the script, Raft was appalled. This role offered precisely the sort of image he sought to avoid.

Over the years, Raft told various stories about why he had turned down *Dead End*. One anecdote had to do with the treatment of Baby Face's mother, who was supposed to slap her son and call him a "yellow dog." Raft was to walk away in a fury. But the specter of his real mother, who was immensely proud of her boy on the screen, rose again, and Raft could not bring himself to play the scene as written. He wanted to walk away with a tear in his eye, so that the audience would know that Mom was right, and Baby Face Martin actually despised his life as a criminal. This ran contrary to the whole character. Nonetheless, Wyler, one of the most respected directors in

Hollywood, pleaded with him to change his mind. Raft, displaying the pig-headedness that was to rise up time and again, refused to listen.

Out of desperation, Wyler and Goldwyn then turned to the bottom of the pecking order when it came to bad-guy actors. Humphrey Bogart had returned to Broadway in 1935 to play the gangster Duke Mantee in the hit play *The Petrified Forest* opposite Leslie Howard. Warner Bros., ever disdainful of Bogart's abilities, wanted to use Edward G. Robinson as Mantee for the 1936 movie version, but Howard had refused to do it without Bogart. Now Goldwyn reluctantly cast him in *Dead End*.

Even though Hellman thought the balls had been cut off the play, and Goldwyn insisted on picking up the garbage used to make the set more slum-like, *Dead End* (1937) was nominated for four Academy Awards, including best picture. The picture raised Bogart's profile considerably: he was no longer merely a stock bad guy on the Warner Bros. lot; an actor of substance and quality was seen to be at work.

If Raft noticed any of this, he gave little sign of it. He was a star, after all, albeit an unhappy one. He had a lifetime contract at Paramount, yet in the past 10 years, he had managed to get himself suspended 20 times by refusing to do the roles assigned him. In 1939, he finally escaped from his contract, but the moment he was free he turned to the last place in the world he ever should have gone near — Warner Bros. The move at once was a grand opportunity and a fateful mistake.

B Y NOW WARNER BROS.' REPUTATION AS THE MOST ACRIMONIOUS studio in Hollywood was firmly established. The studio system as it was constituted in those days bred dissatisfaction all over town, but it was nothing like the brawling that went on at Warners'. What was going through Raft's mind when he decided to go over there beggars the imagination: the actor who did not want to play bad guys and gangsters arriving at the studio that specialized in movies about bad guys and gangsters. He had disliked the way he was treated at Paramount, yet here he was at the gates of the studio with the worst reputation in town for its treatment of contract players.

For its part, Warner Bros. was just as naive in hiring Raft, an actor well known for those suspensions at Paramount as well as for his contrariness and his hair-trigger temper. Yet Warner executives appeared to believe they were solving a problem, not creating one. It was as though they knew nothing of Raft's reputation. Hal Wallis, then executive producer in charge of production, later said Raft was brought over because it was felt the studio needed another strong leading man for its gangster pictures. Cagney and Robinson were always threatening to walk out. Raft would be an insurance policy against that sort of thing. *Raft?* At Warner Bros., he became a classic case of using gasoline to put out the fire.

Raft arrived at the studio in March of 1939 to star in *Each Dawn I Die*, in which he played a tough convict helping wrongly imprisoned James Cagney survive in the big house. The picture was a success, and Warner Bros. exercised its option for an additional picture, *Invisible Stripes*, this time featuring Raft as an ex-con trying to go straight at the same time as he protects his kid brother from a vicious gangster. The gangster was played by Humphrey Bogart — the first, but not the last time the two men would confront each other on the screen.

On 15 July 1939, Raft signed a long-term contract at Warner Bros. calling for three pictures a year — low by the standards of a studio used to working as many as seven movies annually out of its stars. Raft would also be allowed to make one picture a year outside the studio. Amazingly, not only was the number of pictures soon lowered to two a year, but Jack Warner even told his new star that he would not have to play what Raft called "dirty heavies." He declined, however, to commit this assurance to paper. In July of 1940, Raft's agent, Noel Gurney, pointed out to Roy Obringer, Warner's assistant, "George Raft tells me that he never has received the letter promised me by Jack Warner when I was in New York, confirming the fact that he would not be asked to play out and out heavies."

Raft never got the letter, and soon was complaining to Warner, in a memo delivered to his Waldorf Astoria suite in New York, that he was being forced to play a dirty heavy in something called *King of the Roaring Nineties*. He reminded Warner that, "I was afraid the studio would put me into parts that Humphrey Bogart should play, and you told me I would never have to play a Humphrey Bogart part." In light of what happened, that note would take on a particular irony.

Warner let his new star walk away, and *King of the Roaring Nineties* was never made. Hal Wallis now began to see George Raft in a much different light — not as an answer to the studio's problems, but a new source for them. Wallis found Raft hypersensitive to public perceptions of him as a hoodlum, and that, he concluded, was at the root of his refusal to play certain parts. At the same time, Wallis was irritated because Raft's contract was no sooner in effect than he was lobbying to be loaned out to another studio for a movie entitled *The House Across the Bay* (1940), in which he was to play "exactly the tough, low-life type he said he didn't want to play." Raft moaned that his future would be ruined if he could not do the picture. He told Wallis that he was so anxious he could not properly digest his food. Wallis, reluctant to have his employees suffering digestive problems, let him go.

Whatever warning shots were being fired, the studio appeared determined to cast Raft in just about anything that came along. The breadth of the material he was offered in a short period of time was amazing. In part, this was how Warner Bros. operated — keep everyone constantly busy — but it was also because Raft was a certified box-office star whose first Warner movie had been a big success. For a time at least, the studio really did hold Raft in high esteem, particularly Steve Trilling, who was in charge of casting. Trilling believed Raft could act on the screen better than anyone else, calling him "a guy who's got acting for films down cold."

In October 1940, Warner Bros. planned a screen adaptation of Jack London's novel *The Sea Wolf*. Wallis wanted Raft to play the brash seaman who takes on the brutal captain, Wolf Larsen, to be played by Edward G. Robinson. Raft, as usual, was having none of it. The seaman, he grumbled "was just a little bit better than a bit." Wallis wrote him that this "was a great part in a great script, and should be one of the most important pictures of the year, and you should be in it. It is the kind of part you have been wanting to play, namely the romantic lead in a good, gutsy picture. You are not a heavy, and you get the girl."

Raft waffled a bit, then refused. Eventually John Garfield, another actor who hailed from the Lower East Side of New York and had been signed by Warner Bros. the year before Raft, was given the part. Wallis was right. *The Sea Wolf* proved to be one of the most important and prestigious pictures Warner Bros. had ever done, and it helped to establish Garfield as a star.

However, *The Sea Wolf* was a minor incident compared with what came next. As Wallis later pointed out, in the next year or so, Raft made two decisions that "finally sank his career."

I N MARCH OF 1940, JOHN HUSTON, THE SON OF ACTOR WALTER HUSTON and a screenwriter toiling away at Warner Bros., wrote Hal Wallis saying he had just finished a terrific new novel by W. R. Burnett called *High Sierra*. Huston thought the story of the last days of an aging mobster named Roy "Mad Dog" Earle would make a fine, if unconventional, movie. He was so convinced of its potential that, without approval from anyone, Huston started work on a screen treatment.

Immediately, two things happened. George Raft was sought to play Earle, and Jack Warner called director Raoul Walsh to his office. Walsh had run away to sea as a boy, worked as a cowboy in Texas, Montana, and Mexico, played John Wilkes Booth, Lincoln's assassin, in D. W. Griffith's *Birth of a Nation*, and lost an eye while shooting *In Old Arizona*, the first outdoor talking picture, in 1929. He wore an eyepatch and had a reputation as a tough, no-nonsense picturemaker. Warner called him "Irish." He slapped the script of *High Sierra* down on the desk in front of Walsh. "Irish, here's a story right up your alley," Warner said.

Walsh agreed with Warner. He immediately thought of Raft, whom he had just directed in the very successful *They Drive by Night*, in which Raft co-starred with Bogart — the second and last time he worked with his rival. Walsh liked Raft and the way he had stood up to Wallace Beery when Walsh was directing the two of them in *The Bowery*. He thought Raft a pretty brave, gutsy guy and was amazed when Warner told him that the actor had already turned down *High Sierra*.

There was some suspicion that Bogart had gotten to Raft and talked him out of doing Roy Earle. W. R. Burnett later said Bogart did not think the part suited Raft, and Burnett agreed. But in Jack Warner's office, hope persisted that Raft would do the picture. "Go and see him," Warner ordered Walsh. "Perhaps he'll change his mind."

Walsh sat Raft down and talked to him for two hours. But the actor, predictably, could not be persuaded. "I'm not going to die," he insisted.

"But you have to die," Walsh argued. "You're a baddie who killed two people. The censors won't go for it unless we knock you off."

Raft was the last actor in the world who wanted to play someone who killed people and then died for it. "Tell Jack Warner to shove it," he responded.

The next choice was Paul Muni, who had starred in *Scarface*, then in one of Warners' most successful and highly regarded social issue pictures, *I Am a Fugitive from a Chain Gang*. But word was beginning to go around the studio about Raft turning everything down, and no one wanted to play second banana to him. Muni said no, although he might have been persuaded had a drunken John Huston not encountered him at a party and accused Muni of ruining *Juarez*, another picture that he had scripted. Muni was so furious he refused to appear in anything Huston wrote. They even slipped in W. R. Burnett to work on *High Sierra*, but that did not satisfy Muni.

Now everyone on the Warner lot took turns rejecting the script: Cagney because Raft and Muni did not want it, and Robinson because Cagney had it before he did. Even John Garfield, 27 years old at the time and a little young to be playing an aging gangster, was propositioned.

In later years, Walsh took credit for coming up with Bogart's name. "How about Bogart, that bit player? I think I can make him tough enough for the part," he said to Jack Warner.

"He's tough enough already or thinks he is," Jack Warner said. "Goes around with a big chip on his shoulder, and lately he's been telling people I'm a fairy. But if you want to take a chance, go ahead."

It was to be the performance that finally made everyone notice Humphrey Bogart. "*High Sierra* marked a turning point in his career," Huston said later. "It established him." Walsh was even more succinct: "The performance made him a star."

Roy Earle, on the surface, was the typical snarling Warner Bros. bad guy, but there was also unexpected romanticism and humanity, the sense of a lonely, doomed man, nearing the end, cut off from the rest of the world. Bogart somehow embodied all those things. Whether he knew what he was doing is another matter. Walsh did not recall Bogart being exactly overwhelmed with shooting *High Sierra*. The director called his star "Bogey the Beefer." Years later what stood out most in Walsh's mind was Bogart's constant complaining about everything, including the food and the accommodation on location in northern California. More than anything else, the actor playing the toughest of all gangsters lamented the absence of orange juice on the set of *High Sierra*.

Even after he had played Roy Earle, Bogart was still not particularly liked or well regarded at the studio. A memo written 18 September 1940 suggested that Ida Lupino, who played the tough moll, should receive top billing and not Bogart. "Lupino has had a great deal of publicity on the strength of *They Drive by Night*," the memo argued, "whereas Bogart has been playing the leads in a lot of 'B' pictures, and this fact might mitigate against the success of *High Sierra*."

Raft, meantime, promptly took another step in the direction of ensuring that he would be forever typecast as exactly what he did not want to be: a hoodlum.

J OHN HUSTON BY NOW HAD DETERMINED THAT THE ONLY WAY TO PRO-tect what he wrote was to become a director. He employed the clout derived from the success of *High Sierra* to demand that he direct his next picture, a screen adaptation of the Dashiell Hammett detective novel *The Maltese Falcon*. Warner Bros. was not anxious for writers to become directors, but Huston had made a canny choice: the studio liked nothing better than to recycle stories it already owned, and it owned the rights to the Hammett novel. *The Maltese Falcon* had been tried twice before, once in 1931, when it was called *Dangerous Female*, and again in 1936 as *Satan Met a Lady*, featuring Bette Davis. If Huston messed up a third version of the story, so what? The picture cost next to nothing. Nobody was expecting very much. Huston was liked well enough, and certainly he was a flamboyant, larger-than-life character, but only recently, in the wake of his first marriage and his arrival at Warner Bros., had he been credited with any kind of maturity. Before that, producer Henry Blanke described Huston as "just a drunken boy."

The studio put together a list of possible names for the main role, that of private detective Sam Spade — or "Samuel Spade" as he was referred to in memos. Spade is at the center of the movie, coolly and cleverly orchestrating the odd and rather sleazy assortment of characters tracking down the priceless bird statue known as the Maltese Falcon. Among those considered were Edward G. Robinson, Richard Whorf, Franchot Tone, Fred MacMurray, Fredric March, Henry Fonda, Brian Donlevy, Warner Baxter, Paul Muni,

Robert Montgomery, Melvyn Douglas, Preston Foster, Lloyd Nolan, and Anthony Quinn.[5] At the top of the list was George Raft. The number two name was that of Humphrey Bogart. On 19 May, a red star was penciled beside Raft's name. He would play Sam Spade.

As was customary with studio brass, the last person they wanted to learn about any casting decisions was the actor. On 19 May 1941, Hal Wallis sent Roy Obringer a memo which read:

"Please send George Raft his two weeks notice to report for work June 2nd. It will not be necessary for you to tell Raft at this time what his picture is to be, but for your own information he will do *The Maltese Falcon*."

Raft did not actually receive a copy of the script until 26 May. There was a note attached: "We shall expect you to report to our studio June 4, 1941 to commence the rendition of your services in our above referred to photoplay. . . ."

On 28 May, Raft was supposed to report to the producer Henry Blanke to discuss the script and to do wardrobe tests. Raft never showed. By now he had gotten wind of the studio's ambivalence toward the picture as well as its first-time director and had decided he wanted no part of it.

N OW WILLIAM WYLER,[6] WHO HAD UNSUCCESSFULLY TRIED TO PER-suade Raft to play in *Dead End*, once again stepped into the actor's life, trying to calm his fears about Huston. "Huston is a brilliant guy, and you can't miss with him," Wyler said.

---

[5] There was an equally long list of possibilities for Brigid O'Shaughnessy, the femme fatale of the piece. Among the actresses considered: Olivia De Havilland, Loretta Young, Rita Hayworth, Paulette Goddard, Brenda Marshall, Janet Gaynor, Joan Bennett, Betty Field, Ingrid Bergman, Frances Dee, Ruth Hussey, Laraine Day, Annabella, and Dorothy Lamour. However, Geraldine Fitzgerald, whose name was underlined in red on the list, was Warner Bros.' first choice. The Dublin-born actress never did get the sort of breaks necessary for stardom. In this case, she missed her big chance by refusing to do the movie. "If we do not get an okay from Geraldine Fitzgerald," wrote Hal Wallis on 19 May 1941, "we will use Mary Astor." Which is exactly what happened.

[6] Interestingly, Wyler also played a pivotal role in bringing Huston to Warner Bros. He had insisted the young man act as his script consultant on the production of *Jezebel* (1938) with Bette Davis. John Weld, a writer who became friends with Huston in the mid-1930s, credited Wyler with getting Huston into screenwriting, and thus opening the door to everything else. "Without Willy," Weld said, "I don't know that John would *ever* have made it."

"All right," Raft told him. "I'll do the picture, if you'll direct my next picture."

Wyler sensibly replied, "Sure, George, if I have a role that suits you." But Raft interpreted that as a rejection.

Raft tried one final ploy to avoid *The Maltese Falcon*, saying he had been offered a picture at 20th Century–Fox. Warner Bros. apparently went along, but stated that if the Fox picture had not materialized by 3 June, Raft would have to report to work on *The Maltese Falcon*.

Since there was no deal for a Fox picture, the day before he was supposed to report to the studio — and with only four days to go before Huston started shooting — Raft sent Jack Warner a note. "As you know," he wrote, "I feel strongly that *The Maltese Falcon*, which you want me to do, is not an important picture and, in this connection, I must remind you again, before I signed the new contract with you, you promised me that you would not require me to perform in anything but important pictures."

In a sense, Raft was right. Nobody at Warner Bros. considered *The Maltese Falcon* important. Still, if Raft had understood more about movies, had been better able to read the script, had known something of Hammett's work, or even understood the artistry Huston had brought to the writing of *High Sierra* — if he had just *listened* to William Wyler — he might have made another decision entirely. As it was, he walked away from what could have been the pivotal movie in his career. Huston later dismissed him curtly: "He fancied himself an actor, but he was not really a good actor."

Huston now turned to the man he had originally envisaged in the part, Humphrey Bogart. He was not hard to find. Like any Warner Bros. contract player worth his salt, Bogey was cooling his heels on a suspension imposed for his refusal to star in something called *Bad Men of Missouri*. Huston wasted no time in getting Bogart on the set. Six days after Raft wrote his note to Warner, *The Maltese Falcon* was in production. Hal Wallis, viewing the second day's rushes, was critical of Bogart, "who has adopted a leisurely, suave form of delivery. I don't think we can stand this all through the picture." He was also concerned that Bogart's makeup looked phony and that "the hairline on the headpiece [is] pretty obvious in this test. I hope it won't show up that way in the dailies."

Bogart's delivery and his hairline were adjusted accordingly, as was the title of the movie. Briefly, the studio announced it would be called *The Girl from 'Frisco*. That notion was thankfully abandoned and *The Maltese Falcon* was reality — or what passed for reality at the Warner factory. Bogart even contributed the movie's most quoted line. At the end, as Spade is holding the black bird, a detective asks him what it is. "The stuff dreams are made of," Spade replies. The line was not in the Hammett novel or in the script. It was often attributed to Huston, but before he died in 1987, the director admitted that Bogart had ad libbed that bit of dialogue.

*The Maltese Falcon* was released in October of 1941 and, to the pleasant surprise of Warner Bros., became both a critical hit and an unexpected commercial success. Raft got almost as much attention as the movie itself for being so dumb as to turn down Sam Spade. The *Los Angeles Daily News* reported on 6 October 1941 that "George Raft is doing a slow burn over Humphrey Bogart's hit performance in *The Maltese Falcon*, one of the fall season's best films. Raft turned down the role."

On 17 October, columnist Hedda Hopper noted Raft's penchant for turning down roles, and Dorothy Manners reported on 19 October that "Humphrey Bogart, who has played more roles turned down by other actors than any other player in Hollywood, was reading a new script last week. 'Hmmm,' he hemmed to his wife, Mayo Methot, 'this can't be any good. No one on the lot turned it down.'"

Another columnist, Jimmy Fiedler, caught up with Raft himself and asked him about *The Maltese Falcon*. His comment made as much sense as any of his actions at Warner Bros. "There but for the grace of me, go I," he said.

INSTEAD OF *THE MALTESE FALCON*, IN JUNE 1941, GEORGE RAFT WAS assigned to *Manpower*, a melodrama not about gangsters, but about the brave boys who risk their lives to work with high voltage wires. Raft, as usual, hesitated when he got word that Bogart was going to be in it. Edward G. Robinson was cast, but Raft did not get along with him, either. The two men brawled on the set, the only time in his life, Robinson said later, that he ever hit anybody off camera. Raft said they fought because Robinson was always putting him down, but it probably had as much to do with the infatuation both men had for their co-star, Marlene Dietrich, who was accurately described in *Manpower* as "a dame who can only be trouble."

In July 1941, having completed *Manpower*, Raft refused to do a gangster spoof titled *All Through the Night*, in which he was to play a New York gambler named Gloves Donohue chasing the Nazis who killed the baker of his favorite cheesecake. Who else to replace Raft but his old standby and archrival, Humphrey Bogart, fresh from that triumph of replacement, *The Maltese Falcon*. This time, though, Bogart's agent had had enough and pointed out his client's dissatisfaction, adding, "It seems that for the past year, he's practically pinch-hitted for Raft, and been kicked around from pillar to post." But Bogart, as usual, went along, and did the part — not a bad one either. George Raft never let Bogey down; he always left the best roles for him.

Jack Warner referred to Bogart as "an apple polisher," and grumbled that his success came from "licking assholes." He thought Bogart was ugly and had a lisp, and was not much good for anything but gangster parts, although before he did *The Petrified Forest*, Warner could not even be convinced that he was a good hoodlum. For a long time, Bogart was an object of scorn around Warner Bros. "A lot of people disliked him, and he knew it," James Cagney said. "He hated everybody. But when it came to fighting, he was about as tough as Shirley Temple."

Cagney recalled that he once spotted Bogart in the car next to him, picking his nose. Gleefully, Cagney composed a poem, and sent it off to Bogart. It read: "In this silly town of ours/ One sees odd primps and poses/ But movie stars in fancy cars/ Shouldn't pick their fancy noses." Bogart never responded. However, the image of Sam Spade from *The Maltese Falcon* and Rick Blaine of *Casablanca* picking his nose in Beverly Hills resonates through time.

By 1940, the attitude toward Bogart had begun to change. S. Charles Einfeld, the studio's director of advertising and publicity, urged that a campaign be mounted to turn Bogart into a star. "Bogart has been typed through publicity as a gangster character," he wrote. "We must undo this. For Bogart is one of the greatest actors on the screen today and has demonstrated this with his parts in *The Petrified Forest*, *Dark Victory*, *It All Came True*, and *They Drive by Night*. This fellow is a master of technique and can do anything. Sell Bogart romantically. Sell him as a great actor. Let us see if within the next three months we cannot have the country flooded with Bogart art and column breaks, lauding Warner Bros. for their recognition of Bogart's talent and producing a great success for him as a star."

So preparations for the transformation of Bogart from gangster to romantic lead were already under way when *Casablanca* came along. How close Raft — or anyone else, including Ronald Reagan, who, over the years, was often listed as a candidate [7] — ever came to starring in it is questionable. Wallis later said that "Raft turned down Rick," a decision that, given Raft's track record, hardly surprised him. Raft told his biographer, Lewis Yablonsky, that the role of Rick was not right for him.

Certainly when the obscure, never-performed play *Everyone Comes to Rick's* first came to the attention of Warner Bros., there was interest in Raft. Associate producer Jerry Wald wrote to Hal Wallis on 23 December 1941 saying, "This story should make a good vehicle for either Raft or Bogart." Early in April of 1942, Jack Warner sent Wallis a memo asking, "What do you think of using Raft in *Casablanca*? He knows we are going to make this, and is starting a campaign for it."

That hardly sounded like an actor proposing to turn down a role, but it made little difference. On 13 April, Wallis wrote back to Warner saying he had discussed Raft's casting with the director, Michael Curtiz, "and we both feel he [Raft] should not be in the picture. Bogart is ideal for it, and it is being written for him, and I think we should forget Raft for this property."

Not only did Wallis dismiss Raft for *Casablanca*, he also seemed to write him off as far as any future involvement with the studio was concerned: "Incidentally, he [Raft] hasn't done a picture here since I was a little boy, and I don't think he should be able to put his finger on just what he wants to do, when he wants to do it."

Raft, instead of being less trouble than anyone else, was turning out to be the biggest nuisance on the lot. At least the others would make movies. Warner Bros. could not even get Raft in front of a camera. After turning down *All Through the Night* in September, he refused to report for a film called *Juke Girl* (he was replaced by Ronald Reagan). In April of 1942, he failed to report for start of production on a Raoul Walsh picture called *Deadline* (which was

---

[7] Reagan mentions nothing about *Casablanca* in his autobiography. According to Aljean Harmetz in her book on the making of the movie, titled *Round Up the Usual Suspects*, Warner Bros. issued a press release printed in *Variety* 5 January 1942 that Ronald Reagan would co-star with Ann Sheridan. But apparently that sort of thing was done all the time, and Reagan could never have made *Casablanca* anyway, because he was off filming *Desperate Journey* with Errol Flynn.

never made), although he did agree to go over to Universal to dance once again in *Broadway*. By now, even Raft understood the pattern he had fallen into at Warner Bros. "I suppose I'll go back over there, turn down another story, and get suspended again," he said from the *Broadway* set at Universal. "As far as I'm concerned, I don't care if I never make another picture on the Warner lot."

He did make one last picture, a pretty good one, actually, *Background to Danger*. Directed by Raoul Walsh and written by *High Sierra*'s W. R. Burnett, Raft played an American agent trying to stop the Nazis from pulling neutral Turkey into the war. *Background to Danger* tried to summon visions of *Casablanca*, particularly in its casting of Peter Lorre and Sydney Greenstreet in featured parts, but never came to anything more than an entertaining imitation.

After he finished *Background* in December of 1942, less than a month before *Casablanca* opened and became the most prestigious picture Warner Bros. had done since *The Jazz Singer*, George Raft petitioned the studio to release him from his contract. As Humphrey Bogart became one of the biggest stars in the picture that would ensure his status as a screen legend, Raft began his descent toward obscurity. He even paid for the ride — agreeing to reimburse Jack Warner $10,000 the studio head said he was owed. Actually, it was not such a bad deal. Raft had made $288,396.82 between 1939 and 1942 for appearing in only five pictures. That amounted to $57,679 per picture, not bad considering that Bogart had made 18 movies during that same period, receiving only $11,200 for *High Sierra* and $16,500 for *The Maltese Falcon*. Bogart may have been paid less, but thanks to George Raft, he earned much more.

R AFT WAS GIVEN ONE MORE OPPORTUNITY TO AVOID A CLASSIC MOVIE shortly after he left Warner Bros. As usual, he took it. Billy Wilder, the Viennese-born screenwriter who lately had turned to directing, was about to start work on a screen adaptation of *Double Indemnity*. His usual collaborator, Charles Brackett, so hated the James M. Cain novella that he refused to be part of it. Wilder, after a great deal of difficulty, had worked out a screenplay with the novelist Raymond Chandler. Now he was in search of an actor to play Walter Neff, the insurance salesman who enters into a Faustian pact with a beautiful woman (Barbara Stanwyck) to kill her husband. When

▲ *Al Jolson in*
The Jazz
Singer *(1927):
stolen immortal-
ity in the first
talking picture.*

▶ *George Jessel,
around the time
he lost out on*
The Jazz
Singer.

▲ *Humphrey Bogart became a star after he appeared in* The Maltese Falcon *(1941).*

▲ *Meanwhile George Raft turned it down, and was consigned to oblivion.*

▲ *Raft and Bogart together in* They Drive by Night *(1940).*

▼ *(inset below)*
*Robert Donat*
*appeared with*
*Madeleine Carroll in*
The Thirty-Nine
Steps *(1935) then*
*said no to* Captain
Blood *(1935) …*

▶ *… Opening the*
*way for unknown*
*Errol Flynn to*
*become a*
*swashbuckling*
*star.*

▲ *Vivien Leigh: in her screen test (with Douglass Montgomery) and on the set of* Gone With the Wind *(1939).*

◄ *If it hadn't been for Leigh, Scarlett probably would have been played by Paulette Goddard.*

▶ *Ronald Colman (with Jane Wyatt in* Lost Horizon, 1937*) wanted to play Rhett Butler.*

▲ *But the world insisted on a reluctant Clark Gable (with Vivien Leigh).*

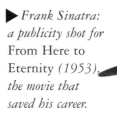

> ▶ *Frank Sinatra:*
> *a publicity shot for*
> From Here to
> Eternity *(1953),*
> *the movie that*
> *saved his career.*

> ◀ *Marlon Brando in*
> On the Waterfront
> *(1954). He won*
> *an Oscar for the role*
> *Sinatra should have*
> *had ...*

> ◀ *... And 25*
> *years later,*
> *in* Apocalypse
> Now *(1979).*

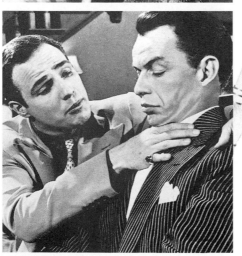

> ◀ *Brando and Sinatra,*
> *together in* Guys and
> Dolls *(1955), didn't*
> *like each other, on screen*
> *or off.*

▲ *James Dean died shortly after completing* Giant *(1956).*

▲ *His death made it possible for a brooding Paul Newman to star in* Somebody Up There Likes Me *(1956).*

▲ *Steve McQueen always resented Paul Newman's success. But the two finally co-starred together in* The Towering Inferno *(1974) with Faye Dunaway.*

◀ *Rock Hudson said he preferred Elizabeth Taylor to Grace Kelly in* Giant *(1956).*

▼ *But he wasn't allowed to star in* Ben-Hur *(1959). Charlton Heston got Haya Harareet, and an Oscar.*

Alan Ladd, then the biggest star on the Paramount lot, passed, Wilder turned to George Raft.

As Wilder recalled it, Raft refused to read the script, saying he did not read scripts. "Tell it to me," he demanded. Raft appeared not to understand the story very well and wanted to know when Neff would flash his badge to make it clear that he was a detective. Wilder was taken aback. Raft, clearly missing the point of *Double Indemnity*, turned Wilder down. "That's when we knew we had a good picture," the director said later. The word about Raft had gotten around. The role went instead to a reluctant Fred MacMurray, who could not believe what he was getting himself into. But he did something Raft always refused to do — he trusted the director — and because he did, he got what he later said was the best role of his career.

Fifteen years later, Wilder returned to Raft, but this time it was for the cliché of himself — the coin-flipping gangster who pursues Jack Lemmon and Tony Curtis in *Some Like It Hot*. By that time Raft had given up any thoughts of eluding his past. "Typecasting again," he said ruefully of the part in the Wilder comedy, "but what can you do? I just never seemed to make the break away to other roles the way Bogart and Cagney did."

Raft had no one but himself to blame for that. Through the 1940s he made a series of increasingly forgettable program pictures until by the 1950s he was reduced to making B movies. The older he got, the less he was remembered as a movie star and the more he became associated with the hoodlum past he wanted everyone to forget.

Humphrey Bogart was sprung from the Warner internment camp in 1947 after finishing *The Treasure of the Sierra Madre* and *Key Largo*, his last great films for the studio. In *Key Largo* he even got to gun down Edward G. Robinson, a kind of revenge for all those years at Warner Bros. when everyone was filling Bogey full of lead. Bogart won an Academy Award for *The African Queen* in 1951, and he got to play the most outrageously different role of his career, the weak, sniveling Captain Queeg in *The Caine Mutiny*. But the majority of the pictures he made in his post-studio period were run-of-the-mill rehashes of what he had done much better at Warner Bros. He could have used George Raft to run interference, rejecting movie roles so that he would know which ones were really worthy of him.

Raft never smoked or drank and therefore could take some satisfaction from his longevity. Bogart died of lung cancer at the age of 57, but even in death he continued to haunt Raft. Beginning in the late 1950s and early '60s, Bogart and his movies — particularly *The Maltese Falcon* and *Casablanca* — attained a cult status that persists to this day. Raft was there to watch as Bogart, the legend he might have been, became even more famous in death than he was in life. If he had any thoughts one way or the other about this, however, he kept them to himself.

George Raft died in 1980 at the age of 85. Lewis Yablonsky saw him in the hospital a week before his death. "He didn't dwell on the past or the errors that he made," said Yablonsky, who believed Raft finished life essentially a happy man. He recalled one day after lunch with Raft at the Beverly Wilshire Hotel, as they were about to cross the street, he heard someone behind them mutter the actor's name. "Hey, George Raft," the voice said. "Hey, he had his day."

But Raft gave no sign that he had heard the comment. He started across the street, and never looked back.

# 4

# "BUT IT'S IN TECHNICOLOR," HE SPUTTERED.
## *The misalliance of Flynn and Davis*

HARRY WARNER, WHO, BEFORE *THE JAZZ SINGER*, HAD WONDERED why anyone would want to hear actors talking, thought just about anybody could be a movie star. In the midst of ranting one day about the evils of stars, he grabbed a handsome young producer in the studio commissary and claimed that Warner Bros. could make *him* a star if they chose to. Why, according to Harry, you could even turn a corpse into a movie star. And that is exactly what happened.

Jack Warner liked an adventure novel by Rafael Sabatini entitled *Captain Blood*. It was Warner's kind of project: the studio already owned the rights, so nothing would have to be paid out in order to mount a production. The novel, originally published in 1922, was turned into a 1924 silent movie starring J. Warren Kerrigan. The story dealt with a young English doctor in the 17th century, wrongly imprisoned, who escaped to become the leader of a band of pirates. Sabatini based his hero on a real-life pirate, Henry Morgan. Such was the excitement about the project at the studio that production supervisor Harry Joe Brown felt there was not an actor in the business "too big to go after. . . . I am confident it is one of the best stories ever written." Jack Warner, as usual, was not interested in big stars who would cost a lot of money. He had his eye on a young British actor named Robert Donat.

Donat, who would come to epitomize on film the charming, courteous English hero, was actually the son of a Polish immigrant father and a British mother. Elocution lessons begun at age 11 enabled him to overcome a stutter, and at 16 he made his stage debut. By the time he appeared on film in 1932 (in something called *Men of Tomorrow*), Donat had amassed an impressive background with touring companies and on the London stage in a wide variety of Shakespearean and classical roles. He was tall, slim, good-looking, but possessed of a rather high, nasal voice. Nonetheless, movie producers almost immediately were interested in him — an interest he took great pains not to reciprocate. He turned down the offer of a contract from Irving Thalberg at MGM, but did agree to work for Alexander Korda in *The Private Life of Henry VIII* (1933). The film not only won its star, Charles Laughton, an Academy Award, it also established Donat.

Hollywood called him again, this time to appear in a screen version of the Alexandre Dumas classic *The Count of Monte Cristo*. Again, he agreed. Like *Captain Blood*, it dealt with a young man wrongly imprisoned. Warner, being able to typecast with the best of them, figured that if Donat had been wrongly jailed once, it could happen again. Moreover, he wielded a sword and had a British accent — perfect for *Captain Blood*. The Warner Bros. man in London, Irving Asher, was ordered to complete negotiations and sign a deal for Donat's services. Meanwhile, in Hollywood, a huge galleon was being constructed on Stage Seven, and the rest of the cast was gathered together, including a young actress named Olivia De Havilland, the daughter of a British patent attorney, who had come to Hollywood at the age of three. She recently had been signed to the usual seven-year Warner Bros. contract on the strength of her first movie appearance in Max Reinhardt's version of Shakespeare's *A Midsummer Night's Dream*.

Back in London, Donat was becoming increasingly uneasy at the reaction to *The Count of Monte Cristo*. "Just because I did a fencing scene in *Cristo* with a small moustache, Hollywood thinks I'm a new Douglas Fairbanks," he grumbled. "Fairbanks was an agile and engaging monkey and is now dead as a doornail. None of his pictures would stand revival. I am certainly not the second Douglas Fairbanks. I am the first Robert Donat. One has to fight to preserve one's individuality."

As wary as he was, Donat agreed to do *Captain Blood*. First, however, he was contracted to star in a British picture, a thriller based on a novel by John Buchan entitled *The Thirty-Nine Steps*. It was to be directed by a rather formal and extremely rotund young man named Alfred Hitchcock. Donat would doubtless have gone off to Hollywood at once had he not encountered Hitchcock. He very much liked working with him, and the director in turn later credited his star for the picture's success. "He is not in any way a comedian," Hitchcock said of Donat. "But he had a beautiful dry quality and that was his great contribution to any particular picture."

*The Thirty-Nine Steps* opened in June of 1935 and was an immediate hit. Donat decided he had no need of *Captain Blood*. His career was precisely where he wanted it to be in England. Hollywood was of no interest to him. When the script arrived, he immediately decided he disliked it, judging writer Casey Robinson's work to be "poor." Given the evidence of the finished picture, that seems hard to believe, but Donat was more convinced than ever that Warner Bros. had seen only the swashbuckling elements in *The Count of Monte Cristo*. He thought those were the least convincing aspects of his performance. Donat did seem wooden during the sword-fighting scenes, and years later his sons, attending a revival of the film, were nearly tossed out, so hard did they laugh at the spectacle of their father in a duel.

Donat would not do *Captain Blood*, but that was not the end of it. After all, he had signed a contract calling for Warner Bros. to pay him $25,000 in exchange for his services in the film. It was at that moment that the studio played into Donat's hands. Somehow, Warner Bros.' Irving Asher misunderstood — intentionally or otherwise — and the amount actually paid to Donat was only $20,000. It was pretext enough for his agent to cancel the contract.

Warner Bros. took Donat to court over the matter, called him "a stubborn young guy," but did not, when all was said and done, have a legal leg to stand on. The studio lost the case, and Donat was overjoyed. He was one of the few actors Jack Warner ever encountered who did not want to be a movie star. "What is a star?" he once mused. "It is a foolish description to apply to an actor. He should, if possible, be a different man every time he appears before the public, changing, pliant, and always different." And that was how Donat played out his career. He turned down another Warner Bros. swashbuckler, *The Adventures of Robin Hood*, and a few years later unexpectedly beat out Clark Gable's Rhett Butler to win the 1939 Academy Award for best actor, playing a gentle English schoolteacher in *Goodbye, Mr. Chips,* the screen adaptation of James Hilton's novel. Aged for much of the movie, outfitted with a wig and a thick gray mustache, he was all but unrecognizable. Which was how Robert Donat always preferred it.

As for the upcoming production of *Captain Blood,* Hal Wallis was now told that Donat could not come back to Hollywood because the climate would aggravate his asthma. Asher lied outright to Wallis, saying that Donat had burst into tears in his office and claimed his girlfriend refused to travel to America. Did Asher tell Wallis that in an attempt to cover up his carelessness over the $25,000? Or did he have something else up his sleeve? Asher may have been working from his own agenda by now. He had discovered an actor he thought would be much better for *Captain Blood* — who had no qualms whatsoever about movie stardom.

T HE YEAR BEFORE, ERROL FLYNN HAD GONE TO VISIT IRVING ASHER IN his office at First National Studios in Teddington, outside London. Flynn had been born in Tasmania of Australian parents. By the time he arrived in England, he had had enough careers for several lifetimes — among them, gold miner, sailor, and plantation manager in New Guinea. The aura of the adventurer clung to him — and of the scoundrel. Flynn had never even thought of acting until he was asked to appear as Fletcher Christian in a rather amateurish Australian film, *In the Wake of the Bounty*. It was enough to whet his appetite for the business, and he promptly decided to pursue an acting career.

By the time he came to see Asher, Flynn had been in London for a year, doing some repertory theater work but unable to land anything in films. Asher was immediately impressed with the handsome, athletic-looking young man who sat before him and put him under contract without so much as a screen test. He wired the home office: "Signed today seven years' optional contract best picture bet we have ever seen. He twenty-five Irish looks cross between Charles Farrell and George Brent same type and build excellent actor champion boxer swimmer guarantee he real find."

Three days later, Flynn was standing in front of a camera. A low-budget British "quota quickie" titled *Murder at Monte Carlo* was urgently in need of a leading man, and Flynn was it. Shortly thereafter, Flynn was dispatched to Hollywood on a salary of $125 a week. Jack Warner ordered all the writers under contract to take a look at *Murder at Monte Carlo* with a view to coming up with other film projects for the studio's newest acquisition. One of the writers, Delmer Daves, saw no sign of Flynn's potential — only a rather self-conscious young actor. "But he *was* the handsome man who was to conquer a few million female hearts," Daves conceded, "and he was signed based more on that attribute than any evident acting ability."

Flynn's first role was in a Perry Mason mystery titled *The Case of the Curious Bride*. He was on his feet for a short silent scene near the end of the eighty-minute film, but his main assignment was to play a corpse seen only in silhouette — an inauspicious debut in American movies, to say the least. That was soon to change. The corpse was about to become a movie star.

At the Warner Bros. front office, panic was beginning to set in over *Captain Blood*. The cast and sets were ready; all that was missing was a leading man. Leslie Howard was suggested, as were Fredric March and Ronald Colman. Hal Wallis briefly considered George Brent, then decided he was not colorful enough. They were days away from shooting.

Minna Wallis, Hal Wallis's sister, was Flynn's Hollywood agent. She suggested him, and Michael Curtiz, who was to direct *Captain Blood* — and had directed *The Case of the Curious Bride* — thought it a good idea. But as far as Jack Warner was concerned, this Errol Flynn was a nobody. Brian Aherne was tested for the role, as was Ian Hunter, a young actor from South Africa who also had been dispatched from London by Irving Asher. Curtiz persuaded Warner to let him do a test with Flynn, and everyone was excited by the results.

"It seemed not to matter whether he could act," Wallis later observed. "He leapt from the screen into the projection room with the impact of a bullet." Warner was equally knocked out. "I knew we had grabbed the brass ring in our two-thousand-to-one shot with Flynn. What's more," the cost-conscious studio head gloated, "he only cost three hundred dollars a week."

Later, Flynn was to give Warner full credit for casting him: "He had the guts to take a complete unknown and put me in the lead of a big production." He might also have thanked Irving Asher, Warners' man in London, who probably had a lot more to do with Errol Flynn's attaining stardom than he ever let on.

Whoever was responsible, Flynn's appreciation was short-lived. Wallis reported that on the first day of shooting, Flynn arrived late without having memorized his lines, and had no idea how to act them. "But as soon as he was on camera, everything was fine," Wallis conceded. "The camera loved everything he did. . . . [Flynn] wasn't an admirable character, but he was a magnificent male animal, and his sex appeal was obvious."

Given his lack of experience, Flynn's grace and dexterity in *Captain*

*Blood* were breathtaking. If Donat looked wooden and uncertain in a sword-fight, Flynn dueling it out with Basil Rathbone in the sands of Laguna Beach — which stood in for a Caribbean island — looked as though he had been born with a rapier in his hand. Donat was an actor, not an athlete; Flynn was a fine tennis player, swimmer, and boxer, who took easily to both fencing and horseback riding. He came complete with a great smile and a roguish twinkle in his eye, and he had no curious opinions about stardom. The moment the movie opened, his future was assured. At a party following the premiere of *Captain Blood* in December of 1935, Flynn's new bride, the petite and lovely French actress Lili Damita, whom he had met on the ship to America, broke down and began to weep. "Don't . . . please . . . tell him how wonderful he was," she begged Delmer Daves. "Tonight, I have lost my husband."

It was already too late. Everyone told Errol Flynn how wonderful he was, and for a long time he believed it. However, it was evident to Hal Wallis almost from the beginning that Flynn was not a disciplined performer and that he had no real interest in what he was doing. He had a wonderful time being a movie star, though, and even Warner could not resist his charm. He called Flynn "the Baron," and he probably saw a great deal of himself reflected in the actor. Warner never wanted to be Bogart or Cagney or Edward G. Robinson. But he would not have minded at all being Errol Flynn. "To the Walter Mittys of the world, he was all the heroes in one magnificent, sexy, animal package," Warner wrote late in his life. "I just wish we had someone around today half as good as Flynn."

Not everyone felt that way. The most talented, contrary, and difficult star in Hollywood viewed him in a much harsher and more critical light, and partly because she did, Bette Davis and Errol Flynn missed out on the greatest roles of their careers.

I N 1934, TWO YEARS AFTER ARRIVING AT WARNER BROS., RUTH ELIZABETH Davis was fed up — hardly a unique emotional state around the studio. Her dissatisfaction stemmed from the studio's failure to put her into anything but indifferent pictures, again, not unusual around Warner Bros. There seemed to be nothing she could do about the situation until suddenly a rival studio, RKO, asked her to co-star as Mildred in a screen version of W. Somerset Maugham's *Of Human Bondage*. The studio might have been indifferent to Davis's unhappiness, but that did not mean it was about to do anything silly like loaning out one of its contract players.

Ruth Elizabeth, as usual, was not playing by rules laid down by a studio that at the time could have cared less if she had dropped dead on a sound stage. She saw opportunity in *Of Human Bondage*, and proceeded to do what she did best, next to acting: fight tooth and nail to get her way.

"Go ahead, bury yourself," Jack Warner finally sneered. But the opposite happened. For the first time since she began acting professionally, Ruth Elizabeth had found a glorious opportunity to demonstrate the kind of strength and independence that would be the hallmark of her most memorable screen performances. Ruth Elizabeth Davis was not buried in *Of Human Bondage*: Bette Davis was born.

Jack Warner did not take kindly to being wrong, and plotted his revenge. Safely returned to the Warner lot, Davis got a call from a young director over at Columbia named Frank Capra who was preparing a new comedy. Davis loved the script and was anxious to work with Capra, but Warner would not hear of loaning out a contract player for two pictures in a row. He decreed that Bette Davis would *not* co-star in *It Happened One Night*.

Denied his first choice, Capra then turned to a number of other actresses, including Claudette Colbert, who reluctantly agreed to do the picture with Clark Gable. It became a runaway smash, and won Oscars for just about everyone involved, including Claudette Colbert. "I was heartbroken at missing *It Happened One Night*, and working with Clark Gable," Davis said years later. "What a thrill it would have been."

Fate is never far away in these matters, and 16 years later it added an ironic twist to the story. Claudette Colbert was preparing to star in a new film for Joseph L. Mankiewicz. But just before production was to start, she injured her back during a ski accident and had to bow out. Davis was finishing a movie entitled *Payment on Demand*. Her career had fallen into the doldrums, and she was very unhappy. Then a call came from Darryl Zanuck. Would she consider replacing Colbert in the Mankiewicz movie, to be called *All About Eve*?

Davis read Mankiewicz's script about an aging Broadway diva named Margo Channing, whose career is savaged by a young upstart actress, and knew immediately it was the role she was born to play. Five days after finishing *Payment on Demand*, she began work on *All About Eve*. The actress who had lost out to Claudette Colbert in *It Happened One Night* replaced her in the film that would revitalize her career. Now it was Colbert's turn to spend a lifetime mourning the loss of a part that could have made all the difference.

E VEN NOW, DESPITE DESCRIPTIONS IN NUMEROUS BIOGRAPHIES, AND AT least three of her own memoirs, the very ferocity with which Bette Davis strove for and then maintained movie stardom comes as a shock. By pure grit and determination, Davis fashioned the most remarkable career of any woman in the history of movies, and did so in the face of countless rejections that began from the moment she decided to become an actress. Eva Le Gallienne turned her down as a student; George Cukor fired her from her first professional engagement with a stock company in Rochester, New York; and she was promptly dismissed from Samuel Goldwyn Productions after a screen test flopped. Even when Davis landed a contract at Universal, studio boss Carl Laemmle commented that she had "as much sex appeal as Slim Summerville."

Eventually, she gained attention and a contract at Warner Bros. when she appeared with George Arliss in *The Man Who Played God* in 1932. But she locked into a man's world at Warner Bros. Outside the Warner gates was another, equally limiting world called Hollywood that demanded beauty and perfection from its women. Bette Davis was neither beautiful nor perfect, but she was immensely talented and stubborn, and, no matter what, she was not to be pushed around — much or often. She later said that her major problem was with Jack Warner, which was no surprise. That was everyone's major problem at Warner Bros. Hal Wallis made it possible for her to survive. "He never personally liked the type of pictures I made," she said. "He bought the best properties he could find for me, and they were done with great care, but he really preferred the hard cynical pictures of Robinson, Bogart and Cagney."

However, in 1936, despite the success of *Of Human Bondage*, and having won her first Oscar the year before for *Dangerous*, a tearjerker forgotten almost as soon as the awards ceremony was over, Davis was still miserable about the kinds of parts the studio was forcing her into. She had appeared in *The Petrified Forest* with Leslie Howard, the movie that helped establish Humphrey Bogart at the studio, but she was also forced into such forgettable items as *The Golden Arrow* and an early version of Dashiell Hammett's *The Maltese Falcon*, retitled *Satan Met a Lady* (1936). When Jack Warner came along with her next project, *God's Country and the Woman*, in which she was to play a lumberjack, that was enough. She stormed into his office.

"But it's in Technicolor," he sputtered, "you'll have George Brent as co-star." Davis would have none of it. Warner tried one more tack. On his desk was a new novel that had yet to be published. The book's heroine appeared to have been created with Bette Davis in mind. If she would just do *God's Country and the Woman*, Warner would be only too glad to buy the book for her. Davis was far beyond believing anything Warner promised. "I'll bet it's a pip!" she snarled, stomped out of his office, and went on suspension.

And that was the first, but not the last time, that Bette Davis turned down the opportunity to play Scarlett O'Hara in *Gone With the Wind*.

NO BATTLE FOR A STARRING ROLE HAS BEEN MORE WIDELY REPORTED than the one over the casting of Scarlett O'Hara. It was the one role that every actress at the time dreamed of and coveted, and it was the part that producer David O. Selznick used to tantalize the public while he tried to make *Gone With the Wind* more than just a publicist's dream project. The search for Scarlett effectively camouflaged Selznick's problems in creating a workable script or even in making a deal with one of the studios.

However, what began as a great publicity stunt eventually degenerated into one more show of indecisiveness on Selznick's part. Was it really necessary to go through all the machinations he did to find Scarlett? Probably not. There were at least three actresses, including Bette Davis, who would have performed magnificently in the part, but it can also be argued that all the doubts and delays resulted in the casting of the actress who best suited all aspects of the role. And after all, the casting of Scarlett is not simply part of the legend of *Gone With the Wind*, but its central, most memorable drama. The finding of Scarlett became a national obsession, and there has not been one remotely like it since.

In late May of 1936, Kay Brown, Selznick's reader in New York, who first read Margaret Mitchell's manuscript, thought Scarlett could be played by either Miriam Hopkins or Margaret Sullavan. Selznick at first was unimpressed with the idea of turning *Gone With the Wind* into a movie. His secretary read the Margaret Mitchell novel and didn't like it, while his assistant, Val Lewton, thought it "ponderous trash." But Kay Brown continued to push him from New York, this time suggesting Bette Davis as Scarlett.

Bette Davis, in fact, could have had the part any number of times in the course of the Scarlett search. She might even have been forced to do it if Selznick had been able to make a deal with Jack Warner for *GWTW*, as he seemed on the verge of doing on a number of occasions. In a poll conducted to ascertain who the public preferred, Davis received the highest number of votes. As Selznick himself admitted in 1939, "it would have been very simple" for all concerned to have cast her.

But Davis herself was a major problem. One of the reasons Selznick wanted to make a deal with Warner Bros. was so that he could cast Davis as Scarlett, with Errol Flynn as Rhett Butler. Despite her determination to play Scarlett, she could not bring herself to accept Flynn as her co-star. "She thought she was the greatest actress who ever lived," Flynn sneered. For her part, Davis felt Flynn had no respect for her as an actress "because I was a worker at my profession, and he was not." Moreover, she was absolutely convinced that Flynn would be miscast as Rhett "and therefore my performance would have been hampered."

Jack Warner did not help matters, as far as Selznick was concerned, by going ahead with Bette Davis in *Jezebel*, a movie based on a play by Owen Davis, Sr., about a passionate, headstrong New Orleans belle named Julie Marsden, in love with an Ashley Wilkes type played by Henry Fonda, while keeping at bay a n'er-do-well Rhett Butler–style rake, played by George Brent. Everyone, Selznick included, saw *Jezebel* as a patent attempt on Warner's part to get the jump on *GWTW*, which, by the time *Jezebel* was released in the early spring of 1938, had been delayed endlessly and still had no Scarlett. Even so, Selznick might well have ended up at Warner Bros. with Davis and Flynn as his stars. Jack Warner offered more money ($850,000 more), a better distribution deal, and more profit participation. But Selznick finally decided to go with MGM in July of 1938, principally because he felt MGM's parent company, Loew's Inc., would do a better job of marketing the film.

When the announcement was made on 20 July 1938 that Selznick had reached agreement with MGM to make *Gone With the Wind*, Bette Davis finally knew Scarlett O'Hara was not to be hers. She remained convinced for the rest of her life that she would have been the best actress for the role. "I was as perfect for Scarlett," she declared, "as Clark Gable was for Rhett. . . .

It was insanity that I not be given Scarlett. But then, Hollywood has never been rational."

As for Errol Flynn, Davis seemingly never changed her opinion of his acting skills. They would co-star in *The Private Lives of Elizabeth and Essex* (Davis had stated flatly that she could picture only Laurence Olivier as Essex), a Michael Curtiz film released in 1939. "To me the only fly in the ointment was the casting of Errol Flynn as Essex," Davis wrote. "He wasn't an experienced enough actor to cope with the complicated blank verse the [Maxwell Anderson] play had been written in."

Eleven years later, *All About Eve* momentarily pumped new life into the career of Bette Davis, but otherwise her movies during the 1950s were mostly mediocre, a far cry from the days when Hal Wallis was tailoring the best scripts to her talents and assigning the finest directors to film her movies. Errol Flynn's popularity began to fall apart in the late '40s, along with his health. He drank too much and he started taking drugs. Captain Blood looked at least 10 years older than his 43 years when he retreated from Hollywood in 1952 to hide out in Europe, where he would make a series of infinitely forgettable films.

# 5

# RHETT TO HER SCARLETT
## Clark Gable, Vivien Leigh, and GWTW

S EVERAL PROMINENT ACTORS WERE INITIALLY SUGGESTED FOR THE ROLE OF
Rhett Butler. One of them was Gary Cooper, and another was Ronald
Colman, whom Selznick had approached at the very start. Colman, a
native of Richmond, England, was in his mid-40s in 1936. He had taken up
acting after the First World War but had not amounted to much until Lillian
Gish chose him to be her leading man in *The White Sister* in 1923.

Selznick spoke at length to the actor about playing Rhett Butler, and
Colman responded with a great deal of enthusiasm. "*Gone With the Wind* is
tremendous and I'd like to play Rhett," he wrote to Selznick. "If you think I
would and should play Rhett, I'd do it like a shot, subject to the character not
being too much emasculated for picture purposes, and conditional on a chat
with you as to Scarlett, etc. etc."

The eagerness for Colman in the part was exceedingly short-lived. The
only person in Hollywood who thought him perfect for the role was Clark
Gable. Of course everyone believed that Gable was born to be Rhett, but he
was convinced they were wrong; after all, he did spend his entire professional
life fighting hard to avoid good parts.

Clark Gable was the purest creation of the studio system of the 1930s
and 1940s, a product of the MGM star-making apparatus working at its most
awesome capacity to shape him into the most popular male star of the time.
This was accomplished by carefully manufacturing vehicles that showed off
the sort of splendidly rough masculinity beloved of both male and female
Depression-era audiences.

Gable was not a fighter the way Bogart and Cagney and Bette Davis
had to be over at Warner Bros. He tended to go along, because going along at
MGM brought him untold fame and fortune. When the studio thought it a

good idea for him to learn to hunt and fish — enterprises that would add to his image of rugged masculinity — Gable learned to hunt and fish, and even found that he enjoyed those pastimes. When the studio fretted about their married movie star running around with Carole Lombard, Gable smoldered, but he kept the affair hidden. And when the studio wanted him to do a movie, he usually went along, grumbling, but he went along, which in his case was just as well. Left to his own shaky devices when it came to choosing material, God knows what he would have ended up in.

Gable tended to treat women badly on the screen, gaining the first gleam of notoriety in 1931 by slapping Norma Shearer around in *A Free Soul*. That sort of rough treatment of women coupled with a flirtatious style — smugly dashing eyebrows dancing above an irritating smirk — today makes him the most obvious and outdated of matinee idols. Gable was never a very natural actor, and there was something forced about his onscreen charm, whereas, by contrast, the naturalness of someone like Gary Cooper seems much more contemporary. However, audiences both male and female adored him, and his popularity at the time was surpassed only by that of Shirley Temple.

Gable had been born in Cadiz, Ohio, in 1901, to a farm family. He was finished with school by the age of 14 and working in a tire factory in Akron, Ohio, when he first became interested in the theater, starting out as a page boy for a local stock company. His stage career was interrupted by a father who dragged him off to Oklahoma to work as an oil driller, but as soon as he turned 21, Gable joined a theater troupe that soon left him stranded in Oregon. There he worked variously as a lumberjack and tie salesman.

After a time, he joined another troupe where he met the woman who would become his first wife. Gable married Josephine Dillon, an actress 14 years his senior, in 1924. The couple settled in Hollywood, but Gable could land nothing more than work as an extra. When he separated from his wife a couple of years later, he went on the road again with a theatrical company and eventually got to Broadway. He was appearing in a Los Angeles production of *The Last Mile* when Lionel Barrymore persuaded MGM to give him a screen test. The studio was unimpressed, as was Warner Bros. However, a year later, after playing the villain in a William Boyd western, *The Painted Desert*, he was signed to a contract by MGM. He would remain at the studio for the next two decades. However, it was not until MGM angrily farmed him out to another studio that anyone began to take him seriously. It was the best thing that ever happened to Clark Gable's movie career; needless to say, he wanted no part of it.

COLUMBIA PICTURES WAS THE POOR SISTER OF THE MAJOR STUDIOS, ONE of the Poverty Row film factories south of Sunset Boulevard, this one supervised by the tyrant Harry Cohn and dependent on the talents not of a stable of stars, but of a single filmmaker, a Californian born in Palermo, Sicily, named Frank Capra. He would become the studio's biggest star and one of most dependable box-office names in an era when most people barely knew there *was* a director.

Frank Capra had begun working for Cohn in 1928, churning out seven pictures that first year. Over the next five years Capra worked on a total of 19 pictures, increasingly desperate to be taken seriously as a filmmaker. Naturally, no one paid him the least attention. Then he made the most inauspicious little comedy imaginable, and that was the picture that changed Capra's life, turned Columbia into a major studio, and elevated Clark Gable to superstardom. It all happened with such dazzling speed no one could quite believe it.

Capra came across a magazine story, "Night Bus," that he thought might make a movie and bought it for $5,000. He and writer Robert Riskin retreated to Palm Beach, Florida, and wrote a script based on the story of a bohemian painter who gets involved with a spoiled heiress. They changed the title to *It Happened One Night* and brought it back to Harry Cohn, from whom Capra already had wrested an impressive autonomy that was almost unheard of at the other studios. Cohn was not about to get in the way of Capra's latest whim.

But Capra encountered trouble when he came to cast the story. Myrna Loy turned it down, as did Margaret Sullavan, Constance Bennett, and Miriam Hopkins. Thinking something wrong, Riskin and Capra rewrote the screenplay, for one thing, changing the bohemian painter into a tough reporter. Capra tried to get Bette Davis from Warner Bros., and, when that was not possible, he approached Claudette Colbert to play the heiress.

Colbert had made her film debut in *For the Love of Mike*, a 1927 film Capra shot in New York. It was such a flop that it had sent her scurrying back to the stage swearing never to have anything more to do with Frank Capra. Now here he was back on her doorstep. About to go on vacation in Sun Valley, she decided to demand such an outrageous fee that it would be impossible to hire her. She would do *It Happened One Night* for $50,000, but she had to be finished in no more than four weeks. To her utter amazement, Harry Cohn agreed. She was stuck. She had to make this awful little picture for this crummy studio with a director she disliked.

Capra wanted Robert Montgomery for the reporter role, but already events were conspiring to alter the makeup of the film drastically. At MGM, Louis B. Mayer was upset with Clark Gable, who had shown early promise but whose career had been languishing of late. Gable was becoming contrary, complaining that he was tired of the tough guy and gigolo roles assigned to him and demanding a raise. Furious, Mayer put him on suspension. A relationship of sorts had already been established with Harry Cohn when MGM borrowed Capra the year before to make *Lady for a Day*. It was not a particularly happy experience for the independent-minded Capra, but Cohn was delighted because it gave him an "in" with the big boys who ran the major studios. Thus the way was open for Mayer to punish Gable properly.

One can only imagine his surprise when Harry Cohn received a call from Mayer, offering the services of one of his major stars. Harry Cohn could have Clark Gable for *It Happened One Night*. This did not sit well with Capra, who still wanted Montgomery, but Cohn gave him no choice. Gable was beside himself with anger at being shuffled off to such an ignominious fate at a truly minor studio. The first meeting between the two men was a disaster. "Mr. Gable," Capra finally snapped, grabbing the script from him, "you and I are supposed to make a picture out of this. Shall I tell you the story or would you rather read it yourself?"

"Buddy," Gable snarled, "I don't give a fuck what you do with it."

So here was Capra with a movie no one believed in, two stars who hated him, and not a lot of time to accomplish the impossible. The picture began shooting, and Gable, to his credit, quickly saw that *It Happened One Night* was something different, that finally he could break free of the kind of one-note thugs he had been playing at MGM. As for the pint-sized Capra, he was entirely impressed with Gable's larger-than-life-masculinity. "He didn't look like anyone else," Capra said. "It was not only physical; he had mannerisms that were all his own; ways of standing, smoking — things like that — and a great flair for clothes."

It is almost forgotten now, but *It Happened One Night* became one of those watershed movies when it was released in February 1934 — an astonishing success that changes the nature of a business. It was not the first screwball comedy, but it was certainly the most popular, and it established the parameters of the genre for years to come. People flocked back to see the movie again and again, not because the critical response was so good, but because everyone was talking about it. The movie played across the country all year, this comic gem gleaming resolutely in the midst of a gloomy Depression, with the working-class stiff, Gable, who could tame a rich and beautiful dame like Colbert. The Walls of Jericho, the protagonists' name for the blankets strung up between them when they slept "that" night, became a national phenomenon — slightly, delightfully risqué — and so was Gable when he took his shirt off. The bare-chested matinee idol sent undershirt sales plummeting.

But more important than what it did for undershirts was what *It Happened One Night* did for Gable's career. He won an Academy Award for his performance, and when he returned to MGM, it was in triumph — and there were no more gigolo roles. Now the studio's machinery was refitted to provide the shining new star with much more important vehicles, and in the next five years, between 1935 and 1940, basking in the afterglow of the Oscar, he would achieve his greatest popularity and film his most enduring pictures.[8]

It was Irving Thalberg, MGM's production head, who thought of Gable for Fletcher Christian in the studio's lavish production of *Mutiny on the Bounty*. Charles Laughton already had been signed to play the villainous Captain Bligh. Gable was convinced Laughton would overwhelm him on the screen, and he was outraged at the idea of having to wear knee breeches and shave off his trademark mustache. Gable tried everything to get out of the picture, until finally Eddie Mannix, MGM's troubleshooter, was dispatched to have a word with the actor. "You've got the personality for Fletcher Christian," Mannix pointed out. "And besides, you're the only one in the picture who has anything to do with a dame." Mannix was certain it was his promise of a romantic involvement that changed Gable's mind.

Thanks in large part to the success of both *It Happened One Night* and

---

[8] *It Happened One Night,* in addition to winning an Oscar for Claudette Colbert, made her immensely popular. After doing various kinds of roles for years, she finally had found her niche in sophisticated comedy.

*Mutiny on the Bounty*, Gable now enjoyed an unprecedented popularity that coincided with the publication of *Gone With the Wind*. The novel and Clark Gable were traveling similar trajectories. By the end of July 1936, when Gable's name first began being attached to Rhett Butler, *Gone With the Wind* had sold more than a million copies. By early 1937, the book was a phenomenon, and so was Clark Gable. Judy Garland sang "Dear Mr. Gable" on the occasion of his birthday in February 1937, and the following year he was actually crowned "King" of Hollywood — the result of a poll conducted in his newspaper column by Ed Sullivan that voted Gable the most popular star in movies by a huge margin (Myrna Loy was chosen "Queen").

Gable would remain the King for the rest of his career, even though his reign at the top of popularity polls was brief. Other actors, notably John Wayne and Gary Cooper, both had much longer runs as the screen's number one actor. But in 1938, the public was convinced the King was the only actor who could do justice to Rhett Butler. Gable thought otherwise. "People didn't just read that novel," he said in the 1950s, "they lived it. They had a pre-conceived idea about the kind of Rhett Butler they would want to see. . . . Suppose I didn't come up with what they already have me doing, then I'm in trouble."

For a time he was determined not to do it. However, even though he was earning $4,500 a week in a period when the average salary in the United States was $1,500 a year, Clark Gable was a king in need of money. Gable had fallen in love with actress Carole Lombard and wanted to marry her, but he was still attached to his second wife, Rhea Langham, a woman 17 years his senior and not enthusiastic about divorce — unless she received $286,000 plus the income tax owed on the money. So Gable badly needed the $100,000 bonus being waved under his nose. He would get the money, and Lombard, if he did *Gone With the Wind*. Finally, on 28 August 1938, Clark Gable agreed to play Rhett Butler, not because he had any desire whatsoever to do it, but so that he could get married.

D AVID O. SELZNICK, *GWTW*'S PRODUCER, WAS MARRIED TO IRENE Mayer, the daughter of MGM boss Louis B. Mayer, but marriage had never stopped him or the other moguls who controlled the movie business from womanizing. After all, women were among the perquisites of the job. The smooth-skinned, mostly anonymous young starlets who littered the studios regularly serviced the great men in their hideaways and offices. In that kind of atmosphere, it is difficult to tell where Selznick's uncertainty over whom to cast as Scarlett O'Hara ended, and where the pleasure of the hunt began. Here was a rotund, unattractive man with something every woman in America wanted. That was a power to be savored, and not to be given up any more quickly than it had to be. In the history of movies, the great searches were almost always conducted for the unknown young *actresses* because historically, older men who wanted to meet those young women ran the movie business. Never had there been such a publicized search as there was for Scarlett O'Hara.

There is no doubt that everyone wanted to play Scarlett, from Hollywood's biggest stars to shop girls daydreaming in a five and dime store in Des Moines. For a time, the role seemed to be open to just about any young woman in America; briefly, everyone could dream that she might be Scarlett, although in reality only Hollywood actresses were looked at seriously. Joan Crawford was an early consideration when Selznick first began talking to MGM. Ann Sheridan was a favorite choice of the public, ahead of Miriam Hopkins. Jean Arthur was tested in mid-December of 1938, as was a young unknown named Edythe Marrener, later to be known as Susan Hayward. Nancy Coleman, who would go on to play second leads in a number of Warner Bros. movies, including *Kings Row* and *Desperate Journey*, was considered, and Anita Louise, an actress who had appeared mostly in costume dramas and was regarded as one of the most beautiful women in films. The 18-year-old Lana Turner was tested, as was a model named Doris Jordan, briefly a Zanuck favorite, and soon to be better known as Doris Davenport, Gary Cooper's love interest in *The Westerner*.

Katharine Hepburn, for one, never thought much of Bette Davis as a choice for Scarlett; "too unpleasant," she decided. Hepburn had something of a front-row seat from which to view the drama, since her close friend, George Cukor, was to direct *Gone With the Wind*. Cukor likewise had misgivings about Davis, although he was not in favor of his pal Hepburn doing Scarlett either. Unbeknown to just about everyone, Katharine Hepburn was, in effect, being held in reserve by Selznick — a curious position for a prominent actress to find herself in, but then she had powerful allies, including the author Margaret

Mitchell. Even though Mitchell professed to have no interest in the *GWTW* casting, she had sent Hepburn a copy of the typescript before it was published. By doing this she signaled that the creator of Scarlett felt her heroine was embodied in, of all people, a Yankee.

Hepburn, a strong-minded native of Hartford, Connecticut, and daughter of a prominent New England family, was educated at Bryn Mawr. When all the fuss began over *GWTW* in 1936, she was 30 years old. At least as tough and determined as Davis, Hepburn also had the advantages of beauty and luck. Unlike Bette Davis, who had repeatedly tried and failed to break into movies, Hepburn professed to care less about them. When RKO offered her a contract, she had responded by demanding an outrageous amount of money. To her surprise, the studio agreed, and the next thing she knew, Hepburn was in Hollywood.

Hepburn was always careful not to express any passion about the Scarlett O'Hara role, perhaps because she was so close to the principals involved. George Cukor had directed her first film, *A Bill of Divorcement* (1932), and her Hollywood agent was Myron Selznick, David's powerful brother. In fact, one day shortly after reading the book, she arrived at Myron's house to pick him up for some function. When she rang the doorbell, David himself answered, holding a copy of *Gone With the Wind*. "Don't read it, David," she curtly advised. "Just buy it."

When Margaret Mitchell sent her the novel, Hepburn showed it to Pandro S. Berman, her boss at RKO, but he thought Scarlett much too unsympathetic. Joe Sistron, Berman's assistant, advised Hepburn that the role would be bad for her career. Cukor was honest enough to tell her that he felt she was not the right type. Selznick, apparently, was not convinced Cukor was right and asked Hepburn to test, but she refused, thinking she was being asked because there was increasing pressure to get the picture started. "I also felt that I would really be a disappointing choice," she later said. "And I knew that if I did the test, they would sign me, but they would go on looking for an unknown and might just find one and then dump me."

In May of 1938, Hepburn made one of the most curious arrangements a major star ever entered into with a producer. She agreed to be a kind of back-up Scarlett for Selznick. If he could not find another actress, then "the day before" the production was to commence principal photography, she would step in and become Scarlett O'Hara.

How seriously anyone took the agreement is anyone's guess. Certainly as time passed, Selznick became less and less attached to the idea of Hepburn as Scarlett. Her undeserved reputation for being "box-office poison" probably did not help her position. "The more I see her, the colder I get on her," Selznick reported. Still, there is some evidence that Hepburn might have been more anxious to play the part than she let on. In 1938, she delayed appearing on Broadway in Philip Barry's *The Philadelphia Story*, the play that was to revive her career, until she was absolutely certain she would not be cast as Scarlett O'Hara.

E VEN AS THE KNOWNS AND THE UNKNOWNS WERE SOUGHT AND INTER- viewed — and, in 35 instances, screentested — Selznick found himself increasingly leaning toward a former Ziegfeld showgirl, Pauline Levee. She became known as the actress Paulette Goddard, although working for Ziegfeld at the age of 14 she was billed as "Peaches." As soon as she turned 16, she married a rich lumberman, but he did not last long because Pauline — Paulette — was after bigger things.

Barely out of her teens, she was radiantly beautiful and cynically witty, but no more than a Hollywood bit player when she met Charlie Chaplin on a yacht. He fell in love with her and cast her in one of his best-loved classics, *Modern Times*. Everyone seemed mesmerized by Paulette Goddard. Jean Cocteau described her as "this thousand-spiked cactus, this little lioness with her mane and superb claws, this great sports Rolls with its shining leather-work and metal."

Chaplin and Goddard finally married in 1936, even as they were beginning to drift apart. It was not hard for Selznick to meet her, since she and Chaplin lived across the street from the Selznicks on Summit Drive in Beverly Hills. Myron Selznick was her agent, and he was the one who initially sug-gested her to his brother for the Scarlett role, even though Irene Selznick thought the idea a joke. Selznick could hardly believe that after all this time Scarlett might be living across the street. Goddard tested three times, two silent tests and one with sound. Selznick was impressed. "Her tests were funny, full of energy," he noted. Still, he hesitated. The former Pauline Levee was Jewish, and he worried about a Jewish Scarlett. But of all the candidates for the role who came and went after it became clear Bette Davis would not do it, Paulette Goddard probably came the closest to becoming Scarlett. She lost out at the last moment to the young actress who, ironically, Goddard had previously bested for another role.

THE NAME OF VIVIEN LEIGH WAS FIRST MENTIONED IN DAVID O. Selznick's presence for the co-starring role in another picture he was preparing, *The Young in Heart*. However, in February of 1937, he had yet to see even a photograph of her. He also wanted to see one of her movies, *Fire Over England*, in which she had co-starred with a young actor named Laurence Olivier who was starting to attract attention in Hollywood. By the following year, Selznick had also seen Leigh in *A Yank at Oxford*, with Robert Taylor as co-star. Selznick liked her performance, but "I don't like her for a part in our picture [*The Young in Heart*]." The role instead went to Paulette Goddard. Now she would lose out to Vivien Leigh.

In the spring of 1938, the former Vivian Mary Hartley, born in Darjeeling, India, was 25 years of age and filming *St. Martin's Lane* (U.S. title, *Sidewalks of London*) with Charles Laughton. She recently had left her husband, Leigh Holman, and her four-year-old daughter, Suzanne, so that she could pursue a turbulent romance with her *Fire Over England* co-star, Laurence Olivier. By now she had read *Gone With the Wind* and decided that she would play Scarlett O'Hara.

For anyone else, stranded so far from MGM, let alone the entire American experience, such determination would be considered ludicrous. But Vivien Leigh was no ordinary woman. She had been acclaimed one of the great beauties of her time, a woman of iron will and tenacity. When she wanted something, whether it was a lover like Olivier or a role like that of Scarlett, she was used to getting it.

Hollywood had not been immediately responsive to her, however. In addition to losing out to Paulette Goddard, she did not fare well in her quest for the role of Cathy in Samuel Goldwyn's production of Emily Brontë's novel, *Wuthering Heights*. Moreover, although Vivien Leigh was soon to become the most celebrated — and envied — woman in the history of movies, she was to lose out on two other parts that undoubtedly would have added even more luster to a legend that basically turns on a single role.

The director William Wyler had spent two years persuading Sam Goldwyn to let him film *Wuthering Heights*. The producer finally was pushed into doing it when he found out Jack Warner might be interested — Bette Davis, having starred for Wyler in *Jezebel*, was after Warner to buy the book for her. Merle Oberon, under contract to Goldwyn, agreed to star in it. It was Ben Hecht, collaborating on the screenplay with his partner Charles MacArthur, who suggested Laurence Olivier for the role of Heathcliff. In July of 1938, Wyler flew to London and had dinner with Olivier and Vivien Leigh at their townhouse. They were living quietly, since both of them were still married to others, Leigh to Leigh Holman and Olivier to actress Jill Esmond.

Olivier was reluctant to have anything to do with Hollywood, since Greta Garbo had unceremoniously rejected him as her leading man in *Queen Christina* in 1933. Only in the last couple of years had he become celebrated either on stage or in films. Wyler had actually tested another actor for the Heathcliff role — Robert Newton, later to become one of the most popular character actors in the British cinema, best known for his roles as Bill Sikes in the 1948 version of *Oliver Twist* and as Long John Silver in *Treasure Island* (1950). But he still wanted Olivier, and that evening in London, the actor made it clear that what he wanted in return for a commitment to play Heathcliff was the co-starring role in *Wuthering Heights* for his true love.

"Vivien, I'll give you the part of Isabella," offered Wyler, referring to a secondary character in *Wuthering Heights*.

"I want to play Cathy," Leigh retorted.

Taken aback, Wyler pointed out that Merle Oberon already had the part; in fact, that was the only reason the picture was even getting made.

"Then I don't want any part."

"Look, Vivien," Wyler said, "you're not known in the States. You may become a big star but for the first role in an American film, you'll never do better than Isabella in *Wuthering Heights*."

But Leigh, headstrong and determined to have it all or nothing, was not interested. Now she set her heart and her ambition on something much larger and much more difficult. Both Scarlett and Olivier were now to be found in Los Angeles, and she was determined to have them both. In September she turned down a role in Cecil B. De Mille's *Union Pacific* (it went to Barbara Stanwyck, complete with Irish brogue), but made preparations for her arrival in America. Olivier, filming *Wuthering Heights* and having a difficult time, nonetheless found a moment to have "a few quiet words" with Myron Selznick to help prepare the way for Vivien.

She arrived in New York in early December and by 10 December was in California, arriving at the David O. Selznick Studio in Culver City where shooting of *Gone With the Wind* was finally under way. Well, at least the burning of Atlanta sequence was being shot, with acres of old sets, including the gate from *King Kong*, to be consumed by flames while cameras turned and stand-ins for Rhett and Scarlett struggled with a horsedrawn wagon. It was a night for fire and drama, from eight o'clock on that evening, and if Leigh had been able to orchestrate the moment herself — which she dearly would have loved to do — she could not have accomplished it better. Olivier later recalled with eloquence the moment Vivien Leigh was introduced to David O. Selznick. "I looked back at Vivien, her hair giving the perfect impression of Scarlett's, her cheeks prettily flushed, her lips adorably parted, her green eyes dancing and shining with excitement in the firelight; I said to myself, 'David won't be able to resist that.'"

He was right. David could not. "I took one look and knew that she was right, at least as far as appearance went — at least right as far as how my conception of Scarlett O'Hara looked."

Olivier remembered Selznick peering intently at Vivien, hardly able to believe what was being played out, watching the two-year search for Scarlett come to an end before his eyes. Cukor escorted her to his office and had her read a couple of scenes. Selznick wrote to his wife two days later: "She's the Scarlett dark horse, and looks damned good."

Still, there was a final flurry of second thoughts and screen tests. Jean Arthur was tested on 17 December and, on 20 December, actress Joan Bennett, a last-minute surprise who had not previously even read for the part. On the 20th and 21st, Paulette Goddard was tested again, and then on the 21st and 22nd, Vivien Leigh. The test was barely finished when it was decided Leigh, who had come all the way from England to get Scarlett, indeed had her. She would work a grueling 125 days on *Gone With the Wind*, for which she would be paid $25,000, a measly sum even in those days. Clark Gable, who would work only 71 days, received $121,454.

WHAT A MAGICAL TIME IT MUST HAVE BEEN FOR THE TWO LOVERS. Olivier was the dashing young Heathcliff, Vivien Leigh the most popular movie heroine of all time. The magic would not last for long. Soon the war would intrude on their happiness, and nothing would be quite the same for them again. But for a moment, everything was theirs, including each other, and the rest of the world was somewhere vaguely in the background. "They screwed constantly," recalled Douglas Fairbanks Jr., "impatient to get the trivialities of everyday life over with so they could just rush madly back to bed. Or anywhere else handy, and preferably private. . . . Vivien was extremely libidinous."

But even passion could not bank Vivien Leigh's ambition. As she began filming *Gone With the Wind*, she already had her eye on the movie she wanted next. And why not? She must have known what *Gone With the Wind* would do for her career. She could have anything she wanted, surely. She was about to find out that she could not.

Even as he prepared *Gone With the Wind*, David O. Selznick was making arrangements to film another popular novel of the day, a Gothic romance written by Daphne du Maurier. The story concerned an innocent young woman who marries a mysterious nobleman named Maxim de Winter, who may or may not have killed his first wife, Rebecca. Selznick had contracted the portly 40-year-old British director Alfred Hitchcock to make *Rebecca*. This was to be Hitchcock's first American picture, and he favored Ronald Colman for the role of Maxim, the same actor Selznick had first approached to play Rhett Butler. Selznick, too, felt Colman "the perfect man" for the role. But he was not available, so Selznick found himself torn between William Powell, who was closer in age to the character, and Laurence Olivier, who "has more obvious edge romantically." Olivier appears to have won one of his best-known film roles, not because he was younger or more romantic, but because he cost less. Powell would have been paid $100,000 more than Olivier, "which means," Selznick pointed out, "we would have to gross $150,000 additional to break even."

Besides, the role of the innocent young woman was much more pivotal to the story, and to that end, Selznick, as he had with *Gone With the Wind*, decided to launch a publicity-drenched search for the right actress. And just as she had determined to play Scarlett, Vivien Leigh intended to co-star with her lover in *Rebecca*. This time, however, she discovered a producer who was all but impervious to her appeals. It must have been particularly frustrating. Here she was the world's most publicized and envied actress playing the role of a lifetime in *GWTW*. What better way to follow up her success than with the starring role in *Rebecca*?

For Selznick's part, the casting would seem to have made sense; it would have allowed him to hang on to an actress who would become more important and valuable than ever once *Gone With the Wind* was completed. But Selznick did not see it that way. He seems to have had no interest at all in casting Vivien Leigh in *Rebecca*, partly because he was looking forward to the kind of star search he had conducted for *GWTW*, and partly because he had a passion for Joan Fontaine and wanted her in the movie, even while the "search" went on. As for Fontaine, she had no interest whatsoever in Selznick, found him physically somewhat repulsive, and was busy planning to marry the actor Brian Aherne.

By August of 1939, Selznick had gotten over his infatuation with Fontaine, but whatever lingering affection he had for her left him convinced that she was the actress for *Rebecca*. Throughout the summer months, he had looked at a score of actresses including Loretta Young, Margaret Sullavan, and Olivia De Havilland, Joan Fontaine's older sister.

Another candidate, Anne Baxter, was only 16, but Selznick had shown more than passing interest. He wanted to test her for a role in his planned production of *Tom Sawyer* that was to star Montgomery Clift. However, Baxter later said, Clift was suffering such a bad case of acne that the test had to be canceled, and Clift was sent back to New York. The next thing, Selznick brought her in to test for *Rebecca*. Recalled Baxter, "Selznick looked in my mouth and examined my teeth, and I felt like I was a prize racing horse."

Hitchcock shot several scenes with her and then took her to one side and said that she was his first choice for the lead. However, Selznick decided the teenage Baxter photographed too young next to Olivier, and she lost the part that might have made her a major star. Her consolation prize was a seven-year contract at 20th Century–Fox starting at $350 a week, offered by Darryl Zanuck after he saw her *Rebecca* test.

As he tested other actresses, Selznick continued to be pressured by Vivien Leigh. He was unmoved. "She doesn't seem at all right as to sincerity or age or innocence," he reported. It was a curious criticism for an actress who would embody a certain youthful innocence, if not in the early stages of *Gone With the Wind*, certainly in her next film, the romantic melodrama *Waterloo Bridge*. But perhaps Selznick could not see past either Scarlett or Joan Fontaine, who certainly was a very different type from Leigh, less beautiful on the screen, more hesitant.

Whatever Selznick's misgivings, he allowed Leigh to test twice for *Rebecca*, once after a day's work on *Gone With the Wind* and, after she pressed him for a second chance, with Olivier in New York. Selznick claimed that neither Hitchcock nor George Cukor thought her right, although his partner in Selznick International, John Hay ("Jock") Whitney, favored Leigh and described Fontaine as a "talking magazine cover" — which is how she comes off in the movie. But Selznick would not be deterred. Joan Fontaine would play the lead in *Rebecca*, and Leigh, en route to New York, would get a radiogram onboard the Île de France on 18 August. "We have tried to sell ourselves right up until today to cast you in *Rebecca*," he wrote, "but I regret necessity in telling you we are finally convinced you are as wrong for role as role would be for you."

Selznick went on to say that he was "positive you would be bitterly criticized and your career, which is now off to such a tremendous start with Scarlett . . . damaged."

Selznick also sent Olivier a wire that in effect stated that the only reason Leigh was now so interested in the part was because her lover was in it. He claimed that when he had first mentioned the movie to her, she showed no interest whatsoever. The radiograms were dreadfully condescending, saying more about the nature of movie stardom at the time than anything else. The star served at the pleasure of the producer; it was a pleasure of glamor and money, but there was virtually no power.

In today's movie-star world, Vivien Leigh would have starred in *Rebecca*. Instead, she was robbed of a role that might have served as a classic companion piece to Scarlett O'Hara, leaving filmgoers to remember her cast forever against the white oaks of Tara. Nothing else she ever did came close to overwhelming that central image of her career, and yet she was one of the most beautiful and talented actresses ever to grace the screen. It is tragic that she did not do more in the movies.

After *Gone With the Wind* won her every conceivable plaudit and award, including the Oscar, she did only two more films, *Waterloo Bridge* (1940) and *That Hamilton Woman* (U.S. title, *Lady Hamilton*) in 1941 (with Olivier), until appearing in the dull *Caesar and Cleopatra* in 1945. She won a second Oscar as Blanche du Bois in the movie version of *A Streetcar Named Desire* in 1951.[9] She was only 38 but already looked fragile and exhausted, her great beauty slipping away into the tuberculosis and depression that plagued her final years. While her obsession with Olivier and her often debilitating health problems had much to do with her paucity of movie roles, one cannot help suspecting that David O. Selznick, the man who bestowed upon her ever-lasting fame, also somehow contrived to rob her of a brilliant movie career. She would star in only three more films, none of them memorable (*The Deep Blue Sea; The Roman Spring of Mrs. Stone; Ship of Fools*) before her death, at only 54, in 1967.

A S FOR CLARK GABLE, NOTHING WOULD MARK THE DISINTEGRATION OF the studio system more dramatically than his exit from MGM in 1954. For 23 years, Gable had been the pre-eminent studio star, created and nurtured, protected by the Hollywood dream factory. MGM had made him King, and now the King was without a kingdom, exiled to the far-off city of Hong Kong in order to make *Soldier of Fortune*. Left to his own devices, without a studio to save him from himself, Gable, aging, drinking heavily, and never really recovered from the death of his third wife, Carole Lombard, in January 1942, made mediocre picture after mediocre picture.

In 1960 he agreed to co-star with Marilyn Monroe in a drama of modern-day cowboys, *The Misfits*, written by Arthur Miller and directed by John Huston.[10] As usual when faced with good material, he hesitated and had to be talked into doing the movie by his agent and Miller. Even so, his friends were appalled that he was playing Gay Langland, an aging cowboy who sells wild

---

[9] Elia Kazan chose Vivien Leigh over Jessica Tandy, who originated the role on Broadway. Thus it could be said that Tandy was robbed of a major career in the movies until she finally landed a starring role in *Driving Miss Daisy* in 1989. She was 80 years old and won the Oscar for best actress.

[10] Huston first offered the part to Robert Mitchum, who, like Gable, couldn't understand the script. Years later, Mitchum also would rather casually turn down *Patton,* the movie that won George C. Scott an Oscar, and *Dirty Harry,* which made a huge star out of Clint Eastwood. Mitchum said he didn't feel so bad about *Dirty Harry,* since Frank Sinatra also passed on it.

mustangs to dog-food companies — and Gable never really understood the script. The arduousness of shooting the movie in the heat of the Nevada desert, the production constantly delayed by Monroe's tardiness, put a terrible strain on a heavy smoker who commonly used the butt of one cigarette to light another, and a drinker who, according to Robert Mitchum, was "drinking two quarts of whiskey a day."

Gable could hardly believe they were allowing him, at 59 years of age, to wrestle wild horses out in the desert. "What surprised me," he said to his fifth wife, Kay Spreckels, "is that no one gave a damn if I got killed or not. We were never allowed to take chances when the studio had us under contract." But there was no studio, and just six years after leaving MGM, and days after he finished shooting *The Misfits,* Clark Gable died of a heart attack. The King was dead; and so was an era.

# PART II
Going Independent

# 6

# "HE DOESN'T TALK, HE MUMBLES."
## Brando and the Revolution

I N 1947, JACK WARNER WAS PREOCCUPIED, AS WAS EVERYONE ELSE IN Hollywood, with the House Un-American Activities Committee (HUAC), the congressional body charged with looking into Communist subversion in U.S. life, which lately had taken a particular interest in Hollywood. Warner had already been interviewed and named people he considered subversive, and he was feeling guilty about it. More threatening than the Commie menace, however, was what was happening to Warner Bros. and all the other studios.

Even though the 1940s — the World War II era — had been the most profitable decade in the history of movies, it was all coming to an end. The factory system that had evolved in the wake of sound not only to provide a roster of easily accessible stars, but also to stand for 20-odd years as a bulwark against the outside world, was beginning to come apart. The following year the studios would be forced by the government to divest themselves of their theaters, and television would become an intrusive reality cutting deeply into motion-picture attendance.

Faced with these new threats to their existence, the studios were forced to cut back, and in so doing discovered they could no longer afford the vast army of workers they had retained. It became more economical to hire people as they were needed — and this applied to movie stars as well as everyone else. At the end of the silent era, a great number of stars were dropped not just because their voices were wrong, but simply because they cost too much. Now a second great shedding began as the studios failed to renew the contracts of some of their most durable but by now aging stars. As for the stars themselves, they were becoming more and more independent. A whole new generation, discontent with the studio system and old-style bosses who told them what to do, was about to emerge.

J
ACK WARNER WOULD PRESIDE OVER WARNER BROS. FOR 50 YEARS, longer than any other studio executive, and despite the Commies and the television screens, he was still in the business of making movies, busily overseeing preparations for a dramatic tearjerker titled *Johnny Belinda*. Set in a Nova Scotia fishing community, *Johnny Belinda* was the heartwarming story of a young deaf-mute girl and the doctor who falls in love with her.

Jane Wyman was cast as the girl, but director Jean Negulesco was less certain about the doctor. He had seen a screen test of a young actor in New York that he quite liked. The actor's name was Marlon Brando, and according to the slateboard that provided details of the test, he was 23 years old, had brown hair, stood 5 feet 10 inches tall, and weighed 170 pounds. His experience consisted of three years of stage work. Brando's screen test was for a movie called *Rebel Without a Cause*, which had nothing to do with the movie James Dean subsequently made, although the irony contained in the title, and its subsequent importance, are inescapable.

Brando looked handsome in a jacket and tie, his hair neatly combed. A woman off camera asked him, "What were the shows you've done in New York?" In a soft, slurry voice, he answered, "I was in *Candida* with Katharine Cornell, and I was in *The Eagle Has Two Heads* with Tallulah Bankhead." He punctuated his answers with a syrupy grin, giving the impression of a young man with a funny voice trying to be solicitous as you checked in at the hotel where he was working for the summer. It was somehow not the voice of a kid from Omaha, Nebraska, and it was not a voice to impress Jack Warner.

"He doesn't talk, he mumbles," sneered Warner. And that was that, as far as Brando's involvement went with *Johnny Belinda*. Warner preferred a 40-year-old actor named Lew Ayres, who had appeared in *All Quiet on the Western Front*. Ayres had virtually ruined his career by declaring himself a conscientious objector during World War II, but he was the kind of actor with whom Warner felt an audience could identify, being known best for his portrayal of Dr. Kildare in a series of movies at MGM. Ayres had played a doctor many times before; the public would be comfortable with him. Who was this young, mumbling punk called Brando anyway?

That same year Brando exploded on Broadway in Tennessee Williams' *A Streetcar Named Desire*, playing Stanley Kowalski, and a revolution of sorts was under way. When Brando walked out on stage, everything began to change. "We who saw him in his first shocking days," wrote actor William Redfield, "believed in him not only as an actor, but also as an artistic, spiritual and specifically American leader." Overnight a line was drawn demarcating what had been and what was to be from now on. Brando was new and he was constantly energizing. "I got worn out after many months [in *Streetcar*]," remembered Kim Stanley, "but I never got bored." That originality that electrified Broadway also sparked the movies, and Brando spearheaded the most startling upheaval since the coming of sound. He did not originate the spirit of independence about to sweep through the studios, but he was certainly that spirit's patron saint. Jack Warner missed the coming of Marlon Brando at his peril.

Brando was the first major star not under a long-term contract. He refused to be a worker in one of the film factories. He would be a king, but he would not be a slave. Restless and rebellious, and often openly hostile toward Hollywood and all it represented, he took great pains to be different and to upset even as he dazzled. There had never been a star quite like him. Movie stars got dressed up and looked their best. Brando reveled in looking his worst, unshaven, wearing a T-shirt and bluejeans, wanting to have nothing to do with Hollywood and what he termed "its putrid glamor."

"The only reason I'm here," he announced, "is because I don't have the moral strength to turn down the money."

Even Bogart and Cagney, who had always represented a certain anti-Establishment stance on the screen, basically toed the line. Brando, however, did not have to listen to anyone. In part he was lucky; the people who might have forced him to listen just a decade before were now disappearing. The disintegration of the studio system already was freeing the slaves; Brando happened to arrive in time to lead the rebellion.

The tradition-bound Hollywood press was slow to understand what was happening and tried to slot him into its outdated molds, dubbing him "the male Garbo." But that simply did not work. *Time* magazine attempted the argument that if Clark Gable was "the King" then Marlon Brando was "the Slob." Brando simply thumbed at everyone a nose one cinematographer said was hard to photograph. He went after legendary gossip columnists Louella Parsons and Hedda Hopper, who in their heyday could make or break a performer's career. Brando called Hedda Hopper "the hat." Parsons was "the fat one." Hopper, perhaps seeing the writing on the wall, was restrained in her assessment: "I don't think Marlon can be explained in terms of the uninhibited brat or the sensitive artist. He's a combination of sham, seeing through sham and defying it, yet a bit guilty of sham himself."

Brando's fiercely demonstrated independence established the standard for future movie stardom. Stars now would be left to their own devices to make their own decisions. They would rise or fall, not according to the whims of a studio, but by the decisions they made about their own careers. When 20th Century–Fox tried to push Brando into a traditional studio-driven vehicle, a big, dumb epic titled *The Egyptian*, he simply failed to show up. Fox was outraged: the cast was waiting, sets had been prepared, a lavishly budgeted Hollywood movie was all set to go. Instead, a letter arrived from the star's psychiatrist stating that the actor could not work for 10 weeks because "he was under a mental strain and facing a personal crisis." Later, Brando gloated that he had "copped a medical plea."

*The Egyptian* went ahead with Edmund Purdom in the Brando role, and today neither the movie nor the actor is remembered. Darryl F. Zanuck was close to apoplexy, and Fox sued, but there was little anyone could do. There was no more adding time spent in suspension to a recalcitrant star's contract, and a court case would take years. Certainly it was the first time in the history of movies that a star had in effect announced that he could not do a movie because he was emotionally disturbed. More important, it served as one of the first demonstrations of modern movie star power. It would not be the last.

In those days, Brando seemed to know instinctively what was right and what was not. It was not, unfortunately, an instinct that long survived. The power of choice, Brando and all other movie stars soon would realize, was a two-edged sword. The freedom now was available to screw up badly, and there was no studio to save you from yourself.

Brando was mercurial and difficult, and as quickly as he achieved greatness he lost it again, and carelessly bypassed some of the best roles ever offered a performer. In the end, his freedom from the studio system allowed him almost to destroy himself by way of a series of increasingly mediocre movies. His legend survived thanks to a handful of pictures he made when the comet of his ascension had briefly stabilized. But the films he could have made, the roles he should have played — when that aspect of Brando's career is considered, it begins to take on the gloom of tragedy.

In the beginning, though, he could do no wrong. His influence was such that he made possible the stardom of any number of other young actors. Without him, it is doubtful there would have been a Montgomery Clift, a James Dean, or a Paul Newman. His lineage can be traced through those performers and into the styles of Hoffman, Nicholson, Pacino, and De Niro. Everyone wanted to be like him, and everyone wanted him, and because there was for a time a desperation to grab this unique being, no matter what the cost, a legendary singer was robbed of a classic film.

F RANK SINATRA WAS RIDING HIGH IN JUNE OF 1953. HE WAS CERTAIN HE had saved his career by fighting for and finally landing a co-starring role in the movie version of James Jones's bestseller *From Here to Eternity*. Set at Pearl Harbor just before the Japanese attack and U.S. involvement in World War II, the movie had attracted an all-star cast that included Burt Lancaster, Deborah Kerr, Montgomery Clift, and Donna Reed. Daniel Taradash trimmed Jones's 816-page book down to a 161-page screenplay directed by Fred Zinnemann. Harry Cohn, the boss of Columbia, having long since put his Poverty Row antecedents behind him, now arrogantly believed he had the movie audience "wired to his ass," and his ass was telling him he was about to make a major hit.

Sinatra had read the book when it was first published and became obsessed with the character of Maggio. Skinny and pathetic as he was, Maggio was possessed of an indomitable spirit; he refused to give up, no matter what the odds. Maggio was not just a character — Frank Sinatra *was* Maggio. At the time Sinatra read the book, his vocal cords were ruptured, his record company had dropped him, and his marriage to actress Ava Gardner was in trouble. No one wanted him, certainly not Harry Cohn, employing his ass and everything else so as to personally oversee production of *From Here to Eternity*.

Over Cohn's objections, Sinatra was tested along with a muscular, dark-haired young New York actor named Eli Wallach, who had never made a movie. Also tested was a popular comedian, Harvey Lembach. No one liked Lembach's performance, and he was quickly out of the running. Attention focused on Sinatra and Wallach.

Wallach was from Brooklyn and had made his Broadway debut in 1945. Since then he had become one of the most respected stage actors in New York, an exponent of the so-called "Method" acting, but without the sound and fury that ordinarily accompanied it. Wallach was a superb no-frills actor, and everyone was knocked out by his test. "Eli Wallach made the best test of the three of them, no doubt about it," Daniel Taradash said. "Sinatra had none of the consummate acting skill of Wallach."

By rights, the actor should have had the part. But then fate, and Wallach's agent, intervened. The agent started making money demands that angered Harry Cohn. Moreover, Wallach himself was ambivalent about Maggio. He had agreed to star on the stage in Tennessee Williams' new play, *Camino Real*, which was to be directed by Elia Kazan and was only awaiting financial backing. Williams was the leading playwright in America, Kazan the most respected director, and no stage-trained New York actor in his right mind would have turned down the opportunity to work with these two creative powerhouses. Movies were just . . . movies. They could wait for another day.

Shooting of *From Here to Eternity* was slated to start in March of 1952. Only Maggio remained to be cast, and everyone was starting to get desperate. Zinnemann, along with screenwriter Taradash and the movie's producer, Buddy Adler, met at Harry Cohn's house to make the final decision. They sat in Cohn's projection room and screened Eli Wallach's test as well as Sinatra's. Still, they couldn't decide. Finally, Cohn went upstairs, got his wife, Joan, and had her watch the two tests. When the lights went up again, she spoke to the group: "Eli Wallach is a brilliant actor, no doubt about it," she said. "But he looks too good. He's not skinny, and he's not pathetic, and he's not Italian. Frank is just Maggio to me."

And that decided it. A few words from Harry Cohn's wife saved Frank Sinatra's career. Legend would complicate the story over the years, particularly when Sinatra's mob connections became better known. Rumors circulated that the mob pulled strings so that Sinatra could play Maggio — rumors that took on a mythic status thanks to Mario Puzo's 1969 novel *The Godfather*. In the book that became the basis for one of the most popular movies of all time, a Sinatra-like singer named Johnny Fontane goes to the Godfather, Vito Corleone, and begs for his help in landing the movie role that would save his career. When the studio boss, a racing aficionado, refuses to let Fontane have the part, he wakes up one morning to find the severed head of his favorite thoroughbred lying in bed beside him. The horrified studio boss, realizing the mob will not stop, gives the part to Johnny, and his career is revived. "There were no horses' heads involved," Zinnemann said years later. "Frank lobbied for the part by sending Harry Cohn and myself telegrams and signing them, 'Maggio.' His test was good and I saw no reason why he shouldn't do it. But there was no pressure. If I hadn't wanted him, he wouldn't have done it."

NOW IN THE SUMMER OF 1953, AWAITING THE RELEASE OF *FROM HERE to Eternity*, for which he would win the best supporting actor Oscar, Sinatra saw the golden opportunity every actor seeks — to follow up a great part with an even greater one. Now Sinatra saw himself in the character of longshoreman Terry Malloy, the washed-up ex-fighter who finally decides to stand up to the bosses who run the waterfront. Maggio saved him; Terry Malloy and *On the Waterfront* could put him right back on top again.

This time there was no opposition. Elia Kazan was to direct *On the Waterfront* and he thought Sinatra perfect for Terry Malloy. "Frank had grown up in Hoboken where I was going to shoot the film, and spoke perfect Hobokenese."

The movie had had a rough time reaching the point where Sinatra could get involved. Kazan had originally attached himself to a waterfront-type script titled *The Hook*, written by playwright Arthur Miller. It had been killed by Columbia's Harry Cohn because Miller refused to change the racketeers in the story to Reds.

Miller eventually gave up, but the idea stayed with Kazan. Several years later, he ran into Budd Schulberg, a novelist and screenwriter. The son of movie executive B. P. Schulberg, he was best known for his controversial 1941 bestseller, *What Makes Sammy Run?* Schulberg, like Kazan, had testified before the House Un-American Activities Committee and named several of his colleagues from the days of his brief association with the Communist party. Thus there was a common bond between them that was only enhanced when Kazan discovered Schulberg had been working on a screenplay based on a Pulitzer Prize–winning series of stories exposing racketeering on the waterfront. He and Schulberg decided to team up to make *On the Waterfront*.

The script would later be viewed in some quarters as a thinly veiled defense of whistleblowers, but whatever it was, Hollywood was not buying. Darryl Zanuck at 20th Century–Fox read the script and declared, "What you have written is exactly what the American people do not want to see."

Somehow Kazan and Schulberg ended up in a suite at the Beverly Hills Hotel, lamenting their bad luck and wondering what to do next. Abruptly there was a knock on the door, and standing on the other side was a small lizard-like man by the name of Sam Spiegel. Actually, in those days, he was going by the name S. P. Eagle, because he thought Eagle had a more elegant ring to it than Spiegel. An independent producer from Austria who had fled Hitler's Germany in 1933, S.P. had briefly been in Hollywood in 1927 working as a story translator. He had produced Orson Welles' *The Stranger* (1946) and most recently *The African Queen* (1952). "On first acquaintance, Sam Spiegel would probably satisfy the popular expectation of the more popular type of film producer," the screenwriter Robert Bolt was to write of him. "He has charm, force of personality, is witty, dresses quietly. He speaks four languages fluently and two more sufficiently well to get his own way in them. He likes good living, knows how to find it in most parts of the globe, and delights in sharing it. He is stout and has a Roman head in which the eyes are still mischievous when the expression is most senatorial. To give a good present and to drive a good bargain afford equal satisfaction."

At that point Spiegel was down on his luck, having been forced to give up his house in Bel Air. For Spiegel, being down meant a retreat to the Beverly Hills Hotel. It did not mean you stopped socializing, however. Spiegel, hearing that Schulberg and Kazan were next door, invited the two men to a party in his suite. Over drinks, Spiegel heard about *On the Waterfront* and, before the night was out, agreed to become involved as producer without even having read the script.

When he did get around to reading Schulberg's draft, Spiegel was appalled. "I wouldn't have touched the original script with a ten-foot pole," he said. Schulberg was forced to spend much of the next year rewriting, a process he resented immensely. Spiegel kept saying to him, "Let's open it up again." Even Schulberg later told the story about his wife waking up to find her husband dressing. When she inquired as to where he was going, Schulberg replied, "I'm going over to kill that son of a bitch." Spiegel was a trifle more diplomatic: "I had a great deal of trouble with Budd." Even Kazan was impressed by the producer's grasp of story, and eventually a script was produced that was to everyone's liking.

Sinatra had been set for the lead, although it was not helping Spiegel much. He was having trouble financing the picture on the strength of the singer's name. He knew that Kazan had directed Marlon Brando in both the stage and screen versions of *A Streetcar Named Desire*, as well as his next movie, *Viva Zapata!* Kazan thought him a "man-boy," and while dazzled by his talents, did not think he was right for Terry Malloy. Besides, they had had a falling out after Kazan testified before the HUAC. Brando had said he would never work with the director again, and for his part, Kazan was hardly enamored of Brando. "I didn't want the son of a bitch in the film," was the way he put it. Besides, as Kazan kept pointing out to Spiegel, they already had committed to Frank Sinatra, and the actor was in the process of being fitted for his wardrobe. But Spiegel was possessed of a legendary stubbornness and he would not be put off the idea of Marlon Brando. With the most talked about actor in movies in *On the Waterfront* there would be no trouble raising the needed financing. "Frank was not a great star yet," Kazan wrote later. "Brando had made *Streetcar*. Sam would have more money to play with."

But Spiegel was having no success getting in touch with Brando. One night in New York, unable to sleep, Spiegel went over to the Stage Delicatessen on 7th Avenue. He was sitting having coffee, he said later, when Marlon Brando walked in the door.

Spiegel, not about to allow outrageously coincidental opportunity to slip away, approached the actor, introduced himself, and proceeded to tell him the story of *On the Waterfront*. Brando was intrigued, but he still refused to work with Kazan. "Professional is one thing," Spiegel told Brando. "Politics is another. Separate them."

At 3:00 A.M., Spiegel got on the phone to Kazan and told him to hurry over to the deli. Brando and Kazan talked for half an hour. At the end of that time, Brando agreed to do the picture with one proviso — he had to be allowed to leave at 4:00 P.M. each day to visit his analyst. The greatest actor of his time agreed to the picture he is most remembered for on the strength of that.

Columbia, which had twice turned down the project, leapt at it now that Marlon Brando was involved. Kazan was not proud of himself. "I confess I ate shit," he said. "Sam had conned Marlon into making the film, and I let him do the dirty work and said nothing."

The "dirty work" consisted of finding a technicality that gave Spiegel reason to dump Sinatra. It was provided by a concert date to which Sinatra had already committed. There was no way the shooting schedule could accommodate it, Spiegel said, therefore Sinatra would have to go. Sinatra was furious and promptly fired his agent, Abe Lastfogel, who advised the singer not to sue over the breach of the contract. "Do you want the world to know Hollywood doesn't want you?" Lastfogel said. Sinatra sued anyway.

Kazan, still feeling terrible about it, wrote the singer, saying how sorry he was, and how good he would have been in the film. Months later, Sinatra wrote back with a graciousness that belies the reputation that has grown up around him over the years: "For me to tell you I was not deeply hurt, would not be telling you my true feelings. However, with the passing of time and after re-reading your letter, how could I do or say anything other than I, too, want to be friends with you. I hope it's going well."

Sinatra was not nearly so kind to Sam Spiegel. Several years later, after *The Bridge on the River Kwai* had been released, Spiegel was dining in a restaurant when Sinatra came by. When Spiegel said, "Hi, Frank," Sinatra snapped, "You say, 'hello, Mr. Sinatra.' I'd prefer it if you didn't say anything at all."

When it was all over, and *On the Waterfront* had been showered with Oscars (it won eight, including those for best picture, best director, and for Brando's performance, best actor), and had long since been acclaimed as one of the true classics of American cinema, Kazan conceded two things: Spiegel's dogged persistence was what made the script right, and Brando's Terry was an unparalleled acting achievement. "If there was a better performance by a man in the history of film in America, I don't know what it is."

The film represented an apogee of sorts for both director and star. Kazan was never to soar to such cinematic heights again, and Brando, after *On the Waterfront*, entered a period of decline interrupted only by the big screen version of *Guys and Dolls* in which he played Sky Masterson opposite, of all people, Frank Sinatra. Brando would spiral downward for almost two decades, and let the roles that might have confirmed his greatness as an actor slip through his grasp.

*Time* magazine, curiously enough, understood what was about to happen. The magazine devoted its cover of 11 October 1954 to Brando and built the story around his role as Napoleon in *Desiree*, a movie that would turn out to be the first of his many flops. The magazine observed with a prescience that was quite startling: "*Waterfront* in short suggests that Brando is getting too big for his blue jeans. But the question arises. What else is he to wear? From Brando's precocious eminence the future may look less like a land of dreams than a highly promising nightmare. If, as he professes, he cares chiefly about acting as an art, there will hardly be enough opportunity in commercial Hollywood to keep him there much longer."

I N "COMMERCIAL HOLLYWOOD," THE OLD-TIME CONTRACT STARS, FREE AT last, were now in the hands of agents and managers, but without a vast studio infrastructure to create stories and evaluate material for them. They were left to figure it all out for themselves, and often that did not work very well. Gregory Peck, for example, was offered a western produced by Stanley Kramer that was to be directed by Fred Zinnemann. "I had made a picture called *The Gunfighter*," he recalled years later, "and it was pretty much the lone fellow against a town. Along came this script a few months later and I must have read it hurriedly, but I do remember my reacton: it's too much like *The Gunfighter*."

Turning down *High Noon* was a decision that has haunted Peck for the rest of his life. Gary Cooper, away from Paramount and somewhat lost, wandering aimlessly from film to unsuccessful film, accepted the role of town marshall Will Kane, and not only won an Academy Award but also revived his career. *High Noon* (1952) was his most memorable movie and became the kind of film classic that lifts an actor beyond stardom and into legend. Peck was never able to make a movie that was its equal, and talking about it over 30 years later, he seemed to understand this.

"I don't know what else was on my mind at the time," he said. "It's too long ago, but it got by me and Gary Cooper was smart enough to take it and did it beautifully. I couldn't have done it, probably, as well, but it still would have been a very good picture with me in it. Maybe not as good as it was with him in it. It was a plum; it was a surefire role."

World War II as much as anything had contributed to rearranging the traditional face of the studio star system. As the stars came back from the war, they were suddenly older, and more sober, and Hollywood was somehow less a dream factory than it had been. James Stewart returned after 20 bombing missions over Germany only to discover that the gawky, amiable everyman he had always played no longer worked. He made Frank Capra's *It's a Wonderful Life*, yet another in the series of sentimental comedies he and Capra had been so successful with. But the Depression was gone, and with it, apparently, America's need for the Capraesque. *Wonderful Life* flopped badly in 1946, leaving Stewart depressed and confused, thinking perhaps he was finished.

Inadvertently, he found a new life outside the studio system thanks to a series of solid, visually spectacular westerns directed by Anthony Mann that toughened his good guy image. *Winchester '73* (1950), *Bend of the River* (1952), *The Naked Spur* (1953), *The Far Country,* and *The Man from Laramie* (both 1955) uncovered a maturity and unplumbed anger that defied the amiable string-bean who had drifted through movies in the '30s and early 1940s.

The war also wiped the smile off William Holden's face, which was fine with him. He had always been the nice guy next door in "Smiling Jim roles," as he called them, and by the 1940s he was sick of what he was doing. He was still under contract at Paramount, and it looked as though little was going to change until Montgomery Clift inadvertently came to his aid to make him a superstar.

C HARLES BRACKETT SUGGESTED A STORY BASED ON A FADED SILENT movie star, and his collaborator, Billy Wilder, added the idea of the faded star falling in love with a man years younger than herself. Brackett and Wilder together had created the sort of richly sophisticated and acerbic movies that helped to give Paramount its distinction among the studios — films such as *Ninotchka* (1939), *Ball of Fire* (1942), and *The Lost Weekend* (1945).

*Sunset Blvd.*, the title they decided upon for their story, would be their final collaboration. Wilder saw the silent star, Norma Desmond, as someone who "lives in the past and refuses to believe her days as a star are gone. She has sealed herself in one of those immense old rundown mansions on Sunset Boulevard amidst a clutter of mementoes, like a Grand Rapids Louis Quinze commode and a huge swan-shaped bed. We see the young man as a screenwriter. He's a nice guy from the middle west, maybe. But he can't make the grade in Hollywood and he's really down on his luck."

Wilder and Brackett, all the time fearing that Paramount would get wind of what they were up to, fought constantly over the shape of the story. They did agree to borrow a key plot point from a Balzac novel, *Père Goriot*, and allow the older woman to shoot her young lover. But there were all sorts of problems with casting Norma Desmond, principally because none of the dowagers of the silent era wanted to be seen as finished. Mae West, Wilder's first choice, would have nothing to do with *Sunset Blvd.*, and neither would Pola Negri. Mary Pickford, to her credit, liked the script, but wanted to be more central to the story, something Brackett and Wilder declined. Wilder complained to George Cukor that he could not find anyone, and Cukor raised his eyebrows and said, of course no actress but Gloria Swanson could play the role. And of course no one could. The silents had been dead barely two decades, although it might as well have been a millennium, and Swanson was just 52 years old. Gable and Cooper, only a couple of years younger, male, and creatures of sound, were still working movie stars in 1949–50. Swanson, as big a star in her era as her male counterparts were in theirs, had all but disappeared.

Now who to cast as Joe Gillis, the young stud who reluctantly moves into Norma Desmond's life? That seemed simple enough. Montgomery Clift had just finished a picture for Paramount, *The Heiress*, and everyone had their eyes on him. At the age of 29, Clift seemed fragile to the point of breaking, yet at the same time possessed of an inner strength that burned out through his eyes. You could beat Monty down, but you could not destroy him — qualities that would find their fullest expression a couple of years later when he played Prewitt in *From Here to Eternity*.

Wilder offered him the part of Joe, and Clift seemed enthusiastic. Thinking he had solved his casting problems, Wilder allowed Monty to fly off to Switzerland for a skiing holiday before starting work. Standing on an Alpine slope, however, Clift began to have second thoughts. He had just done *The Heiress*, about a manipulative young man involved in a relationship with an older woman. Now here he was about to repeat himself, only this time the woman was even older. He was supposed to be this youthful heartthrob idolized by teenage girls. These were hardly the roles that would enhance that sort of reputation. Never mind that he was involved with the singer Libby Holman, a considerably older woman. That was real life. This was the movies. Accordingly, he phoned Herman Citron at Paramount and lamely told him he could not go through with this because he had trouble doing love scenes with older women. He apparently managed the statement with a straight face.

Citron was appalled. If Clift was going to back out, he would have to talk to Wilder personally. Clift managed to get back to Los Angeles without changing his mind, although he did somewhat amend the story he would nervously rattle off to the forbidding Wilder. His audience, he explained, would never accept him making love to a woman 35 years older than he (in fact, Swanson was some 20 years older). Wilder, not one to suffer fools or wishy-washy actors gladly, was apoplectic. "Bullshit!" he thundered to an interviewer on the subject. "If he was any kind of actor, he would be convincing making love to *any* woman!"

Paramount was so upset, the studio dropped his contract. Nonetheless, Clift was gone — presumably in search of a younger co-star[11] — leaving Wilder, one week away from production, hustling to find a replacement. He approached Fred MacMurray, who had filled in so effectively when no one else would do *Double Indemnity*. MacMurray, even though willing to kill for the deceitful woman he loved, could not bring himself to play a kept man. Marlon Brando was already a sensation in *Streetcar* on Broadway, but Paramount did not think him a big enough name yet. Gene Kelly was considered but MGM, where he was still under contract, would not release him. Wilder had no choice but to look around the lot.

William Holden's name came up and, although Wilder did not think much of him, time was running out, so he invited the actor around to his bungalow for a drink. Like most people exposed to Holden's loose, likable charm, Wilder was impressed. Maybe there was more to him than thus far had been exposed to a camera. Holden went home, read the script, then agreed to do something no other actor had done for Wilder — act in the movie. Not without trepidation, though. "I agreed to do this picture," he confessed to his wife, "and now I'm not sure I can deliver."

---

[11] He soon found her in 18-year-old Elizabeth Taylor, with whom he co-starred in George Stevens' *A Place in the Sun*. It was released in 1951, a year after *Sunset Blvd*. Posterity has not been kind to *A Place in the Sun;* it has been magnificent to *Sunset Blvd.*

Wilder had envisaged a 25-year-old and Holden was 31. He looked it on the screen. The war and his drinking, already heavy, had etched into his handsome face premature traces of the world-weariness that soon would overtake him. No matter. He made a great Joe Gillis — a perfect foil to the amazing Norma Desmond provided by Gloria Swanson, who must have understood this would be her last great role.

What nearly ruined the movie, however, was Wilder himself. Brackett had hotly argued that the way to open the story was not in a morgue with Joe Gillis, already dead from a gunshot wound, talking to the other corpses. But Wilder was insistent. When this version was unveiled to a preview audience in, of all places, Evanston, Illinois, it was met with howls of laughter. Shaken, Wilder and Paramount withdrew the picture for six months, creating speculation that it was to be shelved permanently. But Wilder reshot the beginning, the now famous sequence where Joe is introduced, his body floating in Norma's swimming pool, and then narrates the train of events leading up to his death.

L IKE MOST OF THE PICTURES HOLLYWOOD HAS MADE ABOUT ITSELF, *Sunset Blvd.*, despite glowing reviews, was not a hit. However, it did put an end to the "Smiling Jim" roles Holden hated so much. He was to win an Oscar, not for *Sunset Blvd.* but for *Stalag 17*, directed again by Wilder three years later. He was now a movie star, and so when it came time to cast the film version of Clifford Odets' play, *The Country Girl*, there was no hesitation about Holden as the male lead, pushing an alcoholic singer, Bing Crosby, toward a comeback. The question was, who would play the singer's wife.

Originally, the movie's producers, William Perlberg and George Seaton, cast Jennifer Jones as Georgie Elgin, the plain, drab woman who falls in love with Holden as she nurses her recovering husband. When she announced she was pregnant, Jones's husband, David O. Selznick, assured the producers that her condition would not show until after filming was completed. Not entirely satisfied with Jones in the role, anyway, they used the pregnancy as the pretext to get rid of her and go after the actress they really wanted — Grace Kelly, a former model from Philadelphia.

Like Audrey Hepburn, Kelly was making something of a specialty of leading men old enough to be her father. Not yet in her mid-20s, she married

51-year-old Gary Cooper in *High Noon*, seduced 52-year-old Clark Gable in *Mogambo*, became engaged to 46-year-old James Stewart in *Rear Window*, and now the plan was to have her save 50-year-old Bing Crosby from the bottle in *The Country Girl*. Kelly was one of the great Hollywood beauties, but that was not required here. Moreover, she was in the habit of arriving at auditions wearing white gloves, not exactly the image of the country girl. Everyone was smitten with the way she looked, but no one was particularly impressed with the way she acted. Even Bing Crosby, who had had an affair with her, was against Grace Kelly being cast in *The Country Girl*.

Perlberg and Seaton were not to be dissuaded, however, and approached MGM about the possibility of a loan-out. The studio, which to this point was only too happy to let Kelly go off and do movies for other studios, had just seen a rough cut of Hitchcock's *Rear Window* in which she co-starred with James Stewart. Hitchcock had found the fire beneath Kelly's icy exterior, and MGM abruptly realized there might be something special here. There would be no more loan-outs. Plans were made to rush her into their own production, a melodrama entitled *Green Fire* in which she was to play a coffee plantation owner. Robert Taylor took one look at the script and ran away. While MGM fretted over a replacement for Taylor (it would finally be Stewart Granger), Perlberg and Seaton managed to slip Kelly a copy of *The Country Girl*.

"I just had to be in *The Country Girl*," she said later, recalling how she had reacted when she read the script. "That was a real acting part for me." She said she had never really had to act before. Always she was outfitted in glamorous clothes and surrounded by glamorous settings. "And lots of times, too, I was just the feminine background for the male stars who carried the action and the story on their shoulders."

There was a story that Kelly, upon hearing that the studio would not loan her out to do *The Country Girl*, stormed into the office of boss Dore Schary and swore, "If I can't do this picture, I'll get on a train and never come back. I'll never make another film." She later conceded that it was the sort of speech she was urged to make, but never did. The whole thing was handled by her agent, Lew Wasserman, who persuaded Schary to let her go on the understanding that as soon as she finished *The Country Girl*, she would do *Green Fire*. Thus, Grace Kelly became the least likely-looking country girl ever to appear in the movies. She wore glasses, little makeup, and allowed her hair to be pulled back. Of such sacrifices are Academy Awards made, though, and sure enough, Kelly got one in 1954 for her performance. *Green Fire* was probably the least memorable movie she made.

G RACE KELLY AND BILL HOLDEN BOTH HAD THEIR EYES FIRMLY SET ON *Giant*, the adaptation of Edna Ferber's bestselling novel that George Stevens was planning to turn into a movie. Kelly was anxious to play the eastern beauty swept off to Texas by the stubborn rancher, Bick Benedict. That was the role Holden badly wanted. Kelly's competition was Elizabeth Taylor, while Stevens was also taking a look at both Clark Gable and Gary Cooper for Bick, as well as a young actor named Rock Hudson.

Holden met with Stevens a couple of times and was pretty sure that Bick was his. The next thing he heard, it had gone to Hudson. Upset, he decided to take a steambath over at the Universal gym. He walked into the steamroom naked and there, equally naked, was the man who would play Bick. Hudson had just heard the news himself a couple of hours before. Holden swallowed hard, walked up to Hudson, and congratulated him. "I wish you luck on the picture," he said. "It's a very good role."

In fact, it was the best role of Rock Hudson's short, meteoric, and, some would say, hard-to-explain movie career. The studios had not completely abandoned contract players, particularly at Universal where they were signing up young actors cheaply, concentrating more on their beefcake potential than on any talent. Roy Fitzgerald was dark and pretty and driving a truck when the talent agent Henry Willson found him, changed his name to Rock Hudson, capped his teeth, got him acting lessons and a contract at Universal.

Hudson did not act in front of a camera; he suffered. Legend held that Rock Hudson had required 38 takes to get out a single line of dialogue in his maiden picture, a cliché-riddled World War II drama titled *Fighter Squadron* that was released in 1948. Nonetheless, despite determined efforts on the part of Universal to throw him into every piece of junk imaginable, his handsomeness saw him through, and his popularity soared. In effect he became the last — and least charismatic — studio-made star. Whatever else he was, Rock Hudson never was much of an actor. John Huston, who loved real actors, despised Hudson. The director of *Giant*, George Stevens, by contrast, took him by the hand and did something Huston never would have, guiding his young charge through every nuance of playing Bick. In that way, he induced a confidence Hudson had never felt before. Stevens' care and feeding of his star may have been at least partially responsible for Elizabeth Taylor being cast as his co-star over Grace Kelly.

Hudson later recalled Stevens asked him, "Who would you like for your leading lady? Grace Kelly or Elizabeth Taylor?"

At first Hudson did not think the director was serious. When he saw that he was, "I said, 'Elizabeth.'"

"Fine," said Stevens. "We'll get Elizabeth."

*Giant*, which in addition to Taylor starred the charismatic newcomer James Dean, became the movie of Hudson's career. Viewed today, he still seems inanimate and unnatural compared with others in the picture that would later inspire any number of soap-opera imitations, particularly on television. Nonetheless, Hudson was nominated for an Oscar for the performance Stevens managed to pull out of him. *Giant* made him the most popular star in movies, a popularity, thanks to the constraints imposed by the Universal contract, that he was never able to capitalize on properly.

MGM, for example, was preparing a remake of *Ben-Hur* (it had been filmed twice before — in 1907 and in a lavish 1926 production), and wanted Marlon Brando to play the prince who runs afoul of the Roman authorities in Palestine at the time of Christ. That would have been something to see — Brando in a chariot, racing for Christianity.

Any number of stars turned down the movie for one reason or another. Kirk Douglas would have nothing to do with it, and his friend Burt Lancaster disliked like the script's "interpretation" of the Lew Wallace novel. Rock Hudson was anxious to play the part, and MGM wanted him badly enough that it offered $1 million to Universal for his services. The studio, perhaps thinking that one good movie, *Giant*, in a contract player's career was enough, demurred. "We rejected the possibility of lending him at all for the picture," said Ed Mahl, Universal's chief production executive. "Rock was obviously very well established by that time, but it was more important to us to have him for our own pictures. Rock, or anyone else, was never loaned for the sole purpose of making money."

Charlton Heston got the chariot, the Oscar, and the superstardom almost by default. Hudson was devastated according to his longtime friend and confidant Tom Clark, and when he renegotiated his Universal contract, he made sure it contained a clause allowing him to do at least one movie a year outside the studio — an example of closing the studio gate after the good part had escaped, if ever there was one.

Hudson next had to choose between two romantic films, both of which required him to play a soldier, and both of which required him to fall in love. Joshua Logan was planning to direct *Sayonara*, an adaptation from a James Michener story about an American soldier who falls for a Japanese entertainer. Meanwhile, producer David O. Selznick was mounting a lavishly budgeted remake of Hemingway's *A Farewell to Arms* with a script by Ben Hecht and direction by John Huston. Selznick wanted Hudson for the young soldier who is wounded and becomes passionately involved with his nurse. Selznick's wife, Jennifer Jones, now recovered from her pregnancy and the loss of *The Country Girl*, was to play the nurse. On paper, there seemed no contest. *Farewell to Arms* was the more prestigious of the two projects, and so Hudson passed on *Sayonara*. Logan showed the script to — who else? — Marlon Brando, who, in one of the final exercises of good judgment he was to make during the 1950s, agreed after much persuasion and frustration on the part of Logan, to star. It would be one of his most popular movies.

Hudson, on the other hand, made "the worst mistake of my career" in doing *A Farewell to Arms*. It was Selznick's last disaster-plagued hurrah, complete with John Huston, who had no respect for Hudson anyway, walking off (replaced by solid, uninspired Charles Vidor). The movie, with a woefully miscast Rock, was a terrible failure.

Eventually, Rock Hudson found a métier of sorts playing in a series of lightweight romantic comedies, the most popular of which, *Pillow Talk* (1959) and *Lover Come Back* (1962) partnered him with Doris Day. He stayed at Universal for 17 years, built by the studio, and torn down by it, too, thanks to the uninspired vehicles he was shoved into year after year. At the end, when he left the lot, his exit was hardly noticed.

"It seemed to me that the least they could have done was to send some third assistant vice president down to wave at me as I left," Hudson said later. "But no one showed up."

# 7

# THREE ACTORS
# FROM THE MIDWEST
*And a movie of the Far East*

A NEW GENERATION OF ACTORS NOW EMERGED IN THE WAKE OF Brando's success that had nothing but disdain for the oldtime movie stardom represented — at least in the 1950s — by the likes of Rock Hudson. Most of these actors came from New York, trained in the "Method," cutting their teeth on the live productions flourishing in this new medium called television (an astonishing 500 live television dramas were produced in 1952 alone). Television was supposed to destroy movies, but in fact the medium would end up providing film with the most exciting influx of new talent since sound brought dozens of stage-trained actors west to Hollywood in the late 1920s.

Among the actors to be seen around New York theater and television in the '50s were Rod Steiger, Martin Landau, Eva Marie Saint, Grace Kelly, and Anne Bancroft. The group also included three young men from the Midwestern United States, all of whom struggled under Brando's shadow and whose careers would intersect in curious and even tragic ways.

James Dean, Paul Newman, and Steve McQueen often bumped into each other at auditions. All three had been influenced by Brando's emergence, but then so had just about every other young actor in New York. James Dean and Paul Newman both came from middle-class backgrounds. James Byron Dean was from Marion, Indiana, while Paul Newman hailed from Cleveland, Ohio. They were young actors, anxious to make it, and their rebellion was more feigned than real. But Terrence Steven McQueen, raised in Slater, Missouri, was the real goods. The other two could act troubled, McQueen *was* troubled. Abandoned by his father, a navy flyer, when he was a child, McQueen spent part of his youth at Boys' Republic, a reform school in Chino, California. While Dean was attending classes at UCLA and Newman was at

Yale Drama School, McQueen was drifting around the country in jobs as varied as sailor, lumberjack, carnival barker, oilfield worker, and beachcomber. He enlisted in the Marines in 1947, did some time in the brig for being AWOL, and, when he was discharged in 1950, ended up in New York where he became a member of the Neighborhood Playhouse, taking acting lessons under Uta Hagen and Herbert Berghof.

McQueen always carried a chip on his shoulder. He was frustrated and angry, and he resented both Dean and Newman because they were moving ahead with an effortlessness that had never been his experience. Nothing in Steve McQueen's life came easily, not even acting. In 1958, Jimmy Dean was already a movie icon of mythological proportions, and Paul Newman had received his first Oscar nomination for *Cat on a Hot Tin Roof* while Steve McQueen starred in a low-budget horror monster movie, *The Blob*.

What would happen to Steve McQueen was anybody's guess. Paul Newman and James Dean were something else again. There was the real competition, and the debate was over which of them would become the bigger star first.

Following the success of *On the Waterfront*, Elia Kazan prepared a movie version of John Steinbeck's novel *East of Eden*. He was looking for a young actor to play Cal Trask and, as was everyone's wont at the time, briefly considered Brando. Abandoning that notion, Kazan appeared in New York to read a number of the more talked-about young actors and actresses around town. Among those auditioning were Paul Newman and James Dean, as well as Joanne Woodward (who later would marry Newman) and Julie Harris.

Newman and Dean found themselves being tested together. Newman was dressed in a white shirt with a bow tie, a cigarette tucked behind his ear. Dean showed up in a sportshirt. During the test, he jammed his eyeglasses in his shirt pocket. There was no dialogue spoken from the script; the test was designed to see how the two actors looked on camera.

"Hey, you two queers," the director called off camera, "look this way."

Dutifully, the actors turned their profiles to camera. "I don't want to look at him," Newman joked. "He's a sourpuss."

A considerable amount of kidding around went on, but the humor had an edge to it, an echo of things to come. At one point the director, off camera, asked Newman, "Paul, do you think Jimmy will appeal to bobby-soxers?"

"I don't know," Newman replied.

"Is he going to be a sex symbol?" The voice off camera inquired.

Newman gave Dean the once-over. "I don't usually go out with boys. But with his looks, sure . . . sure, I think they'll flip over him."

"What about you, Jimmy?" the director asked. "Do you think the girls will like you?"

"Sure," he replied laconically, flipping something in his hand. "All depends whether I like them."

It took a moment before it was evident that Dean was tossing around a switchblade knife.

After seeing the test, David Dalton, Dean's most eloquent biographer, was certain that what he had witnessed was a test of raw star power between two unknown actors who would someday command the attention of a world-wide movie audience. "What determined the winner was his face," Dalton wrote. "Both Jimmy and Paul were nascent icons with features that were to become as easily recognizable as Christ, Mao, or Mickey Mouse."

But on the screen, and for the role in question, he had no doubt as to the winner. "Newman didn't look like he would do anything unpredictable or uncontrollable, but Jimmy looked like he was about to erupt."

Newman might have played the elder brother in *East of Eden*, but he lost out to Richard Davalos, while Jimmy won the main role of Cal, amidst considerable surprise. "I wouldn't imagine Kazan being initially attracted to Jimmy," said Dean's friend Bill Gunn. Kazan was not. "Marlon was well trained, proficient in technique, character, and make-up," Kazan said. "Dean had no technique."

There was no mistaking Dean's idolization of Brando, however. When Brando showed up on the set of *East of Eden*, Kazan recalled, Dean "was so adoring that he seemed shrunken and wasted in misery." The older actor was unimpressed. "Dean was never a friend of mine, but he had an *idée fixe* about me," Brando told Truman Capote. "Whatever I did, he did. He was always try-ing to get close to me."

Kazan was astonished at what happened during the first screenings of *East of Eden*. Dean, still totally unknown, had only to be on the screen for a few seconds before young women began screaming. Overnight he was a star. Even Dean's agent, Dick Clayton, was amazed by what was happening at that premiere. "I couldn't believe that was Jimmy next to me," he said 38 years later. "The camera really loved him."

The same year that Dean starred in *East of Eden*, he turned down another film role, the lead in an old-fashioned studio epic called *The Silver Chalice*. Instead, Paul Newman made this his film debut. While teenage girls screamed in ecstasy when Dean appeared on screen in *East of Eden*, audiences groaned and laughed at Newman in *The Silver Chalice*. It was one of the most disastrous debuts in screen history. Years later, when *The Silver Chalice* was shown on television, Newman was still so embarrassed that he took ads in the show-business trade papers apologizing for it. Newman's movie career was in trouble even before it started, and it would take a tragedy to turn it around.

WHEN ROBERT WISE AGREED TO DIRECT *SOMEBODY UP THERE LIKES Me*, James Dean already was attached to the movie. He had read Rocky Graziano's autobiography about his hard rise from the streets of New York to prominence as a middleweight boxing champion, liked it, and had told MGM producer Charles Schnee he wanted to do it. "Jimmy was all set to do it," said Dick Clayton. "We'd met with the producers and had some fittings."

Wise, a former film editor on Orson Welles' *Citizen Kane* and *The Magnificent Ambersons*, had established himself as a director of note in 1949 via a well-received low-budget boxing drama called *The Set-Up*. By the time he came to *Somebody Up There Likes Me*, Wise had churned out nearly 20 films in just under a decade, including *The Day the Earth Stood Still*, *The Desert Rats*, and *Helen of Troy*. He was excited about the prospect of working with one of the hottest young actors in movies, although slightly concerned that, physically, Dean was not suited for the part. But he put that notion to one side. "It was quite a coup to have him in it," Wise recalled. "He was being sought by so many of the studios."

On 30 September 1955, after completing work on *Giant* with Rock Hudson and Elizabeth Taylor, Dean climbed behind the wheel of his brand new Porsche Spyder 550 for the drive to Salinas where he was to compete in a car race. En route, his sportscar collided with another vehicle, and Dean was killed instantly. When he died at the age of 24, James Byron Dean was the hottest young star in Hollywood, even though only one of his films,

*East of Eden*, had been released. Both *Rebel Without a Cause* and *Giant* were released after he died. Tragic death made Dean a bigger star than he ever was in his brief life. His friends could never get over the rapturous effect he had had on audiences in that first screen appearance in *East of Eden*. Death turned that adulation into enduring obsession. Only the mystique that grew in the wake of Marilyn Monroe's tragic death would overshadow the public fascination with Jimmy Dean.

In the first days of October, as the shock waves from Dean's death were absorbed, Wise had to deal with the simple fact that, suddenly, there was no leading man for *Somebody Up There Likes Me*. "Then we were up in the air," Wise said, "and started looking around, and I remember having lunch with John Cassavetes." The New York actor was in his mid-20s and just beginning to break into films. Wise did not think he had the right build to play Rocky Graziano. "He took rather strong exception to that, I recall, and basically said 'all true actors could act anything.'"

Nearly 40 years later, Wise does not remember exactly how Paul Newman came to his attention. He did remember meeting the actor by chance a year or two before when he was in a New York costume house looking for clothing for *Helen of Troy*, Wise's single foray into spectacle filmmaking. Newman was probably there being outfitted for *The Silver Chalice*.

Now, searching for another actor who could play Graziano, Wise viewed footage of Newman, not in the execrable *Silver Chalice*, but as a brain-washed soldier in a small, unreleased drama titled *The Rack* (the movie would not be released until after *Somebody Up There Likes Me*). After seeing the footage, Wise was certain he had his Rocky. "He seemed like a much more likely candidate than anyone else," Wise explained in his typically low-key, dispassionate manner. That simple assertion — the intuitive knowing that someone is right for a part — saved Paul Newman's movie career.

"I don't know you could say it saved his career," Wise said. "But it certainly kicked off his career." Dick Clayton, James Dean's agent, disagrees. "*Silver Chalice* had knocked Paul right out, the experience was so bad for him," Clayton said. "He didn't care at that point. He'd had enough of Hollywood."

Still, having to cast a virtual unknown in a lead role after being certain that you had the hottest young star in the movies was something of a comedown. "Paul Newman was just barely getting established as a movie actor, and he didn't really have any movie name at all," Wise said.

Wise now believes Newman was the better choice. He doubts that he could have gotten the same performance out of Dean. "Paul gives such a strong, believable characterization. He really worked on Rocky, he really worked on getting that character up there on the screen."

Steve McQueen also was in *Somebody Up There Likes Me*, playing a bit part in his first movie. It tore at him that his arch-rival, Paul Newman, was the star. He wanted everything that Newman had, and swore to himself that some day he would have it.

As Robert Wise worked to produce *Somebody Up There Likes Me*, the producer Sam Spiegel followed the success of *On the Waterfront* with *The Strange One*, the movie that finally allowed Ben Gazzara to make his film debut. Based on Calder Willingham's novel, *The Strange One* cast Gazzara as a darkly charismatic cadet who holds a mysterious power over his fellow officers at a military academy. The movie was a resounding flop that left Spiegel — by now used to success — shaken. The movie failed, he decided, largely because of director Jack Garfein, who had also directed the stage play. Spiegel was determined not to let this happen again.

Carl Foreman, the writer of *High Noon*, had been blacklisted in 1951 by the HUAC because he refused to confirm or deny his Communist party affiliations. Foreman had retreated to London and, while there, read a book by the French writer Pierre Boulle about a group of British prisoners of war in Burma who were forced to build a strategic bridge over the River Kwai. Foreman optioned the novel for £300, and showed it to producer Alexander Korda.

Complaining that the British Colonel Nicholson who leads the prisoners of war in the story was either insane or a traitor, Korda turned it down. Foreman next pitched it to Spiegel, who perhaps appreciated insanity more than Korda. He bought the property with Foreman attached to it as screenwriter (although Foreman never received screen credit because he was still blacklisted; that credit, along with an Oscar, went to Pierre Boulle who had never even worked on the script). Spiegel had one suggestion: make one of the characters an American. So Foreman came up with an American commando sent to blow up the British-built bridge.

Spiegel had Humphrey Bogart in mind for the commando, but in 1956 he was already committed to another picture, *The Harder They Fall*, the last movie he made before dying of lung cancer at the age of 57. The actor who had appeared in so many classic films thanks to the carelessness of George Raft missed what would have been a great finale.

Spiegel next turned to Cary Grant to play the American. Grant declined, and Spiegel hired William Holden, who had also been last on the list for *Sunset Blvd.* In addition to being one of his most memorable films, *The Bridge on the River Kwai* would make Bill Holden one of the richest actors in movies. Instead of taking a full salary, Holden agreed to a percentage of the profits, a largely unheard-of practice at the time but a precursor of things to come, and more evidence that studio contract players were a thing of the past.

Even though Holden was a star, his role would support whoever portrayed Colonel Nicholson. Spiegel's first choice, Laurence Olivier, was about to direct Marilyn Monroe in *The Prince and the Showgirl*. "Why should I go off to Ceylon, to play a martinet, when I can stay home and act with Marilyn Monroe?" he asked Spiegel. The logic was inescapable, but it meant Olivier missed a splendid role in what would have been the most popular and widely seen film of his career. Other than appearing in Tony Richardson's movie version of *The Entertainer*, Olivier would not again dominate a film the way he might have dominated *Bridge* until he appeared with Michael Caine in *Sleuth* 12 years later.

Spiegel also approached Charles Laughton, whom director David Lean very much wanted. Laughton was 56 years old and had just finished directing his first (and only) movie, *The Night of the Hunter*. However, with his immense girth, Laughton was judged unfit to be insured for the rigors of a movie being shot on remote locations in the jungles of Ceylon. The playwright Noel Coward also turned the part down, although he said later he regretted the decision. Desperate now to find someone, Spiegel approached Alec Guinness, an unusual choice for such a humorless role. Guinness had become a staple of such critically praised Ealing comedies as *The Lavender Hill Mob*, *The Man in the White Suit,* and *The Ladykillers*. He had first attracted wide notice as Fagin in David Lean's 1948 film of *Oliver Twist*, but his last foray into serious drama, *The Swan* (1956), did not encourage anyone to think of him as a dramatic actor.

"Alec Guinness, as Shaw once observed of Irving, has no face," wrote the critic Kenneth Tynan, going on to describe him as "a slight man, balding and bland, with deprecating, sloped shoulders, which he shrugs constantly." Hardly the description of a leader of jungle bridge-builders. Guinness thought the script "rubbish, filled with elephant charges, that sort of thing," and turned it down three times.

Spiegel, as he had with Brando, refused to take rejection. He invited Guinness to dinner. "You're wasting your time," Guinness grumbled. But he acquiesced, and went along. Sam poured on the wine and the charm and "at the end of it," Guinness later reported, "I was telling him, 'what kind of wig will I be wearing?'" Spiegel's assurances that Nicholson could be played with humor won the day. "This was the thing Guinness did not expect," Spiegel said later.

*The Bridge on the River Kwai* made Guinness an international star and won him an Oscar in 1957 for best actor. The character and the actor were forever linked. Not until 20 years later, when Guinness played Ben (Obi-Wan) Kenobi in George Lucas's *Star Wars*, did the public finally shake its view of him as the obsessed, indomitable British army colonel.

Curious what perception does to the ownership of things. Although Guinness was the last actor ever considered for the part, it became his on the screen, and it is hard to imagine anyone else in it. Similarly, it was soon forgotten that Sam Spiegel had anything to do with the picture itself. *The Bridge on the River Kwai* is now thought of as "a film by David Lean," when in fact it was Spiegel who found the project, worked on the script for two years with Carl Foreman, then wooed and cajoled various actors all over the world. Lean was not even his first choice for director. He had first considered Howard Hawks and John Ford (at least according to Spiegel). Then Lean phoned and asked for the job. Impressed with the way he had shown the workings of the military mind in *In Which We Serve* (co-directed with Noel Coward), Spiegel let him have it.

Guinness never particularly cottoned to Lean, even though the two men worked together often over the years. With *Bridge*, Guinness was aware of how badly Lean had wanted Charles Laughton in the Nicholson role, and the coolness struck from that knowledge never truly abated. For his part, Lean was never particularly friendly with Spiegel. Part of that unfriendliness had to do with the tradition that producer constantly cheated director, but part of it may also have had its roots in Lean's knowledge that his greatest triumphs were to some degree inspired by Spiegel. In any event, the two men would endure each other for one final collaboration — their greatest.

"Lean, like Spiegel, is a stubborn man in having his own way," wrote the screenwriter Robert Bolt. "One of the many remarkable things about *Lawrence of Arabia* is that two such stubborn men were able to agree on the making of it."

They were also able to agree on who should play the elusive, legendary leader of the Arab revolt in the desert, T. E. Lawrence. It would be Marlon Brando.

# 8

# THE BRITISH CONNECTION
*O'Toole, Caine, Connery, et al.*

THE HUNGARIAN-BORN PRODUCER ALEXANDER KORDA MADE THE first serious efforts to bring the life of T. E. Lawrence to the screen. Beginning in 1934, it was announced that Leslie Howard would play Lawrence in a film directed by Lewis Milestone, the first in a series of announcements of Korda-produced Lawrence projects that never amounted to anything. A combination of Lawrence's ambivalence, the politics of the day, money problems, and even suggestions that Korda acted as an agent for the British government conspired to prevent *Lawrence* from coming to the screen.

Howard's participation was announced for a second time in 1937, two years after Lawrence's death in a motorcycle accident; then John Clements, who had starred in Korda's *The Four Feathers,* was supposed to do it. Clements heard that Robert Donat also was offered the role, as was Laurence Olivier, but World War II put a stop to any further efforts until the early 1950s when another producer, Anatole De Grunwald, decided to revive the project, enlisting playwright Terence Rattigan (*Separate Tables*) to write a screenplay.

There was speculation that Denholm Elliott, a 32-year London stage actor, would play Lawrence, or Richard Burton, or Alec Guinness. But then, in September 1957, Dirk Bogarde was announced for the role, with Anthony Asquith directing. "I had never, in my life, wanted a part or script, so much," Bogarde later wrote. Filming was to start the next year outside of Baghdad in Iraq. Bogarde was busy with costume and wig fittings, research and script conferences. "Remember, this was never to be Lean's panoramic thing. . . . We were not making a Technicolor blockbuster." They were not, in fact, making anything. Less than a month before the film was to begin shooting, De Grunwald pulled the plug. The British film industry was going through one of its periodic nosedives. The £500,000 needed to make the film simply was not available.

Bogarde was deeply disappointed, but Terence Rattigan sat down and refashioned his screenplay for *Lawrence* into a stage play titled *Ross: A Dramatic Portrait*.[12]

Enter Sam Spiegel.

He later said his interest in Lawrence's life dated back to 1926 when he had read *Seven Pillars of Wisdom*. It was Spiegel who persuaded Lawrence's brother to let him have the rights to *Seven Pillars*, then distracted David Lean from his intention of making a film of Gandhi's life and set Michael Wilson, who had worked on *Bridge*, to begin fashioning a screenplay. Meanwhile, he went off to produce the screen version of Tennessee Williams' *Suddenly, Last Summer*.

The film production of the Williams play was troubled and tense, thanks to Montgomery Clift's increasingly erratic behavior. Clift, drinking heavily and taking drugs, was in such dreadful shape that Mankiewicz could not bear to work with him. The director demanded that his producer dump the star. Katharine Hepburn was so upset with Mankiewicz and the way he treated Clift that on the last day of shooting, she made sure she had nothing left to film, then spat in Mankiewicz's face and stormed off the set.

If it were not for Hepburn's protectiveness, Clift would have been gone from the film. Spiegel even had someone in mind to replace Clift, a young Irish actor named Peter O'Toole. He ambled into the screen test, whereupon he was asked to pretend he was a doctor performing an operation. At the conclusion, O'Toole turned to the camera and intoned with a professional mournfulness, "It's all right, Mrs. Spiegel, your son will never play the violin again." Sam Spiegel was apoplectic. Given the problems he was already having with drunken movie stars and uncommunicative directors, he did not need young Irish smartasses. That was the end of O'Toole in *Suddenly, Last Summer*. Spiegel swore that this fool would never, ever work for him. Not as long as he lived.

"IN A WAY THEY ARE VERY MUCH ALIKE," SAM SPIEGEL SAID AT A London reception where it was announced that Marlon Brando would play the title role in David Lean's upcoming film of *Lawrence*

---

[12] Producer Herbert Wilcox in 1960 bought the screen rights to Rattigan's play for £100,000 and announced that Laurence Harvey would play T. E. Lawrence, and so for a time there were two competing *Lawrence of Arabia* projects. Alec Guinness portrayed Lawrence in *Ross* on the London stage.

*of Arabia*. "Both have that mystic, tortured quality of doubting their own destiny. In 1917, Lawrence was barely thirty. Brando is the same age. There is practically nobody else of international magnitude who could play the part."

A stunned silence nonetheless greeted this declaration, understandable on the part of A. W. Lawrence (T. E.'s brother) since he had no idea who this Brando was. The silence was shared by Brando and his representatives, there having been no contract signed. Dirk Bogarde, who had come within months of being Lawrence himself, remained cynical. "There are so many actors knocking around who have at some time been going to play Lawrence that Alec Guinness and I decided to form a club. We have even designed a tie. Dark background, with motif of burnoose and camel."

How serious Brando was about playing Lawrence is open to question. Brando already had informed Truman Capote in the notorious interview the author conducted with him one night in his hotel room in Japan while shooting *Sayonara* that he only meant what he said about 40 percent of the time, and estimated he had an attention span of seven minutes — not particularly effective for epic picturemaking, as the makers of *Mutiny on the Bounty* were finding out. The luck for Lean and Spiegel was that *Bounty*'s production problems forced Brando to abandon whatever notion he might have had to do *Lawrence*. Finally completed, *Bounty* cost $20 million, double its initial budget. The movie nearly bankrupted MGM when it collapsed at the box office in 1962.

What *Lawrence* would have been like with Brando presiding is open to the desert-sized limits of the imagination. One can also speculate that, given Brando's increasing propensity for delay and difficulty, the movie might never have been finished. Brando as Lawrence would have been . . . interesting. Perhaps even disastrous. Lean himself later hedged and worried, rightly, that it might have become "Brando of Arabia."

But there was no Brando. Spiegel hurriedly swallowed the notion that there was no other actor "of international magnitude" who could play Lawrence and began searching around for a replacement. His eye fleetingly fell upon Anthony Perkins, but just as Lean worried there would be Brando of Arabia, now there was concern that Perkins would make it "Psycho in Arabia." Spiegel began to look at those less known. "Lawrence will make a star of an actor," Spiegel now decided. "For that reason David Lean and I have finally determined to forget the established stars . . . and to choose an unknown."

They were impressed by the work of Albert Finney in the unreleased *Saturday Night and Sunday Morning*. Finney, a bookie's son, was a graduate of London's prestigious Royal Academy of Dramatic Art who had done mostly Shakespeare on the stage.

Impressed but far from certain, Spiegel and Lean next enlisted Finney for the most complicated series of screen tests since David O. Selznick went looking for Scarlett O'Hara. Dressed in full costume on elaborate sets, Finney enacted scenes from Michael Wilson's screenplay with actors portraying various Arab characters. More than 1,400 feet of 35 mm film was shot, widescreen and in color, at a cost of over £100,000.

Spiegel was impressed; Lean not so much. He worried that Finney, who could be independent and difficult, might provide him with the same kind of problems as Marlon Brando. It never got that far. Finney announced his refusal to sign what Lean himself later conceded was "a slave contract" that would have indentured the actor to the irrepressible Sam for five years. Finney wanted a three-year contract and some veto power over future projects. But Spiegel would have none of it, and Finney was gone. Perhaps there was more to it than the contract, though. Finney might have been having second thoughts about his ability to play Lawrence. Speaking on the set of *Rich in Love* over 30 years later, the actor said, "It was a magnificent part but I just didn't feel I was the right actor for it. So not only did I turn it down but I recommended my fellow actor from the Royal Academy for it."

That might have come as news to Lean, who died in April of 1991. His story was that, following the loss of Finney, he hurried out to the cinemas and started looking at actors. He came across Peter O'Toole in a movie called *The Day They Robbed the Bank of England*. "On the screen, I saw this chap playing a sort of silly-assed Englishman, with a raincoat, casting for trout," Lean recalled. "That's it," he decided. "I'm going to test him."

Spiegel apparently either forgave or already had forgotten O'Toole's silliness during the *Suddenly, Last Summer* screen test, and wisely did not try to tie his actor into the sort of slave contract he had attempted with Finney. The test went so well that midway through, Lean stopped everything and announced, "No use shooting another foot of film. The boy *is* Lawrence."

So it was that Albert Finney's unwillingness to sign a contract opened the way for Peter O'Toole to play one of the greatest roles in the history of the postwar cinema. It was not the first time Finney had gotten out of O'Toole's way. In 1959, Willis Hall, a London playwright, had written a play about British soldiers in the jungle fighting the Japanese, called *The Long and the Short and the Tall*. Hall had written the lead role of the cockney loudmouth, Corporal Bamforth, specifically for Albert Finney. However, during rehearsals, Finney became ill with appendicitis and was forced to leave the play. He was replaced by O'Toole, who became a West End sensation in the part. Understudying the celebrated O'Toole was an increasingly frustrated young actor named Michael Caine.

W HEN PETER O'TOOLE WAS CHOSEN TO PLAY LAWRENCE, HE TOOK his leave from *The Long and the Short and the Tall*, and that provided Michael Caine, his understudy, with an unexpected break. When the play toured the provinces for four months, Caine took over the role of Bamforth. It was during that tour that he met another young actor named Terence Stamp. The two of them hit it off, and when the tour came to an end, they decided to settle into a flat together in London.

Caine was 25 years old, a cockney lad who had been born Maurice Micklewhite to a fish market porter and a mother who worked as a cleaning woman. He had spent the better part of a decade trying to find success as an actor. He had done repertory theater, 125 television shows, and had bit parts in some 40 movies. He was tall and blond, full of charm, opinions, and funny stories. Everyone liked Michael Caine at a party. Stamp, who was seven years younger, quite shy and withdrawn, regarded his flatmate as a mentor. Still, Caine was becoming increasingly dispirited. It seemed that everyone was going off to become a star except him, even the retiring Stamp.

"It was the greatest time of my life," Stamp later wrote of that period. "The excitement of the '60s, the discovery of the birth control pill for women and the resulting change in women's clothes — away with those horrible rubber girdles and in with the mini skirt — coincided with my fame." That fame arrived like a bullet in 1962, via the title role in Peter Ustinov's movie version of the Herman Melville novel *Billy Budd*. "When my agent, Jimmy Fraser, told me I was wanted for the screen test, I said: "You're joking. They must be scraping the bottom of the barrel."" His agent replied: "They are. They've seen every young actor in London." Caine, who had had far more experience in film, gave Stamp some pointers on how to perform in front of a camera ("Don't act," he advised, "externalize feelings, that's what the camera picks up."). Even so, Stamp thought he had no chance whatsoever, and so, when he arrived to meet Ustinov, he found himself quite blasé about the whole thing. "But Ustinov's presence was so heavy, so pithy that when I opened my mouth to speak I suddenly felt it wasn't worth saying — so I didn't say anything. And that was what he was looking for."

One moment, Stamp was unknown, the next he was walking over to the Savoy hotel to a press conference where his participation in *Billy Budd* was about to be announced. "Enjoy this," whispered a publicist, "because this is your last day of being anonymous."

"I was in the right place at the right time, doing the right thing," Stamp wrote three decades later. "I think films are mirrors through which the world can view its condition, and in the early '60s movies burst into Technicolor and my life burst into Technicolor, too."

Meanwhile, there was not much Technicolor in Michael Caine's life, just an offer to do the lead in a play titled *Next Time I'll Sing to You*. Little money was involved, and Caine was not enthusiastic. He preferred to spend his time looking for more lucrative movie and television work. But his agent talked him into doing the play, and to everyone's amazement the rather avant garde piece was a success and moved to the West End. After doing almost nothing for the two years following *The Long and the Short and the Tall*, Caine finally was on a West End stage — this time as lead.

One night Stanley Baker, the actor with whom Caine had appeared in his first film, a war movie titled *A Hill in Korea*, a.k.a. *Hell in Korea* (1956), dropped backstage. Baker was about to star in an adventure picture, *Zulu*, that dealt with the British army's standoff against a vastly superior Zulu force at Roarke's Drift. They had yet to cast the part of a cockney soldier, and Baker thought it might interest Caine. He arranged for him to meet his writer/director, a corpulent, plain-talking man named Cy Endfield. The next morning Caine showed up for the meeting with Endfield only to discover that the director had already cast James Booth in the role.

Crestfallen, Caine headed out the door, but Endfield called him back, wondering aloud if he could do an uppercrust English accent. Caine replied that given the amount of repertory TV and film bits he had done, he was capable of anything that was called for. Endfield looked him up and down and concluded that he resembled "one of those snotty, blue-blooded English guys."[13] Endfield decided to test him for the part of the aristocratic but inexperienced officer Gonville Bromhead. The test was so bad that Endfield later claimed Caine was the worst of all the actors who had tried out. Nonetheless he allowed Caine to play Bromhead, and could never say for sure why he did it. Caine had gotten the biggest break of his career, not because he was any good, but in spite of the fact that he was so bad.

ABOUT THE SAME TIME, THE DIRECTOR ROBERT WISE WAS PREPARING A movie version of the Rodgers and Hammerstein musical hit *The Sound of Music*. From the outset, Wise was concerned about the saccharin content of the true story of a novice nun, Maria, who is sent to act as nanny to the children of a widowed Austrian baron named Von Trapp. When the playwright Robert Anderson heard Wise was going to do *The Sound of Music,* he sent him a note saying, "Can't you run those kids through a whore house, or something?"

There was already a script by Ernest Lehman by the time Wise became attached to the project,[14] and they knew who they wanted for a leading lady. Julie Andrews had become a star on Broadway as Eliza Doolittle in *My Fair Lady*, but had been denied the role in the movie because she was not a movie star (Audrey Hepburn was, and she got the part). "We all felt Julie was the one," Wise said, "but there was this little undercurrent around town that questioned how photogenic she was. That gave us just a little bit of pause." Enough so that a list of possible alternative choices was drawn up, including Grace Kelly, Leslie Caron, Anne Bancroft, Angie Dickinson, Carole Lawrence, and Shirley Jones. "But the only one we really had our heart set on was Julie."

Andrews had finished shooting *Mary Poppins* for Walt Disney, although the film was not yet released. Wise persuaded the Disney people to let him see some of the *Mary Poppins* footage. "Boy, as soon as she came on the

---

[13] Caine used to tell an even better version of the story in which Endfield comes over to him and says, "Can I be very personal . . . but I don't think you're very good as a cockney." However, the above appears to be the more accurate version.

[14] William Wyler was originally to direct but he walked out after arguing with the studio over how large a part the Nazis would play in the proceedings.

screen, there was no question [that she was photogenic], no problem there."

Casting the co-starring role of Baron Von Trapp was more problematic. "Yul Brynner wanted very much to do it," Wise said, "but that would have been stock casting for me [he had played a similar role in *The King and I*]. Besides which, he had an accent." Wise was "half way interested" in the English actor Keith Michell, who would go on to notoriety starring in television's "Henry VIII and His Six Wives." He also flew to New York and met with Walter Matthau and Patrick O'Neal. The names of Sean Connery, Stephen Boyd, and even David Niven were mentioned. But Wise was not enthusiastic about any of them. Christopher Plummer, the Toronto-born actor who had been appearing on the stage since 1950 but had made only three movies, was Wise's idea of Baron Von Trapp. "Well, I'd seen Chris a couple of times on the New York stage. I didn't know him but I thought he was a fine actor, and I felt the [baron] was a pretty stock character, and I wanted to get somebody who would get a little edge, a little darkness to it, a little bite."

But Plummer did not want to do it. Peter Finch, Wise's second choice for the role, was unavailable, so he returned to his campaign to woo Plummer. The actor's agent, Kurt Frings, thought the role would give a boost to his client's career. He suggested that Wise fly to London.

"So I flew to London, expressly to see Plummer. Met him at the Connaught hotel — at the bar." He chuckled at the memory. "We had a drink, and I told him what I thought about it, how I thought he would be right, and that we were going to do some work on the script to improve his character." Wise was concerned about Plummer's age, since the actor was only about 35. Could he be the father of a daughter "sixteen going on seventeen"? Plummer refused to do a screen test to find out. He did agree to some makeup tests that could be shot by a stills photographer so that Wise could convince the studio Plummer was right for the part (whether or not the tests were successful is debatable. The one thing that still strikes a viewer of *The Sound of Music* today is that Christopher Plummer does look too young to be the baron).

In early 1964, as a result of Wise's flight to London, Christopher Plummer had agreed to play Baron Von Trapp. That meant he would not be able to do the low-budget spy thriller he had been about to sign for. That upset the film's producer, Harry Saltzman. Now he would have to find another actor to star in *The Ipcress File*.

Increasingly worried about casting someone in the role of Harry Palmer, a low-key British spy who was the exact opposite of the sort of secret agent personified by the now popular James Bond, Saltzman took his wife to see *Zulu*. He noticed the young blond actor who played the aristocratic lieutenant and thought he was rather good. Saltzman wondered if he might be able to play the role of Palmer in *The Ipcress File*. His wife agreed that there was something special about him all right.

After the movie, they drifted over to a fashionable private show-business hangout called Pickwick, co-owned by the songwriter Leslie Bricusse and writer Wolf Mankowitz. Saltzman no sooner was seated at a table than he looked over and spotted Michael Caine, who was having dinner with Terence Stamp. Recovering from his surprise, Saltzman sent word for the actor to stop by his table and congratulated him on his performance in *Zulu*. Both he and his wife thought the actor had the makings of a movie star. Caine was duly flattered. Saltzman wondered if he had read a new spy novel by Len Deighton called *The Ipcress File*. As it happened, Caine was about halfway through it.

"I'm going to make a film of it," Saltzman said offhandedly. "How would you like to play the lead?"

Trying to appear as calm as possible, Caine said he would not mind.

"And how would you like a seven-year contract with my company?"

Caine gulped. Yes, of course. That would be fine.

Staggered, Caine slumped back down beside Stamp. Noting the look on his friend's face, Stamp asked, "What happened?"

"I got a starring role in a movie and a seven-year contract."

Stamp stared at him. "You've only been gone two minutes."

It was a time of the unexpected, when anything could happen. A cockney actor playing an aristocrat could break through onto the world stage. A low-budget spy thriller concerning a secret agent who wore glasses, listened to Mozart, and cooked a lot could become an international hit. Michael Caine was amazed. "I suppose I underestimated the intelligence of the audiences, which people in show business do all the time," Caine said. "We made *The Ipcress File* very cheaply expecting, if we were lucky, to break even or make a little profit. I thought it would be a rather specialized movie. In the United States it was the students and the intellectuals who started the whole picture off."

Saltzman's agreement called for 11 films over the life of his contract with Caine, at least two of them Harry Palmer movies. Michael Caine would be the thinking man's James Bond, and that was just fine with him. "In two ticks I had the security I'd chased for years. Marvellous i'n' it?" He also had movie stardom.

"For the first time since the explosive success of the James Bond movies starring Sean Connery, another secret agent series is muscling in on the "I Spy" territory," reported the *New York Times* in October of 1965.

Meanwhile, Christopher Plummer was off to Austria to star in *The Sound of Music*, the movie he had been talked into over *The Ipcress File*. The musical became one of the all-time hits, and, along with *Mary Poppins*, it turned Julie Andrews into the most popular female star in the world. But in the headlong swirl around the success of *The Sound of Music*, Plummer was all but forgotten. Despite his initial insistence, his voice was not used in the completed film, and just as he feared from the outset, his Baron Von Trapp was rather wooden and one-dimensional. If they had tried to chip away at the material's sugar coating, they had not chipped very hard. For a long time Plummer was deeply unhappy about the movie, and would refer to it as "The Sound of Mucus."

"Chris never quite made it," said Wise with a shake of his head. "He did good roles, and all that, and he was such a good actor, a pleasure to work with. But he never became a major star by any means."

TERENCE STAMP'S PERFORMANCE AS THE ANGELIC BILLY BUDD WAS CRITIcally hailed and the slim, sensitive, foppishly attired actor became the embodiment of swinging '60s stardom. *Billy* was quickly followed by a dreary courtroom drama, *Term of Trial*, and after that, Stamp was persuaded to return to the stage in a play that Bill Naughton had adapted from his radio drama about a heartless young womanizer named Alfie. "Terence Stamp gives a superb portrayal in the role of *Alfie*," said the *Hollywood Reporter* when the play opened in New York at the Morosco theater in December of 1964.

Despite the best efforts of the *Hollywood Reporter*, *Alfie* flopped on Broadway and Stamp returned to London determined to put the play and the character behind him. He was staying with Michael Caine when the director Lewis Gilbert called to offer him the lead in the movie of *Alfie*. To Caine's astonishment, Stamp proceeded to turn it down.

"I actually spent three whole hours trying to talk him into accepting it," Caine recalled later. But Stamp would not change his mind. As far as he was concerned, *Alfie* was finished. "I had done it, hadn't I?" he said. "So why do it over again?" Laurence Harvey also turned the part down, as did Anthony Newley and James Booth. Caine later concluded that it was rejected by so many actors because of an abortion scene that was considered for the time to be extremely frank. Director Gilbert phoned the apartment again, this time to speak to Michael Caine about *Alfie*. "I reached page two of the script, stopped reading, and phoned Lewis. I told him I'd do it."

It never occurred to Caine that *Alfie* was anything but a parochial British movie. Shelley Winters, who appeared with Caine, told him years later that his accent was so thick she never understood a word he said. When Paramount was preparing to release the film in North America, Caine had to redub more than a hundred pieces of dialogue to make them more intelligible. But *Alfie* became an international hit, and one day over lunch, Lewis Gilbert warned Michael Caine that he was going to be nominated for an Academy Award. He could hardly believe what he was hearing. Later, he summed up what had happened: "I had become a Cinderella-type figure — the person from nowhere who becomes a star, rich and famous."

The success of *Alfie* did something else for Michael Caine. It saved him from being a spy. He made two more Harry Palmer movies, *Funeral in Berlin* and *Billion Dollar Brain*, neither one of them particularly successful. It made no difference. Now Michael Caine was *Alfie* and the world of movies was open to him. His friend Sean Connery was not quite so lucky.

MICHAEL CAINE FIRST ENCOUNTERED SEAN CONNERY AT A LONDON party in the mid-1950s. In those days everyone was hungry and underfed, so what Caine remembered most about him was the way he stood out. "Sean was enormous and very fit," as befitted a bodybuilder marooned in the chorus line of a London production of *South Pacific*. Caine admired his confidence and determination, even though Connery had little enough to be confident about in those days. Born in Edinburgh, Connery, like Caine, was from a working-class background, dropping out of school at 15, enlisting in the Royal Navy, then toiling at various odd jobs including those of bricklayer and coffin polisher before entering the Mr. Universe contest that led him to *South Pacific*.

Caine encountered Connery again a couple of years later when they both auditioned for a small role in a comedy, *How to Murder a Rich Uncle*, that was to star Charles Coburn and Nigel Patrick. Caine was chosen over Connery. Later, Caine was nonplussed to find himself doing a bit part in a British TV adaptation of Rod Serling's *Requiem for a Heavyweight*, and there was Connery starring in the production. While Caine stood by in frustrated anonymity, Connery used *Requiem* as a springboard into a career as a character actor and would-be heartthrob. There was, briefly, a 20th Century–Fox contract. He was loaned out for Disney's *Darby O'Gill and the Little People* and cast as Lana Turner's lover in *Another Time, Another Place*. He tried to finish off the Ape Man in *Tarzan's Greatest Adventure* (1959), the last time he would lose a movie fight for the next 30 years.

Connery did not think he was going anywhere in the London of the swinging '60s. As Caine noted, he was bigger and rougher in appearance than his more ascetic-looking contemporaries. There was something almost American about him, in the way he looked and in the manner in which he was trained on the job. He was never anywhere near a venerable institution such as the Royal Academy of Dramatic Art, where so much of the cream of British theater and movie talent had trained. Connery tended to muscle his way in and take command with that almost larger-than-life Yankee brashness personified by Clark Gable — the actor to whom Connery was most often compared. But the look and the style of leading men was changing in both the U.S. and British films. If not for the most fortuitous of accidents, there might not have been much room for Sean Connery in the movie business. As it happened, he stumbled upon the one character who required his larger-than-life persona. Sean Connery and James Bond were destined to meet, and if they had not, it is doubtful if either one would have done quite so well on a movie screen.

HARRY SALTZMAN, A CANADIAN FROM SAINT JOHN, NEW BRUNSWICK, had actually been raised in the United States but found success in Britain as a partner in Woodfall Films with playwright John Osborne and director Tony Richardson. Woodfall had produced ground-breaking kitchen-sink dramas such as *Saturday Night and Sunday Morning, The Entertainer,* and *Look Back in Anger*, but early in 1961, Saltzman left over his partners' determination not to allow commercial considerations to get in the way of making movies. Saltzman wanted to exercise more populist instincts.

The previous year he had persuaded a London *Sunday Times* columnist named Ian Fleming to let him option the movie rights to the spy novels he wrote in his spare time. Fleming said secret agent James Bond was a by-product of the panic that seized him at the thought of getting married at the age of 42. Fleming did marry, but that failed to stop him from producing a new Bond adventure every year from his retreat at Goldeneye in Jamaica. None of the books had attracted a great deal of attention, and Fleming, flattered that anyone would be interested, let Saltzman option the rights to all his novels except the first one, *Casino Royale*, which he had already sold for $7,500 (Fleming blew the money on a Ford Thunderbird). In return, Saltzman promised Fleming $100,000 per picture, as well as 5 percent of the profits. Fleming was delighted.

But as Saltzman left Woodfall, his option on the Fleming books was about to run out, and no one seemed interested in James Bond in the movies. With less than a month to go, Saltzman became involved with American-born producer Albert Broccoli, who was also interested in the Bond novels. The two men agreed to become equal partners, and to that end formed a Swiss-based company called Danjaq (a name derived from the first names of the producers' wives). Together, they approached Columbia Pictures, who passed on the project. However, Arthur Krim, then president of United Artists, signaled his interest. In exchange for financing *Dr. No*, the first of the Bond adventures to be filmed, United Artists acquired distribution rights to all new Bond pictures in perpetuity, even after the Fleming stories ran out. Now all that was needed was someone to play James Bond.

FLEMING SAID HE ORIGINALLY HAD THE SONGWRITER HOAGY CARmichael in mind when he wrote the Bond books. For the movies, though, he suggested either David Niven or Roger Moore, who was popular with British audiences as television's "The Saint." There was even a suggestion at one point that James Stewart might play Secret Agent 007. Albert Broccoli, known to everyone as Cubby, approached his friend Cary Grant, but he declined, saying he did not want to become involved in a series. Neither did Richard Johnson, just beginning to make a name for himself in films. Patrick McGoohan, later to become known as television's "Danger Man"

("Secret Agent" in the United States), had made only a few films when Broccoli and Saltzman approached him. He turned down Bond, saying the films would be too violent.

Sean Connery did not come as a complete surprise. There was actually something of a public groundswell favoring him, remarkable considering that, although he had attained some prominence, he was hardly a household name. The London *Daily Express*, which was running a daily James Bond comic strip, sent columnist Patricia Lewis around to interview the actor. She was the first to publicly suggest that he might make a great James Bond. When the *Express* conducted a readers' poll asking who should play 007, Sean Connery's name topped the list. Meanwhile, Connery had already come to Broccoli's attention. He and his wife Dana screened *Darby O'Gill and the Little People*, after which Dana Broccoli, excited by Connery's screen presence, urged her husband to consider him for Bond. Then Peter Hunt, who would later edit most of the Bond movies, showed up with reels from a new British comedy, *On the Fiddle* (U.S. title, *Operation Snafu*), in which Connery was featured. Broccoli remained skeptical, but he decided to screentest the actor.

Connery shocked everyone by refusing to test. However, he agreed to a meeting with the two producers. That meeting subsequently became the stuff of movie mythology, thanks to the producers' breathless accounts of Connery "striding like a panther" along the street outside their office window, taking full command, alternately — depending on which of various reports was believed — throwing his feet up on the desk or pounding on it with his fists. Connery, impatient with mythmaking, later dismissed most of this as nonsense, although he said he did attempt to reassure Broccoli and Saltzman that he had the presence required for the part, if not the wardrobe; he showed up wearing baggy slacks, suede loafers, and a shirt, all purchased a long way from Savile Row. "The difference between him and the other young actors was the difference between a still photo and a film," Broccoli said. "We knew we had our Bond."

Not everyone was so sure. United Artists was unenthusiastic. "See if you can do better," snapped a studio executive. "He's not exactly what I had in mind," understated Ian Fleming.

*Dr. No*'s director, the Cambridge-educated Terence Young, also was not impressed with the 32-year-old actor. "When I first met Sean he was a wild

Scotsman," he recalled. Young, who had not before demonstrated any particular dexterity with a movie camera, and would not show many signs of it when he deserted the Bond films, did know where to find a good tailor. "I made him wear the clothes, dinner jackets, everything, for a month before he started shooting," Young said. Otherwise, Connery did no research beyond a quick read of Fleming's *Live and Let Die*. Thus Fleming could be forgiven for not quite recognizing the character with the built-in expression of insouciance who casually lit a Dunhill cigarette and introduced himself at that baccarat table in *Dr. No*. This was not to be Ian Fleming's James Bond on film, it was to be Sean Connery's. With a little help from Terence Young's tailor.

# 9
# THE STAR OF *GIGI* AS A TEXAS BANK ROBBER?
*Casting about: from* Doctor Zhivago
*to* Bonnie and Clyde

IN 1964, PETER SHAW, WHO MARRIED THE ACTRESS ANGELA LANSBURY, WAS an agent at William Morris, and one of his clients was David Lean. One day Shaw telephoned agent Dick Clayton to ask about the availability of one of his clients, a young actress named Jane Fonda.

Following the international success of *Lawrence of Arabia*, Lean had parted company with Sam Spiegel, and on his own was now mounting a production of *Doctor Zhivago*. He invited his *Lawrence* collaborator, Robert Bolt, to fashion a screenplay from Boris Pasternak's novel of the doomed love affair between a young doctor and his beautiful mistress, Lara, set against the background of the Russian Revolution. The movie, to be shot in Spain, was a massive undertaking.

Lean had approached Peter O'Toole to play Zhivago, but was turned down by the actor who wanted a lot more money than the director who made him famous was willing to pay. The clash over money caused a rift between the two men that was only healed shortly before Lean's death in 1991. Lean decided on Omar Sharif, the Egyptian actor who had been cast in *Lawrence* at the last moment as Sherif Ali after he had rejected French actors Alain Delon and Maurice Ronet because their eye color was wrong (dark eyes were required as a contrast to O'Toole's blond hair and blue eyes). The movie made Sharif, born Michael Shalhoub in Alexandria, Egypt, an international star. Still, choosing an Egyptian actor to play the Russian Zhivago was considered risky, particularly since Sharif, post-*Lawrence*, had not been impressive either with his choice of roles or his performances.

With Zhivago cast, Lean turned to the hard part — finding an actress who could encompass on the screen Pasternak's vision of the beautiful, enigmatic Lara. It was the search for Lara that occasioned Peter Shaw's phone call to his friend Clayton. He wondered if Jane Fonda might be interested in co-starring in David Lean's new film.

Fonda was in need of the kind of role that would turn the public's sense of her from just being Henry Fonda's daughter into becoming a movie star. Now here was a great director at her door, bringing with him a great novel complete with a mysterious, haunting heroine. Who could resist such an opportunity? Jane Fonda, young and in love and not, apparently, paying a great deal of attention, was able to.

Clayton read the script by Robert Bolt, thought it wonderful, and passed it on to Fonda, busy with a light romantic comedy, *Sunday in New York*. She also liked the script but wondered if she could do it. At the time, she was deeply involved with the French filmmaker Roger Vadim, the director of *And God Created Woman* and inventor of Brigitte Bardot, the first and greatest of the postwar European sex symbols. Fonda hesitated about *Doctor Zhivago*, not sure she could bear to be stranded on location in Spain for the better part of a year without Vadim. "I don't think I can do it, we'll be separated too much," she concluded.

Clayton was not about to let a great movie part slip away in favor of a French movie director. He got back on the phone to Peter Shaw. "Look," he said, "I'm going to keep after her."

Each day, Clayton arrived on the set pushing *Zhivago*. "Have you thought about this, Jane?" he would ask. "This is going to be a big movie for you."

Fonda stubbornly kept saying no, until one day, when Clayton arrived on the set, she turned to him and said, "You know, I think you're probably right. I should do it."

Clayton raced to telephone Peter Shaw. "Oh, God, Dick," Shaw said, "You'd better call David Lean in London."

Clayton got hold of Lean on a Saturday. "Mr. Lean," Clayton began, "you don't know me, but I have a very happy client. Jane Fonda is thrilled that she's going to be working for you."

On the other end of the line, there was a long pause. Finally, David Lean said, "Oh, Christ, man, I think I have somebody for that."

The somebody was a 24-year-old British actress named Julie Christie, who had appeared in only three movies. Lean said he chose Christie for the Lara role after watching a scene in the second and most influential of those movies, *Billy Liar* (1963). Lean had sat alone in a screening room and watched while this slim, rather gawky actress with long blonde hair and incredibly full lips walked along a street, peering into shop windows. At the end of the screening, Lean, adding a touch of melodrama to the retelling of the story, said he sprang to his feet, crying out, "That's the girl I want for Lara!"

Julie Christie appeared as Billy's girlfriend in the movie for only 11 minutes, but they may have been the most important few moments in the career of any actress in modern film. And she almost missed out on them.

According to her mother, Julie had always wanted to be an actress. Even as a child on the family's tea plantation in India, she would go around declaring, "I'm going to be an actress when I grow up."

In pursuit of childhood ambition, she attended London's Central School for Music and Drama, where a young documentary filmmaker named John Schlesinger found her in a production of *Anne Frank*. "She was not very good," he recalled. "But she was one of the people I remembered."

When Schlesinger was preparing his second feature film, *Billy Liar*, based on a Keith Waterhouse novel that had become a successful play about a bored young man who escapes into a world of fantasy, and looking for a female lead, he spotted Christie's photograph on the cover of *Town* magazine, "showing her breasts and everything, marvelous pictures inside." He remembered a much different version of her in the *Anne Frank* production. Intrigued, he ventured onto the set of a comedy called *The Fast Lady*, which happened to be her first major movie. He was shocked at what they were doing to her. "Her hair was very ordinary. . . . There were inches of pancake on her face." Nonetheless, he decided to test her for the role of Liz in *Billy Liar*. Schlesinger was not happy with the results and turned her down. "And then we tested her again," Schlesinger said, "because I wasn't sure that we'd tested her fairly." The second test failed, too. By that time, he decided Liz should be played by a different type altogether and so hired actress Topsy Jane, who had originated the role on the stage.

THAT SHOULD HAVE BEEN THE END OF IT, EXCEPT FOR THE MOST OBVIOUS of show-business clichés — the star, or, in this case, the featured performer, who suddenly becomes ill and must be replaced by the understudy. Halfway through filming, that is exactly what happened to Topsy Jane, and Schlesinger was left to scramble for another Liz. "One Saturday morning we ran all the tests we'd done before; and it was Julie, unquestionably. We said we all needed our heads examined, we can't think what made us so purist about this part. We'd shot two months on this film and on this wretched girl, and suddenly, out of the screen came, zonk!"

*Billy Liar* led to *Darling* and the most demanding and important role of her career. As Lean mulled over his Lara, John Schlesinger, *Darling's* director, found his Diana Scott. First, though, he had to fight off the moneymen who preferred Shirley MacLaine in the role of the amoral London model adrift in the hip London of the mid-1960s. The film opened in New York in September of 1965, before it was shown in London where the critics generally hated it. The applause for the movie and its star was overwhelming. "A performance by Julie Christie which is pure gold," bubbled *Life* magazine. "By turns wilfull and willing, greedy and contrite, intelligent and self-deceiving, innocent and teasing — it is a characterization such as one rarely sees."

The gale force of enthusiasm reached across the plains of Spain to the set of *Doctor Zhivago*. "Could her face launch a thousand ships?" asked *Newsweek* magazine rhetorically. "Perhaps only 900. It is not conventionally beautiful but it is irresistibly alive. By turns it can be radiant, tough, gay, pained, distracted — even, in some compelling way, ugly."

It was the sort of nonsensical hyperbole that could only signal stardom. Diana and Lara could not have intersected in Julie Christie's life at a more appropriate time. As she finished work on *Zhivago* in October of 1965, she found herself "the most sought after young actress in the world," as columnist Sheila Graham described her from Madrid.

JANE FONDA WAS NOT THE MOST SOUGHT AFTER ACTRESS IN THE WORLD IN 1965. That year she married Roger Vadim and they proceeded to collaborate on a number of films, *La Ronde* or *Circle of Love*, *The Game Is Over*, and, most notoriously, *Barbarella*, in which attempts were made to turn her into a Vassar-educated version of a European sex goddess. It was not a role, Fonda would later confess, in which she felt at all comfortable. Certainly she was a long way from the acclaim showered on Julie Christie, which was to include the 1965 Academy Award for best actress in *Darling*. The critics generally were impervious to Fonda in anything, whether it was Vadim's

European sex movies or such U.S. efforts as *The Chase* (1966), *Any Wednesday* (1966), or *Hurry Sundown* (1967). Only when she starred in a couple of comedies, *Cat Ballou*, a western spoof, and *Barefoot in the Park*, the screen version of Neil Simon's Broadway hit, did anyone sit up and take notice. But she was hardly taken with anything like the seriousness that might have been hers had she not fallen in love.

For the moment, Jane Fonda would continue to be known mainly as the daughter of Henry Fonda. That association certainly had not hurt her in getting launched in movies. It was Henry's boyhood friend, director Joshua Logan, who cast Jane in her first movie, a basketball comedy titled *Tall Story* (1960). Opposite her, Logan had wanted another young newcomer, a 21-year-old actor from Richmond, Virginia, named Warren Beatty. "He was," Logan said, "all a director could hope for: tall, humorous, extremely male. He even sat down at the piano and played a song."

If it were up to Logan, he would have cast Beatty in a movie called *Parrish*, but the director so hated the script, he asked to do something else (newcomer Troy Donahue was cast, and briefly shot to stardom). As it turned out, Logan could not have Warren Beatty for *Tall Story*, either. The studio balked at an unknown male lead, and he was forced to offer the role to the more established Anthony Perkins.

Robert Wise was also aware of Warren Beatty in March of 1960 as he mulled over whom to cast as Tony and Maria, the star-crossed lovers in his movie version of the Leonard Bernstein–Stephen Sondheim Broadway musical *West Side Story*. Working with casting director Lynn Stalmaster, Wise put together a list of possibilities, then began to interview prospective actors and actresses.

Jill St. John was "lovely, but she doesn't seem like Maria." Yvette Mimieux was rated "pretty good." Frankie Avalon at the age of 21 was "a nice looking kid, but not for us." Russ Tamblyn gave an excellent reading, but Tom Skerritt was considered too old and, although Richard Chamberlain's reading was good, "looks and voice too mature." Troy Donahue was merely a "blue eyed, blond." George Hamilton was "too dark for us," while Burt Reynolds was considered "a little tough looking" for Tony, and George Segal and Leonard Nimoy were too old. Wise had also looked at Robert Redford and liked his reading. Jack Nicholson was briefly considered, and an enigmatic question mark left after his name — an indication, perhaps, of mysteries to come.

Jerome Robbins, the choreographer who was co-directing *West Side Story*, pushed Wise to cast Carole Lawrence, the actress who had originated Maria on Broadway. They even tested her in New York, but it was obvious when everyone viewed the test that while she was a lovely 25-year-old, she was not the virginal teenager needed for the movie. It was down to actress Elizabeth Ashley, who had won a Tony Award for her very first Broadway play, *Take Her, She's Mine*, but had yet to appear in a movie. For Tony, the actor Wise considered most seriously was Warren Beatty. "Six-feet one inch tall, brown hair, blue eyes," Wise noted. "Excellent quality. Acting two years. Several auditions for *West Side*. Voice not right? TV shows — *A Loss of Roses*. Excellent reviews."

Wise heard that this kid Beatty was special. No less than Elia Kazan was over at Warner Bros. guiding him through his first movie, *Splendor in the Grass*, in which he co-starred with Natalie Wood. Wise went over to take a look at some of the footage. "It turned out it was a scene with Natalie," Wise recalled. "And the minute she came on the screen, we said, 'Hey, that's our Maria. Where've we been? She's been under our noses all the time.' We forgot all about Warren, and settled in on her." Elizabeth Ashley was also forgotten.

*West Side Story* might have been infinitely more interesting had Beatty been cast. Instead, Wise went with a sensitive-looking juvenile named Richard Beymer, who had appeared in *The Diary of Anne Frank*. Casting Beymer as Tony was generally considered one of Wise's worst career decisions, although, more than 30 years later, he stood by it. "He was very good, he was excellent," Wise maintained. "I thought he did a damned good job. I couldn't have been more surprised when the criticism started coming in." Deeply hurt by a series of vicious reviews of his performances, Beymer was gone from Hollywood two years later, but not before Beatty had turned down *The Stripper* and *Hemingway's Adventures of a Young Man*, roles that then went to Beymer.

If everyone wanted Brando in the '50s, in the '60s it was Warren Beatty. Unlike Brando, he was not obviously rebellious; indeed, when he had to, no one played the games of Hollywood more adroitly. Instead, he teased movies, at once drawn to them and leery. He took his time about making up a mind that as often as not never quite reached any decision. He did not do *The Leopard* (but Alain Delon did) or *The War Lover* (it went to Steve McQueen) or *Act One* (George Hamilton played the role). Even so, he professed unhappiness with the roles he did take. "The only picture of mine I have liked," he said in 1962, "was *Splendor in the Grass*. I hated *The Roman Spring of Mrs. Stone*. *All Fall Down* might have been a success if Metro hadn't put it out so quickly."

Early on, Beatty had decided that survival in Hollywood lay in the control of one's own destiny, and so became one of the first major stars since Chaplin, Pickford, and Fairbanks actively to produce his own movies. Those survivalist instincts evolved by necessity more than anything else, and they began to emerge one day over lunch in Paris with the French director François Truffaut and Beatty's girlfriend of the moment, Leslie Caron. Truffaut was involved with a couple of Americans who had written a script based on the life and times of the Depression-era bankrobbers Clyde Barrow and Bonnie Parker. Truffaut did not think he was the right filmmaker to do *Bonnie and Clyde*, although it was an interesting story. Hearing this, Caron, a woman perhaps in search of ways to keep her boyfriend nearby, perked up and suggested that *Bonnie and Clyde* might be a movie she and Warren could do together.

The star of *Gigi* as a Texas bank robber? Well, it was lunch, and it was Paris. Still, Beatty was intrigued enough that he tracked down the two writers, David Newman and Robert Benton, in New York where they were both working at *Esquire* magazine. To the amazement of the writers, a Hollywood star then optioned *Bonnie and Clyde* for $10,000. The script contained a lot of stuff about the Freudian nature of the relationship between the two that did not interest Beatty. What he liked was "the desperation of the little guy to get out of the crowd. . . . Clyde wanted to be somebody."

The crudest dimestore psychology could be employed to suggest that Warren Beatty wanted the same thing. At that point he was not taken seriously. His stardom seemed so effortless, no dues paid at all, and yet his movies induced little panic at the box office. Critics declined to salute his screen performances. He had attracted more attention via his affairs with some of Hollywood's most eligible and alluring actresses. Against this background, Beatty put Newman and Benton to work rewriting *Bonnie and Clyde*, then induced Arthur Penn, who had directed him in *Mickey One*, to take on his gangster movie. From the outset, however, he put himself in complete charge.

"From the first day of shooting, I felt there was one thing I could never run away from in this film," he said. "No matter what was wrong, I was gonna step up and take complete blame for it. For a change there wouldn't be any cop-outs." Originally, Beatty was not going to star in the movie, only produce it. That changed quickly, however. He would play Clyde Barrow, but any notion of casting Leslie Caron as Bonnie Parker was quickly discarded. Natalie Wood, who was involved with Beatty romantically for a time, said no. Carol Lynley was considered, as was Beatty's sister, Shirley MacLaine. Tuesday Weld, who had had her first nervous breakdown at the age of nine, and by the time she was 12 had attempted suicide, might have had the role. She was only 23 years old in 1966, and she could have flourished as Bonnie, but like most things in those days that might have been good for her, she turned it down. Among other films Tuesday rejected: *Lolita*, *Bob & Carol & Ted & Alice*, *Cactus Flower* (the movie that made Goldie Hawn a star), and *True Grit*. In 1970, she said that she had turned down 60 or 70 films. "I turned down *Bonnie and Clyde*," she said, "because I was nursing the baby. I would have played Bonnie more country."

Beatty later said he was all set to sign Sue Lyon, who was from Davenport, Iowa, although that had not prevented columnist Hedda Hopper from describing her as "the child-woman that only Hollywood can breed." At the age of 16, Lyon had been cast as Lolita after Tuesday Weld passed. And she might have inherited Bonnie from her as well had not Arthur Penn attended an off-Broadway performance of a play entitled *Hogan's Goat*.

Seated in the audience, he found himself transfixed by a young actress named Faye Dunaway. She was 26 years old, the daughter of an army sergeant and a devout Methodist mother, who had escaped rural poverty in Florida via acting and Boston University. She became part of the repertory company at Lincoln Center, and two years later was on stage in *A Man for All Seasons*. When she went to audition for William Alfred, the author of *Hogan's Goat*, he provided some indication of the kind of impression Dunaway tended to make. "'This incredibly beautiful woman in a sharkskin suit and long hair to her hips came in," he recalled. "You could almost hear our eyes click."

In *Hogan's Goat*, she played the epitome of the working-class Irish woman dominated by her husband, but Dunaway's image held in Arthur Penn's mind, and a year later, while Beatty considered just about every actress in Hollywood, Penn pushed for the girl from *Hogan's Goat*. By that time, she had appeared in a picture called *The Happening*, so she was not totally unknown to movies. In fact, Otto Preminger in 1966 had signed her to a six-picture contract.

Penn said Beatty had to be talked into bringing Dunaway out to Hollywood. Producer and director met her at the Beverly Wilshire Hotel where Beatty was living at the time. "When Faye came in," Penn recalled, "my eyes lit up. And Warren came around."

Beatty acknowledged that although he liked her, "I didn't think she would be right for the part of Bonnie at all. I had always thought of the girl as being of a different sort physically." This from the producer who had come close to signing Carol Lynley or Sue Lyon for the part — actresses of the same blonde type as Dunaway. Nonetheless, "[Faye] had such an interesting personality, and had such strong feelings about the part, so many ideas about it, that after a while, I realized I was wrong. So I offered it to her, and she accepted."

Beatty was in his car approaching Hollywood and Vine when he spotted the actor who would play Clyde's brother, Buck Barrow. Gene Hackman had worked in a short scene with Beatty in *Lilith*. A sensitive, restless man, often at odds with himself, Hackman was born in San Bernardino, California, and raised in Danville, Illinois, before dropping out of school at the age of 16 to join the Marines. He drifted around, moving from New York to various jobs around the country before settling at the Pasadena Playhouse to study acting. Returning to New York, he roomed with Dustin Hoffman and Robert Duvall, then finally got a break in 1964 when he appeared on Broadway opposite Sandy Dennis in the comedy *Any Wednesday*.

Beatty did not contact Hackman immediately. When he did catch up with him, Hackman was lying in a New York hospital suffering from blood poisoning. "Warren dropped in to see me," Hackman later recalled. "I was not only surprised, but touched. He said he had a film role he wanted to discuss with me. It was Buck Barrow in *Bonnie and Clyde*."

What happened to *Bonnie and Clyde* is hard to imagine in the coldly calculated bottom-line atmosphere in which most studio-made movies exist today, a marketplace decreeing that you must make it the first weekend or you are gone from theaters. From the beginning, no one outside the small circle of filmmakers and actors working away on location in Texas liked the movie. Jack Warner had gone along with it only reluctantly, and when he saw the first rough cut, he remarked, "this is the longest goddamn movie I've ever seen."

Warner Bros. released the finished *Bonnie and Clyde* in August of 1967, then considered one of the worst times to open a new movie. Bosley Crowther, the ancient but still influential movie critic of the *New York Times,* viciously attacked the movie for its combination of violence and comedy, and both *Time* and *Newsweek* magazines followed suit. If a single event saved *Bonnie and Clyde,* it was a presentation at the Montreal Film Festival, where it was greeted with an unexpected swell of excitement by both critics and audiences.

Beatty spent the next eight months trying to pump new life into what threatened to be the corpse of *Bonnie and Clyde.* He traveled all over America talking to exhibitors, persuading them to give the movie a second chance. Then *Time* and *Newsweek* both recanted their original reviews of the movie and now hailed it as a masterpiece. Beatty threatened to sue Warner Bros. if the studio did not re-release the picture. Unveiled for a second time, *Bonnie and Clyde* quickly was elevated into the most controversial and influential American movie produced in the postwar era. No other modern American film has had the same impact — from its effect on the state of violence in movies to the fashions of the day. The French beret industry, for example, increased production from 1,500 to 20,000 berets a week after Dunaway wore one in her role as Bonnie Parker.

The movie transformed everyone connected with it. The portrait of Beatty was hurriedly altered from that of troublesome kid to film genius. The reporting was often breathless. "With Warren Beatty there is no worry over whether seduction is possible, only when and where and who's next," the journalist Thomas Thompson wrote in 1968. "At 31 he is rich and powerful and famous and beautiful, with no ties at all. He is the producer and star of the year's most successful movie. . . . If the view for Beatty from Olympus is sometimes a lonely one, then the American dream is not what it is cracked up to be."

Thompson did take note of Beatty's continuing inability to make up his mind, particularly where movie projects were concerned. "Most of the people who don't like me in Hollywood are the guys whose pictures I wouldn't do," Beatty said. Over the next 25 years he would repeatedly confirm that observation and his inability to make up his mind would open the door to stardom for any number of other actors — most notably Robert Redford. If Marlon Brando made use of the new independence of movie stars after the collapse of the studio system, Warren Beatty capitalized on it, and discovered power that previously was not available to the movie star. "Let's put it this way," he said in 1968. "Right now if I went to somebody and said I wanted to make a musical film of the Last

Supper, they'd probably say, 'Okay, let's talk about it.'"

Faye Dunaway, post-*Bonnie and Clyde*, promptly encountered problems over her contract with Otto Preminger. She had made one turkey directed by Preminger, *Hurry Sundown*, and was not about to do another. She did not show up to start work on the next Preminger picture, *Too Far to Walk* (which was never filmed), then refused to have anything to do with *Skidoo*, a gangster comedy in which Groucho Marx played a mob boss named God. Preminger sued her in January of 1968.

With filming of *Skidoo* due to start in two weeks, Dunaway and Preminger settled out of court, and she was free of the director and her obligation to perform in what would prove to be a disaster. The army brat from rural Florida who had attached weights to her arms, wrists, and ankles in order to drop 20 pounds for *Bonnie and Clyde* then proceeded to turn herself into a bizarre throwback to the regal movie queens of the 1930s and 1940s. Now she jetted around the world with the hip fashion photographer Jerry Schatzberg. She drove Marcello Mastroianni crazy in Rome before throwing herself into a relationship with Peter Wolf, the lead singer of the J. Geils Band. Her reputation for causing trouble on movie sets grew, the movie star act getting its worst reviews during the shooting of *Chinatown* after repeated clashes with director Roman Polanski.

Dunaway was not the first choice for the movie's enigmatic widow. Polanski had wanted Jane Fonda. Previously, Robert Evans, when he was executive vice president of production at Paramount, had offered Fonda the lead role in Polanski's *Rosemary's Baby*, but she had turned it down. Now Polanski wanted her again, and one night in November of 1973, Fonda came around to the house in the Hollywood Hills he had rented from actor George Montgomery. She had just had a baby with her husband, activist Tom Hayden, and she brought the child with her. It was cold that night and as Fonda sat in the office downstairs, she wrapped a Mexican blanket around her head and breast-fed her baby while the director pitched the story of *Chinatown*.

She listened intently, and seemed to be enthusiastic. Polanski was convinced he had won her over, but Robert Towne, who had written the screenplay, was less convinced. A couple of days later, there was a phone call from Jane Fonda's representatives. She would not do *Chinatown*. Furious, Polanski turned to Dunaway.

Much the same thing happened again when Sidney Lumet sought to find an actress who could play the ambitious, ratings-obsessed executive in *Network*. The actresses Lumet approached found the character unlikeable, but he finally narrowed his choices down to Faye Dunaway and Jane Fonda. When Fonda said no, Dunaway got the role and an Academy Award in 1976. The two actresses encountered each other one more time during the 1970s. This time, they both were offered the role of the feisty southern textile worker in Martin Ritt's *Norma Rae*. When they both said no, that opened the way for Sally Field, the star of TV's "Gidget" and "The Flying Nun." Her boyfriend at the time, Burt Reynolds, read the script and quietly announced she would win an Oscar. He was right, and thanks to Fonda and Dunaway, Sally Field was transformed from a bubbly TV ingenue into one of the most popular and respected actresses of the 1980s. The same could not be said of Faye Dunaway. *Norma Rae* was her last chance to escape typecasting. After *Network*, she was with few exceptions always cast as the gimlet-eyed, cold-hearted grande dame. There was something hollow and inhuman about her roles. The endless promise of the kinetic young actress who stopped everyone in their tracks in *Hogan's Goat*, and who electrified movie audiences in *Bonnie and Clyde*, somehow was lost.

"It's very hard to know who you are and where you're going when success hits you," she said many years and a lot of bad choices later. "It's very easy to get carried away from reality and it takes a great deal of effort to come back."

For Gene Hackman, the evolution of stardom came more slowly. He was large and balding, with a working man's face, not the sort of actor who at first glance was a popular crowd pleaser. Moreover, he did not always impress directors with his abilities. Before the release of *Bonnie and Clyde*, his former roommate, Dustin Hoffman, had enabled him to land the role of Mr. Robinson in *The Graduate*. But director Mike Nichols fired him during rehearsals. "That was a painful experience," Hackman remembered. "Hell, it was my own fault. I just wasn't capable of giving the director what he wanted."

If *The Graduate* was not to change the life of Gene Hackman, it would certainly have dramatic effect on Hackman's ex-roommate. His popularity would change the recognized face of movie stardom.

# 10

# "BUT HE'S TOO DAMNED ASSURED."

*Redford and Hoffman and the changing
face of movie stardom*

I N 1964, LAWRENCE TURMAN WAS A 37-YEAR-OLD MOVIE PRODUCER
responsible for the soap-opera-style *The Young Doctors* and a Judy
Garland picture, *I Could Go on Singing*. *The Young Doctors* was a commercial success. *I Could Go on Singing* was a resounding failure. Still, this was not
a bad start in the movie business for someone who originally was only looking for a way to avoid work in his father's textile firm. Turman had answered
an ad in *Variety* and landed a $50-a-week job as an agent for the Kurt Frings
agency. Now, as a new producer in town, and on the prowl for writers,
Turman encountered an intriguing *New York Times* book review. A first novel
by a writer named Charles Webb was liked by the *Times*. Turman tossed the
paper to one side, thinking that Webb might be someone who could write
for the movies.

Turman got hold of a copy of Webb's novel, titled *The Graduate*. It concerned a young man coming uneasily of age in Southern California, involved in
an affair with an older woman, falling for the woman's daughter. "I read it and
quickly concluded he was not going to be a screenwriter," Turman recalled 25
years later. "There was something about the book itself, though. There were
images that stayed with me long after I'd finished reading it."

Reading the novel today, it is hard to see how Turman concluded that
Webb was not a screenwriter. The book reads very much like the screenplay for
*The Graduate*. This was Webb's first novel, and like most first novels it was not
selling well. The story itself bore no relationship to the two movies Turman
had previously produced. For that matter, it was like nothing he would ever
be involved with again. Although the phenomenal success of *The Graduate*
would permit him to make many more pictures over the years, never again did
he find a story close to the one Charles Webb had concocted. In many ways it

was Turman's one-shot wonder — but what a shot it was.

*The Graduate* struck a chord that resonated through an entire generation, and it changed Hollywood's thinking about movie stardom. For the first time since Bogart was unexpectedly transformed into a romantic lead by *Casablanca*, it was not necessary for a movie star to be conventionally handsome in order to be popular. Yet this was the last movie in the world that should have brought about such a sea of change in Hollywood. On its surface, the novel seemed to have been written especially for a typical young Hollywood leading man. Although Webb never described Benjamin Braddock, Turman and everyone else who read the novel at the time concluded that he was tall, blond, and waspish.

That the part ended up being played by a short, plain, 30-year-old Jew could well have been one of the great dumb casting decisions of all time. However, the casting worked so well it was considered a stroke of genius. It was anything but. If the people involved in *The Graduate* often gave the impression that they had no clue as to what they were doing or what kind of movie they were making, it was not surprising. "You do come away with that feeling," said Craig Modderno, the journalist who put together a documentary on the making of *The Graduate* for a 25th anniversary video edition. "A lot of what was done happened purely by accident. Dustin Hoffman told me Mike Nichols never had a plan for the film, but he had a lot of choices." Even Turman conceded, "In retrospect, we were smart — and lucky."

Because he was hardly a proven commodity, Turman lacked the clout to go after a big-shot director. That worked in the movie's favor in helping to create the go-for-broke atmosphere that encouraged outrageous creative decisions. How else to explain the way in which Turman acquired his director? One evening in New York he went to see a Broadway play directed by a young man named Mike Nichols, who was best known as a comedian, along with his partner Elaine May. However, the duo had broken up and now Nichols was directing his first stage show, a Neil Simon comedy titled *Barefoot in the Park*.

It is hard to imagine what Turman saw as he sat in the theater that made him think Mike Nichols could direct a movie. That he saw anything was indicative of the sort of crazy chance that would mark the progress of *The*

*Graduate*. "The direction really stood out," Turman maintained. "The detail he brought to it was really impressive." When approached on the subject, however, Nichols revealed himself to be decidedly ambivalent about directing movies. "I like directing plays," he said. "I preferred to *see* movies."

Nonetheless, Turman sent Nichols a copy of the book, then heard nothing for a long time. "One night I got back to my hotel and there was a message: 'While you were out, Mr. Nichols called to say he likes the book.'" At that point, Larry Turman had never laid eyes on Mike Nichols. The next day they met, and after a 20-minute conversation, an agreement was casually concluded whereby Mike Nichols would direct *The Graduate*. Both men identified with the main character, Benjamin Braddock, not literally so much as psychologically. Turman recalled: "*Life* magazine interviewed me and said, 'tell me about Benjamin Braddock.' And I said, 'that's me.' 'Son of a gun,' said the reporter, 'that's what Nichols said.'"

On 10 December 1964, *Variety* reported that Mike Nichols would make his feature film debut as a director with *The Graduate*. Less than a year after he first read the *New York Times* review, Turman had made good progress. He had acquired a book and a director. Now all he had to do was interest someone in putting up the money to turn *The Graduate* into a movie. That proved to be the tough part.

"Nobody thought it would make a movie," Turman said, recalling that all the studios turned it down. Mike Nichols became impatient and seized the opportunity to direct *Who's Afraid of Virginia Woolf?* with Elizabeth Taylor and Richard Burton. The movie not only caused a great deal of controversy when it was released in 1966, but became a hit that brought Taylor her second Oscar and Nichols the notoriety of a young *wunderkind* who wove creative magic into everything he touched. The heat now generated by Nichols' name helped get *The Graduate* into production at Embassy Pictures, an independent production company run by a flamboyant former clothier and movie exhibitor named Joseph E. Levine. Levine was notorious for having snapped up a couple of cheaply-made *Hercules* pictures starring muscleman Steve Reeves, dubbing them badly into English, then cleverly marketing and promoting them in the United States. "It was the bottom of the barrel," Turman said. "Levine was the last stop. Up to that point, he'd done things like *Hercules* movies. I think the only reason he wanted to do it was because Nichols was involved."[15]

With financing and distribution in place, Nichols was finally getting the screenplay he wanted from Buck Henry who had co-created with Mel Brooks the "Get Smart" TV series. Again it was one of those crazy chances that worked. The only other movie Henry had written was *The Troublemaker*, a film by Theodore J. Flicker shot for $200,000 that disappeared without a trace. But Nichols and Buck Henry were friends who hung out a lot together, and they had the same sensibility about things. "We came from the same background, both educational and geographical," he said. Other writers had worked on versions of the screenplay, including Calder Willingham. However, it was Henry's draft that Nichols was most pleased with, perhaps because it stuck most closely to the book. The movie of *The Graduate* was ready to go forward.

"We haven't cast the title role yet," Nichols told the *Los Angeles Times* early in January of 1967, "but it'll make a star of whoever gets it."

The film was scheduled to commence principal photography in March or April of that year. Ronald Reagan was briefly considered for the part of Benjamin's father, but Henry could not remember if he was actually approached or not. Larry Turman thought of Doris Day as a possibility to play Mrs. Robinson, the older woman who seduces Benjamin. Day was an actress best known for a series of romantic comedies in which she did everything but end up in bed with her male co-star, usually Rock Hudson.

Casting Day was an interesting long shot. "There was something about taking that All-American housewife image and turning it all around," Turman said. But it was not to be. "I sent the script to a man named Martin Melcher who was her husband. We never heard a thing. I don't even know that she ever saw it." Day later said she had seen the script, but could not imagine playing that kind of part.

Nichols was interested in the actress Patricia Neal, who had won an Oscar for her performance in *Hud* in 1963. But Neal had recently suffered a series of massive strokes that left her confined to a wheelchair. He also consid-

---

[15] That is not quite fair. Levine had also backed such highly respected Italian films as De Sica's *Two Women* as well as Fellini's *8½* and *Divorce, Italian Style* by Pietro Germi. Although they were not exactly high art, he had recently been involved with such glossy big-budget Hollywood productions as *The Carpetbaggers* and *Nevada Smith*. He was probably one of the few producers in Hollywood with a sensibility European enough to understand *The Graduate* and the people who wanted to make it.

ered the French actress Jeanne Moreau. That surprised Turman when he heard it years later. "News to me. I mean maybe her name came up in a conversation. But it was such quintessential American material. If her name came up I'm sure I vetoed it at once. Even in the late '60s, for a French woman to have an affair isn't quite the same thing as an upper middle class American woman."

Nichols later said that he had had Anne Bancroft in mind from the beginning. There were plenty of reasons why. Born Anna Maria Louise Italiano, she had started on television in 1950 using the name Anna Marno. Bancroft appeared in a succession of B-movies throughout the early part of the decade. Tiring of the rut she found herself in, she had returned to New York in 1958 where she won a Tony for her stage performance opposite Henry Fonda in *Two for the Seesaw*. The next year she won a second Tony for *The Miracle Worker* in which she played Anne Sullivan, the teacher and lifelong companion to the blind Helen Keller. When she re-created the role on film, both she and Patty Duke, who played Helen, won Oscars. By the time Bancroft was offered the role in *The Graduate*, she was one of the most respected actresses of the day and, at the age of 36, younger than the 42-year-old Mrs. Robinson, and not exactly known as a sexy older woman. Perhaps for those reasons, Bancroft's agent and her friends urged her to have no part of Mrs. Robinson. It was only at the insistence of her husband, Mel Brooks, that she agreed to do it.

"I think she is the most interesting person in the picture," Nichols said. "She is the most *considerable* person." But even with Bancroft, Turman and Nichols were still worried. They lacked the most crucial piece of casting — the actor who could play Benjamin Braddock.

"Our dilemma was, we had conceived of that character, and in fact all of the characters, as being prototypical southern California, big, blond people," recalled Buck Henry. And Mike Nichols had a good idea of whom he wanted as Benjamin.

He had directed a handsome, blond 29-year-old actor from Santa Monica, California, named Robert Redford in *Barefoot in the Park*. Redford certainly fit into everyone's preconceived notions of Benjamin. The actor's film career had been problematic, but almost everyone thought he would amount to something, even though the year before, he had co-starred in three pictures, *Inside Daisy Clover, This Property Is Condemned*, and *The Chase*, none of them well received. Turman had met Redford and admired him, but he did not think him right for Benjamin. Someone who looked like Bob Redford was not going to have Benjamin's problems with either self-esteem or women, he thought. Moreover, Redford did not strike Turman as the kind of guy who would be awkward about meeting his lover at a hotel. Nonetheless, Nichols was pushing for him, and the actor seemed to want the part, although he was playing his cards pretty close to the chest. "We didn't interview Redford," Turman recalled. "I think Mike invited me to dinner one night, and I walked into his house and there was Redford sitting there."

Over dinner, Nichols turned to Turman and with casual slyness said, "Now tell me why you don't want Redford in the movie."

Turman laughed and said, "I'd love him. He's wonderful. But he's just too damned assured. We need twenty-one, going on sixteen."

Turman did not recall Redford being particularly enthusiastic one way or another. "Bob's a very self-contained guy. I'm not a close friend but I've known him for a long time, and he doesn't put out a lot. He has that reserve." Nonetheless, Redford was interested enough to agree to a screen test. Buck Henry recalled that six actors were tested at about the same time. Redford was filmed with a young actress named Candice Bergen, and the test failed to change Turman's mind.

Christopher Connelly, the actor who had captured attention in the TV movie version of *Peyton Place*, was tested, as was Tony Bill, a 27-year-old actor who had made his movie debut as Frank Sinatra's younger brother in *Come Blow Your Horn*, and along with Redford was the best known of the contenders. When Bill read Charles Webb's book, he was so taken with it that he set out to acquire the rights, only to discover Larry Turman had got there first. "I was the graduate," Bill said. "I was two years out of college from southern California coming back to a world that didn't interest me, so I related very strongly to the underlying themes in the book."

Charles Grodin had recently appeared in a small role in the yet-to-be released *Rosemary's Baby*, but was working mostly in television when he went after *The Graduate*. He had read the book and loved it, but at the age of 32, his agent was told that he was too old for Benjamin. Undaunted, Grodin arranged for a meeting with Mike Nichols through a friend at the William Morris agency. "He agreed to let me come in and audition," Grodin later wrote. "About a week later I went in and read twenty-eight pages of the script for him. I had never in my life been received so enthusiastically."

According to Grodin, Nichols called him at home that night and said he had never heard the part of Benjamin read so well. He told Grodin to lose weight so that he would look more like a recent college graduate. "You are our number one choice for the part," he told Grodin. "We have no second choice."

Grodin hung up in a daze. From Pittsburgh, he had studied acting under both Uta Hagen and Lee Strasberg. He had been an actor for 15 years, and now here was the chance of a lifetime seemingly being handed to him after a single reading. But the very next day, everything seemed to fall apart. Before Grodin did the screen test, he was required to sign a seven-year contract that would have paid him $500 a week to star in *The Graduate*. He was appalled. If he did a guest part on a television show, he was paid $1,000 a week. When he said no, Larry Turman phoned him at home to remind him that this was the chance of a lifetime for an untried actor. But Grodin held firm, and two weeks later there was a counteroffer: $1,000 a week. No sooner was that agreed to, than an envelope arrived containing a 10-page scene from the movie. A note from Nichols was attached: Grodin was to be at Paramount next day at 7:00 A.M. for the screen test. That meant he had a single evening to prepare for the part that he hoped would make his career in Hollywood.

"Something had happened," Grodin thought. "They were resentful of me — they thought I was going to be a difficult person to deal with — and, without fully realizing it, I was resentful of them as well. I felt the whole craft of acting was being given short shrift by expecting me to prepare this much material and excel at it in such a short period of time."

The next day, Grodin was argumentative with Nichols, and unhappy with the work he did in the test. When he drove home that evening he was sure he had blown it — and he had. A couple of days later, Mike Nichols called and asked Grodin if he would like to be in his next movie — not *The Graduate*, but *Catch-22*, the film he was planning of Joseph Heller's bestselling novel. Charles Grodin was to be many things in his career, but he would not be Benjamin Braddock.

Buck Henry doubted Grodin was as close to getting the part as he liked to think. "He gave a great reading," Henry said. "In fact it was one of the funniest readings I've ever heard any actor do. But it simply wasn't as interesting as what Dustin did." Tony Bill, who would later become a producer (*The*

*Sting*; *Taxi Driver*) and director (*Untamed Heart*), also was led to believe he had got close to Benjamin. "I was told that it was either me or Dustin. Maybe they said that just to make me feel better."

Dustin was Dustin Hoffman.

Who spotted Hoffman first remains the subject of some debate. Mike Nichols said he saw him on the New York stage. But screenwriter Buck Henry thought he was the only one of the production team who had actually seen Hoffman perform — in 1963 or 1964 in an off-Broadway play called *Harry, Noon and Night*. Hoffman played "a crippled German transvestite," said Henry. "It was impossible to believe he wasn't one or two or three of those things. It was a bravura performance."

This much is certain: Dustin Hoffman was 29 years of age in 1966, and he had just gotten the break of his career playing in an off-Broadway farce directed by Alan Arkin titled *Eh?* Walter Kerr wrote a front-page piece in the "Arts and Leisure" section of the Sunday *New York Times* comparing him to Buster Keaton. Hoffman was flattered, although he had never even seen a Buster Keaton movie. His agent phoned to say Mike Nichols wanted to see him in Los Angeles for a movie. First, however, they wanted him to sign a contract. If he got the part, he would be committed for six more pictures. If he did not get it, there would be no contract. Hoffman could not believe he would have to sign something before he even tested. "Fuck it," he told his agent. Unlike Charles Grodin, no one tried to pressure Hoffman into signing anything, an indication perhaps of the increasing desperation to find Benjamin. Later, someone said it was the smartest business decision he ever made.

Hoffman was despondent after reading *The Graduate*. He was all wrong for Benjamin. Like everyone else who read it, he concluded the book's hero was tall and blond and handsome — all the things Dustin Hoffman most definitely was not. He put the book down on a table beside a copy of *Time* magazine. The cover featured "The Man of the Year" and the honoree for 1966 was "Youth."

"The guy on the cover was handsome, and I thought to myself, 'that's the kind of guy they want,'" Hoffman lamented.

He was to be haunted by those feelings of insecurity throughout his involvement with *The Graduate*. He never did shake the sense that he was not right. He was small and dark and Jewish, with a nose that tended to over-

▶ *Albert Finney seen here in* The Victors *(1963), successfully tested for* Lawrence of Arabia *(1962). However, he walked away from the role of a lifetime.*

▶ *Peter O'Toole inherited the part. This photograph was taken at the time he was signed for* Lawrence.

▶ *Terence Stamp became a star in* Billy Budd *(1962).*

▶ *But when he said no to* Alfie *(1966), his flat-mate, Michael Caine, became an international star.*

▼ *Caine and Stamp together on the* set of Alfie.

▼ *Cary Grant (in* Charade, *1963) was offered the part of James Bond.*
▶ *But it was Scottish actor Sean Connery who became 007 in* Dr. No *(1962) with Ursula Andress.*

▲ *Jane Fonda seen here in* Sunday in New York *(1963), the movie she was shooting when she declined to play Lara in* Doctor Zhivago *(1965). Unknown Julie Christie got the part.*

▶ *A publicity shot of Leslie Caron in the mid 1960s, when she wanted to co-star with boyfriend Warren Beatty in* Bonnie and Clyde *(1967).*

◀ *Tuesday Weld turned down Bonnie Parker.*

◀ *So the role went to Faye Dunaway.*

160C

◀ *Dustin Hoffman and Katharine Ross in a wardrobe shot for* The Graduate *(1967).*

▲ *Young actor Tony Bill briefly thought he might play Benjamin Braddock …*

▼ *… And so did Charles Grodin. He later became a star in* The Heartbreak Kid *(1972), with Cybill Shepherd.*

◀ *Robert Redford's career was going nowhere before he was reluctantly cast in* Butch Cassidy and the Sundance Kid *(1969).*

▲ *Appearing with Paul Newman made him the most sought after star of the 1970s.*

▶ *Meanwhile, Warren Beatty, who was offered Redford's role, basked in the glory of* Bonnie and Clyde.

◀ *Jack Nicholson was fed up with the movie business when* Easy Rider *(1969) made him a star.*

▶ *Rip Torn was supposed to play Nicholson's role. He later claimed he was never even on the set.*

▲ *When Al Pacino played Michael Corleone in* The Godfather *(1972)...*

▲ *... Newcomer Robert De Niro inherited his role in* The Gang That Couldn't Shoot Straight *(1971).*

▲ *Joel Grey, seen in* Cabaret *(1972), badly wanted to be in* Jaws *(1975).*

▲ *But it was Richard Dreyfuss who was talked into the role.*

▲ *Sterling Hayden was the first choice for Quint.*

▲ *But it was British actor Robert Shaw who took on the Great White Shark.*

160G

◀ Moment by Moment *(1978) was the biggest bomb of John Travolta's career, and pretty much finished him in movies.*

▼ He *appeared in* Staying Alive *(1983), left inset, and in* Urban Cowboy *(1980). Even so, stardom slipped away from him.*

◀ *When John Travolta dropped out of* American Gigolo *(1980), he was replaced by Richard Gere and the movie made him a star.*

▼ *Travolta also passed on* An Officer and a Gentleman *(1982). Again Gere was chosen to replace him and, with Debra Winger, he had the biggest hit of his career.*

whelm a face still troubled with acne. He thought of himself as an ethnic Easterner, but in fact he was born in Los Angeles, and his association with movies began when his mother named him after her favorite cowboy actor, Dustin Farnham. Hoffman had dropped out of Santa Monica City College to attend the Pasadena Playhouse, finding his way to New York at the age of 19, determined to become an actor. There, he slept on the floor of another struggling actor, Gene Hackman. "Every morning at three a.m.," he remembered, "the refrigerator would have a heart attack and wake me up."

His father, a furniture designer, bankrolled him to the tune of about $3,000 over the next two years. For a time Hoffman worked as an attendant at a psychiatric hospital, demonstrated toys at Macy's, taught acting at a boy's club in Harlem, worked as a typist (65 words a minute), and even waited tables. Ten years later, having finally broken through on the off-Broadway stage, his feelings about movies were decidedly ambivalent. Nonetheless, he found himself with three days off from *Eh?* on a plane headed for California and a screen test for Mike Nichols. He was certain the trip would be a waste of time. A poor student, he had trouble properly memorizing his lines. Nervous, and wondering why he was returning to a city he had been eager to leave, he spent a sleepless night tossing and worrying. Arriving at the Paramount lot the next day, he was ushered into a palatial office, and there, leaning against the bar, was Mike Nichols. It was, Hoffman thought, right out of a movie. All the time he was meeting with Nichols, he kept thinking, "I'm not supposed to be in movies. I should be where I belong. An ethnic actor is supposed to be in ethnic New York in an ethnic off-Broadway show." Already Hoffman was beginning to sense that Nichols was feeling he had made a big mistake bringing him out here.

Nonetheless, he spent a long day at the studio auditioning with several others, including Katharine Ross, a strikingly beautiful young actress who had already tested with Charles Grodin. Neither one of them could quite believe each other, but for much different reasons. Ross, who was about to turn 25 and who had been appearing in movies for the past two years, was appalled. "He looked about three feet tall, so dead serious, so humorless, so unkempt." She thought the test would be a disaster.

Conversely, Hoffman was in awe. Katharine Ross's beauty left him speechless. He could never, he thought, be involved with someone like that.

Worse still, they were about to do a love scene together — something he was completely unfamiliar with. "I'd never ask a girl in acting class to do a love scene; no girl asked me either."

They did the test together the next day on a Paramount sound stage. Hoffman kept blowing his lines. At one point, trying to lighten up the tense atmosphere, he reached over and awkwardly pinched Ross on the buttocks. Immediately, she turned on him. "Don't you ever do that to me again!" she screamed. "How dare you!"

At the end of a long day that had begun at 10:00 A.M., Hoffman was saying good-bye to the various members of the crew when he accidentally dropped some New York subway tokens. One of the prop men leaned over and picked up the tokens, inspected them, then handed them back to Hoffman. "Here, kid," said the man, "you're gonna need these."

When Hoffman left California for New York, he was convinced he had blown whatever slim chance he had at *The Graduate*. He was not far wrong. Joe Levine, the executive producer, could not believe they were even considering the actor. "Him?" he said incredulously. "I thought he was one of the guys from the building. You know, the guys who fix things."

Nichols was disappointed. "He didn't know his lines, and he was terribly nervous."

Still, when everyone sat down to look at Hoffman's test, they were amazed. "He was good on film," Nichols recalled. "He was special. He made us laugh."

Said Buck Henry, "It was clear from the test, Dustin was really interesting." What about Robert Redford? "Good, but just not as interesting as Dustin."[16]

Lawrence Turman turned to Nichols and said simply, "I'd be happy with that one."

Back in New York, the first intimation Hoffman had that he was to be Benjamin Braddock came from his agent. Mike Nichols had called. He wanted to talk to Hoffman. If Nichols did not want him for the part, the agent sur-

---

[16] Katharine Ross won the role of Elaine Robinson over Candice Bergen. "Dustin and Katharine just seemed to work so well together," recalled Buck Henry. "Katharine was just staggeringly beautiful, yet she was the girl next door. Candy was beautiful too, but sort of like an icon. If she had lived next door, you would have broken down the walls to get at her."

mised, he would not have called, would he? Forgetting the time difference, Hoffman called Nichols in Los Angeles and woke him up. Hoffman, over time, recounted various versions of the ensuing conversation, but basically it came down to this:

"I woke you up."

"That's all right. You got the part."

"Thank you."

"Is that all you have to say?"

"Sorry . . . thank you very much."

When he hung up, Hoffman turned to his girlfriend, Anne Byrne, who would later become his first wife. "I got the part," he said calmly.

"I knew you would," Anne said.

They stared at each other for a long time and suddenly, instead of being elated, they were curiously depressed. "We'd been content before," Hoffman said later, "and now we knew there would be a great change in our lives."

T HE GRADUATE WAS EVERYTHING DUSTIN HOFFMAN AND MIKE Nichols suspected it would be, and much more. Released at Christmas of 1967, it ended up grossing $50 million (about $175 million in today's money), and became the most successful movie of the year. It won Mike Nichols the Academy Award for best director, and Oscar nominations went to Buck Henry and Calder Willingham for the script, as well as to Anne Bancroft, Katharine Ross, and Dustin Hoffman. The film itself lost out to *In the Heat of the Night* as best picture (this in a year that also saw the release of *Bonnie and Clyde*).

But *The Graduate*'s influence went far beyond any awards it did or did not receive. Propelled along by the music of Simon and Garfunkel, it crossed that invisible line where a movie stops being merely an entertainment and begins to reflect the consciousness of the time and in the process becomes part of the culture. *The Graduate* appeared at a moment when a whole generation was feeling disaffected and left out, without a mainstream American movie that accurately caught that disaffection. Moreover, Dustin Hoffman was a hero with whom everyone in the audience could identify. He was not impossibly handsome as was Warren Beatty in *Bonnie and Clyde*, or impossibly good and heroic as was Sidney Poitier in *In the Heat of the Night*. He was flawed, and stupid, romantic and awkward and funny, just like everyone else.

"Taking nothing away from Dustin Hoffman, a lot of his behavior was taken from the scenes, again, right from the book as written by Charles Webb," Turman said. "'Mrs. Robinson — you're trying to seduce me — aren't you?'" Even now the words caused Turman to laugh. "I mean that's right from the book."

Hoffman, almost overnight, was transformed into the most unlikely movie star. After him came a whole series of character actors who became movie stars, including Hoffman's friends, Gene Hackman and Robert Duvall, as well as Jack Nicholson, Al Pacino (who was often mistaken for Hoffman), and Robert De Niro. If he had not played Benjamin, Hoffman was sure his career in the movies would have amounted to no more than a series of supporting roles, yet he remained convinced that he got the part by default more than anything else. "It was like the bottom of the barrel. If [Katharine Ross and I] had tested a year earlier, we would never have gotten the roles."

*The Graduate* made Larry Turman a wealthy man, and established him as a major Hollywood producer. He began working with a young writer from Chicago named William Goldman, who had spent several years researching the life and times of two western desperados named the Sundance Kid and Butch Cassidy. Goldman had written an original screenplay based on their exploits and titled it *The Sundance Kid and Butch Cassidy*. Turman's instincts, which had worked so well at divining far in advance of anyone the merits of *The Graduate*, would not work nearly so well this time. Goldman's script would be turned into a hit movie, but not because Larry Turman had anything to do with it.

# 11

# "I DON'T KNOW WHAT IT IS, BUT I CAN PLAY IT."

*Redford plays Sundance as Nicholson arrives*

---

B Y THE TIME STEVE MCQUEEN WENT TO SEE *THE GRADUATE* IN FEB-
ruary of 1968, he was already aware of William Goldman's script of
*The Sundance Kid and Butch Cassidy*. In San Francisco shooting a police
thriller titled *Bullitt*, he emerged from the theater with his wife, Neile, after
the screening, shaken and disturbed by what he had just seen.

"What's gonna happen to us, do you suppose?"

Neile McQueen was not sure what he was getting at. After a few minutes of prodding, it became apparent that it was Dustin Hoffman. "Gosh,
baby," he said, "I can't believe this guy's going to be a major star, can you? I
mean he is an ugly cat. Good actor, yeah, but he sure is homely."

The public's fascination with Dustin Hoffman baffled McQueen. For
Neile McQueen, however, that evening marked her husband's first intimation
of mortality. The sight of Hoffman on the screen exposed a deep-seated sense
of insecurity and concern about his ability to remain a movie star. The poor,
restless, rebellious reform-school kid who deeply resented Paul Newman and
James Dean, for whom nothing ever came easily, had reached out and grabbed
the brass ring. Now close to 40, he finally had a lock on that ring, and here
was the new gun already in town and threatening to take it away from him.
Dustin Hoffman up there on the screen was the future, and Steve McQueen
did not like it.

At the same time as *The Graduate* enveloped the American moviegoing experience, Robert Redford, one of the actors who did not play
Benjamin Braddock, co-starred with Jane Fonda in the film version of *Barefoot
in the Park*. The movie was only a middling success, and Redford's reviews, as
usual, were so-so. Once again he was blond and bland — this time as the
young attorney, Paul Bratter, adjusting to a new wife (Fonda) and a leaky loft

apartment in Greenwich Village.

By the time *Barefoot in the Park* was released, Redford was considered an actor who, as a movie executive once said to director George Roy Hill, "had been to the post too many times." While Dustin Hoffman dealt with the emotional bends involved in shooting to the top overnight, Redford stomped out of a western titled *Blue*[17] and was sued for breach of contract by Paramount Pictures. Instead of becoming a movie star, Redford would not work again for two years. His future was problematic, not helped by his ambivalence toward acting. He liked to say he derived more satisfaction from building a house in Utah with his wife, Lola, than from anything he had done on either the stage or the screen.

That ambivalence was reflected in his work. He had appeared in a string of failures — *War Hunt* (1962), *Situation Hopeless — But Not Serious* (1965), *Inside Daisy Clover* (1966), *The Chase* (1966), and *This Property Is Condemned* (1966). He was present in those movies, to be sure, but never seemed connected either to the role or to the movie itself. Mike Nichols had a terrible time with him during the pre-Broadway tryout for *Barefoot in the Park*. While co-star Elizabeth Ashley effortlessly embraced the audience, Redford demonstrated no empathy whatsoever. "I just didn't want to be there," he said. ". . . And I was lousy in the part, really bad, I just couldn't get with it, and I wanted to quit."

But Nichols would not allow it. During the play's tryout in New Haven, he took Redford to dinner across the street from the theater and told him flatly that he was not going to let him out of the play. He would insist Redford go to New York, and if he was going to fail, he would do it in front of a Broadway audience. "So make up your mind," Nichols snapped. After that, Redford smartened up, and his character finally came to life. The play was a hit in New York, and Redford had the biggest break of his career. It was the first but certainly not the last time a director would defy the prevailing wisdom and push for him.

Paul Newman was thinking of Steve McQueen in the summer of

---

[17] He was replaced by the British actor Terence Stamp, who at the time was considered to be much hotter. Stamp had already turned down *Alfie* and had been fired from *Blowup* a couple of years before by the director Michelangelo Antonioni. He was replaced by newcomer David Hemmings. *Blue's* director, Silvio Narizzano, said he felt much more comfortable with Stamp than he would have with Redford. "He was worried about Redford," Stamp said, "thought he was a bit too much of a Brooks Brothers suit type."

1967. He had read the initial draft of *The Sundance Kid and Butch Cassidy*, liked it, and thought he and McQueen would make an interesting combination in the starring roles. After all, they had struggled together in New York back in the 1950s, though McQueen had come a long way since Robert Wise chose him for a small role in *Somebody Up There Likes Me*.

"I saw a lot of kids come in to interview for this little bit part," Wise said of that film. "I just remember he came in kind of cocky, this little cap set on his head. I liked that cocky attitude he had." Years later, when Wise was preparing a Far East epic called *The Sand Pebbles*, he thought of Steve McQueen for the starring role of Jake Holman, a navy engine-room mechanic on board a gunboat patrolling the Yangtze River on the eve of the Boxer Rebellion in 1926. McQueen still was not a star, and 20th Century–Fox, the studio financing *The Sand Pebbles*, wanted a bigger name. Before the casting could be resolved, Wise decided to shelve the picture so that he could go off and do *The Sound of Music*. By the time he returned to *The Sand Pebbles* in 1965, McQueen was a major star. "I never met any actor, any star, that knew what worked for him on the screen as well as McQueen did," Wise said. "He really had studied himself, and he parlayed that into quite a career."

It was Larry Turman, the producer of *The Graduate*, who developed the *Sundance Kid and Butch Cassidy* script with William Goldman. When it was finished, Turman decided to let it go "because there's something sadder, should be something sadder, in the relationship between those two men and that woman. Maybe what I wanted would have been less successful or less good, but I didn't want that 1970 hip dialogue, that smooth surface. I told Bill, 'You've got the most buyable screenplay in the world, let's stay friends.'"

Paul Newman arrived for lunch at Steve McQueen's home on a clear, perfect California afternoon. He sat by the pool with McQueen and his wife, Neile, and described how he saw the relationship between Butch and Sundance. Neile McQueen later recalled him talking about the posse that "glowed and shimmered in the distance." McQueen was intrigued. Here was the man whose stardom he coveted more than anyone else's, sitting beside his pool suggesting a movie together. It must have been a moment of supreme triumph.

Steve McQueen agreed to look at the script when it was ready, then went off to San Francisco to make *Bullitt.* When he got back to Los Angeles several months later, he was visited by David Foster, a partner in the public relations firm that represented him. Accompanying Foster was Bob Sherman, a talent agent. This time they had the Goldman script with them. McQueen read it and liked it, which brought 20th Century–Fox into the picture. Richard Zanuck, who was about to become president of the studio, and David Brown, his vice president of creative operations, knew that Newman wanted to do the script, and had heard rumors that Steve McQueen was also interested. "We had reason to believe that Steve McQueen would commit to it if George Roy Hill directed," Brown said. "We geared up our courage and offered the then unheard-of price of $275,000[18] for the script. It was presumed that Newman and McQueen would co-star together."

McQueen had waited for over a decade to savor this moment. Finally he was the equal of Paul Newman, and now he was determined to capitalize on everyone's anxiousness for him to co-star. He demanded top billing over his longtime rival. Neile was appalled, but her husband was adamant. His name would come first or he would not make the movie.

Freddie Fields, Newman's agent at the time, came around to see McQueen. Fields proposed a unique way out of the billing dilemma. McQueen's name would indeed come first, at the left, while Paul Newman's name would be placed to the right, but slightly higher. McQueen could even decide on which billing he preferred — to the left and slightly lower or to the right, and slightly higher. McQueen thought about this. What would Fields suggest? The agent recommended that he take the billing on the left. McQueen agreed to do that. The matter seemed to have been settled. Fields was at the door when McQueen changed his mind. The actor now abruptly proposed that they flip a coin to decide top billing, but Fields dismissed the suggestion. A moment later the agent was gone, and Steve McQueen was finished with *The Sundance Kid and Butch Cassidy*. The chip he would always carry on his shoulder where Paul Newman was concerned had prevented him from co-starring in one of the biggest hits of the decade.[19]

---

[18] Actually, Fox paid a record $400,000 for Goldman's script — the most that had ever been paid for a screenplay to that time.

[19] Paul Newman and Steve McQueen finally co-starred together in 1974 in *The Towering Inferno,* a big-budget disaster epic produced by Irwin Allen. And McQueen was billed first. As Freddie Fields had suggested, his name appeared first, but positioned slightly lower than Newman's.

George Roy Hill was delighted to see the end of McQueen. He had already decided on the actor he wanted to play opposite Newman — Robert Redford. While McQueen was being wooed, Hill had sat in Joe Allen's restaurant in New York with Redford and over hamburgers made the actor swear patience. Hill, somehow, was going to get him that movie.

Redford was not so sure, and he had enough pride to refuse even to read the script until there was a firm offer. Initially, based on seeing him in *Barefoot in the Park*, Hill thought of the actor as the more passive and easygoing Butch Cassidy. But as they talked, Hill decided Redford would be better as the Sundance Kid — everything coiled tight, intermittently igniting the sparks that warned strangers to keep their distance.

Redford had encountered William Goldman years before when the writer was researching a nonfiction book about Broadway called *The Season*. The two men liked one another, which helped when they met to talk about the script, and Goldman asked point-blank, "Can you play Sundance?" Redford replied, "I don't know what it is, but I can play it."

But there was a problem, succinctly articulated by George Roy Hill: "Nobody wanted Redford in the movie." Fox was still reeling from McQueen's abrupt exit. "It's hard to recall, but it must have been a disappointment," David Brown said years later. "McQueen and Newman together were a surefire package. Redford we didn't know about."

THUS, WHEN IT BECAME APPARENT THAT McQUEEN WAS A LOST CAUSE, Fox next went after Marlon Brando. At the age of 44, the actor who had done more to change the nature of stardom than anyone since the beginning of the sound era now found his career floundering. There had not been a successful Brando picture in years, and after the fiasco of *Mutiny on the Bounty* in 1962, he was considered box-office poison. How surprising that Fox would want him for this sort of commercial enterprise, but the studio was anxious to make an offer — if he could be found. "They made phone calls and they sent messengers," Hill remembered, "but Brando wouldn't see anybody, wouldn't answer anything."

Finally, the actor was located in Oakland, where he was working with the Black Panthers. Craig Modderno, then a young reporter for the *Oakland Tribune*, was sitting in the Panther offices trying to get an interview with the group's leader, Huey Newton, when he came across the *Butch Cassidy* script, addressed to Brando, lying on a desk. He read half of it while waiting for Newton. "I remember thinking it was terrific," Modderno said. "It didn't read like a script at all, but this great story Goldman was trying to tell." Later a *Tribune* photographer went back and found the script still lying where Modderno had left it. He read the other half, and was equally impressed.

"They sent some damned vice president up there [to Oakland] to tell Marlon that this was important for his career," Hill said, "and you know what he said? 'America's important too, and I'm working for America.'"

Finally, the studio gave up. There were discussions with Warren Beatty, who proved to be as elusive as Brando. Hill decided to rally a final assault, and flew out to California to confront studio executives. "The director exerts a great deal of leadership in casting," explained David Brown. "You don't want to cast someone the director can't work with." Even so, Hill discovered his clout still was not enough to sway the studio. "I used up all my muscle and I asked Paul Newman to step in and by that time he was convinced about Redford, too, so that he used his muscle, and Goldman, who wrote the script, sent a six-page telegram saying that if the whole creative team — or some such phrase — agreed on Redford, then why the hell couldn't management go along with it? And finally we got him in."

"I owe him," Redford said of Hill after *Butch Cassidy and the Sundance Kid* had made him a star. "I owe him a lot for *Sundance* — and Newman and Goldman."

Redford over the next 10 years carefully constructed his career using the combination of golden looks and larger-than-life romanticism. He embodied the by now ancient traditions of movie star as All-American guy — beautiful, flawed, but ultimately triumphant. Paul Newman, once he shook himself clear of Brando, hewed to much the same mythos and, like Redford, often claimed he found it restricting. Newman strayed more from his image as he got older, but Redford, 12 years younger, having reluctantly tasted stardom, toed the line throughout the '70s in a series of successful pictures that included *The Candidate* (1972), *The Hot Rock* (1972), *The Way We Were* (1973), *The Sting* (1973), *The Great Gatsby* (1974), *The Great Waldo Pepper* (1975), *Three Days of the Condor* (1975), *All the President's Men* (1976), and *The Electric Horseman* (1979). There were no stumbles at the box office — although *Gatsby* refused to live up to its advance hype — and no great risks either as an actor. Redford understood that it was all about movie stardom, not great performance, and there was no better example of the limits he set for himself than what happened with *The Verdict*.

The producers, David Brown and Richard Zanuck, acquired the rights to the novel by a Boston lawyer named Barry Reed, and as soon as they did, the word went out over that jungle telegraph that ignites Hollywood whenever there is a rumor of an extraordinary role. Soon every actor in town was after Frank Galvin, the boozy Boston attorney mounting a malpractice suit and involved in the fight of his misspent, ambulance-chasing life against the power of the Catholic archdiocese. Dustin Hoffman expressed interest, and so did Roy Scheider, who later was furious when he did not get the part. To the further amazement of Zanuck and Brown, Frank Sinatra called, and most unbelievable of all, Cary Grant, who had retired from movies in 1966, made inquiries. "Never before in our careers have we had the kind of property that attracted that kind of attention," Zanuck said.

But of all the actors who hungered for Frank Galvin, the most potent box-office force was Robert Redford. The producers who once fought so hard at 20th Century–Fox to keep him away from *Butch and Sundance* now courted the golden boy of the movies. It was Redford's time; his movies were hits, and the great powers of Hollywood all were anxious to work with him. Redford could have the part that everyone else desired without even asking. Except that Galvin did not quite match his image. "When he realized he'd have to let the warts show, let it all hang out, then he backed off," Zanuck said. "Every time a scene was written in which he looked boozy and ill-kempt, unshaven, he resisted. He wanted to be a family man. Frank Galvin, in his estimation, had kids and was a nice, clean-cut guy — a kind of boy scout version of the character. This was not what we conceived at all."

Director Arthur Hiller became impatient with the constant delays and rewrites and deserted the project. He was briefly replaced by James Bridges, who also departed, leaving the golden boy lost among at least 10 script rewrites. And still he vacillated. Finally, Zanuck and Brown lost patience and took action almost unheard of in modern day movie-star-obsessed Hollywood — they dumped the movie star. "We were sick of it, quite frankly," recounted Zanuck.

Paul Newman was finishing *Absence of Malice* when Zanuck and Brown sent him the script. Fifty-five years of age, shedding the godlike pretensions of his more youthful stardom, he saw Galvin not as a drunk but as an opportunity to stretch the envelope — a real character for a real actor. Newman even got the rasp in his voice right; not only did he look like he was caught in the hangover's clutches, he sounded it, too. The completed film, directed by Sidney Lumet, was not only one of the big money earners of 1982, it also won Paul Newman an Academy Award nomination. Redford, it can be politely stated, did not receive an Academy Award nomination that year. He preferred to continue the pursuit of golden romanticism in *The Natural* and *Out of Africa*, all the time insisting he was trapped by an image over which he had no control.

B Y THE TIME ROBERT REDFORD BECAME A STAR IN 1969, JACK NICHolson was considering a retreat from Hollywood altogether. Nicholson, from Neptune, New Jersey, had arrived in town in 1954 to "see the stars," he said, only half jokingly — all the stars you could see from MGM's animation department where he landed his first job. He had appeared in a succession of B movies for Roger Corman, beginning with *The Cry Baby Killer*, and continuing with a dizzying array of horror movies, action pictures, biker flicks, and westerns. It was the kind of on-the-job training actors used to get at the studios in the 1930s and 1940s, but was almost unheard of by the end of the '60s. Moreover, Nicholson had written movie screenplays (*The Trip* and *Head*), and he had produced them (*Ride in the Whirlwind* and *The Shooting*). In a decade he had achieved as fully rounded a career as any actor in town, but he was almost completely unrecognized, existing at the edges of the mainstream, watching the likes of Beatty, Redford, and Hoffman beat him out of A-picture roles and become movie stars. Nothing quite jelled, and repeated attempts to go over the wall out of the schlock movie cellblock in which he had been serving a long time seemed doomed to failure.

Roman Polanski had been uninterested in him for Mia Farrow's husband in *Rosemary's Baby*. His name was mentioned in connection with *Bonnie and Clyde*, but the part of Buck Barrow had gone to Gene Hackman. Now here he was hanging around a newly formed independent production company hoping to get a directing gig off the ground. The new company, BBS, represented the initials of its three founders, Bert Schneider, Bob Rafelson, and

Steve Blauner. Their intention was to produce upscale variations on the sort of exploitation drive-in pictures Roger Corman was overseeing at American International Pictures (AIP), the company owned by Samuel Z. Arkoff.

Nicholson, along with his friends Dennis Hopper and Peter Fonda, had already suggested one picture to BBS, something called *The Queen* in which the three actors in those ferociously anti-Vietnam War days would play LBJ, McGeorge Bundy, and Dean Rusk. The three architects of the U.S. involvement in the war were to be shown sitting around a table, each dressed in a white, off-the-shoulder gown, plotting the assassination of John F. Kennedy. There was an embarrassed silence after that particular scenario was pitched, and the subject switched to another project Hopper and Fonda were working on — a biker picture to be an amalgamation of *The Trip* and *The Wild Angels*, two very successful AIP pictures in which Fonda had starred. The picture was to be called *Easy Rider*, and already the duo had been in to talk to Roger Corman about financing. "I was sure they had a hit on their hands," Corman later recalled.

The trouble was Hopper. He had made his movie debut in *Rebel Without a Cause* with his friend James Dean while still a teenager, and also appeared with him in *Giant*. In the late 1960s, more than a decade after he had started to act, Hopper was considered violent, difficult, and self-destructive. Samuel Z. Arkoff was not about to put up money for anything that Dennis Hopper planned to direct. Still, on second thought, the *Easy Rider* project seemed so commercial that Arkoff backed off a little, agreeing that Hopper could direct, and AIP would put up $360,000. However, if the production fell behind schedule, Hopper would be fired. Fonda, who was as close to being a star as any of them in those days, refused to go along with that arrangement.

So with Jack Nicholson acting as a kind of broker, the trio was now in the BBS offices pitching *Easy Rider*. Bert Schneider stuck his head in the door, liked what he heard, and agreed on the spot to put up the $360,000. Fonda and Hopper would play characters called Billy the Kid and Captain America, two dudes off to find America on their choppers. Along the way, they would pick up a straight lawyer, a role that another longtime member of the AIP student faculty, Bruce Dern, was supposed to do. Then, it seemed, Rip Torn had the role. Over the years, two stories grew up over what happened to Rip Torn on *Easy Rider*. The first story, told most often, had him on location in New Orleans, discovering that *Easy Rider* was going to be a lot more work than he had figured and demanding more money. When that was not forthcoming, he left town.

The second story, the one Torn angrily told, had him nowhere near the *Easy Rider* set, let alone walking off it. "Look, you can say a guy shoots up every day or that he goes to orgies or whatever, and that doesn't have anything to do with the work," he said. "But if you say a guy's professionally irresponsible, that he 'walked out' on a film, that's the worst rap you can give him."

Torn said there was "some talk about me doing that role, but I never signed a contract. I was never on the set. I just had other obligations, and couldn't do it, that's all." The part of the lawyer had been written for him by his friend, writer Terry Southern, but he was doing a Broadway play at the time and simply was not available.

In Los Angeles, alarm swirled through the BBS offices. *Easy Rider* had barely started shooting and it was behind schedule, and there were reports of fights. Bert Schneider dispatched Jack Nicholson south to act as production troubleshooter. And since he was already there, it was decided he might as well take the role of the lawyer in the movie. In short order, Nicholson got the production under control, using a few tricks he had learned doing all those low-budget pictures for Corman. He also brought in Laszlo Kovacs, the cinematographer who gave *Easy Rider* its mesmerizing look. Later, after filming was completed, Nicholson also worked on the scoring of the picture.

Imagine Nicholson's surprise when *Easy Rider* was released and overnight turned him into a movie star. After 10 years of hitting his head against the high wall around the compound where they held the A pictures, suddenly the door opened and he walked right in. Somehow he was just more accessible in the movie than either the aloof Fonda or the freaked-out Hopper. He was the wounded, cynical drunk, but playing it laid back and with lots of quirky humor. On the screen, Nicholson became what he had been for *Easy Rider* in real life — an anchor, the one guy in the movie you could gravitate toward. You knew Jack as soon as he bounced into view behind bars, and you immediately liked him. He was a maverick, wearing a jacket and tie, trying to stay straight, but kind of failing, like most of the young people sitting in movie theaters watching the movie.

Literally overnight, Nicholson was a star, and because he had worked so long in films in almost every capacity, over the next three decades he would use that knowledge of the business to remain one of the movies' more powerful and influential actors.

T HE ACTOR MICHAEL DOUGLAS, WEARING HIS PRODUCER'S HAT, ADMITted that, of course, Marlon Brando had turned down the role of McMurphy in *One Flew Over the Cuckoo's Nest* — hardly unexpected, given Brando's penchant for turning down anything that might have enhanced his career. That was fine with Milos Forman, the Czech filmmaker who had been hired by producers Douglas and Saul Zaentz to direct the movie. Forman said that from the beginning he had wanted Nicholson — not Brando or Gene Hackman or Burt Reynolds, who was also considered.

Reynolds came close to getting the role. Forman had breakfast with the actor one morning and told him it was down to two people. "If the other guy isn't Jack Nicholson, I've got the part," Reynolds said. Forman stopped eating, and Reynolds knew right there that it was all over. Nicholson, the streetwise former B-player, understood all the tricks of playing against the grain, the kind of underdog the audience always liked. In *Cuckoo's Nest*, he had found his ultimate rebel with a cause role.

Nearly a decade after he received his Oscar for *Cuckoo's Nest*, Nicholson, turning 46, came to the realization that "I could not go on playing 35-year-olds." James L. Brooks, the creator of television's "Taxi," sent him his script for a movie in which he would make his directorial debut. Adapted from a Larry McMurtry novel, *Terms of Endearment* dealt with the relationship between a mother and her daughter. What it lacked was a leading male role. Instead, Brooks wanted Nicholson to play the washed-up astronaut Garrett Breedlove, who lived next door to the widowed Shirley MacLaine.

Burt Reynolds, for whom Brooks had written the part in the first place, to everyone's astonishment turned it down. But Nicholson *knew* from the moment he read the screenplay. "How many scripts make you cry?" he asked rhetorically. "I read hundreds of screenplays every year and this one made me think, 'Yeah, I know just how this guy feels.' It was a terrific play." He also understood that the flamboyant yet sympathetic Breedlove constituted a mid-course career correction. After *Terms of Endearment*, the 35-year-olds Nicholson had been portraying would be gone, their exit celebrated with a second Oscar, this one for best supporting actor.

For Burt Reynolds, who had read the same script, but who did not cry, who did not *know*, there was no mid-course correction, simply the end of a superstar movie career. Moreover, Reynolds knew it, the way he knew he did not have *Cuckoo's Nest* as soon as Milos Forman stopped eating. This time, though, there was no one to blame but himself. "I was an idiot," Reynolds later said. "I promised someone else I would do a film [Blake Edwards' *The Man Who Loved Women*], and I couldn't break the promise. If I had to do it again, maybe I'd ask to get out, but I've never been that kind of person. It was a huge mistake, though. It would have fixed and changed all the things I wanted to fix and change."

A T THE BEGINNING OF THE 1970S, GENE HACKMAN REMAINED A SUPporting actor. Twice, he had been nominated in that category for his performances, first in *Bonnie and Clyde* and the next year for playing the ailing Melvyn Douglas's son in *I Never Sang for My Father*. Even with the ascension of his old roommate Dustin Hoffman and the sudden success of Jack Nicholson, the face of movie stardom still had not been altered to the point where it would resemble Hackman's Everyman countenance. He could not stop being astonished every time he was asked for an autograph. "I'm not someone people come up to," he said. "I look so common."

Certainly, he was the last person either the producer Philip D'Antoni or his director, William Friedkin, considered for their new police thriller. D'Antoni had produced *Bullitt*, with Steve McQueen as a tough San Francisco cop. The movie was the biggest hit of McQueen's career, mostly because of a slam-bang car chase up and down the hills of San Francisco — a chase that inspired dozens of imitations. D'Antoni was looking for something in the same vein as *Bullitt* that might also serve as the excuse for another high-speed auto chase.

He thought he had found it in a book by Robin Moore titled *The French Connection*, the true story of two New York narcotics detectives, Eddie Egan and Sonny Grosso, who stumbled across the biggest shipment of heroin ever to enter the United States. But D'Antoni then had trouble getting the script he wanted until he hired a writer named Ernest Tidyman. Very quickly Tidyman solved the script problems. Nevertheless, everyone in town turned it down until finally Richard Zanuck and David Brown, who were then running 20th Century–Fox, decided to go ahead.

Roy Scheider, a New Jersey actor who had made his professional stage debut as Mercutio in the New York Shakespeare Festival production of *Romeo and Juliet*, was cast as Sonny Grosso, called Buddy Russo in the movie. But the all-important lead detective, Jimmy 'Popeye' Doyle, remained elusive. Friedkin, a former TV station floor manager from Chicago whose movies included a filmed stage play (Pinter's *The Birthday Party*), a comedy (*The Night They Raided Minsky's*), and a somewhat controversial homosexual drama (*The Boys in the Band*), had had no previous experience with the sort of fast-paced action movie D'Antoni envisaged. Friedkin wanted *French Connection* to have a gritty, documentary quality, and perhaps for that reason he was interested in casting someone who was not an actor. For Friedkin, the essence of Popeye Doyle was embodied in New York's *Daily News* columnist Jimmy Breslin. "A big, fat, slobbering guy who looked like that, and had a big gut and he was trying to run down the street tripping over himself." That was how Friedkin saw Popeye.

Breslin, of course, was fascinated with the idea, and Fox actually went along with it until Friedkin started to rehearse the newspaper columnist. "In the action stuff, he was great," remembered Roy Scheider. "But when he had to say, 'Pass the sugar,' not too good. Desperate."

Friedkin was more diplomatic. "It was clear that [Jimmy] couldn't sustain from one day to the next, which is what an actor can do. He also couldn't drive a car. It was one of those deathbed promises to his mother that he would never drive. So that became an overriding factor."

Steve McQueen did not want to play another tough cop. Paul Newman and Robert Mitchum both said no, while Peter Boyle and even comedian Jackie Gleason were considered before the casting people came up with Hackman's name. D'Antoni and Friedkin were not enthusiastic about the suggestion. However, at this point there was not much of an alternative. With filming due to begin in December 1970, they reluctantly decided to go with the actor. He was Friedkin's last choice, and D'Antoni was reluctant even to tell Richard Zanuck what they had decided. "You won't believe this, but we're down to Gene Hackman," D'Antoni said. Zanuck grimaced.

Hackman, unaware of any of this, liked the idea of Popeye because, "It seemed like a chance to do all these things I watched Jimmy Cagney do as a kid." But then he realized this was the starring role, which had never before been entrusted to him, and worried that he was in over his head. "On the second day of shooting, I asked the director to replace me because I just didn't feel I could do it. I was popping these guys in the mouth and playing this tough guy, and I'd never played a role quite that demanding. However, after a while if you punch someone enough, you get used to it. So I kind of came around a bit."

The picture's instant success when it was released in 1971 caught Hackman by surprise. "I had no idea it was going to be such a good film when I accepted it," he said. "I didn't think the characters would be as well rounded. It's a brilliantly edited film. The cutting did a great deal to help. I can't take too much credit for my performance."

Instead, his peers provided the credit in the form of an Academy Award in 1971 for the year's best performance by an actor. The second lead, the understanding best pal, the guy least likely to succeed, had finally led the cavalry charge and, to his amazement, won the day. Maybe it was not so unusual after all. Spencer Tracy lurked in his performances, the natural hand on deck, steady at the wheel, stripped of any artifice. There was a size and toughness to his work, qualities a movie star should always carry with him. None of this was what Hackman expected when he looked at a movie screen. "I can't stand looking at that guy up there," he remarked in 1972, a variation on similar statements issued and reissued over the next 20 years. "He's too fat and he talks too slow."

# 12
## "LIKE A FURNACE DOOR OPENING"
### *Brando rising; Brando falling*

"**M**ARLON WAS AS DEAD AS DEAD COULD BE," WAS THE WAY Robert Evans characterized Brando's career in the early 1970s. Twenty years after he had begun to obsess Hollywood with his unorthodox approach to movies and movie stardom, Brando was all but finished as a box-office name. He had rejected role after role that might have redeemed him with a new audience, opting instead to do such increasingly marginal pictures as *Reflections in a Golden Eye*, *The Night of the Following Day*, *Burn!*, and *The Nightcomers*. It was not that Brando was bad in these films. In the case of both *Reflections* and *Burn!*, a maverick brilliance was at work, yet the pictures themselves failed to inspire either audiences or, for the most part, critics. That there was still greatness in him, there was little debate. John Huston certainly could see it when they did *Reflections in a Golden Eye* (1967) together.

Montgomery Clift was supposed to play the part of a homosexual southern major married to Elizabeth Taylor in the adaptation of the Carson McCullers novel. Clift had agreed to work with Huston again despite two previous bruising encounters making *The Misfits* and then *Freud*. But before work could start, Clift was dead in New York at the age of 45, and Huston had to find someone else. He had previously tried to persuade Brando to do *Heaven Knows, Mr. Allison* (1957), but he did not like the script (Robert Mitchum was more easily talked into it). This time Brando was easy, perhaps because he had just had a bad time with Charlie Chaplin making *A Countess from Hong Kong*.

For Huston, Brando was something of a dream come true. "He's an extraordinary, amazing actor," the director said. "He reaches down to some recess that's unexpected and shocking. You feel something smoldering, explosive, like a furnace door opening, with the heat coming off the screen." For all that, Huston believed that Brando had truly come to hate acting — and that, as much as anything, was responsible for his decline.

In his late 40s, Brando was slipping further away from the mainstream of American moviemaking, drifting, largely neglected. Even so, the writer Mario Puzo thought him perfect for the movie that might be produced from the novel he had just completed. Puzo, who had published two previous works of fiction without great success, spent three years fashioning a gangster saga called *The Godfather*. After being rejected by one publisher, *The Godfather* finally was published by G. P. Putnam's Sons in 1969. Paramount Pictures bought the film rights, then became leery about more gangster pictures after the thud created by a Kirk Douglas movie, *The Brotherhood*.

With the movie and paperback rights to *The Godfather* sold, Puzo, in his mid-40s, was suddenly a wealthy man for the first time in his life. One day he picked up the paper and there was comedian Danny Thomas, saying he wanted to play the lead in *The Godfather*. Puzo was shocked. The notion that someone like Thomas might end up playing Don Vito Corleone, the Godfather, propelled him into action. Somehow, he got hold of Marlon Brando's telephone number — a not inconsiderable achievement when major studios lately had been failing to track him down — and talked to the actor on the phone. Brando had not read *The Godfather*, but advised its author that, given his reputation, a major studio like Paramount would never hire him.

Brando was right. Paramount, when it thought about *The Godfather* at all, had visions of someone like George C. Scott or the veteran B-movie actor Richard Conte in the starring role. If the movie was to be filmed, it would be done in modern dress and shot for $2.5 million in St. Louis. Robert Evans, Paramount's executive vice president of production, approached director Peter Yates, who had been successful a couple of years before with *Bullitt*. When he was not interested, Evans turned to Richard Brooks of *In Cold Blood* and Costa-Gavras, who had directed *Z*. Neither one of them wanted to do it.

Peter Bart, a production aid to Evans, suggested a 30-year-old film-maker named Francis Ford Coppola. Evans liked the idea because Coppola was down on his luck, came cheap, and was Italian in a town not renowned for its abundance of Italian filmmakers. That was about all Coppola had going. Briefly, he had been anointed a Hollywood whiz kid, won an Oscar for his screenplay of *Patton*, and directed a nicely offbeat youth comedy, *You're a Big*

*Boy Now*. Graduating to big-budget filmmaking, he had tripped over *Finian's Rainbow*, setting Fred Astaire to dancing with British pop singer Petula Clark toward box-office disaster. Coppola was in danger of being finished before he even properly got started when Peter Bart brought up his name. Word seeped out that Evans was planning to hire Coppola to direct, and various studio executives were on the phone issuing warnings. "Bob," producer Richard Zanuck cautioned, "they're going to throw you off the picture, that guy's *nuts*."

Not that Coppola was fired up with ambition to direct *The Godfather*. Wading through 50 pages, he decided "it was a popular sensational novel, pretty cheap stuff." He said no, and there it stood for five months, until Bart telephoned again. Coppola had started up his own production company, Zoetrope, a few years before, and now it was $300,000 in debt. Coppola put Bart on hold and turned to his friend George Lucas. "What should I do? Should I make this gangster picture or shouldn't I?"

Lucas, forever the pragmatist about these matters, answered: "Francis, we need the money."

Francis Coppola agreed to direct *The Godfather*.

When Coppola met with Puzo to begin reworking the script, they discovered they had a number of things in common, not the least of them a desire to see Marlon Brando play Don Vito Corleone, the Godfather, although Coppola came to that decision much more slowly.

"I must have interviewed two thousand people," Coppola recounted. "We videotaped every old Italian actor in existence. But it became apparent that the role called for an actor of such magnetism, such charisma, just walking into a room had to be an event. We concluded that if an Italian actor had gotten to be seventy years old without becoming famous on his own, he wouldn't have the air of authority we needed."

There was no shortage of prospects. Since the book was by now a huge bestseller, every actor of a certain age was angling for the role of the Don. Coppola's thinking ranged far and wide, from the flamboyant San Francisco lawyer Melvin Belli to Carlo Ponti, the Italian producer and husband of actress Sophia Loren.

"What we had to do was hire the best *actor* in the world," Coppola concluded. "It was that simple. It boiled down to Laurence Olivier or Marlon Brando, who are the greatest actors in the world."

Olivier, according to Evans, was never approached, but Paramount was adamant about one thing: no Marlon Brando in their movie. The head of the studio, Stanley Jaffe, made it clear: "As president of Paramount Pictures, I assure you that Marlon Brando will never appear in this motion picture and, furthermore, as president of the company, I will no longer allow you to discuss it."

Coppola refused to back away from the idea of Brando. If a single brave gesture saved an actor's career, this was it. Puzo was amazed by Coppola. He seemed so jolly and easygoing, yet suddenly he could get tough and draw the line in the sand. Evans intervened with Jaffe on Coppola's behalf: Give Francis five minutes to make his case. Allow him to name names, and argue why those names would work. Jaffe agreed, and Coppola was ushered into the president's office on the Paramount lot.

The shaggy, rotund filmmaker stood in the center of Jaffe's office, a trial lawyer making his case. He carefully outlined the reasons Brando must become the Godfather. Say what you will about him, there was a mystique and aura that clung to Brando that was unique, Coppola argued. That was what was needed in this movie, an actor who "would inspire precisely the right kind of awe that the character of the Don needed." Never one to neglect the right melodramatic touch when it was needed, Coppola, at the conclusion of his speech, pretended to collapse to the floor.

Even in the crisp, cool world through which the corporate reaches of Hollywood move, a bit of grand opera, a little passion can carry the day. Jaffe was persuaded — but not without a price. Coppola and Puzo and Bob Evans and the producer Albert S. Ruddy could have their Brando, but now it was son-of-a-bitch time, so Brando would have to audition, and guarantee with his own money any overruns that his shenanigans might cause.

Brando, the man who had informed the style of a whole generation of actors — *auditioning?* Coppola approached this gingerly, placing a friendly telephone call to the actor. He thought they might meet and explore the role together. An unexpected confession: Brando was not even sure he could do the part, so just as well if they found out one way or the other right away. "Wonderful," Coppola said quickly. "Let's videotape it."

What happened next has spun into casting folklore, right up there with Vivien Leigh introduced to David Selznick as Atlanta burned in the background. Coppola arranged for a photographer as well as actor Salvatore Corsitto, playing the undertaker who appears at the beginning of the film to ask the Godfather for a favor. All of them hurried to Brando's place the next day.

Brando met them at the door dressed in a Japanese kimono, his hair pulled back into a ponytail. Coppola caught on tape Brando's transformation. The furnace door that John Huston talked about was opened, and by all accounts there commenced an awesome journey deep into the heart of Vito Corleone. Brando produced black shoe polish and darkened his hair, added a fake mustache, lastly stuffing tissues into his cheeks. "I want to be like a bulldog," he said.

"It was fantastic," Coppola recalled. For once, studio executives agreed. When Coppola showed them his amazing videotaped screen test the next day, there was no actor in sight. What they saw instead was the man who *was* the Godfather. Brando had the part, and his price was certainly right. He agreed to star in *The Godfather* for only $50,000.[20]

Truly amazing in retrospect is the canniness demonstrated by Brando with the tissues in his mouth and his back up against the wall. He understood intuitively that if his career was to be salvaged, games must be played, the magician must demonstrate the magic. Within him lurked the ability to stop the nonsense when he had to. It was as those Hollywood pundits had so long ago divined: much of him was pose. When the pose required him to behave, he could bring it off brilliantly. But supposing Brando had not done *The Godfather*. Who could have stood in for him? As adamant as the Paramount hierarchy was against him, there does not appear to have been any real alternative. Despite all the jockeying around, no one strong candidate for Vito Corleone other than Brando seems to have emerged.

To his credit, Brando the good did not disappear once filming started. Coppola had all kinds of problems, including the fact that no one thought he could pull this off, and he nearly got himself fired. But whatever the hurdles, for once they were not constructed by Brando. He was the boy scout leader, taking the younger cast members under his wing, breaking up tension on the set with his joking, encouraging fellow thespians to drop their drawers and show off their asses — the mooning of the Godfather. He was even Godfather

---

[20] Despite his paltry salary, Brando did have points in the gross revenues of *The Godfather*. Desperately in need of $100,000, he had to give up some of those participation points in order to get the money out of Paramount. Robert Evans estimated, "That $100,000 cost Brando $11 million."

to Francis himself, threatening to quit the picture if, as Paramount seemed to want, the director was fired. If there was a problem, it was with memorizing dialogue. Brando never did learn his lines, but instead had to read them from cue cards hidden around the set just out of camera range — a small price to pay for his performance.

WARREN BEATTY, JACK NICHOLSON, AND ROBERT REDFORD WERE all considered for the film's other pivotal role, that of the don's youngest son, Michael, the clean-cut, Ivy-League-educated boy who becomes a man when he takes over the family business. Robert Evans was enthusiastic about the French actor Alain Delon. "He was the type," Evans said, "but he couldn't speak English well."

Coppola had seen footage of Al Pacino in his second movie, playing a junkie in *The Panic in Needle Park*. It was an impressive performance. Pacino at the age of 30, less than four years after attending Lee Strasberg's Actors Studio, had become something of a presence on the New York stage. An Obie winner for his performance as a drunken psychotic in the off-Broadway production of *The Indian Wants the Bronx*, the following year Pacino had won a Tony for his portrayal of a drug addict in the Broadway production of *Does a Tiger Wear a Necktie?* Once more the studio was not convinced. Pacino was small and dark, and Michael was supposed to stand out from the rest of the family. Coppola once more was adamant, and once again a screen test was agreed to. This time, however, it was a disaster. Pacino did not know his lines or seem to fathom the character. Puzo was ready to get rid of him and move on to someone else.

"Pacino's a self-destructive bastard," snarled Coppola, then went to work on the actor, testing him all day long, forcing the performance out of him. Still, no one was happy with the result. "Francis," Evans sighed, "I must say you are alone in this." There was talk of postponing the March 1971 start of production until someone else was found. Then Marlon Brando, as much as anyone, saved Al Pacino. "We didn't speak much, but he called me about this," recalled Evans. "He said, 'Listen to me, Bob. He's a brooder. And if he's my son, that's what you need because I'm a brooder.' It was Brando's insight that made me understand why Al would work."

There was one more hurdle. Paramount no sooner announced Pacino's casting in March 1971 than MGM filed a complaint saying the actor already was under contract to perform in another gangster picture, *The Gang That Couldn't Shoot Straight*. For a moment it looked as though Al Pacino might make a gangster picture all right, but it would not be called *The Godfather*. A few days later, the matter was settled out of court, Paramount reportedly agreeing to transfer an unnamed property to MGM, and Pacino himself agreeing to appear in another MGM film. Pacino was being paid only $35,000, and the MGM lawsuit left him broke. "I paid for the lawyers, I paid for everything," he said. "I was broke after that, even in debt. But I didn't care. I've been broke before, but from the beginning, I knew I'd have more money than I'd ever need."

Pacino's intuition was correct. *The Godfather* would make him an overnight star, and although he was upset at being nominated for best supporting actor in a film he so obviously dominated, he was astute enough to realize that "they may have come to see Brando, but I guarantee you it was me they remembered."

With Pacino gone from *Gang*, and production to begin the following month, the producers frantically searched for another Italian-American actor. They found a 27-year-old from New York who had also trained with Lee Strasberg. Thanks to Al Pacino and *The Godfather*, Robert De Niro was cast in *The Gang That Couldn't Shoot Straight*, his first major studio movie.

CARL GOTTLIEB WAS SITTING AT HOME ONE SUNDAY AFTERNOON IN MAY of 1974 when he got a call from his friend Steven Spielberg. Spielberg was 26 years old and had majored not in film, but in English at California State University at Long Beach, because his marks were too bad to get in anywhere else. That had not stopped him from becoming a filmmaker, however, first on television, and more recently with his first feature, *The Sugarland Express*. Spielberg previously had asked Gottlieb for his comments on a script he was going to direct and Gottlieb obliged, sitting down and drafting a memo on what might be done to make *Jaws* a better movie.

Basically, Gottlieb saw the movie as "Moby Dick Meets Enemy of the People" and, among other things, suggested that a cumbersome Mafia subplot be cut. He had not thought much more about it until the call from Spielberg. Could Carl get over to the Bel Air Hotel? When? Right now. "It was like where do you get a screenwriter on a Sunday afternoon?" Gottlieb chuckled years later. He arrived at the Bel Air to find Spielberg huddled with the film's producers, Richard Zanuck and David Brown. *Jaws* was about to start shooting at Martha's Vineyard, and not only was no one particularly happy with the script, only one of the major parts had been cast. Roy Scheider was to play the landlubber police chief who begins to suspect that a great white shark is menacing the New England town of Amity.

Gottlieb huddled with the producers and Spielberg, and they spent the afternoon talking about the script and how it might be improved. Soon Gottlieb, who wrote television series and specials and had never written a produced screenplay, was en route to Martha's Vineyard where in 10 days *Jaws* was to commence production. It turned out to be the movie adventure of a lifetime — a couple of guys sharing a house that overlooked the sea, virtually putting together a movie as they went along. Casting it, too.

When Spielberg became involved with *Jaws*, Universal, the studio that had bought the rights to the book by Peter Benchley, had no particular hopes for the movie. A series of disaster-type movies were being produced, including *Airport 1975*, *Earthquake*, and *The Hindenburg*. *Jaws* was just another disaster picture in the lineup, and the studio thought of Jan-Michael Vincent as the young shark expert and Charlton Heston, who was becoming something of a mainstay in Universal's disaster movies, as Quint, the Ahab-like shark hunter hired to kill the Great White. It was typical by-the-numbers Universal action-movie casting, and Spielberg had no interest in it. So, as *Jaws* moved toward production, there still was no satisfactory cast. Lee Marvin was considered for Quint, but later no one could remember if he was actually offered the part. Joel Grey, Academy Award winner for *Cabaret* a couple of years before, was anxious to play the marine biologist. How close did Grey come to getting it? "Close isn't good enough," snapped David Brown nearly 20 years later. Richard Dreyfuss, who had created a sensation in *American Graffiti*, glanced at an early version of the script, then ignored it. But by the time they arrived on Martha's Vineyard, Spielberg and Gottlieb, both Dreyfuss pals, were convinced they needed him for the movie.

Born in Brooklyn, New York, Dreyfuss had actually been raised in what he jokingly called "the poor section of Beverly Hills." At the age of nine, he appeared in a production at the local Jewish center and after that, he said, "I never got less than the lead." That wasn't quite true. He had played small roles in *Valley of the Dolls* and in *The Graduate* before George Lucas chose him to play Curt Henderson in *American Graffiti*, the role that set him on the road to stardom. Recently, he had starred in *The Apprenticeship of Duddy Kravitz* and was after more challenging things than what he later called "a fish story." By the time Carl Gottlieb got him on the phone, Dreyfuss had already twice turned down *Jaws*. He was on the road promoting *Duddy Kravitz* when Gottlieb reached him. "It's all rewritten, it's all changed," Gottlieb assured the actor. Moreover, he promised that Dreyfuss could collaborate on the creation of his character. The actor agreed to take a shuttle flight to Boston and meet with Spielberg and Gottlieb. "As soon as he walked in the room, he had that beard, those glasses, that hat — the same as the movie — and he *was* the character." When Dreyfuss saw what it was Spielberg and Gottlieb were up to, he decided to come along for the ride.

Gottlieb lobbied for Sterling Hayden as Quint. He had met the actor a couple of times socially while working on Robert Altman's *The Long Goodbye*. Hayden, who lately had acquired a reputation as a fine writer, had run away to sea at the age of 16 and was captain of a schooner by the time he was 22. At Paramount, where he was briefly under contract before going off to World War II, he was dubbed "the most beautiful man in the movies," but the years and hard drinking had reworked the beauty of his face into a craggy, weather-beaten relief map, marked by eyes that glimmered with madness. He was a peculiar customer by any reckoning, and if anyone was born to play Quint, it was surely Sterling Hayden. He probably would have had the role if the U.S. government had not been in the way. Hayden, beset by tax problems, risked losing everything if he returned to the United States as an actor. Better to stay in Paris writing, hunkered over a typewriter on his barge in the River Seine. Writing did not cost him anything; acting did. So there he stayed while David Brown came up with the idea of Robert Shaw.

A British actor with brawny shoulders and piercing eyes, Shaw had been raised in Scotland, trained as an actor at the Royal Academy of Dramatic Art, and made his stage debut in 1949. He was best known in film as the cold-eyed Russian assassin pursuing James Bond in *From Russia with Love* and had been nominated for an Academy Award in 1966 for his performance as Henry VIII in *A Man for All Seasons*. The year before, Zanuck and Brown had discovered the pleasures of Shaw when they cast him as the Irish gangster —

object of the confidence game hosted by Paul Newman and Robert Redford —
in *The Sting*. Shaw had taken the role after Richard Boone[21] refused it. *The
Sting*, along with *Jaws*, would open up a career for Robert Shaw in big-budget
Hollywood movies that required no more than a large presence and a gruff
manner.

Gottlieb found him poetry in the midst of the straightforward prose of
the intense young filmmakers gathered on Martha's Vineyard. "Shaw was a
British actor of the old school," Gottlieb said. "He had a personal servant who
accompanied him. He drank, he lived in a grand style — in fact he supplied all
the grand style that there was to be had on that location."

He also provided the movie with its most powerful dialogue scene.
The creation of the sequence in which Quint describes the torpedoing of the
destroyer *Indianapolis* during World War II and the subsequent mass shark
attack that decimated the survivors is one of the most powerful and chilling
ever put on film, all the more so because it is contained in what otherwise was
supposed to be a run-of-the-mill scare picture. Over the years various people
have taken credit for the scene, including Howard Sackler, who worked on the
original screenplay with author Peter Benchley, and John Milius, who later
contributed dialogue rewrites.

Gottlieb said that Howard Sackler, an avid sailor and diver himself,
remembered the *Indianapolis* incident and added it to a short speech in the
original script. As Spielberg drew close to shooting the scene, it came under
renewed scrutiny, and Gottlieb made a note: What was needed was the sort of
lull-before-the-storm speech always heard from the guys in the trenches prior
to the big battle. Shaw was not happy with the scene as written, so phone calls
were placed to both John Milius and George Lucas, begging for suggestions.
Milius came up with the macho notion of Dreyfuss and Shaw comparing scars
in the first part of the scene. But still the sequence was not to Shaw's liking,
and so finally the actor gathered up all versions, the notes, research material
that had been put together, and went off to have a go at it himself.

The night before the scene was to be shot, he returned to the house
that Gottlieb and Spielberg shared. They had just finished dinner with

---

[21] The former Paladin of television's "Have Gun Will Travel" grumbled that the character was a patsy —
which of course was the whole idea.

Dreyfuss and Verna Fields, the film's editor, as well as her son, Rick, who was Spielberg's assistant. Dessert was on the table when Shaw made his entrance, carrying a single sheet of paper. He announced that he would like to read the scene the way he thought it should be done. With the lights dimmed, the moon over Martha's Vineyard pouring its light through the windows, and the roar of the ocean nearby, Robert Shaw became Quint and remembered the sinking of the *Indianapolis* and the sailors who died in the sea. Everyone was reduced to stunned silence as he finished. That was it. That was the scene, perfectly written. Not a word was changed when Spielberg shot it the next day. In addition to his performance, that scene as it was realized on film became Robert Shaw's enduring contribution to *Jaws*. Fours years later, at 51, he was dead, felled by a heart attack on an Irish roadside.

A S *JAWS* WAS RELEASED IN JUNE OF 1975, ROBERT DE NIRO MOVED from New York to Hollywood to begin work on a new movie. De Niro had begun his film career in 1968 in the low-budget *The Wedding Party*, directed by Brian De Palma, and in 1974 had won an Academy Award for his performance as the young Vito Corleone in *The Godfather, Part II*. Shy, intense, and almost painfully inarticulate, at least when talking to journalists, De Niro was on his way to becoming the most respected actor of the era. He had played a comic thief in *The Gang That Couldn't Shoot Straight*, the role that Al Pacino was supposed to do before Francis Coppola cast him in *The Godfather*. Otherwise, De Niro was known for the intensity of his performances. You did not think of Robert De Niro and think of laughter. Nonetheless, he was in Los Angeles to start work on a Neil Simon comedy, *Bogart Slept Here*, that was to be directed by Mike Nichols.

Simon's script, at one time titled *Gable Slept Here*, was said to be based on Dustin Hoffman's life as a struggling young actor prior to *The Graduate*. Marsha Mason, the actress who was married to Simon, was to co-star. Supposedly, Hoffman had wanted to star but had been turned down because "he was not right for the part." That might have been another way of saying the 38-year-old Hoffman was too old to be playing a struggling young actor.

With De Niro in *Bogart Slept Here*, filming started in September. For two weeks, everything seemed to be fine. Then abruptly, the production was shut down. *Variety* reported that "artistic differences" between De Niro and

Nichols were such that the actor was leaving the cast. Either De Niro was not funny enough — widely believed — or he did not get along with Marsha Mason. Simon promoted the idea that he lacked the requisite humor. "Robert De Niro is a very intense actor," he said. "He doesn't play joy very well." Nichols, in the wake of the huge success of *The Graduate*, had made *Catch-22*, which was not much of a success, either with the public or with critics. It had been followed by two failures, *The Day of the Dolphin* and *The Fortune*. Apparently, Nichols did not want to risk another failure. *Bogart* would not be sleeping anywhere for the forseeable future.

Various names were mentioned as replacements for De Niro, including James Caan and Jack Nicholson, who seemed to be mentioned for everything just then, as well as actor Tony LoBianco, who had a small role in the original production. Dustin Hoffman, previously "not right" for the role, now looked pretty good. But he was committed to doing *Marathon Man* for director John Schlesinger.

When filming resumed in New York the following year, *Bogart Slept Here* had been retitled *The Goodbye Girl*. Marsha Mason was still in the movie, but now her co-star was *Jaws'* Richard Dreyfuss. *The Goodbye Girl* became his second hit that year, following the huge success of *Close Encounters of the Third Kind*. At the age of 29, he became the youngest actor ever to win an Academy Award — for the role Robert De Niro could not find the joy in.[22]

*Jaws* became a phenomenon over the summer of 1975 that grossed over $200 million and changed movies. Carl Gottlieb saw the change at the moment it occurred — at a sneak preview in an Orange County movie theater one evening in May of that year. Standing with Spielberg, he watched while Lew R. Wasserman, the former agent who was now chairman of MCA, and Sid Sheinberg, the president of Universal Studios, decided to play *Jaws* not just in a few hundred movie theaters, but in nearly a thousand. That way the studio could more effectively capitalize on the excitement and maximize revenues more quickly.

---

[22] A couple of years later, Dreyfuss was set to play a TV reporter in *The China Syndrome* opposite Michael Douglas, who was to play his cameraman. When Dreyfuss decided to drop out, Jane Fonda, the movie's producer, stepped in and took the reporter's role. Dreyfuss was also supposed to play the Bob Fosse–like director in *All That Jazz*. When he fled that project at the last moment, Fosse hired Dreyfuss's *Jaws* co-star, Roy Scheider, who was nominated for an Oscar for his performance in the 1979 film.

What happened next was not so much strategy as it was a revolution in the way movies were released. Jaws opened on 20 June 1975 in 450 theaters across North America and within the month had grossed $60 million. By mid-July, it was showing on almost a thousand screens. It would soon become the most successful movie in history in the shortest period of time, with grosses of over $200 million. As the money poured in and records were broken, Hollywood sat up, greedy, seeing the future. That future embraced kids, and funny-looking creatures, and ships whizzing through space. *Jaws*, coupled with the release two years later of *Star Wars*, inflated Hollywood's financial expectations into the stratosphere. As the '70s slipped into the '80s, it was no longer possible merely to make a profit. Movies now would have to break records, amass hundreds of millions of dollars. They would be events, vast profit centers, the success or failure of which would be known, not over the course of several weeks or months, but by the end of the first weekend of release. Everything — risks, profits, losses — was suddenly escalated. Movies were no longer mere product to be moved in and out of theaters, but gigantic rolls of the dice upon which rode the fate of studios, careers, and even, on occasion, the entire industry.

Curiously enough, considering that neither *Jaws* nor *Star Wars* was a star-driven vehicle, all of this had the effect of making the movie star much more important and powerful, not less so. Who could induce the customers to rush out to 1,500 theaters on an opening weekend not only in America but around the world to see a picture that did not feature a mechanical shark or a spaceship? Movie stars.

By the time Francis Coppola realized his long-held ambition of making a movie that reflected the war in Vietnam, it was becoming almost impossible to produce a major American film without a star attached, even if you were the acclaimed director of *The Godfather* and *The Godfather, Part II*, responsible for two of the great financial and artistic success stories of the decade. Francis Coppola's struggle to make *Apocalypse Now* came down, at least in the early going, to a fight for a movie star who would make the enterprise financially viable. The fight involved Steve McQueen, who would miss his final moment of greatness, and Marlon Brando, the man in whose shadow McQueen and his ilk had so long existed. Unlike McQueen, Brando would have his last great film, and at the same time — as he was prone to do — nearly destroy it.

T HE IDEA FOR A MOVIE ABOUT AMERICA'S INVOLVEMENT IN THE WAR IN Vietnam came to Francis Coppola and his friend George Lucas at the height of the conflict in 1969. They saw Joseph Conrad's novel *Heart of Darkness* as the perfect metaphor with which to illuminate the war in Southeast Asia. In Coppola's retelling, a Special Forces officer named Willard is dispatched up the river to assassinate a renegade, Colonel Kurtz, a heroic, highly decorated officer driven to insanity and now running his own private war somewhere in the Cambodian jungle. *Apocalypse Now* was to be produced by Coppola's fledgling production company, Zoetrope, written by John Milius, and directed by George Lucas.

In 1969 the idea had to be dropped because, as Lucas put it, "studios would not finance a film about the war." Following the success of *The Godfather*, however, Coppola had the clout to restart Zoetrope and get *Apocalypse Now* into production. Wanting complete autonomy, Coppola raised most of the projected $14 million budget through pre-sales to United Artists as well as to distributors around the world. Inherent in those pre-sales was the promise of big-name stars to portray Willard and Kurtz. In November of 1975, Coppola called Steve McQueen, his first choice for Willard, the Green Beret sent to kill Kurtz. McQueen had not been in a movie since *The Towering Inferno* a couple of years before. By this time he was divorced from his first wife, Neile, and had married actress Ali MacGraw, his co-star in *The Getaway*. What no one knew, certainly not Coppola, was that McQueen was in the early stages of the fight with cancer that would kill him. McQueen, increasingly obsessed with curing himself, had little interest in work. He liked the script, but Ali MacGraw's son could not leave the country for the 17 weeks Coppola would need McQueen to be on location in the Philippines, and besides, his own son, Chad, was about to graduate from high school, and McQueen wanted to be there.

Coppola next turned to Marlon Brando, for whom he had put his career in jeopardy and challenged an entire studio four years earlier. Now Brando's agent reported that his client was not interested in *Apocalypse*, did not even want to dicuss it.

Coppola tried Al Pacino, for whom he had also put career and reputation on the line so that, post-*Godfather*, he was a major star. Pacino mulled over the script at length. But he had become sick after only a few weeks on location in the Dominican Republic for *The Godfather, Part II*, so how could he ever endure 17 weeks in the jungle?

Coppola approached yet another actor he had enabled to become a star. James Caan, from the Bronx, had begun acting at the Neighborhood Playhouse in New York in 1960. He had played Sonny, Don Corleone's volatile elder son, in *The Godfather*. Over the years, Caan would become minor legend in the industry for the roles he did not do. The hit movies he rejected included *M*A*S*H*, *Love Story*, *One Flew Over the Cuckoo's Nest* (before Milos Forman was attached to it), *Superman*, and *Kramer vs. Kramer*. Caan was willing to play in *Apocalypse Now,* but he wanted $2 million. Coppola offered $1.25 million. "Fuck, all you guys want is money," Coppola said angrily. Caan retorted that Coppola had made $11 million from *The Godfather* while he and the other young actors made only $35,000 apiece. Ultimately, however, Caan would not take the role because his wife was pregnant, and he did not want her having a baby in the Philippines.

Robert Redford liked the script, but he was busy finishing *All the President's Men* and had promised his family he would not soon go away on another long location shoot.

By early 1976, Coppola was looking at unknown actors for Willard. Meanwhile, he again courted McQueen, tempting him this time with the renegade Kurtz. McQueen, pushing for big paydays now that his cancer was spreading, wanted $3 million for three weeks' work. Enraged, Coppola withdrew his offer entirely. Next he tried to persuade Jack Nicholson, who had already turned down Willard, to do Kurtz. Sandy Bressler, Nicholson's agent, said no. Then Coppola was on a plane to New York, trying to talk Pacino into Kurtz. "Trust me," Coppola said to Pacino, "together we can make it great." The prospect of greatness did not sway Pacino; he refused to commit. Back home in northern California, Coppola was so angry that he threw his five Oscars out the window, breaking four of them.

Coppola was getting a firsthand view of what would become the norm for the 1980s — too few big name stars with too much power. "The problem is not really actors like Steve [McQueen] being outrageous and greedy," Coppola said in February of 1976. "It is that the studios are crippling the industry by not developing talent. Actors today are like salmon swimming upstream. If they make it, they are worth a fortune and who can blame them for asking what they can get?" Coppola lamented the absence of a studio system, the stars working in-house and instantly available. Zoetrope would work to change this, he said, by attracting talented actors who could be placed under long-term contracts. He suggested that each studio put $500,000 a year into a fund to give actors the opportunity to do experimental theater and workshops. "But," he concluded with a sigh, "the studios are short-sighted. They want to know what they are going to get this year.

"I would hate to think that at this stage in my career, I need a star to get financing," he continued. "A star functions more as an insurance policy for what might happen if the film is bad, but look at *Jaws* and *Godfather*. They had no stars except for Marlon Brando, and they are the highest grossing films ever." It was a view that would be repeated with increasing wistfulness over the next decade.

Despite Coppola's public protests, no major star would commit to him. Even Clint Eastwood declined, correctly divining that what Coppola estimated to be 17 weeks of production would drag on much longer. After the agony of one overblown Hollywood epic, *Paint Your Wagon*, Eastwood never wanted to get involved in another. Coppola was forced finally to make good on his promise to consider an unknown. He picked Harvey Keitel, and he seemed perfect.

Keitel was from Brooklyn, New York, and unlike anyone else approached, had actually had military experience — a stint in the Marine Corps after he left high school. Moreover, there was an aura of repressed violence about him that had found its most effective expression when Martin Scorsese cast him as Jodie Foster's murderous pimp in *Taxi Driver*. Everyone said Keitel could be a movie star. Now here was his chance. What was more, he would be accompanied to stardom by none other than Marlon Brando. In February 1976, Brando suddenly phoned and said he wanted to meet with Coppola. He would play Kurtz. For each of the three weeks Brando worked, he was to receive $1 million, one of those million payable in advance.

Coppola and his family arrived in the Philippines in March 1976 to prepare for the production of *Apocalypse Now*. Filming began the following month, and everything seemed to be going smoothly. Then on 16 April, Coppola looked at a rough assemblage of footage from the first week of shooting, featuring Keitel as Willard on board the patrol boat as it headed upriver to begin the mission. Afterward Coppola sat with co-producers Fred Roos and Gray Frederickson. "We bit the bullet and did a very, very unpleasant thing, which is replace an actor in mid-shooting," Roos said. A spokesman for Coppola, publicist Dick Guttman, announced that "Francis said he wasn't right for the role." However, Keitel's agent, Harry Ufland, offered a more complicated story that had nothing to do with his ability to play Willard.

According to Ufland, the possibility was raised that *Apocalypse Now* would stop production for the summer to accommodate Brando, who wanted to be with his children. Then shooting would resume again in September. This upset Keitel, because Coppola had promised him shooting would be finished by September so that he could do another movie for which he was already contracted. This made Keitel think twice about the long-term contract Coppola wanted him to sign with Zoetrope. By the time shooting started, there was only a verbal agreement between the two and now, hearing of possible delays, Keitel hesitated to sign anything. Soon thereafter, Ufland received a five-page letter from Zoetrope's attorneys stating that Keitel "had repeatedly refused to fulfill his obligation to execute a written memorialization, therefore Coppola Cinema Seven hereby terminates said employment agreement."

Ufland was the one who had to tell Keitel he was fired. "His reaction was a mixture of shock and fury," Ufland said. "Here he is stuck in the jungle. He said it confirmed his feeling that Francis could not be taken at his word."

Years later, Keitel was still smarting over the incident. "I wanted to make that movie badly," he said. "I'm an ex-marine from before Vietnam. I knew the essence of the part. I knew it from both points of view, from that of a marine and from that of someone who was an actor." However, Keitel said it had been a mistake for him to get involved without having resolved what was being demanded of him in the contract with Coppola. "I discovered afterward that I could not give what was demanded, which was someone saying, 'I will give you the job, then I will control you for the next seven years.' . . . It was painful to leave *Apocalypse Now*. But the price of my freedom would have cost me more."

Coppola tried Jack Nicholson one final time, but a spokesman said it conflicted with a movie titled *Moontrap* that the actor was scheduled for. No such movie was ever made. Coppola was on a plane back to Los Angeles over the Easter weekend to meet at the airport with Martin Sheen, who was flying in from Rome where he had just finished *The Cassandra Crossing*. Sheen, born Ramon Estevez in Dayton, Ohio, broke through as an actor in the 1964 Broadway production of *The Subject Was Roses*, then starred in a highly respected TV movie, *The Execution of Private Slovik*. He was best known for his work as a young drifter on a killing spree in Terrence Malick's *Badlands*, released in 1973.

Coppola and Sheen talked at the airport, and he agreed to play Willard even though, as he later admitted, he was 36 years old, in terrible shape, smoking three packs of cigarettes a day, and worried about his health. An open and warm-hearted man who impressed Coppola's wife Eleanor with his "humanness," Sheen, less than two weeks after that airport meeting with Coppola, found himself in the Philippines portraying a cold-eyed professional killer.

Sixteen weeks later, *Apocalypse Now* had become the great white whale and Coppola its Ahab, restlessly, obsessively pursuing it, running behind schedule and over budget. Even before he arrived, Brando became a problem: if his scenes were delayed, he would not show up at all, and he would keep the $1 million advance. Brando eventually was placated, and arrangements were concluded whereby he would arrive in the Philippines at the beginning of September 1976 — Keitel's concerns about the movie being delayed to accommodate Brando having been realized. By that time Coppola was barely hanging on. "It's like a great war in itself," he said. A war punctuated by a typhoon in May that had destroyed most of the sets and forced the production to shut down, and a major heart attack suffered by Sheen that put him out of commission for five weeks. Compared to Brando's arrival, typhoons and heart attacks were anticlimactic. Those sorts of catastrophes Coppola could handle. It was Brando who almost pushed him over the edge.

The first shock was Brando's size. "He was already heavy when I hired him," Coppola said, "and he promised me he'd get into shape." Just the opposite was the case. Brando was downright fat and extremely self-conscious about it. When Coppola suggested they play up Kurtz's corpulence, Brando refused to go along. With only three weeks in which to shoot his scenes, Coppola now discovered Brando had not read *Heart of Darkness*, did not know his lines, and did not want to shoot anything until there was some discussion of his character's motivation.

In fairness, Coppola had been struggling with the ending to the story for a year and still had not come up with anything that satisfied him. That made him vulnerable to Brando's demand that the script, in effect, be tossed out. The actor in his corpulent greatness would improvise. Thus, Coppola would feed him a line, "What is blood lust?" And Brando on camera would pause and say something like, "They say the human animal is the only one who has blood lust." He began another take, and then grimaced. "I swallowed a bug," he announced. Later, the actor arose, wandered over to a doorway, said something, then declared, "I can't think of any more dialogue today."

While Brando worked his way through this, the crew sat and waited, to the growing horror of everyone, including Fred Roos who knew that unless Brando finished in three weeks, the financial consequences could become horrendous. "Whole days would go by [with nothing happening], and this was at Marlon's urging, and yet he was getting paid for it." Coppola was beside himself. "I'm feeling like an idiot," he groaned, "having set into motion stuff that doesn't make any sense, stuff that doesn't match, and yet I'm doing it. And the reason I'm doing it is out of desperation because I have no rational way to do it." Eleanor Coppola said later that it was during this period that her husband came as close to the edge of insanity as he ever did during the long production of *Apocalypse Now*.

In the finished film, Brando's rambling, improvised dialogue made little more sense than it did on the set, and the great man cast constantly in shadow lends to Kurtz the air of a confused, self-indulgent Buddha seated in darkness, rather than that of a highly dangerous outlaw. The last third of *Apocalypse* is the weakest part of the movie, and yet the film itself is such an achievement, such an incredible monument to a filmmaker's single-minded determination to reach out for greatness, that the Brando intrusion — for that is what it ends up being — is brief enough and ultimately so irrelevant that it is forgivable. After all, Willard was on a journey toward the heart of futility and waste, and here it was slumped in the darkness, mumbling incoherently and looking like Marlon Brando. As a symbol of greatness lost, Brando stood out in the jungle like a ruined, vine-covered temple. If you had followed the churning river of his stardom across three decades of the movie landscape, here was where it ended — badly — at the finish of a great movie, on the edge of a new decade.

# 13

## "IT WAS AS IF WE COMMITTED A CRIME."
### John Travolta and the tough act to follow

I N 1972, AN 18-YEAR-OLD HIGH-SCHOOL DROPOUT FROM ENGLEWOOD, New Jersey, auditioned for a role in a Jack Nicholson film, *The Last Detail*. John Travolta was on the brink of landing the first big role in a career that so far had progressed no further than off-Broadway, commercials, and the national touring company of the hit musical *Grease*. It had come down to him and another actor for the part of the kleptomaniac seaman being escorted to the brig by two tough shore patrol officers. To Travolta's vast disappointment, it was the other actor, Randy Quaid, who was chosen. "They thought I acted the part well," he said, "but that Randy was the part."

Still, having come so close, Travolta attracted the attention of casting director Lynn Stalmaster, and a few years later when TV producer James Komack was looking for students to fill the high-school classroom for a situation comedy called "Welcome Back, Kotter," Stalmaster recommended Travolta. As the dim-witted Vinnie Barbarino, Travolta was supposed to be no more than one of the kids in the class. But by some curious alchemy set into motion when certain faces are in front of a camera, the audience began to take notice of John Travolta. Although the star of the TV series was ostensibly Gabe Kaplan, as was to happen a few years later with Michael J. Fox in "Family Ties," the audience was not interested in what was supposed to be. It just wanted to see John Travolta. Having been launched from the back of a TV classroom, the speed of Travolta's ascent was dizzying. The last star of the 1970s burned brighter and was extinguished with a speed that demonstrated not only the increasing fickleness of the audience but also the severity of the price that was now to be paid for mistakes.

After missing out on *The Last Detail*, Travolta found himself cast in a couple of feature films, *The Devil's Rain* and *Carrie*, as well as a popular television movie, *The Boy in the Plastic Bubble*. From the beginning, there were signs that even as Travolta was catapulted toward superstardom, he was not certain of either himself or the movies he was being offered. Terrence Malick wanted him for a co-starring role in *Days of Heaven*, and initially Travolta agreed to it, "but because of the 'Kotter' schedule I couldn't do it." A week later, Robert Stigwood, the British record and movie mogul, offered him a deal that was, as Travolta himself described it, "mind boggling." Stigwood, ignoring the fact that he had yet even to star in a movie, signed him to a three-picture deal involving more than $1 million.

"I don't think Stigwood would have signed me if he didn't think I was somewhat bankable," Travolta reasoned. "But being perfectly honest, that wasn't the sole reason. The reason stated to me was that he really liked my talent and signed me because he thought I could be a film star. I can only go on what he told me. He auditioned me for *Jesus Christ Superstar* way back when I was seventeen, right? And he showed me what he had written on a yellow pad he had saved from that audition. 'This kid will be a very big star' or something like that."

In his first Stigwood-sponsored starring role, Travolta more than lived up to the promise that was being held out for him. When his companion, actress Diana Hyland, read the script for *Saturday Night Fever*, she knew immediately what was about to happen. "Baby," she said, "you are going to be great in this."

Tony Manero in *Saturday Night Fever* was the role of a lifetime for a young actor. Tony was an uninformed boy/man, choked with uncertain ambition, seeing the future across the Brooklyn Bridge, and discovering release for his passion, frustration, and talent on the dance floor of Brooklyn's 2001 Odyssey discotheque. Tony was full of Latin hustle and charm fitted into a white suit that was to become a combination trademark and object of a thousand parodies, sparkling in the light of a rotating glitter ball, a disco icon to a generation snapping up the movie's Bee Gees soundtrack album as fast as it could be pressed into vinyl.

The movie, released in 1977, might have been a metaphor for the decade to come: Tony staring from the '70s toward the '80s, wanting it all, but not sure how to get it. Suddenly, John Travolta had all the success in the world. Now, what to do with it? He represented something, the disco phenomenon that was disappearing even as the movie made millions (and the Bee Gees soundtrack album millions more — the bestselling album of its time earned four times as much as the movie).

How do you cast a passing fad? For a moment, there was no problem. The Robert Stigwood Organization set about filming *Grease*, the stage musical in which Travolta had perfomed, first on tour and then on Broadway. It was the perfect follow-up vehicle for a freshly minted star, smartly camped up and modernized so that the '70s did not look so far away from the 1950s, the musical's setting. Following as it did on the heels of *Saturday Night Fever*, *Grease* was an extraordinary hit, and John Travolta's stardom seemed confirmed. Never had a single performer enjoyed such huge back-to-back successes. Now Travolta seemed to be at the top of everyone's casting list. He was reason enough to get *The Godfather, Part III* started up. He would star in movie versions of *Hair* and *A Chorus Line*. On and on it went.

But nothing ever came of those movies. Instead, steps were made gingerly away from musicals, toward a very Hollywood kind of romantic fantasy with Travolta as a gigolo who becomes entangled with a bored Malibu woman portrayed by Lily Tomlin. A comedienne whose talent for characterization verged on genius, Tomlin's initial success was with her Ernestine, the telephone operator on television's "Rowan & Martin's Laugh-In." TV opened the way to a movie career and critical acclaim for her portrayal of a gospel singer in *Nashville*, then as a kooky client making life difficult for private eye Art Carney in *The Late Show*. However, Tomlin had never appeared in anything remotely romantic, so suddenly here she was playing the romantic interest of the hottest young star in the movies. It was a notoriously bizarre coupling, not helped by the fact that Tomlin's friend and longtime associate, Jane Wagner, was the movie's first-time director.

The release of the film in 1978 was accompanied by a great deal of snickering and innuendo about the sexual persuasions of the principals, so that before anyone even got a look at it, *Moment by Moment* was considered a bad joke. The movie was panned with extraordinary viciousness, and the audiences who could not wait to see *Saturday Night Fever* or *Grease* stayed away as if in fear for their lives.

Travolta was stunned. "Everyone has a right to say what they think, but I just feel that the criticism after *Moment* became abusive," he said. "It went beyond mere criticism; it was as if we committed a crime." How could he be so popular one moment and the object of such universal ridicule the next? Even as he grappled with that question in December of 1978, he was due to begin work on another film, *American Gigolo*. Once again he was playing a kept man, although this time the character, Julian Kay, was older and much more sophisticated than the hustler of *Moment by Moment*. In pursuit of that sophistication, Travolta took lessons in the art of elegance from Francis Lederer, a Czech-born septuagenarian who had been a matinee idol in Berlin before coming to Hollywood in the 1930s. Twice Travolta flew to Milan where Giorgio Armani personally fitted him for his wardrobe. "It will be hot," promised director-screenwriter Paul Schrader. "It will generate a lot of sexual heat."

But something was wrong. Travolta, as he went through the motions preparing for the start of *American Gigolo*, was increasingly troubled by a number of things: the gnawing failure of *Moment by Moment*; the death of his girlfriend, Diana Hyland, and of his mother; his father's heart attack. It was during this period that Travolta embraced the philosophy of Scientology, which may have further fueled his doubts about *American Gigolo*. Also, it could not have escaped his notice that he was about to play another hustler, the same kind of character that got him into so much trouble in *Moment by Moment*. "When I first read the script I thought that I would do it," he later said. "I was attracted to the flashiness of the part, on the surface it looked very good. But then I read it again and I decided that I just couldn't see what they were trying to say."

On 24 January 1979, *Variety* announced: "John Travolta has exited Paul Schrader's *American Gigolo* for Paramount, in which he was set to play a Los Angeles hustler being framed for murder." The paper pointed out that this was the third time within the past year that a major star had dropped out of a film at the last moment. George Segal had left *10*, a Blake Edwards comedy, and was replaced by Dudley Moore, a move that virtually put an end to Segal's career as an easygoing leading man in lightweight comedies. But *10* enabled Moore, a British comedian little known until then in North America, to become one of the busiest comedy movie stars of the early 1980s. And Richard Dreyfuss had decided he wanted no part of Bob Fosse's *All That Jazz* and was replaced by Roy Scheider. Dreyfuss's career was not hurt by the decision, but it did allow Scheider, in the role of a tortured

Broadway director (modeled on Fosse himself), to show a side of himself he had not been allowed to demonstrate in previous adventure roles. His display of versatility was duly rewarded with an Academy Award nomination.

J ERRY BRUCKHEIMER, THE PRODUCER OF *AMERICAN GIGOLO*, DISCOVERED on a Friday night that he no longer had a star. With only a month to go before production, and with thousands of dollars already spent on a wardrobe specifically designed for one actor, there was a certain amount of panic over what to do next. Paramount considered dropping the picture altogether, except that the studio had received enormous advances from distributors all over the world on the strength of Travolta's name.

Bruckheimer convened a meeting to discuss who might replace Travolta. The only name that caused any excitement was that of Christopher Reeve, a 26-year-old New York actor who had starred in a lavishly mounted version of *Superman* that had been a tremendous international success the year before. Reeve had been chosen after a much hyped search for the Man of Steel, conducted by father-and-son wheeler-dealers Alexander and Ilya Salkind.

In 1975, their intention was to cast a major star as Superman, and that search kept gossip columnists occupied for months speculating over such names as Paul Newman, Clint Eastwood, Dustin Hoffman, and Al Pacino. Never mind how either Hoffman or Pacino would have looked in blue tights, not to mention Eastwood. The Salkinds managed to attach just about every box-office star of the day to *Superman*. Robert Redford said it would take too much time out of his life, even though he was offered $2 million. James Caan, who was avidly wooed by the producers, eventually said no, claiming he did not like the Salkinds' idea of shooting a sequel at the same time as the original. Burt Reynolds was unsuccessfully pursued, as were Nick Nolte and Sylvester Stallone (the producers claimed to have passed on Sly because he did not have "the right kind of look for Superman, that kind of All-American, apple pie-and-Clark-Kent-look"). Unsuccessful with major stars, except for Gene Hackman and, of all people, Marlon Brando, who agreed to play, respectively, the villainous Lex Luthor and Superman's dad, the Salkinds took a new tack.

"If we had cast a well-known star, as he soared over the city of Metropolis," now reasoned Ilya Salkind, "you would never have been able to forget his star personality. It would have been the star up there, not Superman."

With that logic in hand, the role fell to Reeve, who had made only one other picture, *Gray Lady Down* (1978). Six months was then spent getting Reeve pumped up and into shape so as to fit properly into Superman's tights. The search and the work had proved to be worth the time. Reeve made an unexpectedly charming and charismatic Man of Steel. Now the demand for him was such that Paramount thought he was the other young star name who could save *American Gigolo*. "Unfortunately," said Bruckheimer, "he turned us down."

Paul Schrader later said he had wanted Richard Gere for *American Gigolo* all along, and that it was the studio that insisted upon Travolta. Gere was 29 years old, from Philadelphia, and he had already inherited one Travolta reject, a role in Terrence Malick's *Days of Heaven*. But that movie had not been a success, and neither were other Gere vehicles, *Bloodbrothers* and *Yanks*. Still, there was a great deal of excitement surrounding him. His appeal was both androgynous and dangerous. Being attracted to Gere was like being drawn into dark and uncharted territory.

"Paul and I always liked Richard Gere enormously," Bruckheimer recalled. "We sent Ed Limato, his agent, the script. Ed read it right away, as did Richard. Ed called me, and he said, 'Look, I want to meet with you. I want Richard to meet you guys, and we want to do this picture.' Now nobody knew this but us. Paramount had already told us that they weren't going to make the picture with anybody but Reeve."

Bruckheimer met with Gere, and by Sunday night, the actor had committed to do *American Gigolo*. Now Bruckheimer was faced with selling this to the studio. On Monday morning he walked into Don Simpson's office, and said, "Richard Gere just committed to the movie." Simpson looked at him in astonishment. "What?" he exclaimed. "You can't have Richard Gere committed to the movie! How am I gonna sell this to my bosses?"

But Simpson prided himself on his ability to bring a street savvy con man's finesse to his job. He marched into the office of Michael Eisner, who was then president of Paramount. Money, it turned out, was more persuasive than anything. With Gere, Simpson argued, cost of the $11 million picture could be considerably reduced. This made sense to Eisner. At a subsequent meeting that included Schrader, he turned to Bruckheimer and asked, "Jerry, can you make this picture for $5 million?" Bruckheimer agreed that it could be done; after all, they were paying Gere only $350,000, considerably less than

Travolta's fee. "You didn't have a lot of the entourage John had at the time," Bruckheimer said. "You were paying higher fees to the costume designers, make-up, hair, on and on. Everybody was top of the line. We got Richard and things got more cost effective."

They also got a movie star. Within the conservative milieu in which most American filmmaking existed, *Gigolo* was considered edgy and erotic, showing off the new young hunk in town. The moment Richard Gere appeared on the screen as Julian Kay, lingering thoughts of John Travolta were erased. Schrader and the movie's producer, Freddie Fields, soon dropped a suit claiming Paramount had failed to live up to its promise to deliver Travolta. The suit appeared to reflect suspicions on the part of the producer and director that the studio shifted Travolta out of *Gigolo* and into its upcoming production of *Urban Cowboy*. There was nothing in the recollections of either Bruckheimer or Simpson to suggest that was the case, and the suit became academic in the face of *Gigolo*'s success. Travolta's absence did not precipitate a failure. Instead, it might have contributed to a hit.

Travolta attempted a comeback with *Urban Cowboy*, a movie that essentially attempted to revamp *Saturday Night Fever*, so that this time a young oil worker finds his identity via an urban cowboy lifestyle, complete with mechanical bulls, line dancing, and pretty girls (in this case country girl Debra Winger and city slicker Madolyn Smith). Travolta announced himself to be much more pleased with his new movie than he ever would have been with *American Gigolo*. *Urban Cowboy*, released in 1980, did business but was certainly not a hit of *Saturday Night Fever* or *Grease* proportions. Already the audience seemed to be tiring of him, as though he were outdated, part of another decade. Then Travolta passed over his chance to slip smartly into the '80s by yet again pulling out of a hit movie at the last moment.

Director Taylor Hackford was after him to play a maverick naval officer trainee in a romantic melodrama titled *An Officer and a Gentleman*, about a tough young punk, Zack Mayo, whose life is turned around at Naval Officer Candidate School. Paramount was anxious for him to be in the movie, and so were his managers. Once again, Travolta vacillated, as time grew short. *An Officer and a Gentleman* had to go into production in advance of a threatened Screen Actors Guild strike. Finally, Hackford got a call from Travolta. He could hear the sound of planes taking off and landing in the background and asked him where he was calling from. Travolta said he was at an air base learning to fly a jet plane. It was part of a survivalist training course he had undertaken in order to protect himself in the event of a nuclear war. He added that he had decided not to do *An Officer and a Gentleman*, having concluded that it glorified war. With the sound of jet engines ringing in his ears, Hackford hung up the phone, shaking his head.[23]

For the third time in two years, Travolta had passed on a major starring role. Twice before, with *Days of Heaven* and *American Gigolo*, he had been replaced by Richard Gere. Now, for a third time, Gere became Hackford's choice for the lead in *An Officer and a Gentleman*. Debra Winger, who co-starred as the party girl desperately searching for a naval officer she could marry, later said the production was one of the worst experiences of her life. Gere said it was the only movie he did just for the money, but in rather telling contrast to Winger, he added that it turned into "certainly one of the two or three best experiences in my life."

The movie that might have given Travolta's career new life instead demonstrated to Hollywood that Richard Gere was a heartthrob capable of generating a $100-million hit. In turn, Travolta was all but finished as any kind of box-office threat. He had staggered from movie to movie in the '80s, but the heat he had generated was gone; the comet that had soared so dramatically and briefly at the end of the 1970s now fell to earth, and he became the last thing any movie star cares to be — ordinary.

Travolta allowed himself to be talked into a lamentable sequel to *Saturday Night Fever* titled *Staying Alive*. It was a bizarre movie, sort of "Rocky Goes to Broadway," directed by Rocky himself, Sylvester Stallone, not a filmmaker exactly renowned for his handling of musical drama. However mismatched Stallone and Travolta were in filming *Staying Alive*, they turned out to have more in common than they might have thought. They had both encountered a character named John Rambo, and because Travolta, as usual, rejected him, Sylvester Stallone was able to have the movie career in the 1980s that John Travolta so carelessly tossed away.

---

[23] Scott Glenn turned down the part of the drill instructor. It went instead to Lou Gossett, Jr., who won an Academy Award for best supporting actor.

# PART III

The Power Players

# 14
## RAMBO MEETS THE BEVERLY HILLS COP
### *Stallone and Murphy and the movie stardom of the '80s*

A T THE AGE OF 28, JOAN SINGLETON WAS A SECRETARY AT WARNER Bros., but like everyone else in Hollywood, she longed to make movies. Her mother was an actress, her father a producer, and her aunt was the actress Joan Caulfield. Singleton had taken the job at Warner Bros. working for Jack Freedman, head of business affairs in charge of acquisitions, in order to get her foot in the door of the movie business. She was young, smart, ambitious, and she thought anything was possible.

One day she came across a script that had been lying around the studio for some time. It was by a writer named Michael Kozoll, from a novel called *First Blood*, by David Morrell. By that time Singleton had read a lot of scripts, none of them very good as far as she was concerned. When she finished reading *First Blood*, she decided this was far and away the best thing she had seen.

The story concerned a Vietnam veteran named John Rambo who goes to a small town to look up an old army buddy. He discovers the friend is dead, but before he can leave town, he is harassed by the local sheriff, a man named Teasle, because he is a stranger, and because he has a beard and his hair is long. What the authorities do not know is that Rambo is a trained killer, tortured repeatedly by the North Vietnamese, a human time bomb that explodes when he escapes into the wilderness, eluding authorities by using methods he learned in Vietnam. Despite the intervention of his old friend and mentor, Colonel Trautman, Rambo is a killing machine out of control.

Singleton took the script to her boss, who dismissed her enthusiasm. "You don't know anything about scripts," she later recalled Freedman saying. "This will never be a movie." Freedman said *First Blood* had been sent over to the TV department where it was being considered for the actor David Soul.

Singleton was stung by the criticism, but undaunted. To her, the *First*

*Blood* screenplay conformed to all the rules of what constituted a viable property in the Hollywood emerging out of the 1970s and into the 1980s. There were three sharply defined acts, characters with whom the audience could easily identify, and most important, a strong central character thrown against the Establishment: "David against Goliath," as Singleton saw it — a perfect star vehicle in an industry that was increasingly nervous and therefore reliant on the perceived box-office power of movie stars to attract audiences.

Singleton was not alone in her conclusion. As she would discover, *First Blood* had a long and truly amazing history. What now languished on a shelf at Warner Bros., all but forgotten, had been through some of the most important, powerful, and influential hands in Hollywood. Everyone was convinced it would make a terrific movie, but no one was quite prepared to make it.

The eventual success of *First Blood* saved the career of a failing movie star who was not only savvy enough to take on the part after some of the biggest names in the business had let it slip through their fingers, but also knew intuitively how to mold it into something that not only fit his persona, but also the needs of the culture of the day, thereby creating one of the most popular characters in modern movies. It is doubtful that any of this would have happened if Joan Singleton, then known as Joan Ross, had not come across the script sitting in her office. Without her, the history of the movies throughout the 1980s would have been much different.

John Calley, then head of production, had first brought the book to Warner Bros., having bought the project from Columbia for $125,000. It was Lawrence Turman, producer of *The Graduate*, who had brought the book to the attention of Columbia, which then purchased the rights from author Morrell in 1972, the same year the book was published. Ironically, the creator of one of the most famous Americans was actually a Canadian, born in Kitchener, Ontario. At the time, David Morrell was working as an assistant professor at the University of Iowa and supporting his family on an income of $1,000 a month. The $90,000 Columbia paid for *First Blood* was a godsend. Certainly the novel itself had earned nowhere near that kind of money.

Morrell had drawn his hero's name from Arthur Rimbaud, the 19th-century French poet. Inspiration for the story came from the images that drenched television screens in the late 1960s: fire fights in Vietnam and scenes of National Guardsmen quelling riots on U.S. streets. "I thought, what if I wrote a novel about bringing Vietnam to America? What if I showed what the war would be like if it happened in this country?"

Once *First Blood* was in Columbia's hands, the veteran Richard Brooks became the first of many directors to have a crack at it. Brooks, the director of such movies as *Blackboard Jungle* and *The Professionals*, thought it a good adventure story, the kind of film he did well. He worried most about the sheriff who hassles Rambo, saying that he had personally traveled to half a dozen different states and talked to various law enforcement officers, all of whom had beards exactly like the one Morrell described Rambo as having. Why would they bother someone who looked just like them? Nevertheless, Brooks wrote a script of 115 pages, but with the war in Vietnam still in progress, Columbia was not in a mood to make *First Blood*, no matter what the sheriff looked like. Brooks dropped the project and went on to make *Bite the Bullet* and *Looking for Mr. Goodbar*.

So the project came to Warner Bros., where John Calley immediately thought of Robert De Niro for John Rambo. He also gave the script to Clint Eastwood, at the time the world's number one action star. Eastwood had a look at everything on the Warner lot, but apparently was uninspired by *First Blood*. By now, Calley had a director, Martin Ritt, well known for the seriousness of his pictures; he was not a man for the making of mindless adventure movies. Sure enough, Ritt viewed *First Blood* as a comment on the mentality of the military. The army and what it stood for had produced John Rambo, and Ritt wanted to reflect that in the story. He worked with screenwriter Walter Newman on three drafts of the script, and then gave it to Paul Newman. Ritt and Newman had made a series of highly successful, socially conscious films together, including *The Long, Hot Summer; Hud;* and *Hombre.*

But Newman did not seem particularly interested, and Ritt's attention soon drifted. It went next to Steve McQueen via director Sydney Pollack. He thought the movie would be a way of coming in the back door at the Vietnam War, a subject that otherwise still scared Hollywood. Pollack's interest was brief, however. He gave up the project for no other reason than that he could not see spending two years of his life on it. McQueen's interest faded along with Pollack's.

In 1975, *First Blood* fell into the hands of Al Pacino, thanks to the producer Martin Bregman. They had worked together on two previous movies,

*Serpico* and *Dog Day Afternoon*. Bregman hired playwright David Rabe to write a screenplay. Rabe had already written a controversial Vietnam play, *The Basic Training of Pavlo Hummel*, and Pacino had starred in it. The Rabe version of *First Blood*, as might be expected from the writer of not only *Pavlo Hummel* but also *Sticks and Bones* and *Streamers*, was a grim, dark journey. His Rambo was "more of a madman. He was pretty far gone. . . . People would have understood the character but they wouldn't have had empathy for him. There is a kind of violence that excites an audience and makes them feel that it's a lot of fun. Mine was not."

Rabe worked on the screenplay for six months, consulting often with Pacino. But when the actor saw the finished script, he thought it too extreme, and passed. John Calley still had hopes for it, though. In the next couple of years, director Mike Nichols was interested, and so was producer Ray Stark, and again, briefly, Martin Ritt.

Then it was John Travolta's turn to be considered for Rambo. Not for long, though. Among the small platoon of stars whose fingerprints could be found on various *Rambo* scripts, his were the most unlikely. But in the first heat of Travolta's brief stardom emanating from the explosion caused by *Saturday Night Fever*, he was offered everything imaginable — even a psychopathic Vietnam veteran crawling around the bush with a bandana tied around his head. By now it was 1977, and producer William Sackheim had worked on yet another version of the screenplay, this one by Michael Kozoll. It was the Kozoll-Sackheim script that would become the basis for the eventual movie — the script that Joan Singleton found at Warner Bros.

B Y THE TIME SINGLETON BROUGHT *FIRST BLOOD* TO THE ATTENTION OF her boss, Jack Freedman, the project once again had fallen into limbo. There is little reason to believe it would not have stayed there were it not for Singleton's eagerness. Foolishly, given the odds of accomplishing such things, she wondered if it might be possible to get hold of the rights. She was a lowly secretary, totally inexperienced in the film business. What chance did she have in the wake of the failure of so many high-powered producers, directors, and stars to get the project off the ground? Still, she could not shake it off. This was *good*. It could make a real movie. She took the script to Alex Schaefe, an actor who was also interested in getting into production. He liked it immensely. They decided to see if it was not possible to put the movie together. They turned to Larry Sugar, the founder of the American Film Market and a whiz at international sales. He in turn brought in an agent named Peter Sabiston.

It was decided to make the studio an offer that it would hopefully find difficult to refuse: $25,000 for a three-month option. It was chutzpah of the most delirious kind. Singleton was earning $400 a week. She had nothing like $25,000, and neither did any of her cohorts. They made up with audaciousness what they lacked in money: the studio was given the weekend to reply to the offer. On Monday morning, Warner Bros. came back: the offer was accepted. Singleton was stunned. Now what? Peter Sabiston, the agent, knew a producer named Carter De Haven. He agreed to get involved in the project, and now each of the participants anted up $6,400 toward the option. De Haven sewed up the director John Frankenheimer, known for such masterful political thrillers as *The Manchurian Candidate* and *Seven Days in May*.

Various actors were considered for the role of John Rambo. Frankenheimer spoke to Powers Boothe and Michael Douglas, and De Haven sent the material to Nick Nolte's agent. Steve Railsback, who had played Charles Manson in a TV movie, was also discussed, as was Sylvester Stallone, best known as Rocky. Stallone was dismissed fairly quickly. He was not considered box-office. Besides, "Stallone looked like a muscle guy," Joan Singleton said. "The character of Rambo was a thinker; the character in *Rocky* comes off as brawn, not brains."

An actor named Brad Davis was settled upon. At the time, he was riding high on the 1978 success of *Midnight Express*, the true story of a young man imprisoned in a Turkish jail for drug smuggling. Davis was the right age for the part, and he had the right physical qualities. At the same time, there was something pleasingly vulnerable about him (sadly, he would later become best known as an actor who died of AIDS). Davis, like everyone else, was fascinated by the material.

Now the project began to heat up. A budget of $12 million was settled upon, with $6 million to be provided by a company called Cinema Group. Paramount was interested in releasing the movie, but then the industry was hit with an actors' strike, and no decisions were being made. However, the option on *First Blood* was running out and more money was desperately needed. Cinema Group came up with the funds, and quite suddenly everyone was housed at the Samuel Goldwyn studios. Singleton even had her name on a parking spot. It all seemed so easy. She was associate producer on the project, although De Haven did not want her going on the location scout in Georgia where Frankenheimer was to shoot the movie because she was a woman. In fact, it increasingly seemed De Haven was not interested in either Singleton or Alex Schaefe.

The problems began to multiply. With the strike still on, De Haven and Frankenheimer became restless and began to look around for other pro-jects. Singleton's marriage was falling apart. Then Cinema Group announced that it wanted out. Investors from Chicago were coming in to replace them. More troublesome was the fact that the option once again was due. By now, it was Christmas of 1981, and Singleton was frantically looking for an extension. She telephoned her old boss, Jack Freedman, who was skiing in Sun Valley. He told her not to worry, that Warner Bros. could wait for the money until after the holidays.

But on phoning someone she knew at the Warner Bros. business affairs office, she was told that the rights had been sold two days before. They had gone to a pair of young producers named Andrew Vajna and Mario Kassar, who had recently put together a company called Carolco and were looking for their first project. Singleton knew that Vajna and Jack Freedman were friends and that Carolco previously had shown some interest in *First Blood*. But until now, the company had been unwilling to put up any money. At the moment when it looked as though someone else was about to make the movie, Carolco had found the opening and taken it. Singleton suspected that Jack Freedman, who had originally dismissed any suggestion that the *First Blood* script was viable, had tipped off Vajna and Kassar that the option had run out and the rights were momentarily available.

She was shattered. They had come so far, and now suddenly it was all over. They had failed. There was just one small piece of driftwood to cling to: the Michael Kozoll script was still theirs. If Carolco wanted that script, then it would have to deal with Singleton and her group.

Unfortunately, they had given the right of final decision about such matters to Carter De Haven. He did not have to consult with anyone in order to sell the script. He let the rights go to Vajna and Kassar for $50,000. After all her work, Singleton's share of a movie that would go on to gross hundreds of millions of dollars worldwide was $2,500.

FROM THE OUTSET, VAJNA AND KASSAR SAID THEY HAD SYLVESTER Stallone in mind to play Rambo. "He was the number one choice, because in a way this was a kind of *Rocky* movie," Vajna said. The two producers saw Rambo neither as a thinker, the way Joan Singleton saw him, nor as a psychopathic madman running around killing people — as he had been portrayed in most of the scripts — but as the underdog, a man fighting to survive.

And there were parallels between what happened to Rambo and what was happening to Stallone. He, too, viewed himself as an underdog — a man fighting to survive in a town that neither liked nor understood him. His personal life was a shambles, his career was shaky at best. Stallone needed something to rejuvenate him at the box office. But what? The public, it seemed, wanted only to see him in *Rocky* movies.

Stallone had already been the subject of one of the great modern-day Cinderella-in-Hollywood stories. He was born in 1946 and grew up in New York's Hell's Kitchen, the son of a Sicilian immigrant. His parents worked hard to escape the city, and when Sylvester was five years old, Frank and Jacqueline Stallone moved to Silver Spring, Maryland, where they opened a beauty salon. When the marriage broke up, Stallone went to live with his mother and her new husband in Philadelphia. His childhood was not particularly happy. An accident at birth had left the motor nerves on the left side of his face immobilized, so that his mouth hung slack to the right and caused him to slur. At school he was teased a lot and called slantmouth by the other children.

By the time he was 16, Stallone was getting himself into enough minor trouble that he was sent to the Devereux-Manor Hall High School, an institution for kids with learning and behavioral problems. Around this time, he discovered bodybuilding, thanks to his mother, who had opened a gym called Barbella's. Stallone later claimed his mother could bench-press 170 pounds. He was impressed by Marlon Brando's appearance in *On the Waterfront*, but what intrigued him even more was a bodybuilder named Steve Reeves who had starred in the low-budget Italian epic *Hercules Unchained*. The combination of Brando's style and Reeves' larger-than-life physique would greatly influence Stallone.

While on an athletic scholarship at the American College in Switzerland, he got his first taste of acting, playing Biff in a college production of *Death of a Salesman*. When he returned to the United States, he enrolled as a drama student at the University of Miami. By 1969, Stallone was in New York trying to get noticed. He spent five years working at menial jobs — among them cleaning the lions' cages at the Bronx zoo — and failing as an actor. His only film experience had been in a porno movie titled *Party at Kitty and Studs* until he landed a part in *The Lords of Flatbush* (1974), a low-budget movie filmed in New York. After that Stallone, his wife Sasha, and their bull mastiff Butkus headed for California in a 10-year-old Oldsmobile he had purchased for $40. If he was going to starve, he concluded, at least he would go out with a suntan. He had some success with small parts in movies such as *Bananas*, *Capone*, *Death Race 2000*, *The Prisoner of Second Avenue*, and *Farewell, My Lovely*. Then the phone stopped ringing, and he was out of work for nine months.

The way Stallone would describe it later, he decided to spend what little money he had left on some entertainment: They were showing a closed-circuit heavyweight fight between the then reigning champion, Muhammad Ali, and an unknown challenger named Chuck Wepner at the Wiltern theater on the corner of Western Ave. and Wilshire Blvd. What impressed Stallone about the fight was the fact that Wepner, who was supposed to collapse quickly, showed tremendous spirit and unexpected resilience. When Ali tripped and momentarily fell, the crowd went wild. Everyone was suddenly rooting for the underdog. Ali managed to win the fight on a TKO in the last round, but, in a sense, the real winner was Chuck Wepner because he went the distance. He was better than anyone thought he could be.

The fight provided Stallone with the inspiration he needed. There was a story here, incredible drama. In little more than three months in 1975, while various producers and directors were trying to launch *First Blood*, Sylvester Stallone wrote a first-draft screenplay about a failed Philadelphia boxer who has never lived up to anyone's slightest expectations of him. By chance, the boxer is given a shot at a title fight, and despite overwhelming odds and the ridicule of everyone, he is determined to get himself in shape and give the arrogant Ali-like boxing champ some real competition. The script was titled simply *Rocky*.

Stallone's agent, Herb Nanas, shopped *Rocky* around for a couple of months, and finally in August that year, United Artists offered to pay $75,000 for it. Then Stallone did something amazing: he said no. He had decided that only one person in the world could play Rocky Balboa — himself. United Artists offered $100,000 and then $200,000. Finally the offer stood at $315,000. There were promises that a major star would play Rocky. The names of James Caan, Paul Newman, Ryan O'Neal, Robert Redford, Al Pacino, Burt Reynolds, and Gene Hackman were mentioned. But Stallone stood his ground. He was determined to play Rocky.

Finally, to the amazement of both Stallone and his agent, United Artists caved in: the actor could star in his own creation. No major director was interested, and so John G. Avildsen — best known as the director of a low-budget independent film called *Joe* — was hired. There were no expectations whatsoever for the movie, and that made what happened all the more magical. When Stallone saw the daily rushes, he predicted the movie would earn $20 million. By the time he saw it all put together, he upped the ante, predicting that it would gross over $100 million. The producers laughed at his arrogance. If the movie made *that* much, they would buy him any car he wanted.

The car Sylvester Stallone got was a Mercedes-Benz 450 SEL, Hollywood's status symbol of choice. Stallone also got overnight stardom, and *Rocky* itself received three Academy Awards including one for best picture of 1976. For his labors, Stallone ended up being paid the Writers Guild minimum of $20,000, and even though he was the star of the picture, he was paid only the Screen Actors Guild scale. But he had managed to secure 10 percent of the net profits of *Rocky*. They were a while in coming, but eventually a check for $1 million arrived in the mail. The year before he made *Rocky*, Stallone had earned a total of $1,400. Now he had the satisfaction of becoming a millionaire in a single day.

If Stallone knew from the beginning that *Rocky* would be a hit, he also suspected that he would have trouble repeating its success. What he did not understand was how far he was capable of falling. "I'll just make small winners, because I really don't think I'll ever make a bomb," he said confidently. "As long as I can remain in some sort of creative control of my films, that will *never* happen."

His first post-*Rocky* movie, *F.I.S.T.*, in which he played a Jimmy Hoffa–type labor organizer, was slammed by the critics, as was his next movie,

*Paradise Alley*, which he also directed. While those movies were not outright failures, they were not hits, either. The suspicion began to grow that perhaps Stallone was a one-hit wonder. He had Rocky Balboa in him and nothing more.

By the time producers Kassar and Vajna thought of him for Rambo, Stallone's career was in trouble. He had made two *Rocky* movies, each more successful than the last. But his other films usually turned out to be the bombs he had claimed he could avoid. He was a victim of his own stardom, breaking up his marriage, running around after tall blonde starlets, then patching the marriage back together again. In the process, there was a lot of attention in the tabloid press and a growing reputation for being egotistical, difficult, and arrogant. It was not a good time.

S TALLONE HAD HEARD VAGUELY OF THE *FIRST BLOOD* PROJECT BUT HAD not thought of it for himself. Then Vajna and Kassar got in touch. He immediately recognized Rambo's possibilities, but the nature of the material gave him second thoughts. "The original Rambo was so bloodthirsty. . . . the story was so hard, so terrifying every step of the way," he said. Still, there was something about the character with which Stallone instinctively empathized. He could understand the guy, and what he could not understand, he could change. Rambo became more universal as he became more like Sylvester Stallone.

"He gave us the character," said Buzz Feitshans, who eventually produced two of the *Rambo* movies. "It's like the Rocky character. Rocky is a definite person. I'll wager that you could get the best writer in Hollywood and sit him down and say, 'Here, write *Rocky VI*' and he couldn't come up with Rocky. It's the same with Rambo. Stallone knows him."

Stallone changed the focus of the screenplay so that the story mostly unfolded from Rambo's point of view. He also began cutting dialogue. Rambo became a man of fewer and fewer words. In one draft, Stallone went so far as to give him no dialogue at all. "What I did with Rambo was to try to keep one foot in the Establishment, and one foot in the outlaw or frontier image," he said. "I wanted him to be accepted by the mainstream — but to also be a criminal."

In addition, Stallone imbued Rambo with something no one else thus far had given him — a strong sense of patriotism. This was the beginning of the Reagan era. The terrible memories of Vietnam that haunted the American psyche for so long and effectively scared Hollywood off the subject were fading in the carefully orchestrated glare emanating from the new morning in America. Pride was renewed, the American flag once again was waved. Rambo and patriotism, whether Stallone really understood it or not, were meeting one another at precisely the right moment. In Stallone's hands, Rambo now possessed a nobility of spirit; like Rocky he might lose, but he would never give up. He was a fallen hero — but he was a hero.

Between July and November of 1981, Stallone worked on no less than seven versions of the script. At one point he even changed the title so that it was called *Once a Hero*. Still, the filmmakers were uneasy. When Canadian director Ted Kotcheff, who had never before done an action movie, was hired, he brought in Larry Gross, who had worked with action director Walter Hill on the script for *48 HRS*. Gross was followed by David Giler, who also worked a good deal with Hill and had been one of the writers of *Alien*. Even so, Stallone continued to rewrite all through the movie's difficult production on location near Vancouver. Mostly, the focus was on the ending, which had posed a problem for just about everyone. In the book, Morrell made sure Rambo was dead at the end. And in many of the scripts written over the years, he also ended up dead. When the script fell into Joan Singleton's hands, it was decided Rambo should live, and that view essentially held, even though Larry Gross, working on revisions in a Vancouver hotel room, argued for Rambo's demise.

Such was the uncertainty over what to do that two endings were shot. In one, Rambo's mentor Trautman[24] confronts him. Rambo pulls Trautman's gun to his chest and it goes off. In the second ending, Rambo breaks down, makes a long, agonized speech about the mistreatment of Vietnam veterans, and then he and Trautman walk out of a demolished police station together so that Rambo can surrender himself to the very Establishment he has fought so hard to defeat.

Both endings were test screened. Amazingly, the audience was split 50–50, half wanting John Rambo to live, half wanting him to die. In tried and true Hollywood fashion, living — and what passed in *First Blood* for a happy

---

[24] George C. Scott and Burt Lancaster were thought of for Trautman. Kirk Douglas was actually signed for the part, but left after a dispute during production. He was replaced by Richard Crenna. The role of Teasle, the local sheriff who goes after Rambo, might have been played by Lancaster or Lee Marvin, Gene Hackman, Robert Mitchum, or Charles During. It eventually went to Brian Dennehy.

ending — won the day. That was not the end of Rambo's difficulties, however.

The $18 million film had been shot without a distributor. The prevailing feeling was that Stallone without *Rocky* equaled box-office poison. There was little enthusiasm among the majors for a non-*Rocky* movie; certainly an 18-minute reel failed to impress 20th Century–Fox or, curiously enough, Warner Bros., the studio that had set the project into motion in the first place.

Worried, Vajna and Kassar produced a 55-minute reel of the movie, which was shown at the American Film Market. Stallone himself got up and introduced it. At the conclusion, distributors from around the world gave the movie a standing ovation. For the first time since production began, there was abruptly a sense that Vajna and Kassar had something other than a failure on their hands.

*First Blood* finally was picked up by Orion Pictures and released with little fanfare in the summer of 1982, a decade after Lawrence Turman first bought the book for Columbia Pictures. Stallone still had doubts. Long gone were the days when, full of youthful bravado and enthusiasm, he could confidently announce that one of his pictures was a hit. In front of the press, he termed the plot noble, and the movie a gamble. Privately, he was convinced that despite all the changes, Rambo was still too dark a figure for the U.S. public to embrace.

To everyone's surprise, *First Blood* started doing business. It did very well in North America, but in Europe and Asia it went through the roof. By the time it was finished, *First Blood* had grossed $120 million from worldwide ticket sales, video, and pay television licensing fees. Vajna and Kassar knew two weeks after its release that they had a big success on their hands. By the time *Rambo: First Blood Part II* appeared three years later, the suggestions of darkness swirling around the original Rambo had all but disappeared; John Rambo was a full-bore hero, doing what the American military could not accomplish — winning the war in Vietnam.

Filmed in Mexico on a budget of $28 million with George Pan Cosmatos directing — although there was little doubt in anyone's mind that Stallone was the man in charge — *Rambo II* went on to gross over $200 million worldwide. Rambo was no longer a character in a movie; he was an international phenomenon. In the midst of the civil war in Lebanon, Christians and

Shi'ites took time out from fighting one another to watch Stallone mowing down North Vietnamese soldiers. The love of Rambo was the only thing combatants on either side had in common. In North America, Rambo became the subject of a raging debate that swept off the entertainment pages and into the editorial sections of daily newspapers. Depending on your point of view, he either exemplified America's renewed strength or he stood for the worst kind of jingoistic gung-ho militarism.

Rambo's success rescued Stallone's career, not only demonstrating that the public would respond to Stallone as someone other than Rocky, but making him one of the most popular and highest paid stars of the era. Moreover, Stallone's Rambo provided the prototype that inspired other action stars who emerged during the 1980s. By removing most of the dialogue and emphasizing the action, the way was open for a group of well-muscled stars who were not proficient actors, but who could move well through an increasingly varied array of pyrotechnics. They included Arnold Schwarzenegger, whose success would eclipse Stallone's, as well as a number of lesser clones, such as Jean-Claude Van Damme and Dolph Lundgren. Bruce Willis, who had been a television actor in "Moonlighting," was transformed into an action hero by the success of *Die Hard* in 1988. Like Stallone, Willis promptly found himself typecast. When he made a non-action film, such as *In Country*, *The Bonfire of the Vanities*, *Hudson Hawk*, or *Billy Bathgate*, it invariably was not successful. Only with a gun in his hand in *The Last Boy Scout*, or *Striking Distance*, could Willis attract an audience.

JOAN SINGLETON HAD MIXED FEELINGS ABOUT THE ORIGINAL *FIRST BLOOD*. "The focus they took was more action adventure," she said. "It was less complicated than the movie we had in mind." She later consoled herself with the thought that out of the experience had emerged a new husband, Ralph Singleton, who had been hired by Carter De Haven as the movie's production manager, and two daughters. Singleton ended up with things most people in Hollywood, including Sylvester Stallone, did not have — a successful marriage and two adorable children. She even became a producer in 1990 when her husband, making his directorial debut with the horror movie *Graveyard Shift*, adapted from a Stephen King story, called her in to help. Becoming a producer at that point was the last thing she expected, but then things tended to happen that way in Hollywood.

Every so often, Singleton would pass the big brick and glass building on Sunset Boulevard where Carolco was headquartered and where Sylvester Stallone often sat brooding over his career. This was the house that John Rambo literally built, the house that specialized in big, expensive movies fueled by big, expensive movie-star deals. It might not have been constructed had Joan Singleton failed to come across that screenplay. As she drove by, she sometimes thought back on the heady days of trying to make *First Blood* a reality.

"It was just so amazing to me we ever got the rights in the first place," she said. "I was flabbergasted. It was wonderful. For a brief period we were like kids who somehow got the key to the candy store."

As for Sylvester Stallone, superstardom continued to be both a blessing and a curse. He had embraced the character of Rambo when so many other major stars had rejected him, reshaped him into his own heroic image. Now, however, it was all turning sour. The incredible backlash against Rambo after the release of the second movie caught Stallone in a whirlwind of controversy and anger, much of it focused on him. The criticism left him hurt and confused. By the time he started shooting the third adventure, with Rambo this time winning the war in Afghanistan, Stallone was coming to the realization that perhaps the critics were right. "We are in trouble," he thought one day just before he was about to shoot a fight scene on location in Thailand. "We are in *trouble*. Because this man *can't be defeated*. I feel *sorry* for the guy who's fighting him. In *Rambo I*, he was always running, always scared. But now there's no jeopardy. That's what turns people off. Why didn't I see it? Why didn't I see it?"

T HE SAME YEAR STALLONE STARRED IN *FIRST BLOOD*, HE ALSO WROTE, directed, and appeared in the third installment of the *Rocky* series. With two of the year's biggest hits, he was once again one of the most powerful and popular stars in the movies. Stallone now entered into a relationship with Paramount Pictures. The studio had a script Sylvester Stallone liked. This time, however, the instincts that served him so well with *First Blood* would fail, and he would inadvertently open the way for the ascension to superstardom of a 22-year-old standup comedian named Eddie Murphy.

The genesis of *Beverly Hills Cop* went like this: Don Simpson, who would go on to become one of the most successful producers in the business, had just arrived in Hollywood with not much more than a good deal of ambition. He had traveled a long way from Alaska, where his father was a hunting guide and where, in spite of — or perhaps because of — the fact that his family was fundamentalist southern Baptist, he had been convicted of four felonies before he turned 16. The way Simpson would later tell the story, he was driving through Beverly Hills one day in his beaten-up old Camaro when he was pulled over by two police officers. As might be expected from a kid who referred to himself as the "Baby Face Nelson of Anchorage," Simpson was in possession of what his friend and partner Jerry Bruckheimer described as "a bit of an attitude." He started to mouth off to the cops, and the next thing he knew, he was yanked from his car and frisked right there on the street. Eventually, he was allowed to go free, but as he drove away, still furious, it occurred to him that this might make a great idea for a movie.

Not long after that, Simpson found himself working on a project with director Floyd Mutrux, and the two of them ended up in a Chicano bar in East Los Angeles. The place was full of big, tatooed bruisers, and Simpson was sure they were the bad guys. It turned out, however, that they were actually police officers. Simpson was amazed. What would happen if one of these guys was rousted in Beverly Hills, just as he had been? Simpson had his idea for a movie.

Initially, Don Simpson thought of Mickey Rourke for *Beverly Hills Cop*. By that time Simpson had become wildly successful in the movie business, having moved over from being president of production at Paramount to become an independent producer. He had had a huge hit with a small dance movie titled *Flashdance* that he had developed with his new partner, Jerry Bruckheimer. It was Bruckheimer who kept at him about the *Beverly Hills Cop* project. "Jerry always remembered it," Simpson recalled. "He said, 'Don, this is too good a project; we should really get going on it.' He inspired me." Still, when Simpson and Bruckheimer met for lunch with Rourke, there was no script with which anyone was happy, so Simpson verbally pitched the actor. "I must tell you I made up most of it in my head. And he committed. He was great. He would have been terrific, by the way." The deal called for Rourke to receive $65,000 whether or not the movie was ever made.

However, the script was still far from right, and while writer Daniel

Petrie worked on various drafts, Rourke went off to do *The Pope of Greenwich Village*. Rourke's memory of his involvement with *Beverly Hills Cop* was simply that he turned the movie down. "With all due respect to *Beverly Hills Cop*, there were lots of movies they offered me $1,000,000 or more to do, but, hey, I didn't believe in what the message was."

Paramount, as part of its commitment to Sylvester Stallone, then showed the script to him, and before Simpson and Bruckheimer could object, he had committed himself to the picture. Paramount was delighted, Simpson and Bruckheimer less so. "Sly was a friend," Simpson said, "he's a good guy; but I don't think he was right for the movie we made. We and the studio had a big, *big* brouhaha over that."

Nonetheless, Stallone was to be Beverly Hills Cop, except he disliked the way the cop spoke. "He came in and said, 'Look, I have to change the dialogue because I don't talk this way, this is not me. Let me change it.' He did."

As soon as Stallone delivered his version of the script, it was obvious to everyone that this was not the movie they wanted to make. Not only was the main character much different, but the picture had become much more an action movie than a comedy, full of expensive sequences including a train wreck.

By now, however, the producers were in a bind. With production only weeks away, a meeting was called that involved Barry Diller, the chairman of Paramount, Michael Eisner who at the time was president of the studio, and Jeffrey Katzenberg, head of production. Also present was the director Martin Brest, along with Simpson and Bruckheimer. It was decided there was no way they could make Stallone's script into a movie. Eisner and Katzenberg then visited Stallone at his home. "Look," they said, "we want to go back to the original script. You can take what you want from this script [that you wrote], and we'll give it to you." With Paramount refusing to make the changes he wanted, Stallone suddenly was out of *Beverly Hills Cop*. [25]

But now there was the problem of whom to cast. Simpson and Bruckheimer tabled an idea they had been kicking around for some time: Eddie Murphy. Michael Eisner later said Eddie Murphy was the idea of production chief Jeffrey Katzenberg. However, according to the Bruckheimer-

[25] Stallone did indeed take his script and do something with it. His version of *Beverly Hills Cop* was released in the summer of 1986 under the title *Cobra*. Although anticipation was high, the movie grossed a disappointing $40 million — nothing like the revenues that poured in from *Beverly Hills Cop*.

Simpson version of the story, the Paramount brass saw Murphy as many things, but they did not see him as a cop in Beverly Hills.

If that was indeed Paramount's attitude, it was curious, seeing as how Murphy had made one of the fastest transitions from comparative obscurity to major movie stardom anyone could recall, as a result of the phenomenal success of *48 HRS.*

S IMPSON, TOO, HAD BEEN DEEPLY INVOLVED IN THE DEVELOPMENT OF *48 HRS.* Originally, the story of a cop who bails a crook out of jail for 48 hours in order to track down a vicious killer was conceived for Clint Eastwood and Burt Reynolds. When Simpson saw the script, he thought of Eastwood and Richard Pryor, with whom he had had a working relationship on the movie called *Some Kind of Hero.* By that time Paramount was in desperate need of a picture for Christmas of 1982, and Simpson had begun scrambling to get *48 HRS.* into shape. However, because the script was not right, they could not get commitments from either Eastwood or Pryor. Simpson had frantically begun casting around for other possible actors.

"In the midst of this, 'Saturday Night Live' was reaching a point of kind of critical mass in terms of its success," Simpson said. "Eddie had come along on the scene and with each successive week he was getting hotter and hotter, and better and better on the show." It was not Simpson's idea to cast the young comic in *48 HRS.* — he cannot remember who suggested it — but as soon as he heard it, he went to his boss, Michael Eisner. "He had never heard of Eddie Murphy. As a matter of fact, when I heard the idea and went to him, he said 'Who's Eddie Murphy?' I had to show him the television show and say, 'This is Eddie Murphy.' He went, 'Oh, that guy's interesting.'"

Eddie Murphy was born in Hempstead, Long Island, and as a kid was a cut-up who could get laughs and do great imitations. When he was 17, he went to a nearby club called the Comic Strip and auditioned for its owner, Bob Wachs, who saw immediately that he had possibilities. "This kid has instincts you cannot believe," he said. "I mean I couldn't believe it. His material was a little rough, but he had this smile and this voice."

Murphy remembered things somewhat differently. "[Wachs] threw me out of the club the first time. But then he finally saw my act and put me up for 'Saturday Night Live.'" He began appearing on the show in the fall of

1981, among the replacement crew for the original Not Ready for Prime Time Players that had included Chevy Chase, John Belushi, Dan Aykroyd, and Bill Murray. By the time Don Simpson flew to New York to talk with the young comic, he was growing increasingly unhappy with the show and wanted out.

Simpson met with Murphy in a bar across the street from the CBS headquarters building that was known as Black Rock. From the outset it was obvious the young comic was excited about the possibility of doing a movie. When he discovered Simpson knew Richard Pryor, he was anxious to talk to his idol. Simpson put through a call, then got the two comedians together on the phone. "Basically," Simpson recalled, "Eddie was really wide-eyed about being in a movie, and was extremely excited. So the deal was made."

With Nick Nolte in place as Murphy's co-star, and Walter Hill directing, *48 HRS.* went into production. Nolte would receive $2,000,000; Murphy was getting $200,000. The experience of shooting his first movie was not a happy one for Murphy. He had difficulty sustaining his performance through a scene. After each take he would phone Bob Wachs, who by now was his manager, and complain that he had been crazy to get involved in the first place.

As Christmas of 1982 approached, Paramount was not enthusiastic about *48 HRS.* Murphy was an untried television comedian, while Nolte was coming off a string of flops that included *Who'll Stop the Rain* and *Cannery Row.* As Murphy made his way into the East Side theater where *48 HRS.* was having its premiere, he could not shake the feeling that the evening was headed for disaster. Then the movie started, and Murphy could scarely believe what was happening on the screen. "It was wild," he reported later. "It blew my mind." And everyone else's. When Murphy went to leave the theater, he was mobbed. In less than two hours, he had become a movie star.

The next day, Eddie Murphy bristled with confidence as he talked to the press. "It's wild. If you have a hit movie, you can ride on that for five years. You're hot." He flashed what was soon to become his trademark grin. "All of a sudden, I'm hot."

4 *8 HRS.* HAD BECOME A HUGE AND UNEXPECTED HIT FOR PARAMOUNT, grossing over $200 million. "*48 HRS.* is the most imitated movie of the eighties," Murphy said at the beginning of the 1990s. "You can draw a

line from it to *Commando* to *Lethal Weapon* to *Red Heat* to *Running Scared*. And none of them was as good as the original."

*Trading Places*, Murphy's second movie, was just about as successful. Even so, the studio refused to listen to Simpson and Bruckheimer. Eddie Murphy was not going to appear in *Beverly Hills Cop*. "It's just interesting in terms of hindsight," Simpson mused, years later. "I mean you had a studio that had a deal with him and they did not see Eddie as the Beverly Hills Cop. As a matter of fact, they actively campaigned against it."

Simpson and Bruckheimer, however, were convinced that Eddie was their man. They put in a call to Murphy and told him, "We're sending you a script." They couriered the screenplay to the actor, then got on a plane with Martin Brest and flew to New York while Murphy and his two managers gathered in an office. "They read the script," Bruckheimer recalled, "and they passed the pages around."

"I like this," Murphy said. But then he wanted Brest, Simpson, and Bruckheimer to come out to his $3.5 million estate known as Bubble Hill in Englewood Cliffs, New Jersey. They passed through wrought-iron gates and came up a drive shaped like the number nine to the colonial-style house. Everyone sat at a table, and Murphy said to the two producers, "Tell me what the story is."

"Marty kind of froze for a moment," Bruckheimer recalled, "couldn't say anything. Then Don, who's a great storyteller, just pitched in and told how we saw the movie." When Simpson was finished, Murphy thought for a couple of moments, and then announced, "I'll do it."

*Beverly Hills Cop* was the biggest hit of Eddie Murphy's career and it made him, at the age of 24, one of the most powerful stars in Hollywood. After its success, Murphy, who previously had expressed amazement at the huge amounts of money demanded by some stars, negotiated a five-picture, $15 million deal that was renegotiated upward throughout the '80s as Murphy turned out hit picture after hit picture. By the end of the decade, he was denouncing the deal and making it clear he was in search of a better arrangement elsewhere. "Whoever's gonna give me the most lucrative deal, that's where I'm going," he said. "I'm no fucking idiot who's gonna go, 'I'm gonna stay with Paramount and work for less money because I've been here since the beginning.' Get the fuck outa here!"

# 15

## "THEY KNEW WHERE TO FIND ME."

### *Harrison Ford and the story of*
### Back to the Future

I N 1972, MIKE FENTON AND HIS PARTNER FRED ROOS WERE CASTING A movie for director George Lucas called *American Graffiti*. Roos was handling most of the auditions, but Fenton was also involved, with his associate Jane Feinberg. They were working out of an office at MGM. One day Roos called excitedly. "Don't go to lunch," he said. "I've got an actor I want you to meet."

Fenton and Feinberg had been housed in the Irving Thalberg building at MGM for a year and a half, and they had seen every size and shape of actor under the Hollywood sun. The time had long since passed when anyone was going to surprise them, and the same went for their secretary, a longtime fixture at the studio named Jeanette Walker. She was legend for her unflappability. She had seen them all come and go, so, as Fenton said, "Nothing fazed Jeanette. I mean nothing. Nothing moved her. Nothing stirred her."

Just before noon, Fenton and Feinberg were waiting impatiently for Roos' actor, when suddenly Jeanette Walker burst into the office and slammed the door behind her. She stared at Jane Feinberg and said, "Jane, you are not going to believe this young man. This young man is the most phenomenally attractive person I have ever seen."

Walker left and the door opened. The young actor entered and sat down in front of Fenton's desk. "Did you ever get the feeling you're a third wheel," said Fenton with a chuckle, remembering the incident years later. "Well, I got the feeling Jane wants to take this guy to her bosom."

The actor in question was a 17-year-old from San Diego, California, named Paul Le Mat. "He was as handsome a young man as there was around," remembered Fenton. "He had fought in the Golden Gloves, a light heavyweight, he must have been six feet tall, dark hair and flashing eyes — and really and truly handsome."

Le Mat had drifted to New York, where he had studied acting with Milton Katselas, and had been taken under the wing of the actor Anthony Zerbe. Everyone admired his talent, but there had been trouble casting him because Le Mat tended to turn down the roles he was offered. "I did a television show once," he said. "Never again. The director said, 'Do this, this, and this,' and that was it."

When Le Mat left their offices, Fenton and Feinberg traded looks. They were convinced, as was Fred Roos, that this young actor was on his way to stardom. For a moment, it looked as if they might be right. Le Mat was cast as Milner, the rebellious drag racing high school dropout who spends graduation night 1962 trapped in his hot rod with a snotty 12-year-old (played by Mackenzie Phillips). Le Mat indeed received a lot of attention, along with his co-stars Richard Dreyfuss and Candy Clark. But while it was generally conceded that *American Graffiti* (1975) made Richard Dreyfuss a star in his first film appearance, it did not do much of anything for Paul Le Mat. "He came close, he had some wonderful roles," Fenton said, "and he ran into some problems of a personal nature, but he never became the star we thought — no, were *convinced* — he was going to become."

One of the other actors who, thanks to Fenton's partner, Fred Roos, got himself cast in a small role in *American Graffiti* was Harrison Ford. Taciturn and rather grouchy on occasion, Ford was from Wheaton, Illinois, outside Chicago. He had settled in Los Angeles in the mid-1960s. Ford and his wife had taken a month to drive to the coast. They got as far as Laguna Beach, saw the ocean for the first time in their lives, and decided this would be as good a place as any to get an apartment. Ford did a local play, *John Brown's Body*, for which a man named E. M. Bernard had composed the music. Bernard was also doing the music for the television series "Rowan & Martin's Laugh-In" and had links at Columbia Pictures. He got Ford in touch with the head of the studio's casting department.

"It was the first time I had ever been in a movie studio," Ford recalled. "I went into this huge paneled office, and there was this guy talking on two phones, and another guy behind him on another two phones, literally, and I sat in a straight-back chair for about ten minutes while they talked big bucks, big names. They kept switching from one phone to another, covering one mouth-piece, then the other mouthpiece, shouting back and forth — just like in the movies."

It turned out that neither casting director had even heard of E. M. Bernard, but they duly took down Ford's particulars on an index card, including the fact that he was six feet, one inch tall and weighed 190 pounds. They thanked him for coming in and Ford left the office. On his way to the elevator, he decided to go to the bathroom. When he emerged, he found the casting assistant coming down the hall looking for him. "Come back, he wants to talk to you," Ford was told. When he returned to the office, the head of casting asked, "How'd you like to be on a contract?" Ford wanted to know how much they paid. "Seven-year contract for one hundred and fifty dollars a week," came the reply.

It was not great, but thanks to his bladder, Harrison Ford was now an actor under contract at Columbia. He figured it was a good way to learn the business. If he appeared in good movies, he thought, that was the way to become an actor. Columbia first cast him as a bellboy in *Dead Heat on a Merry-Go-Round* (1966). His job was to hand James Coburn a telegram, and that was accomplished without bumping into anything, but he certainly made little impression. Soon after *Dead Heat*, he was called into the office of a studio executive who said to him, "Listen kid, let me tell you a story. The first time Tony Curtis was in a movie he walked on the screen delivering a bag of groceries. You took one look at the guy and you knew there was a star. Well, you ain't got that, kid."

Nonetheless, Ford soon was doing a lot of television. "I was either the sensitive brother or the bankrobbing brother or the business brother. . . . or the guy that didn't do it — the guy they think in the beginning did it."

When Ford was not acting, which was most of the time, he kept himself busy as a carpenter, a trade he had picked up simply by borrowing a couple of books on the subject from the public library. That was his life for the better part of the years between 1968 and 1976; carpentry interrupted by the occasional acting job. He was a very successful carpenter, too, so much so that when Fred Roos, for whom he had done some woodwork, called him with the offer to play in *American Graffiti*, Ford was able to hold out for $500 a week. Playing Bob Falfa in the movie was the most pleasurable experience he had

had as an actor, mainly because George Lucas, the director, actually listened to what he had to say — the first time that had ever happened.

"Harrison was not conventionally good-looking," Roos said. "He was also tight-lipped, standoffish and most people thought he had an attitude. He's an incredibly cranky guy. But I thought he was going to be a star."

Roos became something of a mentor, making sure Ford was cast in a small part in Francis Coppola's *The Conversation*. However, Ford did not think he had much of a chance at Lucas's next picture, a big-budget science fiction adventure titled *Star Wars*. Lucas, as he would with the *Indiana Jones* films, made it clear from the outset that no one from his last movie would be cast in his new production. "So I didn't think about it," Ford said. "I didn't enter into the picture until about three or four weeks before they were due to make the decision."

He was building an entrance to Francis Coppola's office at Goldwyn studios, when in walked Coppola and Roos with George Lucas and Richard Dreyfuss. "I was asked to do a videotape test, which I did, and then they asked me to help them with other people's videotape tests. . . . it seems like I must have done seventy-five."

Carrie Fisher remembered arriving for her test as Princess Leia[26] and being impressed as soon as she saw him. "I knew he was going to be a star — someone on the order of Bogart and Tracy." Meanwhile, Ford was becoming increasingly irritated. Lucas wanted Nick Nolte or Christopher Walken or William Katt for the part of Han Solo. But Fred Roos kept pestering him about Harrison Ford. "He wasn't high on George's list," Roos said. "He did not know [Harrison] like I did." [27]

For Ford, the part of Han Solo came down to nothing more dramatic than "I was told they wanted me to do the part. I didn't even have a script."

When he did see the screenplay, he was far from impressed. "You can type this shit, George," he reportedly said to the director, "but you can't say

---

[26] Fisher was up against Amy Irving and Jodie Foster, as well as a former *Penthouse* Pet, Terri Nunn, for the role of Princess Leia.

[27] For a time, Lucas considered Glynn Turman, an African-American actor, for Han Solo, but ultimately decided against him because he was nervous about the interracial aspects of his relationship with Princess Leia. "I didn't want to make *Guess Who's Coming to Dinner* at that point," Lucas said, "so I sort of backed off."

it." Somehow he and the rest of the cast[28] did say it, and in the early summer of 1977, *Star Wars* became more evidence that, in the wake of *Jaws*, movies were becoming carefully rigged and constructed celluloid rollercoaster rides. If those rides were appealing enough, the kids would climb on board them again and again. Hollywood saw the vast sums to be realized from these movies and set about furiously trying to imitate them. What Hollywood did not necessarily see were the actors who filled the screen when the special effects spaceships were out of view.

The world was duly attentive to Mark Hamill, who played Luke Skywalker, as well as to Carrie Fisher, but no one was breaking down their respective doors to get them to do other things. Only Ford wriggled free of the comfortable but dangerously smothering cocoon into which the *Star Wars* phenomenon wrapped its cast. But he escaped by way of a series of movie clinkers: *Heroes*, *Force 10 from Navarone*, and *Hanover Street* (a World War II melodrama in which he and Lesley-Anne Down replaced Kris Kristofferson and Genevieve Bujold, who walked away just before the picture was to start production in London). During this time he turned down *Butch and Sundance: The Early Days*, in which he would have played the young Butch Cassidy. Ford said he had no wish to be compared to Paul Newman, who had originated the role in the 1969 film. Instead, newcomer Tom Berenger got a major feature break, although the film was a resounding failure.[29]

O N THE DAY BEFORE THANKSGIVING 1979, MIKE FENTON'S SECRETARY poked her head in the door and said, "There's someone on the phone claiming to be Steven Spielberg." Fenton had worked years before casting Spielberg's first movie, *The Sugarland Express*. Then the filmmaker had announced he was going to train his own casting director for subsequent films, so Fenton was somewhat surprised to hear from him.

Spielberg and Fenton traded pleasantries, then Spielberg asked if he

---

[28] An actor named Will Selzer was in the running for the movie's youthful hero, Luke Skywalker. But ultimately the role went to Mark Hamill. Lucas thought of the Japanese actor Torshiro Mifune for the role of the mystical Jedi leader, Ben (Obi-Wan) Kenobi. However, he offered the part to Alec Guinness and was amazed when the veteran British actor accepted.

[29] William Katt, who had competed with Ford for the role of Han Solo, was the young Sundance Kid.

would like to work with him on a film. Fenton said of course, and they agreed to meet at Hollywood's Egg Company restaurant with George Lucas. It was at that point that Fenton got the script for *Raiders of the Lost Ark*. Already the movie was steeped in secrecy. Spielberg asked Fenton not to discuss the character of Indiana Jones, who was to be the movie's protagonist, but he put no limitations on who might play the role. "We wanted an unknown originally — a total unknown," Spielberg said. "Conceitedly, George and I wanted to make a star of Johnny the construction worker from Malibu. We couldn't find a construction worker in Malibu, so we began looking at more substantial people in the industry."

Casting sessions were held in the kitchen at Lucasfilm, and candidates who arrived from nine to one helped cook, while those arriving between the hours of two and seven ate what had been cooked. "Everything was baked from scratch," Spielberg recalled, "from charlotte au chocolat to homemade pumpkin bread." The word spread — Army Archerd (in *Variety*) and a few of the other columnists were carrying the story in the papers, so the actors were calling their agents saying, "I only want to come after two. Everyone wanted to eat; nobody wanted to work."

It was not recorded whether a 35-year-old actor named Tom Selleck came to work or to eat. Whatever, he was loaded with plenty of ambition. Betty McCartt, Selleck's agent, had been pushing her client hard to everyone in town. A tall, handsome former model from Detroit, raised in the San Fernando Valley, Selleck had attended the University of Southern California on a basketball scholarship. Although he landed a recurring role in the James Garner detective series "The Rockford Files," and had appeared in small roles in a number of movies (he was a corpse in *Coma*), Selleck was best known at the beginning of the '80s as the Marlboro man, the model for countless cigarette ads in print and on billboards across North America.

Selleck was tested for Indiana Jones, as were a number of other young actors, including Nick Mancuso, a Canadian who had recently starred in a thriller titled *Nightwing*. Fenton was sitting in a projection room with Spielberg, Lucas, and his wife Marcia, running through the tests. At the end, Marcia turned to her husband and said she thought it should be Selleck, and everyone agreed.

Privately, Fenton did not think Selleck the right choice. He preferred

Harrison Ford. "Harrison, having done the *Star Wars* films and *American Graffiti*, was certainly a known commodity," Fenton said. "We always knew Harrison existed for that part. George and Marcia Lucas, Steven Spielberg and [producers] Kathleen Kennedy and Frank Marshall, we all felt we had Harrison in our hip pockets, should we not find somebody who was closer to the character of Indiana Jones."

Fenton thought after going through the casting process that there was nobody better than Harrison Ford. However, as he later explained in guarded words, "Tom Selleck tested quite well for the film," and this was May and the picture was to start shooting in June. Selleck had done a pilot for a new CBS private detective series, but he had done any number of pilots and none of them had sold. There was no indication that this one, "Magnum, P.I.," would be any different. "However, as soon as they opened negotiations with the actor," Fenton recalled, "it became apparent CBS was not going to release him from his commitment."

One day Selleck was Indiana Jones, the next he was Magnum, television's newest private detective, and there was nothing he could do about it. "I got real melancholy after I did not get *Raiders*," he said later. "Every actor dreams of doing motion pictures and I thought I was going to be a TV actor forever." Selleck's career never really recovered. He became immensely popular as TV's Magnum over the next eight years, but he never truly established himself as a movie star, despite one runaway hit, *Three Men and a Baby*. The attempts to create a movie career for him were carefully orchestrated, but even so, the public would continue to resist him throughout the '80s in films such as *High Road to China*, *An Innocent Man*, *My Alibi*, and into the '90s in *Mr. Baseball*.

Meanwhile, "there was not a lot of scrambling to find someone else," Fenton said. "As soon as they went back to the projection room and looked at the other tests, everybody said, 'Well, you know something, Harrison's the best we got left, we should go with Harrison.' And I silently cheered."

Where was Ford during all this? Pretending not to be interested. "They knew where to find me," he said cryptically. But there was little doubt he knew how valuable the role could be to his career. "It was clearly the most dominant single character in any of George's films," he said, "quite in variance with his theories about movie stars and what they mean."

With less than a month to go before start of production, and four days after it was announced that Selleck would not be appearing in the movie, Harrison Ford was cast as Indiana Jones. The story of how Ford got the part was altered somewhat for public consumption. In an interview for the official *Raiders of the Lost Ark* souvenir book, Spielberg said: "We were stuck. We had three weeks left to cast the part of Indiana Jones, and there was nobody close. Then I saw *The Empire Strikes Back* and I said Harrison Ford is Indiana Jones. I called George Lucas and said, 'He's right under our noses.' George said, 'I know who you're going to say.' I said, 'Who?' and he said 'Harrison Ford.' 'Right.' 'Let's get him,' he said. And we did."

As it turned out, Selleck could have done the part after all. There soon followed a Screen Actors Guild strike, and Selleck ended up sitting around all summer. Meantime, *Raiders* was shooting in Europe and North Africa with an English company over which the Guild had no jurisdiction. "Had anyone known how long the strike was going to be, Tom Selleck could possibly have done the movie," Mike Fenton concluded.

IN THE SUMMER OF 1984, MICHAEL J. FOX WAS STANDING ON A SIDE STREET in Los Angeles when he saw them. The actor was 23 years old, from Vancouver, British Columbia, and featured in a situation comedy called "Family Ties" that was not doing well in the ratings. One of the five children of a retired Canadian army officer, Fox had arrived in Hollywood five years before, after dropping out of school. On hiatus from the series, and concerned about the show's future, he grabbed at a low-budget movie comedy titled *Teen Wolf*. Now here he was, part of the production team rushing around trying to grab scenes, and who should show up in the midst of everything but the location scouts from a rival production.

The word was whispered around the *Teen Wolf* crew: the scouts worked for Steven Spielberg, and they were planning to use this same neighborhood for a new Spielberg production to be called *Back to the Future*. Here was Michael J. Fox down in the trenches sweating out this low-budget comedy and just a few feet away were the representatives of another kind of filmmaking altogether. He watched, saucer-eyed, thinking how nice it would be someday to work for a well-financed movie production like the ones Spielberg invariably mounted. Then he dismissed the thought and went back to work on *Teen Wolf*.

*Back to the Future* was to be the fantasy story of a teenager named Marty

McFly who ends up piloting a DeLorean automobile back to 1955 where he encounters his parents as teenagers. Robert Zemeckis, a film graduate of the University of Southern California, and his partner Bob Gale had been turned down by every studio in town when they pitched the idea. Most thought it too soft a concept, except the people at Disney who accused *Back to the Future* of being far too risqué since one of the plot twists had to do with Marty's teenage mother coming on to her son.

The two writers were increasingly desperate. They had written two movies for their mentor, Steven Spielberg — *1941*, the biggest failure of his otherwise untarnished career, and *I Wanna Hold Your Hand*, a film that Spielberg had produced about a group of young girls on their way to a Beatles concert. "The only one who wanted to do [*Back to the Future*] from day one was Spielberg," Zemeckis said. "But I had already had two flops that he had produced and I thought it would be detrimental to do another with him at that time."

So Zemeckis went off on his own and after a great deal of difficulty directed *Romancing the Stone* (1984), an Indiana Jones–type adventure with Michael Douglas and Kathleen Turner that became a huge success. More confident, Zemeckis and Gale returned to Amblin with their *Back to the Future* project, and this time it became a favorite of Sid Sheinberg, the president and CEO of MCA Inc., the company that owned Universal. *Back to the Future* was now in excellent hands, with Spielberg producing and the Universal studio solidly behind it. There were plans to release the completed film in the early summer of 1985.

The role of Marty McFly went to a young actor named Eric Stoltz who had first appeared in *Fast Times at Ridgemont High* ("What did we know," he said of the movie's surprising success, "we were just a bunch of kids having a party and making a film") and caused a minor sensation in *Mask*, playing Cher's disfigured son. That role had called for a serious actor who could bring to it a certain grace, quality, and dignity. *Back to the Future*, on the other hand, required a light touch on the part of everyone involved.

Production began 26 November, and was due to shoot for 12 weeks. With nearly half the filming completed, director Zemeckis put together a very rough cut of the footage that already had been shot and began to see that something was seriously wrong. Stoltz was an intense young man, and that was how he was coming across on the screen. "I made a very serious casting error,"

Zemeckis concluded. "Stoltz wasn't in synch with my vision. . . . That only became clear on film." Zemeckis felt he had a good actor on his hands, but in the wrong film. Stoltz would have to go. In the middle of January, Stoltz's manager, Helen Sugland, got a call from Zemeckis. "His performance wasn't consistent with the original concept of the film," Sugland said later. She said that the firing had come as a total surprise and that she had heard only positive things about her client's performance.

"It is such a fickle business, not kind to talent," Stoltz said years later. "You hope that everything you do turns out terrific, but reality insists on a different outcome."

Michael J. Fox, in the meantime, had gone back to work playing the yuppie, conservative Alex Keaton in "Family Ties." The series had been rescheduled to follow the phenomenally successful "The Cosby Show" on Thursday nights and had shot to the top of the ratings. Now, as "Family Ties" entered its last six weeks of production for the season, Fox found himself unexpectedly getting a lot of attention.

One night he went over to watch the taping of a new series, also being produced by "Family Ties" Gary David Goldberg. It was called "Sara," and Fox was always ribbing Goldberg that *Sara* was "the other woman" in his life. As a show of faith, Fox had decided to be present at that evening's taping. As soon as he arrived at the studio, Goldberg intercepted him, and called him into his office. Fox thought he wanted to talk about one of the other TV projects they had been discussing, but as soon as they were alone, Goldberg put a script down in front of him. Across the cover was written *Back to the Future*. Fox stared at it in disbelief. "I just got a call from Steven," Goldberg said, referring to his friend Spielberg. "They want you, and they want you to start on Monday."

"Wait a minute," Fox said. "They've already got a guy."

"There have been some creative differences, and they want you to do it."

Fox's first reaction was to say he did not want it. But Goldberg sent him home with the script, and about 2:00 A.M. the next morning received an excited phone call from his star. "You've gotta phone Steven and tell him I'm gonna do it," Fox exclaimed. "Don't let change him his mind."

"Mike," Goldberg replied calmly, "he's not gonna change his mind, he wouldn't do that."

"Well, just make sure, okay? I'm ready, I'm gonna do it."

The following Monday, Fox reported to work on the *Back to the Future* set. For the first six weeks, he worked on "Family Ties" from 10 :00 A.M. until 6:00 P.M. Then he acted in *Back to the Future* from 6:30 P.M. until 2:30 A.M. "It got to the point where they'd bring me and carry me and put me to bed, wake me up in the morning, throw me in the shower, take me out, take me to work. It got really surrealistic for a while."

A month was lost while the production stopped and Stoltz was replaced. That necessitated the picture's release date being pushed back to 19 July 1985. By then Universal had a good idea of *Back to the Future*'s potential. "Maybe I'm a fool," said Sid Sheinberg, "but I think it's the most commercial movie since *E.T.* . . . We have the potential to catch lightning in a bottle."

He was right. *Back to the Future* eventually grossed over $200 million to become the biggest box-office hit of 1985. Michael J. Fox found himself not only featured in one of television's most popular shows but also starring in the year's biggest hit movie.

For Eric Stoltz, it was a different story altogether. He continued to work as an actor, and his performances in movies such as *The Waterdance* and *Bodies, Rest and Motion* received good notices. But he also appeared in such out-right box-office failures as *The Wild Life, Lionheart,* and *The Fly II.* Eight years after he was summarily bounced from the picture, Stoltz characterized himself as a hard-working actor, a survivor. Still, the pain must have lingered. Each time Fox was profiled, there invariably were a couple of lines devoted to the fact that he had replaced Eric Stoltz in one of the biggest successes of the '80s. The memory refused to go away.

In July of 1993, Stoltz attended a party on a street in TriBeCa in New York with his girlfriend, actress Bridget Fonda. The party was held outside the diner that had been built for Fonda's new movie, *Cop Gives Waitress $2 Million Tip.* A fan approached at one point during the evening and told Stoltz he had seen everything the actor had done and was a great admirer. "One role I'd like to have seen you in," concluded the fan, "was *Back to the Future.*"

Eric Stoltz just smiled.

# 16

# "I WENT TO THE MOVIES FOR A LONG TIME . . ."
## *The Kevin Costner approach*

<br>

IN JANUARY OF 1987, SYLVESTER STALLONE WAS IN LAS VEGAS TO ATTEND A heavyweight championship fight between Mike Tyson, the reigning champ, and James "Bonecrusher" Smith. As Stallone moved through the Hilton casino on his way to a private party after the fight, he was accompanied by a stunning, long-legged blonde and surrounded by an entourage of eight bodyguards, one of them festooned with tattoos. That night Stallone was the embodiment of the powerful American movie star, exuding energy and charisma as he moved through the crowd, waving to onlookers, shaking hands.

Watching nearby was a young actor from Compton, California, who had grown up wanting to be a baseball player. He had discovered acting while attending college at California State University at Fullerton, and although he graduated with a degree in business, he surprised everyone who knew him, including his fiancée, by announcing that he was going to act. In fact, from the beginning, Kevin Costner was confident that he would become a movie star.

Costner had been thwarted, not by lack of opportunity, but by bad luck that had left him, literally, on the cutting-room floor any number of times. Nonetheless, he retained a self-confidence that under the circumstances was nothing less than astonishing. Recently, that confidence had been rewarded with co-starring roles in two films, *Fandango* and *Silverado*. In just six more months, his appearance as crime fighter Eliot Ness in *The Untouchables* would catapult him into major movie stardom. But for now he was ignored by the crowd pressing around Sly. Costner strained to get closer so that he could see firsthand how a major star deported himself. As Stallone passed, Costner momentarily caught his eye, and the present stared into the eyes of the future. Without acknowledging him, Stallone moved on. Costner watched him go.

"Better pay attention," suggested a friend standing with Costner, nodding in the direction of the departing Stallone. "Pretty soon, you're going to be in the same position."

"If I make it big," Costner promised, "you can bet that's the last thing you'll see me doing."

FOR A TIME, KEVIN COSTNER WAS THE INDUSTRY'S BEST-KEPT SECRET, A star in the making who needed only the right picture to push him over the top. However, the right film kept eluding him. He auditioned for the male lead in *Flashdance*, but lost out to actor Michael Nouri. He was rejected for parts in both *Mask* and *The Killing Fields*. He came close to getting the male lead in a Debra Winger picture, *Mike's Murder*, but again missed out, although he was sufficiently impressive to casting director Wally Nicita that she put him up for a new movie directed by Lawrence Kasdan called *The Big Chill*. This time Costner got lucky, and was cast as Alex, the character whose suicide had Kevin Kline, Glenn Close, William Hurt, Tom Berenger, and JoBeth Williams in their respective roles gathering for a weekend of remembrance and introspection. Alex had a pivotal 15-minute scene at the end of the movie.

Costner was so certain he had the transforming role his career required that he turned down a good supporting part in another picture, *WarGames*. "He never had a major part in a movie," Kasdan remembered, "and suddenly he's in a room with Bill Hurt and Kevin Kline. He knew what he could be. He knew what he could gain from it. He totally used that period. He listened and experienced it in the fullest possible way."

However, when the film was completed, and Kasdan tested *The Big Chill*, the audience responded to everything but the flashback scene involving Alex. Kasdan decided to cut the offending sequence. Other than a few closeups of him as a corpse, Costner had been effectively cut from the movie that was intended to provide him with his biggest break. Moreover, it was not the first time that had happened. For a guy who was supposed to be a star at any moment, Costner had a great deal of difficulty remaining in a finished film. He had been cut from Francis Ford Coppola's *One from the Heart*, from *Frances* with Jessica Lange (both 1982), and he was left out of a Jon Voight movie, *Table for Five* (1983). Rather than being upset by these setbacks, Costner remained more convinced than ever that his time would come. He felt the same way after Larry Kasdan called him with the bad news about *The Big Chill*. "Two years from now if I emerge," he thought, "it will be an interesting story."

The story was certainly all over Hollywood. There was this tall, handsome guy, a kind of unassuming Gary Cooper type for the '80s, who had been cut out of one of the big hits of 1983. Costner instinctively understood what had happened. "I knew the day I got the role that I was in, that I had made it. I was exactly where I needed to be and this was the start for me," he said later. "Although I must say the fact that it was a hundred million dollar hit bugged me a little bit."

Kasdan, for his part, felt badly enough about leaving Costner out that he wrote a role in his next film specifically for him. The hotshot gunslinger in *Silverado* was a smart, showy role, and coupled with a coming-of-age movie, *Fandango*, Costner suddenly found himself on the screen. Not so that anyone would particularly notice, though. *Fandango* died at the box office, and *Silverado* turned out to be a disappointment in the summer of 1985.

Still, the buzz on Costner coming off *Silverado* caused the producer Art Linson to have lunch with him at the Farmer's Market restaurant in Hollywood one afternoon. Linson was preparing a movie version of the old "Untouchables" television series, about the treasury agents led by Eliot Ness who had taken on the Al Capone mob in Chicago in the 1930s. Linson was interested in Costner playing Ness. To his surprise, Linson found the actor was more interested in another project in which the producer was involved, called *Arrive Alive*. Nonetheless, Linson was intrigued. "He was wearing a bomber jacket and air force shades," Linson remembered. "Steve McQueen was written all over his forehead."

In those early days, Costner employed his innate belief in himself to tremendous advantage. Even when it was easier just to play along, Costner stuck to his guns — a quality that would later well serve his movie stardom. On the set of *Frances*, for example, as a bit player he refused to say goodnight to Jessica Lange, who was playing actress Frances Farmer. He thought it was wrong for the character. Adrian Lyne, the director of *Flashdance*, had been sufficiently impressed with Costner that when he came to shoot an Apple computer commercial, he decided to do the young actor a favor and hire him.

Costner, who had sworn to himself that he would not do commercials, turned up unshaven and stumbled over his lines. Lyne could not believe it. As Costner exited, following the audition, Lyne went after him. "Kev, what's the matter with you?" he demanded. "This is twenty fucking grand. I'm trying to get you this thing."

Costner turned up the next day for another go at it. Clean shaven now, he sat in a pool of light. With Apple executives looking on, and the camera turning, Costner picked up a telephone and said, "Listen, honey, I can't get this fucking computer to work."

Somehow, Costner's easygoing self-confidence, his willingness to firmly thumb his nose at authority figures, mostly worked for him. Rather than being put off by his ambivalence toward *The Untouchables*, Linson dispatched a rewrite of the script by playwright David Mamet along with the news that Brian De Palma had become attached to the project as director. Now Costner was interested, but De Palma had second thoughts. He liked Costner, but he was basically an unknown young leading man who meant nothing at the box office.

De Palma had started as a maverick independent filmmaker of low-budget items such as *Hi, Mom!* and *Greetings*. But with Hitchcock-inspired thrillers such as *Carrie*, *The Fury*, and *Dressed to Kill*, he had moved into the mainstream. *Scarface* (1983), his remake of the 1932 Howard Hawks gangster picture, had turned him into a big-time Hollywood director. However, his last two films, *Body Double* (1984) and *Wise Guys* (1986), had flopped badly at the box office, and De Palma was in need of a hit. He understood the value of stardom. Little-known actors were big risks. "He was worried Costner did not have enough star power to ensure a hit," Linson recalled.

De Palma considered Harrison Ford for Ness, but his attention focused on Mel Gibson, the American-born, Australian-raised actor who had established himself as the action star of *Mad Max/The Road Warrior*. Despite a couple of career missteps recently with seriously intentioned movies like *Mrs. Soffel* and *The River* (both 1984), Gibson was considered a hot leading man. De Palma and Linson met with the actor, and for a time it looked as though he might do the Ness role. Then Gibson decided to pass, choosing instead the action movie *Lethal Weapon*. For a time, De Palma kicked around the idea of actor Don Johnson, best known as the star of TV's "Miami Vice." But he could not quite bring himself to go with Johnson. Finally, he threw up his hands and decided on Costner. [30]

*The Untouchables* established Kevin Costner as a leading man in a hit movie. But it was with his next picture, *No Way Out*, that the industry acknowledged him as a superstar. After *Silverado*, Eric Pleskow, the CEO of Orion Pictures, certain that Costner would amount to something, offered him his choice of any properties in development at his company. To everyone's amazement, Costner chose the script for *No Way Out*, a Washington-based political thriller that was actually a remake of a 1948 Ray Milland movie, *The Big Clock*. The script had been at Orion for years without inspiring much attention. When *No Way Out* was released in the fall of 1987 on the heels of *The Untouchables*, it became a hit. Costner was no longer an actor in the movies, but a star who had carried two successive box-office hits.

*No Way Out* once again demonstrated how Costner's contrariness could be made to work to his advantage in choosing material everyone else passed on. "You know, I went to the movies for a long time before I was ever in them," he said. "And I always knew what was a good movie for me — something that was original. Where the language, the tenor, the tone, was strong."

When it was considered box-office suicide to make a baseball movie, Costner made two of them back-to-back, and both *Bull Durham* (1988) and *Field of Dreams* (1989) were hits. At a time when no one in Hollywood would make a western, Costner went out and raised the $18 million financing for *Dances with Wolves* himself, then directed and starred in the movie. While it was shooting, the industry sneered and dubbed the film "Kevin's Gate," a reference to the disastrous western *Heaven's Gate* (1980).

*Dances with Wolves* (1990) not only became the most successful movie of Costner's career to that date, but went on to win seven Academy Awards, including best picture and best director. Now no one made fun of his choices,

---

[30] The British actor Bob Hoskins initially was cast as Al Capone, but when it became evident Robert De Niro would do the part, Hoskins was paid off in full, and De Niro cast. From the beginning, De Palma wanted Sean Connery for the role of Ness's Chicago mentor, Malone. Connery had had little U.S. box-office appeal since the days of James Bond. *The Untouchables* not only won him an Academy Award for best supporting actor, but established him as a potent box-office force with North American audiences. Moreover, when Paramount refused to pay Connery's usual $2 million fee, the actor was persuaded to take a percentage of the movie's gross. *The Untouchables* went on to earn more than $100 million, making Connery a much richer man than he ever would have been had Paramount merely paid his fee.

not even when he dusted off an old Lawrence Kasdan script called *The Bodyguard* and in 1991 put it into production. Kasdan had written the script about a former secret service agent hired to protect a famous comedian 15 years before. "After five unsold scripts and five years as an advertising copywriter, *Bodyguard* got me an agent who then submitted it sixty-seven times over a two-year period," Kasdan recalled.

In the late '70s, Warner Bros. finally optioned it for $20,000, and the comedian became a pop singer to make the project appealing to Diana Ross. Steve McQueen was interested for a time in playing the male lead, but then it looked as though Ryan O'Neal would do it. However, it was Ross who stopped the movie from going into production. "She did not want to do the sex scenes, did not want to swear and did not want to be seen as being too black," O'Neal recalled. The project died amidst a welter of rewrites until Costner came along and chose the pop singer Whitney Houston to co-star, even though she had never acted in a movie. Like Ross, Houston insisted that most of the sex scenes be cut, and she would not take off her clothes. Nonetheless, despite almost universally negative reviews, *The Bodyguard*, powered by one of the most successful soundtrack albums in the history of pop music, became a phenomenal hit at Christmas of 1992, reasserting that even in a weak vehicle, Costner's popularity remained unassailable.

"I'm surprised that people did not recognize that Lawrence had written a good script," Costner said with a shrug. "Then again, I'm always surprised by what people think are good scripts. I get a lot of them sent to me and I don't find them well written at all." As a result, Costner has turned down an astonishing number of movies, and in the process helped, among others, Tom Berenger, who had starred in *The Big Chill*.

When Costner rejected the role of the morally corrupt sergeant, Barnes, in Oliver Stone's *Platoon* (1986) because his brother had been in Vietnam, Berenger was cast. Two years later, he said no when director Costa-Gavras asked him to be in *Betrayed* (1988), and again Berenger replaced him. Costner also passed on *Mississippi Burning* (the relationship with Gene Hackman was too close to the one he had with Sean Connery in *The Untouchables*; Willem Dafoe was cast); and *The Accidental Tourist* (the role went to William Hurt); and *Everybody's All-American* (Dennis Quaid did the part). On a single weekend in 1989, he rejected the starring role in four movies adapted from bestselling novels: *The Prince of Tides* (Nick Nolte eventually did it); *Presumed Innocent* (Harrison Ford took the part); *The Hunt for Red October* (it went to Alec Baldwin); and *The Bonfire of the Vanities* (Tom Hanks was cast).

COSTNER HAD JOINED SUCH CONTEMPORARIES AS ARNOLD SCHWARZEN-egger, Sylvester Stallone, and Michael Douglas, among other movie stars, who had become Hollywood power brokers. He could not have come along at a more propitious time. The movie industry, more conservative and nervous than ever in the face of skyrocketing production costs, had never relied so heavily on stars. The biggest commanded astronomical salaries. A Michael Douglas would be paid $14 million for *Basic Instinct*. Tom Cruise received $12 million for *The Firm*. Arnold Schwarzenegger pocketed $17 million for *Last Action Hero*.

These salaries often threw the equation of moviemaking way out of kilter, meaning that everyone else earned less, and downsized, and produced fewer movies that were inhabited by a tiny coterie of increasingly powerful and expensive superstars. Not since the days of silent movies had stars been in such complete charge of their destinies. They were bolstered by high-powered talent agencies such as Creative Artists Agency and International Creative Management, who often functioned for their clients in the way the studios once operated for their contract players — finding the best material, assigning directors and screenwriters to fashion vehicles that would enhance the box office and therefore the power of the stars. The slaves had taken over the plantation in ways that would have shocked the old-time moguls. If someone had told Jack Warner that Bette Davis or Humphrey Bogart might be more powerful than he was, he would have howled with laughter.

"Nobody trades people like ballplayers now," observed veteran producer David Brown. At the beginning of 1993, 40 years after he started in the business, he was among the producers of *A Few Good Men*, a courtroom drama starring Tom Cruise, one of the most in-demand stars in American movies.

"A Tom Cruise doesn't want a studio working for him now," Brown continued. "It was a different world in those [studio] days. Today, agents such as Mike Ovitz [head of Creative Artists Agency, the most powerful talent agency in Hollywood] have become what the studio patriarchs used to be — guiding their clients as to what roles to take."

In the old days, observed veteran casting director Mike Fenton, the studios created the stars and molded the public's desire to see them. "Today, the desire to see the stars comes about through the process of public relations, television, and exploitation," he said. "The studio system taught people how to walk, to talk, how to ride a horse, how to carry themselves, how to be classy enough to be a star. For me, today, what I miss is classy people. It is different, because so many of our people are self-made. I don't think that's bad, but is Sylvester Stallone really a star? I suppose he is, but how do you compare Sylvester Stallone to a Laurence Olivier or a Cary Grant or Clark Gable? There was a kind of unreachable veneer about those people that no longer exists."

Despite the power of stardom, the real ability of stars to attract audiences was largely illusory. If anything, the box-office power of movie stars had diminished. Long gone were the days when audiences would flock to a movie simply because a Bette Davis or a Shirley Temple was in it. A star was only as good as his or her next movie. Jack Nicholson could appear in *Man Trouble* and in *Hoffa* and nobody would go near them. Yet if he co-starred in *A Few Good Men* with Tom Cruise and Demi Moore, he was suddenly participating in a $100 million hit. Jack Nicholson was a star when he appeared in a movie everyone wanted to see. Otherwise, he had no more power to attract an audience than any other actor in Hollywood. At the beginning of 1993, there were only two stars whose very presence seemed to be a guarantee of success — Kevin Costner and Arnold Schwarzenegger. As the summer of 1993 approached, Schwarzenegger was about to demonstrate an historic truism of the movie business — that even the most powerful stars are fallible.

# 17

# "HASTA LA VISTA, BABY."

*Arnold Schwarzenegger's*
*summer of discontent*

A WEEK BEFORE HIS FIRST MOVIE IN TWO YEARS WAS TO OPEN, ARNOLD Schwarzenegger, a former bodybuilding champion from Graz, Austria, swept into a meeting room inside the Four Seasons Hotel on Doheny Drive in Los Angeles. He wore a white shirt over his superbly muscled torso, and pale linen slacks. His square, comic-book hero jaw was tanned and set for action. Arnold Schwarzenegger was in trouble, but he was damned if he was going to show it. He had been reading and hearing nasty stories and innuendos about the problems surrounding his latest movie, *Last Action Hero*, for weeks now, and those reports, questioning the quality of the movie and the box-office viability of its star, made him furious. But if Arnold Schwarzenegger knew anything on that June morning, it was how to play the press. He took one look around the meeting room — and decided it was too crowded. He turned and headed for the door. "I'll be back," he quipped. "We've heard that before," someone called out.

"But this time," said Arnold, "I gave it a new inflection."

No sooner had he disappeared than the room filled with attendants moving tables, throwing open doors to a garden, and minutes later the journalists who had traveled to Los Angeles from all over the country to sit at Arnold's side found themselves regrouped onto a patio. When all was set, Arnold again burst into view, the tanned jaw widened a bit to accommodate the smile of a man used to getting his own way. "Now," he pronounced as he seated himself, "isn't this better?" The sheen of confidence remained impeccable, immovable. No matter what the journalists had heard, he was still Arnold. The months of agony and worry, of trying and retrying to get *Last Action Hero* right, had not altered that certainty.

It seemed only a moment before that it was March of 1993, and not a soul in the world doubted Arnold's box-office power. He was, as he sat in his trailer on the New York set of *Last Action Hero*, the fortress movie star — impregnable. Puffing away on one of the Romeo y Julieta Cuban cigars he loved, Arnold had mulled over the nature of his movie stardom. "I do movies people like to see," he stated. "It's that simple. You try to make sure the movies are memorable. Not just another movie. You've got to have a certain feel for hipness. You milk certain lines. 'Hasta la vista, baby,' or 'I lied.' You go over the top. People love it. Kids love it. And you do some athletic stuff, some fitness, and people think you're cool."

Outside his trailer, pressure was mounting on director John McTiernan and his crew to complete *Last Action Hero* in time for its scheduled 18 June release. But here in the comforting cocoon of his trailer, Arnold radiated nothing but confidence. After all, as he pointed out, his two previous movies, *Total Recall* and *Terminator 2: Judgment Day*, had been completed under similar time constraints, and they had gone on to become huge hits around the world, confirming Schwarzenegger as a box-office phenomenon unlike any other in the modern history of movies. There was no sense on this March evening that Arnold could do anything but succeed. *Last Action Hero* might go vastly over its $60 million budget (at this point it was rumored to be costing from $80 to $100 million), and if it turned out to be a tight finish to get the movie into theaters, so what? Arnold's audience was out there and waiting. The summer was expected to be a duel between Arnold and the dinosaurs of Steven Spielberg's *Jurassic Park*. Arnold would win. Arnold always won.

There was no sense that the movies' most powerful box-office star was in trouble or that he was on a path leading to the biggest flop of his 10-year career. The failure of Arnold Schwarzenegger in the summer of 1993 demonstrated not only the continuing precariousness of movie stardom, but also its wide-ranging ramifications. *Last Action Hero* was to become much more than a movie star vehicle that failed to deliver. It symbolized what was wrong with the movie business in general as it shook a studio to its foundations and caused Hollywood once again to question itself and the kind of pictures it was making. If Arnold could rise higher than any other star, then he would also fall further — and with an impact of atomic proportions.

The finger of blame subsequently would be pointed in many directions, but the plain fact was that *Last Action Hero* would not have existed had Arnold not wanted to do it. Most movies could always accommodate another actor, and were designed that way, but not this one. It was a vehicle hand-tooled for the world's most popular action star, and consequently nearly $3 million had been spent on its development, not because Arnold had agreed to do it, but in the hope that he would. It is doubtful that a studio had ever spent so much money in order to persuade a single star to say yes. One would think that for a project to attract the attention of a major Hollywood studio and the town's most powerful star, its pedigree would have to be impressive. Surely the finest writers in the industry must have worked on it. Certainly the brightest producers and directors in town would have shaped it. As it turned out, that was not at all the case.

WHAT WOULD ALWAYS AMAZE THE UNKNOWN, UNTESTED AUTHORS of *Last Action Hero*, Zak Penn and Adam Leff, both 25, was that what they had written out of a sense of pure fun got to be taken so seriously. Graduates of Wesleyan College in Connecticut, they were living in a crummy Hollywood apartment in the fall of 1991 when they finished the screenplay, their third, that they had been working on for the past four months. *Extremely Violent* was both a sendup and a celebration of all the action movies they had grown up with. They had sat through 36 action films in order to concoct this adventure of a young boy who is swept into a movie screen and becomes involved with his favorite action hero. The story was a variation on a Woody Allen movie, *The Purple Rose of Cairo*, in which a movie hero came down off the screen and into real life.

At the time they finished writing it, Penn and Leff thought *Extremely Violent* might suit any number of action stars — Sylvester Stallone, perhaps, or maybe some lesser practitioner of the genre, such as Jean-Claude Van Damme or Dolph Lundgren. Of course, the star they would have preferred was Arnold Schwarzenegger, but they rejected the notion. It would be impossible. "It's like if you plan a dinner party," Zak Penn said. "You hope in the best of all possible worlds the president of the United States will show up, but what are the chances of it really happening?" Still, while at college they had become friends with Matt Winston, the son of special effects wizard Stan Winston, and he knew Arnold Schwarzenegger. Winston, who was now working on *Jurassic*

*Park*, had offered encouragement to the two young screenwriters, and when they finished their script, they gave him a copy, which he in turn showed to Schwarzenegger. Even before anyone else had a look at it, Arnold Schwarzenegger knew about the script that was to become *Last Action Hero*.

However, in the fall of 1991, following the worldwide success of *Terminator 2*, Schwarzenegger was in no hurry to go back to work. He recently had started a family with his wife, television journalist Maria Shriver. Moreover, he had been working hard for the past three years churning out one hit movie after another. Now he was coming off the biggest success in a career that had begun as something of a good-natured joke — a muscle man, the son of an Austrian policeman who had been sympathetic to the Nazis, a foreigner hobbled with a funny name and thick accent; nonetheless, Schwarzenegger had arrived in Hollywood announcing he would one day become a movie star, much like his hero Clint Eastwood. This assertion was not taken seriously, bodybuilders being freaks, not movie stars.

But Schwarzenegger had fooled everyone. Totally focused and absolutely determined, he had arrived at the summit from which he now looked down on the narrow movie world by way of his sense of humor and a canny reading of what both Hollywood and the moviegoing public wanted to see. Schwarzenegger, refreshingly, had been frank about both his desire for stardom and his unalloyed enjoyment of it once it was attained. "You can't dislike him," declared actress Mercedes Ruehl, one of his *Last Action Hero* co-stars. "He wears this enormous fortune so gracefully — the richest man in the world, and he's having such a good time."

In the autumn of 1991, Arnold considered at least a dozen different projects, some of them improbable to be sure — an explorer in a yellow hat who gets involved with a monkey in Africa, and a comedy for his friend Ivan Reitman, in which he would become pregnant. There were also suggestions of a new version of *The Count of Monte Cristo*, or a remake of the Frank Capra classic, *Mr. Deeds Goes to Town*, or a costume epic directed by Paul Verhoeven concerning the Crusades. Beginning in November of 1991, however, it became clear that the most determined campaign for Arnold was being orchestrated by Columbia Pictures and its new head, Mark Canton, who had taken over the studio the month before and was determined to score fast. He had chosen to do this via "the business of getting into business with Arnold." Columbia executives, furthermore, felt that they had the project best suited to the actor's talents.

Zak Penn and Adam Leff had by this time attracted an agent to represent *Extremely Violent*. He had sent the script around to various producers, including Steve Roth at Columbia. "It had a wonderful first act when this disenfranchised kid is sucked into the movie," said Roth. He turned it over to Barry Josephson, Columbia's executive vice president of production, who also was intrigued and saw immediately who the story was intended for. If the two young writers had hoped against hope that Schwarzenegger might be interested, now Columbia began feeling the same way. The difference was, they were willing to pay for it — an initial $100,000 against a total of $350,000 if the movie was made.

The screenplay next found its way to Lou Pitt, Schwarzenegger's agent, and there were hopes the star might read it over the Christmas holidays. But before Christmas, Pitt was on the phone to his biggest client, and Arnold, having already been alerted to the story by Stan Winston, now signaled his interest in talking about it with Columbia. "Having a kid come into a movie awakened certain fantasies I had as a kid in Austria," Schwarzenegger said. "What would it be like to sit in John Wayne's saddle or have him come with this huge horse right out of the screen?"

But although he liked the idea, Schwarzenegger did not think the script was professionally written. That did not matter to Columbia. Having seen their star attracted to the bait, the trick now was to reel him in. "When you're dealing with Arnold Schwarzenegger, you go into a high stage of alert, Defcon 1," reported Barry Josephson. "You can't let anything fall between the cracks."

To please Arnold, the script would be rewritten, and to that end, Arnold wanted Shane Black, the youthful creator of the *Lethal Weapon* movies. Black and his writing partner, David Arnott, were paid $1 million to begin rewriting in February 1992. Zak Penn and Adam Leff finally got to meet their hero at a conference of all the principals held on the Sony lot. "I thought he was a good guy," Penn said later. "He was really funny, with a terrific amount of charisma — a movie star."

Both Penn and Leff thought they detected a certain level of machination at work, but in general, although several of the participants were critical of the script, it was a congenial meeting. It was the first and last time either of the original writers was included in the production loop. From now on, what would be called *Last Action Hero* was in the hands, not of two young guys who loved action movies, but of the professionals who made them. And that would make all the difference to the execution and tone of the film.

E VEN AS THE REWORKING OF *LAST ACTION HERO* PROCEEDED, OTHER studios were in attendance at the court of Hollywood's new king. Ron Underwood, fresh from the success of *City Slickers*, was committed to a script about the tooth fairy and was anxious that Arnold do it. John Avildsen (*Rocky*) would direct a comedy called *Cop Gives Waitress $2 Million Tip* if only Arnold would agree to star. In all, five major directors sat waiting for Arnold.

In retrospect, Schwarzenegger may always have been a lot closer to doing *Last Action Hero* than he made out. Now that he was in his mid-40s, it was apparent there were limitations when it came to choosing material for him. In part, those limitations had been imposed on actors since the beginning of movies. The public sees a performer in a certain way and desires, with certain variations, to see that performer the same way again and again. Historically, movie stars have gotten into trouble by not giving the moviegoing public what it wants. Schwarzenegger prided himself in his intuitive understanding of what was wanted from him. "Never change," was his recipe for maintaining stardom. "*Never.* Everything I have ever done in my life has always stayed. I have just *added* to it. The muscles will always be in the movies. I will never ignore or avoid them. I will add to them. I will add to the acting ability. I will add to the types of roles that I play. I will add to the kinds of responsibilities I take on with my movies. But I will not change. Because when you are successful and you change, you are an idiot."

Although he might entertain the idea of playing a pregnant hero or a guy in a yellow hat in the jungle with a monkey, in the end Arnold would satisfy his constituency. The public wanted him in action, lots of shooting and explosions, and there was very little Schwarzenegger could do to alter that formula without putting his stardom into jeopardy. He was on top, and *Last Action Hero* seemed the most obvious vehicle with which to ensure that he remained there.

By July of 1992, the Black-Arnott rewrite had attracted a major director, John McTiernan, who had established his reputation as an action filmmaker with *Predator*, one of Schwarzenegger's earlier successes. Since then he had directed *Die Hard* and *The Hunt for Red October*, box-office megahits.

However, his previous film, *Medicine Man*, a romantic adventure set in the South American rain forest that co-starred Sean Connery and Lorraine Bracco, had not been a success. *Last Action Hero* would provide McTiernan with a needed hit.

He and Schwarzenegger wasted little time deciding they were unhappy with the final third of the script. More work was needed, and so there was still no commitment. Now he wanted more of a sense of bonding between action hero and boy, and in order to accomplish this, Arnold thought of the two-time Oscar-winning writer William Goldman. Goldman was the novelist who had written the script for *Butch Cassidy and the Sundance Kid* in 1969 and seven years later had successfully adapted the screenplay for *All the President's Men*. Recently he had become one of Hollywood's foremost script doctors, contributing to *A Few Good Men*, *Chaplin*, and *Indecent Proposal*. Schwarzenegger had had experience with him via the rewrites Goldman had contributed to *Twins* (1988), a movie that marked Arnold's first foray into outright comedy.

When he was approached in July of 1992, Goldman declined the job. But Arnold was adamant, and Goldman was persuaded to work on the *Last Action Hero* script for four weeks in return for $750,000. In the course of the next month, the number of villains was reduced and a sense of vulnerability was added to Arnold's character, Jack Slater, thereby strengthening the relationship with the movie's 11-year-old hero. "Goldman gave Arnold a character to play," McTiernan said. "And he excised a hundred and fifty toilet jokes."

There was also another dynamic at work. Arnold wanted to be the last action hero, but what he no longer desired was to be the *violent* action hero. The new movie, if he did it, would introduce a kinder, gentler Arnold for the '90s, one you could take the whole family to see. "This is a softer movie," he said later, "not really soft, but it's more acceptable to all kinds of audiences, young and old."

Goldman's rewrite worked its magic, even though at least two more writers would do still more work on the script — Larry Ferguson (*The Hunt for Red October*) and Sally Robinson (*Medicine Man*), who was said to have written dialogue for Mercedes Ruehl as Danny's mother. Arnold would not be pregnant or wear a yellow hat in Africa, nor would he attempt to persuade his audience that he would make a great tooth fairy. He would be what the world wanted him to be, the last action hero.

Because of the delays in Arnold's decision, production did not start until the end of October 1992 on various locations in and around Los Angeles. The announced budget was $60 million, but by March 1993 there was talk of a budget skyrocketing toward $80 million and a production already running behind schedule. This was not unusual for a Schwarzenegger picture. As Arnold himself pointed out, his movies were bigger and cost more because that was what his worldwide audience wanted. Besides, it all paid off in the end. Mark Canton himself addressed the concerns about budget at ShoWest, an annual convention of theater exhibitors held in Las Vegas in March. "We've adopted the mantra of all well-run businesses: We want it but only if the price is right — or Arnold's in it." Arnold was in it. Therefore the price — any price — was right.

On the *Action Hero* set, all seemed to be love and optimism, with Arnold totally calm and in command. "My wife says I'm more relaxed on this movie than I've ever been," he said. "It's been a most pleasant shoot." Not just the star of the movie, he was also its executive producer. If he disliked something, he changed it. For example, Arnold did not like the one sheet that would be used to advertise *Last Action Hero* on billboards and in newspapers. It did not look dramatic enough, and, moreover, his hair was not flying around him. The poster was made more dramatic. Arnold's hair flew. This new exercise of power was very much to his liking. He had ordered the script rewritten until he was satisfied, he had handpicked McTiernan to direct, now he was overseeing the marketing campaign as well. "Before," he said, "I always felt a little bit like I was butting in. I was saying, 'Let me see the drawings, let me see the poster. Let's check out which photograph we should use.' I always felt I was stepping over the line." Not any more. Now it was very much Arnold as auteur.

How did Columbia Pictures feel about all this? "When you have Arnold, you have Arnold *plus*," said Sid Ganis, Columbia's president of marketing and distribution, with great enthusiasm. "Arnold plus his total understanding of his public. And he knows how to market himself within that awareness. It's amazing. I mean I've worked with a zillion movie stars, and I've never seen anything quite like this."

By the time *Last Action Hero* finished shooting in March 1993, the Hollywood rumor mill had the budget pushing past the $100 million mark, making it about the most expensive movie in history. Still, there was no panic in evidence. Arnold was in it. The price continued to be right.

Zak Penn and Adam Leff had been to the set of *Last Action Hero* a couple of times, and Arnold was always cordial and friendly. But they were concerned, not about the movie itself, but by what they were hearing from their friend Matt Winston. He had been working on Spielberg's *Jurassic Park* and could barely restrain his enthusiasm about what had been accomplished with the state-of-the-art effects created by his father and others. The dinosaurs of *Jurassic Park* would be more real than anything ever seen on the screen. Everyone would go crazy when the movie was released. Zak Penn knew that *Jurassic Park* would open 11 June, one week before *Last Action Hero*. Could Arnold withstand the competition for a movie that might well capture everyone's imagination the way it had captured Matt Winston's? Penn began to wonder.

T HE FIRST INKLING THAT SOMETHING WAS AMISS WITH *LAST ACTION Hero* came on Saturday night, 1 May, when Columbia held a test screening in a suburban Lakewood, California, multiplex — the first time the movie had been shown to the public. Among those present were Arnold himself, Mark Canton, who had worked so hard to convince Schwarzenegger to do the picture, producer Steve Roth, and Columbia's Sid Ganis. The lights went down amidst much enthusiastic cheering from the audience, and the first showing of *Last Action Hero* got under way.

The print shown to that Saturday night crowd was little more than a rough assemblage of scenes that ran close to two hours and 20 minutes. Special effects were missing, and much of the dialogue on the temporary soundtrack was incomprehensible. Halfway through the showing, it was obvious that enthusiasm had turned to restless boredom. When the movie was over, audience members were asked to fill out cards. Canton took one look at the written responses, then collected them and never prepared an official report, almost unheard of in an industry obsessed with test marketing. The cards were forgotten. Even without them, however, it was evident that the audience did not like *Last Action Hero*, and, seven weeks before the film was due to open, something would have to be done.

By Monday 3 May, the word was all over town: the reaction to Arnold's first movie in two years was not enthusiastic. The gossip began to heat up, fueled by the news that Schwarzenegger and McTiernan were back on the streets of Los Angeles shooting new scenes. "They did reshoots for *Terminator* just *two* weeks before it came out," McTiernan argued. "It's become part of making an Arnold movie."

Maybe so, but now there was talk that the movie could not make its release date. Columbia was considering flipping *Action Hero* with Clint Eastwood's summer thriller, *In the Line of Fire*. The Eastwood movie would open on the date designated for *Last Action Hero*, while the Schwarzenegger picture would be pushed back to occupy *In the Line of Fire*'s 9 July date. Even Arnold, whose abilities at media spin control were second to none, could not keep an edge of bitterness out of his voice as he fought to counter such rumors. "Every movie I've done, there was always a buzz about how it was over budget, how it couldn't come out on time, how it was a disaster. That's because everyone in this town is jealous of the next guy. They're all a bunch of jealous bitches sitting around and saying, 'I hope he takes a dive!'"

As the 18 June release date approached, editors frantically worked triple shifts in order to get the movie ready, and in case anyone faltered, a masseuse was on standby to provide relief for sore muscles. However, no masseuse was available inside Columbia's corporate offices to offset the rising sense of panic. Canton was said to be increasingly furious over what he saw as an organized vendetta against the movie. There were reports that the studio had hired a private detective to look into the matter. Such was the level of frustration and anger that when a *Los Angeles Times* story reported rumors of a second disastrous screening, Columbia officials were so enraged that a letter was sent off to the newspaper threatening to sever all relations unless the offending reporter was publicly prohibited from any further reporting on Columbia Pictures. Nothing like it had been seen around Hollywood for years.

Nevertheless, Schwarzenegger and Columbia executives put on a bold and brave face for the movie's premiere on Sunday 13 June at two Westwood theaters, the Village and the Bruin. It was a lavish affair dominated by the same 70-foot-high helium-filled Arnold doll featured in the movie — a throwback to the sort of glamorous premiere that Hollywood used to toss regularly. *Variety* columnist Army Archerd, a veteran of these affairs, was moved to describe the party as "the biggest bash ever seen in these parts." Streets around the theaters were roped off in order to provide the stage for throngs of press, klieg lights, and a grinning, exuberant Arnold. After the movie was over, invited guests walked along a red carpeted route to a parking lot where skater/actress Sonja Henie's ice palace once had stood. Attendants in medieval costume, positioned before a mockup of the Elsinore castle that played a small part in the movie, were serving pizzas and shrimp. Everyone was impressed with the 100-foot-long dessert table, not to mention the three troupes of dancers and the spectacular fireworks display launched from the roof of a nearby parking garage that ended the celebration. Everyone talked about everything but the movie they had just seen.

As celebrants exited the party that night, word was coming in of a phenomenon even more spectacular than *Last Action Hero*'s fireworks. Steven Spielberg's dinosaur epic, *Jurassic Park*, had opened that weekend, amassing grosses of $50 million, the biggest non-holiday opening on record. The line had been marked in the sand. Could *Last Action Hero* match those kinds of revenues? Privately it was conceded that Arnold, as potent as he was, could not beat Spielberg's dinosaurs. Still, Columbia executives were predicting an opening weekend gross of $20 million, half of the $40 million that originally had been thrown out as a possibility.

The trade paper reviews of *Last Action Hero* were devastating the day after the premiere. "A joyless, soulless machine of a movie," said *Daily Variety*. The *Hollywood Reporter* was equally unimpressed: "A noisy monstrosity." On 18 June, the movie's opening day, the daily newspapers were a little kinder, but still disliked the movie and placed responsibility at the foot of Arnold's throne. In the *Los Angeles Times*, critic Kenneth Turan detected "traces of an idea that was very appealing once upon a time . . . but once an entity of Arnold Schwarzenegger's dimensions became attached to the project, any chances of it being done on an appropriate scale went south." In the *New York Times*, long-time critic Vincent Canby noted that, although John McTiernan was credited as director, "the auteur of it all was Schwarzenegger. It's his aggressively self-assured personality that shapes it. He may not have thought it up, designed the sets or photographed it, but he certainly approved of everything that went into it." Canby went on to say that, "it's to Mr. Schwarzenegger's credit that *Last Action Hero* is the riskiest film he has ever made. If it succeeds he may well run for public office. Icons of his stature get easily restless."

By Sunday afternoon 20 June, it was apparent Arnold would not soon

▲ Rocky *(1976) made Sylvester Stallone a star in the 1970s.*

▶ *But no one wanted to see him in anything else until he played John Rambo in* First Blood *(1982) and* Rambo: First Blood Part II *(1985).*

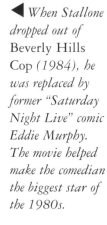

◀ *When Stallone dropped out of* Beverly Hills Cop *(1984), he was replaced by former "Saturday Night Live" comic Eddie Murphy. The movie helped make the comedian the biggest star of the 1980s.*

256A

◀ *Tom Selleck was cast as Indiana Jones in* Raiders of the Lost Ark *(1981). When he had to drop out, Harrison Ford replaced him. Selleck tried an Indiana Jones-type adventure,* High Road to China *(1983), but it was not a success.*

▲ *(Top) Michael J. Fox replaced Eric Stoltz in* Back to the Future *(1985), in which he co-starred with Lea Thompson.*

▲ *Stoltz got to co-star with Thompson, too, but it was in the little-seen* The Wild Life *(1984).*

▶ *Mel Gibson decided not to play Eliot Ness in* The Untouchables *(1987).*

▲ *Instead the part went to little-known Kevin Costner. The movie made him a star.*

When Arnold Schwarzenegger kissed his horse on the set of Conan the Barbarian (1982) he had not yet become the movies' number one action star. He established himself in The Terminator (1984), *left, and in* Total Recall (1990), *below right. But he experienced his biggest failure with* Last Action Hero (1993), *above right.*

256D

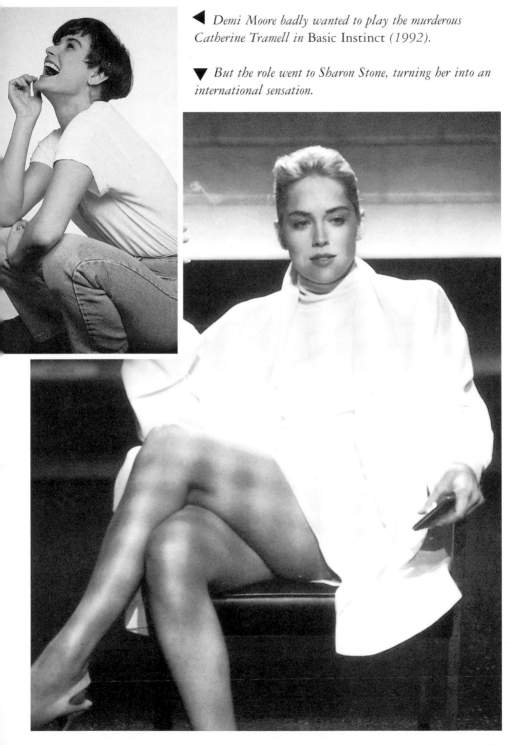

◄ *Demi Moore badly wanted to play the murderous Catherine Tramell in* Basic Instinct *(1992).*

▼ *But the role went to Sharon Stone, turning her into an international sensation.*

▲ *Jodie Foster fought hard to play the FBI agent in* The Silence of the Lambs *(1991). She got the role after Michelle Pfeiffer turned it down.*

▼ *Pfeiffer had already appeared in (from left)* Scarface *(1983),* The Witches of Eastwick *(1987), and* The Fabulous Baker Boys *(1989).*

▲ *Debra Winger trained hard to play the catcher of the Rockford Peaches in* A League of Their Own *(1992). However, she was pushed out of the movie. Geena Davis (right) got the role, and superstardom.*

*Meanwhile, Davis turned down the part of the gum-chewing girlfriend in* My Cousin Vinny *(1992). Newcomer Marisa Tomei (above right) was cast and she won an Oscar.*

▲ *Meg Ryan had the biggest success of her career in* Sleepless in Seattle *(1993), playing the role originally intended for Julia Roberts.*

▶ *Roberts, meanwhile, reaffirmed her status as the biggest female star of the 1990s in* I Love Trouble *(1994), top inset, and in* The Pelican Brief *(1993).*

be running for public office. *Last Action Hero* was not performing even close to expectations at some 3,000 theaters across North America. *Variety* summed up what had happened the next day in a headline that was as succinct as it was devastatingly accurate: "Lizards Eat Arnold's Lunch." The biggest movie star in the world had been trounced by mechanical dinosaurs. *Jurassic Park* retained the number one spot with a weekend gross of $37.5 million. In second place, *Last Action Hero* was not even close — $15.2 million, less than even the most conservative Columbia estimates. In public, the studio put the best face possible on the looming disaster. "Just watch, this is going to be a very fulfilling summer for the studio," promised Sid Ganis. "We feel great about the opening."

But things got worse. In its second week, the number of people attending *Last Action Hero* tumbled by close to 50 percent — a disastrous dropoff for any movie — and it fell into fourth place, beaten this time not just by *Jurassic Park*, but also by a new romantic comedy, *Sleepless in Seattle*. Starring Tom Hanks and Meg Ryan, two attractive but hardly surefire box-office draws, the picture had been expected to do well, but *Sleepless* outdistanced even the most optimistic projections, grossing over $17 million — more than *Last Action Hero* had made on its opening weekend. Even *Dennis the Menace*, a comedy film based on the Hank Ketcham comic strip, did better. After little more than a week in release, *Last Action Hero* was essentially dead, even though Columbia marketing executives frantically shifted the advertising campaign away from Arnold and his blowing hair to Arnold holding a gun. So much for the kinder, gentler action hero for the '90s that the whole family could see.

Depending on how the movie did in foreign markets, it was expected that Columbia would take a loss anywhere from $15 to $35 million. In September, after everything calmed down, the loss figure was amended to about $20 million. But whatever the amount, *Last Action Hero* now was considered a disaster of the proportions of *Hudson Hawk*, a bloated and shapeless Bruce Willis comedy that had taken a similar dive in 1991. But *Hudson Hawk* was just another overblown Hollywood flop. Because initial expectations for *Last Action Hero* had been so high, its demise was seen as something much more worrisome. Hollywood was increasingly unhappy with the big, loud, empty extravaganzas it was so obsessed with producing, and *Last Action Hero* now stood as an example of an industry that had gone terribly wrong in its thinking. "We hate ourselves and the work we are producing," the *Los Angeles Times* quoted one motion picture executive as saying. "And this film is the most obvious manifestation of that problem."

Said another studio executive: "It's the worst I've seen since *Heaven's Gate*. This is as bad for the business as *Jurassic Park* is good. It creates a groundswell of negativity."

Zak Penn, who along with Adam Leff had started all this in the first place, felt that what they had created with a great amount of affection had been turned into a movie by people who mostly had no affection for the material at all, and that it showed on the screen. He might have come closer than anyone to detecting what was wrong with *Last Action Hero*. Nobody seemed very committed to what was on the screen. Everyone had a sense of the commerce involved, but somewhere along the line the original vision of a couple of young writers who loved action movies got lost amidst the noise and the money.

Curiously, despite the fact that the movie would never have existed without him, little of the blame for its failure was aimed at Schwarzenegger himself. Such was the nature of his stardom that, although stories of despondent studio executives looking for new jobs proliferated and the possibility of Mark Canton's demise was discussed, little was said about Arnold. Part of this was because nobody was willing to count Schwarzenegger out, even in the wake of the biggest failure of his career. What went wrong, Arnold concluded, was that he had ignored his own first dictum as a movie star: Don't change. He *had* changed, trying to give his audience something for the entire family, and that had left everyone confused. Arnold's fans like him violent, and when he failed to give them the violence, they stayed away. The family audience he was trying to attract simply never showed up. They all went to see *Jurassic Park* instead.

Shortly before *Last Action Hero* opened, Arnold announced that he would star in yet another action-oriented adventure for his friend James Cameron, who had guided him through the two *Terminator* movies. The movie was to be called *True Lies*, and the budget was reported to be $35 million. Shortly thereafter, new reports surfaced that the budget had jumped to $50 million, weeks before Arnold even stepped in front of a camera. After *True Lies*, Arnold said, he would play a man who is pregnant. He said nothing about the possibility of a guy in a yellow hat with a monkey.

# 18
# TOM AND HARRISON OPEN
## *But Alec doesn't*

B Y THE TIME TOM CRUISE ARRIVED IN FRONT OF MANN'S CHINESE theater on Monday, 28 June 1993, Hollywood, deftly executing an exercise in mass psychology, had erased *Last Action Hero* from its collective thinking. The movie was out there somewhere in a couple of thousand theaters, but it was best to forget and get on to other things. Arnold was not the end of Hollywood, the thinking seemed to go, and here was Cruise stepping from a long black Cadillac limousine to provide the continuum of stardom, the reassurance that if one star was falling, another was on the rise. And at noon hour on that sun-drenched Monday, with crowds the like of which had not been seen for years pressing to get a look at him, Cruise was definitely a young man on the rise.

He was at Mann's Chinese theater to participate in one of the few rituals of movie stardom left over from Hollywood's bygone days. Grinning broadly and dressed in a cherry-colored shirt and jeans, accompanied by his pale, lovely wife, actress Nicole Kidman, Cruise was present for the laying of his hands into the specially prepared wet cement of the Chinese theater's forecourt. Here was a last tenuous link to the days when movie stars denoted the sort of storybook glamor that did not much exist anymore. The legendary Sid Grauman had opened his Chinese theater in 1927. A showman who loved bigness and glitz, Grauman originated the idea of the lavish premiere with movie stars getting all dressed up and klieg lights splashing the garish facades of his theaters. There was some controversy over who exactly originated the idea of the stars immortalizing themselves in cement, but there was no doubt it happened on Sid Grauman's watch.

Lots had changed since those days, but the renamed Mann's Chinese somehow survived, a trifle tacky certainly, its crimson pagodas rising over the

T-shirt emporiums and fast food dives that constitute today's Hollywood Blvd., a far cry from the glamorous thoroughfare the theater had presided over in the 1920s. Even attempting to conjure memories of old Hollywood was fraught with the machinations of today's corporate world in which movie stars such as Cruise now existed.

Because the Mann's theater chain was jointly owned by Paramount Communications and Time Warner, the biggest media conglomerate in the world, any new addition to the forecourt of the theater had to be approved by the partners. Therefore, if an actor was not appearing in either a Paramount picture or a movie produced by Warner Bros., he or she could not become part of Hollywood history. Since Cruise's new movie, *The Firm*, due to open in two days, was produced by Paramount, his handprints were an acceptable addition to posterity. However, posterity had to be positioned properly. When it was discovered Tom Cruise would be located in a cement slab next to Mickey Mouse, that was deemed inappropriate, even though it could rightly be argued that the irrepressible Mickey was already a much bigger and more enduring star. The location was moved.

As music from *Top Gun*, the movie that had transformed Cruise into a superstar in 1986, blared across Hollywood Blvd., cameras snapped away while Sydney Pollack, *The Firm*'s director, and Sherry Lansing, president of Paramount's motion picture group, looked on admiringly, along with producer Scott Rudin. Cruise wrote his name into the quickly hardening cement, pressed his palms, and left behind the imprints of his feet, a trifle difficult since he was wearing shoes that were too big for him, so someone had to help press them down into the cement.

Then, movie history taken care of, Cruise hurried across Hollywood Blvd. to shake hands with the hundreds of fans gathered behind metal barriers. The crowd shoved forward, pressing into his hands copies of *The Firm*, the John Grisham novel on which Cruise's movie was based, for him to autograph. Everyone remarked how beautiful his wife was in her straw sunhat and summer frock, and how "cute" the couple looked together. They were bright, sunny people on a warm California day, and for a moment, it was possible to believe that Hollywood was the way it used to be, and movie stars truly were America's royalty.

Everyone present was slightly taken aback by the size of the crowd that had turned out to see Cruise, and that was interpreted as yet another good omen for *The Firm*. The town had been so preoccupied by the astonishing grosses of *Jurassic Park* and the misfortunes of *Last Action Hero* that no one had paid much attention to *The Firm*. Wags sneered, dubbed Cruise "Tom Terrific" and "Tom Thumb," and snickered about the squeaky clean heroes he insisted on playing. But if nothing else, the ceremony at Mann's Chinese theater reminded everyone that there was an old-fashioned movie star out there who did not need dinosaurs or explosions to sell tickets.

True to the promise held out in front of the Chinese theater, Tom Cruise two days later delivered the audience that historically has been required of movie stars. On its opening day across North America, *The Firm* grossed $7.2 million, and by the end of the July 4th holiday weekend, it had taken in revenues of $44.5 million, unseating *Jurassic Park* as the number one movie. Everyone was frankly amazed — and relieved — that a movie that did not rely on special effects or action sequences could open so power-fully. "It's good news for us and the industry," said Barry London, president of the Paramount motion pictures group. "Pictures like this don't usually open to this level of business."

As Hollywood sought to rid itself of the bitter aftertaste of *Last Action Hero*, what seemed to be re-emerging was the kind of meticulously crafted movie fueled by the power of a popular star that Hollywood tradi-tionally has done best but had lately eschewed in favor of more obvious pyrotechnics. The suspicion that old-fashioned moviemaking once again was in vogue was confirmed a week later with the opening of *In the Line of Fire*, a well-crafted thriller starring 63-year-old Clint Eastwood as a secret service agent trying to stop a presidential assassin, John Malkovich. The producer, Jeff Apple, had been trying to bring *In the Line of Fire* to the screen for years. Dustin Hoffman had been interested in one version, Robert Redford, briefly, in another, before the screenplay was written yet again to accommodate Sean Connery, who decided to star in *Rising Sun* instead. Then in April of 1992, the script by Jeff Maguire was sold to Castle Rock Entertainment, and shortly thereafter Clint Eastwood committed to the movie. Names such as Robert Duvall and Jack Nicholson were mentioned before John Malkovich agreed to play the assassin.

All this was particularly good news for producer Arnold Kopelson and his director, Andrew Davis, completing production of a thriller based on "The Fugitive" television series, so popular between 1963 and 1967. It was to be an action movie, but like *The Firm* and *In the Line of Fire*, it would function on plot and character — and movie stardom as personified this time by 51-year-old Harrison Ford.

If Arnold Schwarzenegger was the superbly muscled comic-book hero sprung to life, and Tom Cruise the well-chiseled young heartthrob, Ford was the all-too-human being up there on the screen. He could be heroic, but entirely vulnerable as well. "Far more than Stallone or Schwarzenegger," journalist David Halberstam wrote of him, "Ford is a cinematic hero with the kind of courage that ordinary citizens can identify with. His big screen character stands at the very center of American myth and represents one of our most cherished self-images. For it is the quiet man who minds his own business, who does not seek trouble but who should not be pushed around."

Any actor who can readily embody those qualities has always been in demand in Hollywood. Initially, though, Arnold Kopelson did not have Ford in mind for *The Fugitive*, and therein lies a David and Goliath story, bearing in mind that in the Hollywood version of such a story, there can be only one outcome — Goliath wins.

FROM SHEEPSHEAD BAY IN BROOKLYN, NEW YORK, KOPELSON, A FORMER lawyer and banking attorney, had first become involved in film distribution, then in production. He won an Academy Award in 1986 as the producer of *Platoon*. Since the 1970s, when he was the lawyer representing Quinn Martin, executive producer of the TV series, Kopelson had longed to turn "The Fugitive" into a movie. Warner Bros. had bought the project, then placed it in what was known in Hollywood as "development hell." When Kopelson finally waded in to retrieve it, he had a director attached to the project — Walter Hill. Now he needed a star. A young actor named Alec Baldwin came to mind.

When Kopelson met with Baldwin, the timing could not have been better. The handsome, dark-haired young actor was 30 years old and had recently filmed *The Hunt for Red October*. This was a post–Cold War thriller, taken from a novel by Tom Clancy, in which Baldwin co-starred with Sean Connery. It had become a hit, grossing more than $100 million.

Baldwin landed the role of CIA agent Jack Ryan in the film after Kevin Costner had turned it down — yet another example of the part one star turns down opening the way to stardom for someone less tried. Baldwin already was respected for the astute manner in which he had developed his movie career. From Massapequa, New York, the eldest of six children, Baldwin had transferred into an acting program at New York University, then, while working as a waiter/lifeguard at a Manhattan health club restaurant, attracted the attention of a casting agent who landed him a part in a TV soap opera called "The Doctors." After five years, he moved to Los Angeles, where he was cast in a nighttime soap, "Knots Landing."

Dissatisfied by the ease with which he had fallen into the TV actor's life, Baldwin retreated to New York, did *Serious Money* and *Prelude to a Kiss* on stage, and at the same time carefully began to make his way into films, taking small roles in large pictures directed by important directors. He was in Jonathan Demme's *Married to the Mob*, Tim Burton's *Beetlejuice*, Oliver Stone's *Talk Radio*, and Mike Nichols' *Working Girl*. The ploy worked. By the time Costner turned down the part of Jack Ryan in *Red October*, Baldwin had come to the attention of Gary Lucchesi, who at the time was president of Paramount production. Lucchesi turned him over to Mace Neufeld, *Red October*'s producer, who immediately saw the possibilities and hired Baldwin for the lead.

Baldwin, talented, clever, outgoing, and well liked by everyone, had been handed the right opportunity at the right time. He was about to join the ranks of the powerful elite of male stars who dominated movies — Tom Cruise, Kevin Costner, Harrison Ford, and Arnold Schwarzenegger. Baldwin was to follow *Red October* with a sequel, *Patriot Games*, in which he again would play Jack Ryan.

S UCCESS IN HOLLYWOOD CAN HAVE A TRANSFORMING EFFECT ON AN actor. The nicest guys in the world become monsters. Baldwin until now had been known as one of the former, but reports began to surface of a darker, more temperamental actor. The monster was on the rise, abetted by his new co-star and girlfriend, actress Kim Basinger. From the set of *The Marrying Man*, a comedy written by Neil Simon, reports began to emerge of fights over the script, temper tantrums, and late arrivals. "Here's this guy, about whom there'd never been a whisper of trouble," said one Hollywood producer. "He's on everybody's A-list. We couldn't believe it was the same guy." Baldwin did not help matters when he gave interviews after *Marrying Man* was completed describing Jeffrey Katzenberg, the head of production at Disney, as "the eighth dwarf — Greedy."

The budget of *Marrying Man*, set at $15 million, had jumped to $23 million. When the movie was released, it was almost universally panned and went on to gross only $11.5 million, far short of what was needed to break even, let alone make a profit. However, difficult movie stars with an unsuccessful movie on their resumés were hardly a new phenomenon. Baldwin was committed to start work on *Patriot Games* in October 1991 with his pricetag at $4 million (he had received $1.5 million for *Marrying Man*). He was to earn another $6 million for a third Jack Ryan adventure, *Clear and Present Danger*. Thus, for two movies, Alec Baldwin stood to make $10 million. That summer, however, Brandon R. Tartikoff, who had been running the NBC television network, took over as head of Paramount from the ousted Frank Mancuso, and suddenly the studio was in a state of disarray and uncertainty. The October start of *Patriot Games* was postponed.

In the meantime, Baldwin had been offered the part of Stanley Kowalski in a Broadway revival of Tennessee Williams' *A Streetcar Named Desire*, with Jessica Lange playing Blanche Dubois. For any stage-trained actor, such an offer comes once in a lifetime. Baldwin would later grumble that Hollywood did not understand the difference between an actor and a movie star — that was true enough. One seldom had anything to do with the other. Baldwin, flexing the power of his recently bestowed movie stardom, wanted Paramount to allow him to keep his commitment to *Streetcar* and somehow work the production of *Patriot Games* around it. What choice did the studio have, after all? Who else was Paramount going to get on such short notice?

Tartikoff, new to the job and not anxious to put up with any nonsense, delivered his answer: Harrison Ford. The actor had just dropped out of another Paramount project and the studio, anxious to keep him on the lot, gave him the *Patriot Games* script. Ford agreed to play Jack Ryan — and when one of the most bankable stars in Hollywood says yes, things change very quickly. Baldwin, not being one of Hollywood's most bankable stars, suddenly was nothing but trouble, and out of *Patriot Games*.

"The day things fell apart, I remember telling Alec, 'I hope this Broadway show does everything for you that you want it to,'" said Mace Neufeld, the producer of *Patriot Games*.

Baldwin later said he could never understand why it took Paramount so long to get a sequel into production after the huge success of *The Hunt for Red October*. "The deal dragged on and on," he remembered. "Then all of a sudden they said, 'Decide by Thursday afternoon, and that's it,' pressuring me to choose between the movie and the play."

Baldwin went off to Broadway and was critically acclaimed for his performance in *Streetcar*. Hollywood barely noticed. Great theater reviews had nothing to do with the care and maintenance of the kind of box-office clout that successfully launched an expensive commercial movie. In June of 1992, *Patriot Games* was released, with Harrison Ford playing Jack Ryan. There was grumbling from Tom Clancy, Jack Ryan's creator, that Harrison Ford was too old for Ryan, but nonetheless, *Patriot Games* proved to be the kind of success Paramount anticipated. Eventually it earned $80 million in North American box-office grosses, and went on to make another $100 million worldwide. Ford had come through with the most important function of modern-day movie stardom — he had opened the movie, which is to say his name attracted an audience on its first weekend, setting the groundwork for the film's eventual success.

A month after *Patriot Games* opened, Baldwin co-starred with Meg Ryan in the movie version of the romantic comedy *Prelude to a Kiss*, in which he had played off-Broadway. Even though the movie received generally good reviews and starred two young actors considered "hot," *Prelude to a Kiss* was anything but a box-office hit. The people who kept an eye on such matters could not help but notice that Harrison Ford had opened his movie while Alec Baldwin, charged with the same function, had not.

"With the movies," Baldwin ruefully noted, "everybody loves you when you do exactly what they want you to do. And when you don't, they hate your guts."

IN AUGUST OF 1992, SIX MONTHS BEFORE *THE FUGITIVE* WAS TO START production, Arnold Kopelson still favored Alec Baldwin for the Richard Kimble role. But now, suddenly, there was a problem. Warner Bros., the studio investing $40 million in the production, was increasingly uncertain about Baldwin. Evidence was required that he could open a big-budget summer picture. The opportunity to demonstrate that ability had presented itself in *Patriot Games*. But Baldwin was not in *Patriot Games*. He had done *Prelude to a Kiss*. Someone who inspired more confidence was needed. A familiar face was about to reappear in Alec Baldwin's life.

Faced with Warners' hesitation, Kopelson sent the script of *The Fugitive* to Patricia McQueeney, the agent who represented Harrison Ford. She liked what she read and passed it on to her client. Ford later claimed he had never watched the original television series starring David Janssen, and, although he felt the script still needed work (there was no third act, not enough jeopardy, and the villains needed to be more clearly defined), he committed himself to the movie. As no formal arrangement had been reached with Baldwin, he was unceremoniously out. For the second time in two years, Harrison Ford had replaced him in a high-profile Hollywood movie. There was, however, little sympathy in the film community for Baldwin's dilemma. He had made the worst mistake an actor can make in his career: he had said no when he should have said yes. Now he was paying for it.

When *The Fugitive* opened on 6 August it grossed $23,758,855, the biggest opening ever for a movie at that time of the year. Kopelson was blunt-spoken about what had happened: "Harrison Ford opens movies. Alec Baldwin is clearly not an actor who can open a movie."

HARRISON FORD HAD DONE HIS JOB SPECTACULARLY. IN THE MEANTIME Alec Baldwin completed work on a remake of a Steve McQueen action movie, *The Getaway*, then began talking to producer Martin Bregman about starring in a movie version of the old radio series *The Shadow*. Bregman said he had three actors in mind when he set about casting the movie's anti-hero, Lamont Cranston: Al Pacino, Jeremy Irons, and Baldwin. "I discussed it with Al, but it just wasn't his kind of thing. He did not quite understand it. He's too old. It needs a young man." Nonetheless, Bregman also thought of the noted British actor Jeremy Irons. "He wanted to do it, but it was a question of timing, and he wasn't available. But also as I got further and further into this thing, I wanted a younger actor. Youth brings energy, it brings charisma, it makes it more accessible to a younger audience."

So instead of losing this time, Alec Baldwin, who had youth and charisma on his side, won the role of *The Shadow*, and Martin Bregman was elated. "Alec Baldwin is a great choice," he said, "and I never thought I would get him." Why not? Bregman looked nonplussed. "Why, because Alec Baldwin really is a movie star." For the moment, Harrison Ford was nowhere in sight.

# 19

# A LEAGUE OF THEIR OWN
## *Women and starring roles in the '90s*

I N EARLY MARCH OF 1993, AN EXCITED BUZZ RAN THROUGH THE PASTEL-
hued interior of the Paramount dining room. Sharon Stone was about to
have lunch. She did not simply enter a room. Sharon Stone was the
celebrity of the moment, therefore she *made an entrance*. Tall and striking, her
short blonde hair flying away from high cheekbones and bright, humorous
eyes, Stone was like a big, slim, particularly contented cat as she made her way
across the rear room. She was finishing work on her first movie since creating a
sensation a year before with her appearance in *Basic Instinct*.

The native of Meadville, Pennsylvania, had been in Hollywood since
1980 and had been the designated blonde starlet in 15 movies without causing
much of a stir. But all of that had changed virtually overnight thanks to her
portrayal of Catherine Tramell, a wealthy, bisexually amoral novelist who may
or may not have murdered her lover with an icepick. In the movie's most
talked-about scene, Stone as Tramell was interrogated by San Francisco police
officers. At one point in the sequence she shifted slightly and crossed her legs,
allowing audiences all over the world, as Stone herself later conceded, to "see
right through to Nebraaaska!" If a single scene in the history of movies could
be said to have created a movie star, the crossing of those long legs created
Sharon Stone. She later claimed, somewhat ludicrously in the view of people
who know anything about the complicated process of moviemaking, that she
had not realized director Paul Verhoeven was going to film her like that.
Unexpected camera angles notwithstanding, having been turned into an
overnight sensation, Stone understood the ramifications and knew how to
exploit her new status. She was an actress who had just starred in an international hit that had grossed $350 million.

But as she picked at her lunch in the Paramount dining room, a nagging question had not been answered. *Was* she a movie star on the strength of one controversial movie? The perception in the business in March was affirmative — that her presence in the right kind of movie could draw an audience eager to see what she was going to do next. That perception was based on advance word about her new movie. *Sliver* was to be another erotic thriller, and in the long, hot, male-dominated summer of 1993, it had been adroitly promoted as the year's sexiest and most controversial thriller, the sort of movie you could expect from the *Basic Instinct* girl.

Stone knew that, in her mid-30s, she was late to all this and that this immense good fortune had been bestowed on her more by accident than by any design. She had attempted for years to orchestrate her stardom with no success; now abruptly it was hers not so much because of what she did, but because of what virtually every other major actress had refused to do. Anyone with any kind of name had turned down the part of Catherine. Michelle Pfeiffer was appalled by the script and what it required of an actress. Geena Davis had taken a pass. Even a little-known actress named Kelly Lynch had said no. Verhoeven said he had Stone in mind from the beginning, but that she did not have the box-office clout deemed necessary to complement Michael Douglas, who was playing the obsessed cop.

It was Paul Verhoeven who had fought for Stone in *Total Recall* (1990), in which she had briefly played Arnold Schwarzenegger's violent, duplicitous wife. There were suggestions that Verhoeven's relationship with her went beyond that of director and actress. "She does a lot of flirting," he said. "One of the most threatening things about her is that she can change in a split second so that in her eyes there's either a loving person or the devil. I have hated her with all my heart, and I have loved her, too. She can be so goddamned mean."

That description sounded a lot like the character Stone played in *Basic Instinct*. Had the right part accidentally found the actress born to play it? "That's not me," Stone insisted. "I'm a girl at home in my glasses and flannel pajamas." Perhaps, but long before the arrival of stardom, her personality and her snappy way with a sentence had caused problems. "In Hollywood," she astutely observed, "you can be tall, you can be blonde, you can be pretty, but you can't be smart."

*Sliver* turned out to be a major disappointment when it was released in May of 1993. By the July 4th weekend it had grossed only $36 million, far short of the $100 million revenues originally predicted. Nevertheless, having deftly navigated the complexities of suddenly entering the spotlight, Stone had demonstrated her willingness to trade seriousness for box-office clout.

In the 1980s, women in the movies generally had been passive, more interested in winning awards than they were in amassing power and gaining box-office clout in the way their male counterparts did. Actresses such as Meryl Streep, Jessica Lange, Sally Field, and Sissy Spacek fought to get small, intimate dramas made, and often were willing to sacrifice their salaries in order to do it. Although those movies won plaudits and awards, they were seldom widely seen.

Since Jane Fonda had appeared in *On Golden Pond* in 1981, virtually no dramatic actress had had the sort of runaway hit that male stars inspired. Only Bette Midler, appearing in high-concept Disney studio comedies, was able to command a sizable audience, but her pre-eminence would be short-lived as the result of a major misstep that all but ruined her movie career.

Midler's All Girl Productions had developed a comedy titled *Sister Act*, in which Bette was to play a Las Vegas lounge singer on the run from her mob boyfriend and forced to hide out in a nunnery. However, instead of that role, Midler opted to play a singer who entertains troops through three wars. *For the Boys* (1991) was a seriously intentioned old-fashioned weepie that became her obsession. *Sister Act*, meanwhile, was put through the development mill at the Disney studio, where it underwent so many rewrites and changes that its original author, playwright Paul Rudnick, had his name removed from the credits.

Eventually, Whoopi Goldberg would play the lounge singer-turned-nun, battling all through production with producer Scott Rudin as well as studio executives. By the time it was finished, the feeling was abroad that *Sister Act* would be a disaster. Goldberg all but disowned it and refused to do any publicity in connection with its May 1992 release. Then it became one of the surprise comedy hits of that summer.

Midler's *For the Boys*, released the previous Christmas with a great deal of fanfare, was a box-office dud. Before 1992, Whoopi Goldberg had been a popular performer who won a best supporting actress Oscar for her performance in *Ghost*. *Sister Act* turned her into a comedy superstar and one of the highest paid actresses in movies, receiving $7 million for the movie's sequel.

Meanwhile, Bette Midler returned to Disney to star in the sort of comedy that had made her so appealing to audiences in the '80s. But *Hocus Pocus* was only a middling success in the summer of 1993, and Midler decided to give up on movies, at least for a time.

"When I think of all the money Whoopi made on *Sister Act*, I want to kill myself," she observed ruefully.

SHARON STONE NOW FOUND HERSELF PART OF A COTERIE OF YOUNG actresses that included Jodie Foster, Demi Moore, Geena Davis, Meg Ryan, and Julia Roberts — all determined to draw audiences to their movies and demonstrate a power in the movie business that women had not possessed since the 1960s, even though the overall statistics remained discouraging. At the end of the 1980s, according to the Screen Actors Guild, only 29.1 percent of all feature film roles went to women, and the average male actor earned 60 percent more than his female counterparts.

These actresses refused to be cowed by statistics, however. They and their agents were certain that they could find and develop the kinds of movies that could be as popular as anything done by men. In order to succeed, they engaged in rivalries that were often much more fiercely competitive than any of the fights that went on among their male counterparts. "I want stardom," Demi Moore stated flatly. "I'm not like, 'Oh, yes, well, if it happens, it happens.' I really want this. I want to learn more. I want to be a great actress."

Jodie Foster echoed the same sentiments. "I've always had to fight for the movies I wanted to be in. That's what actors do. I had to fight tooth and nail for *The Accused*, and I did not find it humiliating — it's like, so what? I got the performance, and the Oscar — so what?"

It was Jodie Foster who inadvertently began the process that changed the way actresses regarded their careers and introduced the fierce competition that has resulted. She knew how to fight for a part, and she had no hesitation about doing it. By the time she turned 28 in 1991, Foster had appeared in close to 30 movies. No contemporary actress had worked as hard, made as many movies, or had so much experience. Yet she was the first to concede that she had never been anyone's "flavor of the month"; there had never been a moment in her career when she was on the cover of all the popular magazines and all scripts flowed to her. Granted, she had had her moments of notoriety.

271

Martin Scorsese's casting her as a 12-year-old prostitute saved by Robert De Niro in *Taxi Driver* (1976) had caused a great deal of public debate. Then she became something of a household name for all the wrong reasons in 1981 when a demented would-be assassin, John Hinckley, shot President Ronald Reagan in order to "express his love" for her. But for the most part, Foster had toiled away quietly, perfecting a craft that began for her at the age of three when she beat out her older brother to star in a Coppertone suntan lotion commercial. Still in her teens, she had been featured in Disney movies (*Freaky Friday*) and was cast in her first Scorsese picture (*Alice Doesn't Live Here Anymore*). When *Paper Moon*, the movie that won young Tatum O'Neal an Oscar, was turned into a short-lived TV series, it was Foster who was cast.

Foster briefly abandoned acting to attend Yale, where she graduated magna cum laude in English Literature, before resuming a career that had previously included marginal movies like *Foxes*, *Carny*, and *The Hotel New Hampshire*. In these films, she was vaguely appreciated, but the movies themselves came and went with little fanfare or impact. She might have been no more than a hard-working actress who had navigated the pitfalls of childhood into a middling adult career had it not been for *The Accused*.

The film was fictionalized, but it had been based on the true story of a woman who had wandered into a pool hall to buy cigarettes and ended up being gang-raped. Foster portrayed a promiscuous bar girl who, with the aid of an uptight district attorney (Kelly McGillis), refused to back down from prosecuting her attackers. It was a brave, complex role in a movie that also possessed commercial appeal. *The Accused* did not just win Jodie Foster an Academy Award in 1988, it also made money. Notice was taken in Hollywood, but not a great deal of notice. Despite her Oscar, there still was no heat around Jodie Foster's name.

Certainly Gene Hackman did not think of her in October of 1988 when Orion Pictures optioned *The Silence of the Lambs* for him. Thomas Harris's bestselling thriller concerned an FBI agent-in-training who tracks down a serial killer with the aid of a mass murderer named Hannibal "the Cannibal" Lecter, a brilliant psychiatrist who not only enjoyed killing his patients, but eating them, too.

Orion acquired the project, because Hackman wanted to direct and write the screenplay. He had not done either before, but he had just completed

*Mississippi Burning* for Orion, and the studio was anxious to continue its relationship with the actor. Moreover, Hackman himself would play the FBI boss, while John Hurt portrayed Lecter. For the role of Clarice, he wanted Michelle Pfeiffer, the former Miss Orange County, who had recently made a name for herself in films such as *Scarface*, *Ladyhawke*, and, most recently, *Married to the Mob*.

Hackman soon dropped the idea of playing the FBI agent and decided to take on the much juicier role of Lecter. Hackman the screenwriter was short-lived, too. Ted Tally, a playwright who had written the screenplay for the movie *White Palace*, knew Harris through his wife, loved the book, and was interested in the possibility of adapting it for the screen, but when he discovered Orion had bought the rights for Hackman, he put the matter to one side. However, his agent, Irene Donovan, kept at it. One day she phoned and said, "Gene's decided he doesn't want to work on the screenplay."

In November, Tally found himself meeting with the actor at his home in Santa Fe, New Mexico. He was halfway through the screenplay in May of 1989 when Hackman dropped out of the project entirely. "For what reasons, I'm still not sure to this day," Tally said. An acquaintance of Hackman's thought, "He always gets cold feet." A report in *People* magazine said Hackman wanted to dissociate himself from violent characters. Maybe so, but shortly after he dropped out of the project, Hackman signed to do a thriller called *Narrow Margin*, in which he portrayed a man outwitting killers aboard a train winding its way through the Canadian Rockies. It died a quick death at the box office.

Suddenly without a director, Mike Medavoy, head of Orion, approached Jonathan Demme and asked him if he was interested in doing *Silence*. Demme had recently done *Married to the Mob* for the studio. He had begun directing in 1974 with *Caged Heat*, a low-budget exploitation movie he shot for just $180,000. Demme was not known either as a mainstream Hollywood director or as the sort of filmmaker who could bring off a suspense-charged thriller. Demme himself later conceded he was the last person in the world anyone would think of for *Silence*, although he had recently worked with Michelle Pfeiffer in *Mob*, and now he, too, wanted her as Clarice Starling. In July of 1989, it was actually announced that she would play the lead role in *The Silence of the Lambs*.

Pfeiffer personified the sort of dedicated, tough-minded actress who had flowered during the 1980s, determined to be taken seriously but not particularly interested in the consequences of their choices at the box office. Pfeiffer, for all her talent and industry, seemed to have no grasp of what might be popular with audiences, and in fact was proud of it. "Most of my movies haven't made money," she observed. "I'm always afraid to say that, 'cause I think the studios haven't figured it out, and they keep letting me work."

Pfeiffer had grown up in a working-class area of Orange County in Southern California, where one of her high-school teachers described her as "a surfer chick." She was remarkably beautiful in the blonde, blue-eyed manner in which young women from California are expected to be beautiful. Shy and uncertain, she nonetheless had been drawn into show business via a beauty contest.

At the age of 21, she was cast on the short-lived TV version of *Animal House*, a series called "Delta House." Then producer Allan Carr chose her, after an exhaustive search for the right blonde, to co-star in his 1982 production of *Grease 2*. However, her big break came thanks to the efforts of Ed Limato, her agent at Creative Artists, who worked tirelessly to get her cast as Elvira, Al Pacino's coke-snorting girlfriend in *Scarface*. A couple of attempts at commercial pictures, *Into the Night* and *Ladyhawke*, did not work at the box office, so she concentrated on a series of well-received movies that increased the critical appreciation of her abilities without creating any great stampedes at the theaters where her films played. Only when she appeared with Jack Nicholson, Susan Sarandon, and Cher in *The Witches of Eastwick* did anything change dramatically. *Witches* was a hit in the summer of 1987, and suddenly people recognized her walking down the street, and the scripts she received were of better quality. "That's when things began to escalate," she said, "because it made a lot of money."

By the time Jonathan Demme became involved in *The Silence of the Lambs*, Pfeiffer was having second thoughts about the subject matter. "Michelle read it and it became apparent she was unable to come to terms with the overwhelming darkness of the piece," Demme said.

Which was exactly what Jodie Foster loved about it. Foster knew Pfeiffer was everyone's first choice for *Silence*, but refused to give up on it. A writer interviewing her for *Vanity Fair* magazine had recommended the book, and Foster knew as soon as she read it that this was the role with which to follow *The Accused*. She also knew that Demme wanted Pfeiffer. Nonetheless, she flew to New York and met with the director. "I just won an Academy Award," she blurted to him, "and this is the only thing I've wanted to do for a really long time."

By now it was September of 1989, and Demme was also said to be considering the actress Meg Ryan for the role. Foster kept pressing. "I basically said, 'I want to be your second choice. These are the reasons I want to do this movie. They are very personal reasons. Not just that it's a good part. So give me a call.'"

The decision to go with Foster may ultimately have had more to do with Orion's Mike Medavoy than anyone. While Demme vacillated, Medavoy became convinced that Foster was right for Clarice. He had suggested Robert Duvall to Demme for the part of Hannibal Lecter. Demme thought Duvall would be better for the FBI boss,[31] preferring the noted Welsh actor Anthony Hopkins for Lecter. Hopkins, not particularly aware of the book when his agent Jeff Conway telephoned, was more interested in working with director Michael Cimino on his remake of *Desperate Hours*. But Conway was excited about the Ted Tally script. Hopkins' wife, Jenni, sat down with a copy, but could not read it because of the gore. When Hopkins finally took a look at it, he flipped through quickly, not wanting to commit himself one way or the other. It was only when Demme flew to England and talked to him that Hopkins agreed to do it.

Back in New York, Medavoy was taken aback at Demme's intention to sign "an Englishman" for Lecter. He made Demme a proposition: the director could have Hopkins if he cast Jodie Foster as Clarice. Demme agreed, and Foster had the part. Meanwhile, Pfeiffer went off to Russia to co-star with Sean Connery in the movie version of John le Carré's *The Russia House*.

Foster won her second Academy Award in a row for *Silence*. The success of the movie also established her as one of the most powerful stars in Hollywood. Meanwhile, Pfeiffer's reputation for rejecting the hits and embracing the misses remained intact. While everyone lined up to see *The Silence of the Lambs*, *The Russia House* was ignored by audiences.

In February of 1990, as Pfeiffer worked at Pinewood studios outside London on *Russia House*, and Jodie Foster completed *Silence* on location in Pittsburgh, director Ridley Scott was casting his next movie. *Thelma & Louise* was a departure for a filmmaker who had started in the business directing

---

[31] Ultimately, the part went to actor Scott Glenn.

commercials, and who was known for such action-oriented fare as *Alien*, *Blade Runner*, and *Black Rain*. While Scott's other pictures had barely acknowledged the existence of women, *Thelma & Louise* amounted to a female *Butch Cassidy and the Sundance Kid* — two friends who become outlaws accused of murder, on the run across the southwestern United States, bonding together as they are hotly pursued by the police.

It was so different from anything else Scott had done that at first he was only going to act as the picture's producer. However, the more he talked to other directors about the script, the more he thought he would be crazy not to direct it. In late February, his first thought was to cast Goldie Hawn as Thelma and Meryl Streep as Louise. They seemed perfect for the roles. Streep had defined the 1980s for most actresses, who aspired to the sort of career she had developed. Streep was offered the most interesting female roles available, and she responded to the opportunities provided to her by winning two Academy Awards (for *Kramer vs. Kramer* in 1979 and *Sophie's Choice* in 1982). Let the men do the frivolous roles. Meryl Streep pursued Seriousness of Purpose, and most other actresses followed her lead — except Goldie Hawn.

Hawn personified the screwball daffiness that had been her stock in trade since she was introduced in the mid-1960s as the ditzy blonde gamine on TV's "Rowan & Martin's Laugh-In." In 1980, she appeared in *Private Benjamin*, a comedy about a widowed Jewish American Princess who enlists in the U.S. Army. It grossed $100 million at the box office, put Hawn on the cover of *Newsweek* magazine, and established her as the only actress through most of the decade whose name alone could attract an audience.

Toward the end of the '80s, however, Hawn's choice of material had become problematic. Audiences failed to respond to such carefully constructed Hawn vehicles as *Swing Shift*, *Protocol*, *Wildcats*, and *Overboard*; the reigning comedienne by then was Bette Midler. As for Streep, despite her influence and the accolades showered upon her, her movies had never done well at the box office. Only *Out of Africa* was a bona fide hit during the decade.

Although they had never worked together, Streep and Hawn were personal friends, and they often talked of working together. Streep believed she had talents as a comedienne that had never been tapped. *Thelma & Louise* appealed to them both, if only because movies with two strong female leads mounted by a highly commercial director were few and far between. However, there was a hitch. Both actresses were commited to other projects. They wanted Scott to delay *Thelma & Louise*, but he was not willing to do that. "We weren't available right then," Hawn later remembered with a trace of bitterness. "It was a matter of six weeks, and he wouldn't wait."

By now, a six-foot-tall actress named Geena Davis had gotten wind of the project and decided to go after it. Davis had inherited many of the same adjectives that attached themselves to Goldie Hawn over the years — zany, loopy, goofy, and ditzy were favored descriptions. She was anxious to shake them off, although winning an Academy Award as best supporting actress in 1988 for *The Accidental Tourist* did little to persuade anyone to look at her differently. Muriel Pritchett, the role Davis played, was a dog-trainer best described as eccentric to the point of exasperation. When she set her sights on William Hurt in the movie, it was hard to determine whether this was supposed to be a romance or the date from hell. The experience of *Accidental Tourist* taught Davis the value of patience and perseverance when it came to going after a part. She had had to fight hard for Muriel, beating out actress Melanie Griffith, no slouch when it came to ditziness.

Davis was born in Wareham, Massachussetts, as a child studied piano and flute, and had been sent off to Sweden for a year to school. Not well known as a country that inspires actors, Sweden was where Geena Davis decided on her career. She enrolled in Boston University's professional actors training program, although it was while modeling in New York for the Zoli agency that she landed her first movie role. In *Tootsie* (1982), she was the sexy soap-opera actress sharing a dressing room with Dustin Hoffman, who had disguised himself as a woman in order to land an acting job. Davis was introduced to the world — and a flustered Hoffman — in her underwear.

*Tootsie* was one of the first auditions Davis had ever been on. Casting director Lynn Stalmaster wanted to see what she looked like in a bathing suit, so she wore the suit under her clothes, convinced nothing would come of it. This was, after all, heady stuff — a movie starring Dustin Hoffman, directed by Sydney Pollack. "Fat chance," she thought. No one even bothered to see her in the bathing suit. Dispirited following the audition, she got on a plane and flew to Paris for some modeling assignments.

After she was gone, Pollack saw her audition tape and liked it. He mistook her certainty that she had no chance of getting the part for confidence.

"In the interview I was very impressed with her and thought she was unusually comfortable in her skin — not trying to make an impression, not trying to be someone she wasn't," Pollack recalled. Still, no one had seen her in that bathing suit. As it happened, she had shot layouts for a number of Victoria's Secret lingerie advertisements. When Dustin Hoffman saw those photographs, he exclaimed, "Oh, my God, you've got to get this girl."

"It was one of those fabulous life experiences," she recalled. "It's not been the same since. I've had great parts, but that was the only time in my life that I'd wake every morning and say, 'Oh, yeah, I get to work on the movie!' It was absolutely like when you're in love and you're just floating and everything is wonderful and your whole life is perfect."

In 1989, Davis was shooting a Bill Murray comedy called *Quick Change* when she heard about *Thelma & Louise*. "Someone had said there was a script with two fabulous women's parts, so I got hold of it right away and read it." At that point, Scott was only producing and was looking for a director. Over the next while, Davis heard all sorts of names mentioned. Her agent at the time, David Eidenberg, kept calling Ridley Scott, reminding him of his client's availability. Rather than being put off by this, Scott was impressed. He appreciated the way Eidenberg was able to keep Davis's name afloat without being irritating about it. Each time Davis heard there was a new director attached to the project, she was on the phone to Eidenberg. "Can I meet him? Does he like me? Who else are they thinking about for the other part?"

To her it seemed to go on forever. Then Scott made it known that he would direct *Thelma & Louise*. He had heard so many directors express enthusiasm for the Callie Khouri script that he began to think he was crazy not to do the movie himself. Having decided to direct, Scott began nosing around for other actresses who would mean more at the box office than did Geena Davis. In addition to Goldie Hawn as Thelma and Meryl Streep as Louise, he approached Michelle Pfeiffer, offering Thelma, and Jodie Foster, proffering the role of Louise. He also spoke to Cher. "Michelle obviously had read the script and was interested, and Jodie the same thing," recalled Eidenberg, "but when it came down to it, they did other projects."

In the end, Geena Davis got the role that made her a bona fide movie star because she hung in there and toughed it out. While the other actresses waffled about whether or not they could do it, or how it would fit into their schedules, Davis stayed true to an unwavering desire for the movie. "She kind of hung in there through thick and thin," marvelled Ridley Scott.

"We were serious," Eidenberg shrugged. "That's what made the difference."

Originally, *Thelma & Louise* was to have been released in March of 1991, but its distributor, MGM-Pathé, was having financial problems, and the release was delayed until May. Even so, the movie was not a huge box-office hit, certainly not compared to the other movies in release that summer, including *Robin Hood: Prince of Thieves*, *Terminator 2: Judgment Day*, and *City Slickers*. But *Thelma & Louise*, like its feisty star, hung in there, eventually grossing $42 million. More tellingly, however, it became a cult movie for female audiences that summer, featured on the cover of *Time* magazine and producing more discussion and controversy than any other movie released in 1991. Davis, with the showier of the two roles, found herself the focal point of all the attention swirling around *Thelma & Louise*, much more so than co-star Susan Sarandon, who had been making films since she appeared in *Joe* in 1970.

Could Geena Davis capitalize on all the fuss being made over her? Lots of actresses throughout the '80s found themselves momentarily in the media spotlight. But few had been able to parlay the publicity into the sort of star power that actors enjoyed. Davis, however, was able to capitalize on her success and become one of the most in-demand actresses, not by any grand design, but because of a fight between a director and her star.

D IRECTOR PENNY MARSHALL, IN MARCH OF 1991, WAS PREPARING TO shoot a comedy movie about female baseball players during World War II. *A League of Their Own* was to star Tom Hanks as the manager of the Rockford Peaches and Debra Winger as his star catcher. Winger was regarded as one of the most talented actresses in Hollywood — and one of the most difficult. According to Hollywood journalist Paul Rosenfield, "She was the girl who almost always said no." Within the industry she was something of a legend, not for what she had done, but for what she did not do. Movies she turned down included *Arthur* (Liza Minnelli did it); *Raiders of the Lost Ark* (Karen Allen); *Peggy Sue Got Married* (Kathleen Turner); *Broadcast News* (Holly Hunter); *Nuts* (Barbra Streisand); *Bull Durham* (Susan Sarandon); and *Music Box* (Jessica Lange).

Even when she did take a role, she was often acutely aware that someone had been there before her, and that someone usually was a blonde. During the filming of *Betrayed* (1988), for example, she knew that the director Costa-Gavras had tried hard to get both Michelle Pfeiffer and Melanie Griffith to take the part of an FBI agent who goes undercover to expose a white racist organization. On location in Alberta, Canada, Winger would finish a scene, then turn to Costa-Gavras and sneer, "How would Michelle do it?" A few years later, however, she met with director Steve Kloves about starring as a lounge singer in *The Fabulous Baker Boys*. When she decided against doing it, the part went to her arch-rival, Michelle Pfeiffer, who was nominated for an Academy Award for the performance Winger might have given. "That role really put Michelle out there," Winger accurately stated later. "It never would have done anything for me."

Winger believed the only power she had as an actress was the power to say no. If that was how she measured it, then at the time, she was the most powerful woman in Hollywood. "I can't remember a time I couldn't say no or walk away," she said. "You have to have standards you won't lower. To be able to say there are things you won't do, and know what they are."

At least part of her obstinancy had roots in the almost mystical sense of how she became an actress in the first place. Winger had been born in Cleveland, Ohio, into an Orthodox Jewish family that operated the Winger Bros. Meat Co. She was six when the family moved to Los Angeles. She graduated from high school at the age of 15, spent some time on a kibbutz in Israel, and briefly joined the Israeli army. She was back in California working at an amusement park called Magic Mountain when on New Year's Eve 1973, she fell off one of the park's vehicles, suffering a cerebral hemorrhage and temporary blindness. For a time, doctors were uncertain whether she would ever walk again.

Lying in a hospital bed, she said later, she decided that no matter what happened, she would become a movie star. Her ambition was soon realized after it became apparent in preparing *Urban Cowboy* that there was no chemistry between John Travolta and Sissy Spacek. Winger later said she was the 200th actress to read for the part of the woman who marries Travolta and gets involved in a lifestyle of country music, Texas honky tonk bars, and mechanical bulls. "The shit was hitting the fan," she recalled, "cause it was like the Scarlett O'Hara wars. They were flying actresses in and out of Houston [where the movie was to be shot]."

The director James Bridges wanted her, but producer Robert Evans was adamantly opposed. "I wouldn't fuck her with a ten-foot pole," he reportedly said. But Bridges prevailed, and *Urban Cowboy* opened the way for *An Officer and a Gentleman* and *Terms of Endearment*, both of which became huge hits in the 1980s. In *Terms*, she was Shirley MacLaine's cancer-stricken daughter in a high-toned tearjerker that won the Academy Award for best picture of 1983 as well as a nomination for Winger and Oscars for MacLaine and Jack Nicholson.

Despite her success, Winger refused to play the Hollywood game. She attacked her directors, co-stars, studios, anyone who got in the way of what she wanted to achieve as an actress. And she continually used that word *no*. Trouble was, the movies she said yes to often did no business at the box office, among them *Cannery Row* (in which she was a last-minute replacement for Raquel Welch), *Mike's Murder, Betrayed, Everybody Wins*, and *The Sheltering Sky*. By the time she began to work with Penny Marshall on *A League of Their Own* in 1990, she had burned a lot of bridges in Hollywood. Ivan Reitman, who had had an unhappy experience directing her in *Legal Eagles* (1986), a limp comedy in which she co-starred with Robert Redford, succinctly summed up the prevailing attitude: "People feel she's talented. I do, too. And the critics especially like her. But her choices of films haven't been the best, and her personal eccentricities hurt her." In short, she was a star in need of a hit; *League* promised to be her most commercial film in years.

A LEAGUE OF THEIR OWN BEGAN LIFE IN 1988 AS A DOCUMENTARY ON public television. The All-American Girls Professional Baseball League was formed in 1943 by Chicago Cubs owner Phillip Wrigley after most of the men had gone off to fight in World War II. It flourished until 1954 when the teams were disbanded. Director Penny Marshall saw the PBS documentary and bought the rights to the story.

If *League* had gone into production in May of 1990 at 20th Century–Fox as it was supposed to, it would have starred Demi Moore and Jim Belushi. But Joe Roth, newly arrived to head production at Fox, was anxious to get movies into production. Marshall was scheduled to direct a movie called *Awakenings*, and Roth did not want to wait for her. He asked her to step aside.

"That was my fatal error," he conceded later. He then assigned the project to David Anspaugh, who had directed another sports movie, *Hoosiers*.

Roth soon became disenchanted with Anspaugh and his cast, which now included, in addition to Belushi, Daryl Hannah and Laura Dern. They were due to start filming in July of 1990, but Roth believed "the casting just wasn't coming out as expected." He canceled the movie altogether, enabling Marshall to pick it up again and take it over to Columbia.

Marshall was still best known as an actress — principally for her role as Laverne De Fazio in the television situation comedy "Laverne & Shirley" — when she and Debra Winger became friends in 1984. She was supposed to make her debut as a director with the comedy *Peggy Sue Got Married*, in which Winger would co-star as a woman who finds herself transported back to her old high school. Eight days into production, Marshall was told she was too inexperienced and was fired. "It was like being kicked in the stomach," she said later. Winger was gone, too, replaced by Kathleen Turner. Francis Coppola replaced Marshall, and *Peggy Sue* became his first commercially successful picture in several years when it was released in 1986.

Marshall finally became a director that same year with another comedy, *Jumpin' Jack Flash*. Ironically, she got the job by replacing director Howard Zieff, who was not getting along with the movie's star, Whoopi Goldberg. *Jumpin' Jack Flash* was not a hit, but it did establish the fact that Marshall could direct a major Hollywood movie. She became a hot property in the business with her second movie, *Big*, a fantasy comedy starring Tom Hanks as a boy who finds himself inhabiting the body of a man. Now she was talking to Debra Winger about working together on *A League of Their Own*. By the time Marshall relocated the picture at Columbia, Winger was deeply involved, having undertaken a rigorous training schedule in order to get herself into shape to play Dottie Hinson, the catcher of the Rockford Peaches.

But what had started as a collaborative friendship between Marshall and Winger began to deteriorate in the spring of 1991. Winger refused to find anything but fault with the script, to the point where Columbia became concerned with what was going on. In an unprecedented move, the studio demanded that the actress's contract include fines if she delayed the production or caused difficulties on the set. At the same time, there were whispers that other actresses were being considered. One of the actresses who reportedly was interested in *A League of Their Own* was Geena Davis.

Matters came to a head in June 1991 when the pop singer Madonna became one of the Rockford Peaches. This infuriated Winger. The two of them rehearsed together, but Winger could not stop herself from sniping away in public. "I'm afraid of the press zoo," she told *Variety* columnist Army Archerd in a report published 11 June. "I don't approve of stunt casting." Winger noted that this time she did not have her usual cast approval, the inference being that if she had, Madonna would not have been part of the team. Meanwhile, Madonna also had a thing or two to say, particularly when it came to the subject of Winger's latest movie, *The Sheltering Sky*. Directed by Bernardo Bertolucci, the film had not been a success. "Debra was so wrong," Madonna sneered. "Oh, it was so wrong, so wrong. It was so unsexy. It was horrible."

On 18 June, little more than a month before shooting on *League* was to start, Winger was out of the film. She denied that she left because of the casting of Madonna, and her agent, Rick Nicita, stated, "She's been prevented from rendering service. She's ready, willing and able to do the movie and is being told not to do it." Later, however, Winger hinted that her unhappiness with the casting had played a major part in her departure. "It hurts when a project that could be special becomes compromised for no good reason, and I was devastated, briefly, but I bounced back."

Marshall wasted little time getting on the phone to Geena Davis. "Can you come to Chicago tomorrow?" she asked, and by the time production started on 10 July 1991, Geena Davis was in uniform and swinging a bat.

"I ordinarily never do that," Davis later said of the speed with which she had made her decision. "It's the first time I ever leapt into something without a lot of thought and care going into the decision. But it just seemed like the thing to do."

Did Columbia orchestrate these events, knowing that *League* could star either the hottest young actress in movies or an older, more difficult one hobbled by her personal demons and a career that was quickly cooling off? Certainly the studio's outrageous contract demands seemed designed to force Winger out of the picture, but she also appeared to play right into her detractors' hands by refusing to ignore Madonna's casting in the movie. What was so ironic was that in the wake of *A League of Their Own*'s immense success, Madonna was all but ignored. She neither added to nor detracted from the picture. In the end, her casting could not have mattered less.

For Geena Davis, however, walking into the role Debra Winger had spent years preparing for, the picture's popularity in July of 1992 assured her major stardom. Not only was she in a movie that pushed across that magic $100 million mark in grosses, but a movie devoted to women in baseball. It was an amazing achievement, considering that no one had held out much hope for a "period" movie dealing with women and sports. Promoting *League* that summer, Davis was carefully ambivalent when the subject of Madonna came up. "No, uh, she was fine, she . . . was part of the team, you know. Most of our scenes were in a big ensemble, and uh, she was part of all that."

*Hero*, the social comedy with which Davis followed *League*, flopped even though it co-starred Dustin Hoffman. But it did no damage to the view that she was now a star. If anyone was hurt, it was the aging Hoffman, as *Hero* confirmed suspicions that the 55-year-old actor now required a powerful young co-star such as Tom Cruise (*Rain Man*) or Robin Williams (*Hook*) in order to open a movie.

DAVIS NOW HAD HER OWN PRODUCTION COMPANY AND THE POWER not only to pick and choose her own projects, but also the directors attached to them. If Geena Davis did not like a certain director, then someone of whom she approved was found. But with power comes the ability to make wrong career decisions, as Davis discovered when she was hotly pursued for the co-starring role in *My Cousin Vinny*. The comedy concerned a Brooklyn lawyer who must defend his cousin on a murder charge in the Deep South despite never having practiced law.

Joe Pesci was to play the lawyer, with Davis, it was hoped, as the gum-chewing, miniskirted Brooklyn girlfriend, Mona Lisa Vito, who turns out to be a lot smarter than Vinny. Despite the showiness of the part, Davis did not think it was right for her and turned it down. So did everyone else. "Here was this terrific, funny role and we couldn't get any actress interested, and believe me, we offered it to everyone," recalled the movie's British director, Jonathan Lynn.

Finally, he took a look at some footage of Marisa Tomei, an actress in her mid-20s who was born in Brooklyn. Tomei had made her movie debut in Garry Marshall's *The Flamingo Kid* (1984). If she was known at all, it was as Denise Huxtable's roommate in the situation comedy "A Different World." Lynn looked at some footage of her in Sylvester Stallone's 1991 comedy, *Oscar*, and was impressed enough to bring her in for an audition.

"It was clearly evident from her first reading that she was perfect for the role," said producer Paul Schiff. However, there was a problem. The studio continued to insist that an actress with some sort of name fill the role. Schiff kept arguing for Tomei. "It took myself, the director, and the casting director to make a case for her, even though the evidence was right there in front of them," he said.

"What the audience saw on the movie screen was what we saw — that this was a funny and offbeat comic performance that literally leapt off the screen without stealing anything from Joe."

Tomei became the only American actress nominated in the best supporting category in the Academy Awards of 1992, in competition with Judy Davis, Miranda Richardson, Joan Plowright, and Vanessa Redgrave. When Tomei won, Geena Davis was said to be devastated. Marisa Tomei was to benefit again when Davis said no, this time to a romantic drama, *The Baboon Heart*. After Davis turned it down, the slightly retitled *Untamed Heart* featured Marisa Tomei in her first romantic lead, opposite actor Christian Slater.

Now Davis was once again to encounter her old baseball teammate, Madonna, who had also created her own production company. One of its film projects was an adaptation of an Avra Wing novel, *Angie, I Says*, about a tough Brooklyn woman who gets pregnant and decides to have the baby without marrying the child's father. Madonna felt a close kinship with the novel's heroine and had worked with screenwriter Todd Graff when it was at 20th Century–Fox. But a star's fortunes can change overnight. In January of 1993 came the release of a highly anticipated erotic thriller, *Body of Evidence*, starring the Material Girl.

Even before it was released, the word was out that *Body of Evidence* was a stiff. Hollywood's perception of Madonna as an intriguing pop phenomenon rather than a bona fide movie star was confirmed. It was that perception as much as anything that caused her to lose *Angie, I Says*.

When Joe Roth, then head of production at 20th Century–Fox, departed the studio to become an independent producer at Disney with his own company, Caravan Pictures, one of the projects he took with him was *Angie, I Says*. No sooner had he established himself at Disney than he was announcing that there was a scheduling conflict and Madonna would not be able to do the movie.

The pop singer was hurt and angry and fired off a letter to Roth that was promptly leaked to the press. "I'm just grateful that I had the chance to inspire the writer to write the screenplay that is sure to make you happy fellas in Hollywood," she wrote caustically. Madonna's replacement? Geena Davis, who in the world of movies remained a much more potent box-office attraction than Madonna, and who was proving herself to be increasingly adept with her newly acquired clout. Madonna's choice for director, Jonathan Kaplan, found himself out of a job, replaced by Martha Coolidge, who was favored by Geena Davis. Still, Roth was taking no chances if Davis said no. He had Marisa Tomei, who had replaced Davis in *My Cousin Vinny* and *Untamed Heart*, standing by to do it again.

WHILE EVERY ACTRESS OF ANY NOTE IN HOLLYWOOD IN 1991 — including Geena Davis and Michelle Pfeiffer — was turning down *Basic Instinct*, there was one actress who wanted it badly. Demi Moore was regarded as one of the most beautiful women in the business. Originally introduced on the television soap opera "General Hospital," Moore for a time was known as something of a promiscuous party girl. Then director Joel Schumacher offered her a role in his production of *St. Elmo's Fire*, providing she cleaned up her act. Demonstrating for the first time the sort of determination that would drive her career, Moore did just that. Being clean and sober did not help her avoid a series of forgettable movies, however, including *About Last Night*, *One Crazy Summer*, and *The Seventh Sign*.

In 1990, she had appeared in *Ghost*, a fantasy about a young woman whose dead husband (Patrick Swayze) tries to protect her from a killer. To the surprise of everyone in the industry, *Ghost* became one of the sleeper hits of that summer, but despite the movie's success, neither she nor her co-star Patrick Swayze had been transformed into stars. *Ghost* was considered a fluke, not a star-driven vehicle. Moore searched for something to capitalize on her unexpected success, and she sensed immediately that whoever played Catherine Tramell in *Basic Instinct* was going to receive a lot of attention. "What struck me . . . was that it was about a woman in control of her life, however sick it was," she said. But she could not get director Paul Verhoeven to see her for the part. "And I was even blonde at the time," she lamented. The failure even to get a hearing on *Basic Instinct* was somewhat the story of Demi Moore's career. She never seemed to be in quite the right place at the right time or if she was, she found Meg Ryan or Michelle Pfeiffer already there. For example, when Meg Ryan dropped out of *The Butcher's Wife*, Moore, complete with blonde hair, took her place.

She also went after the part of Catwoman in *Batman Returns*. "I kept saying, I can get in shape, I can." However, Annette Bening already had been cast. Then in August of 1991, Bening had to drop out of the movie because she had become pregnant by her soon-to-be husband, Warren Beatty. But instead of Demi Moore, it was Michelle Pfeiffer who inherited Catwoman's tights. For once Pfeiffer did not say no and therefore found herself, thanks to Warren Beatty and Annette Bening, in the most commercial film of her career. Moreover, she displayed a sensuality and comic playfulness that brought an otherwise dark and joyless enterprise to life. For the first time in her career, Pfeiffer was able to generate some heat in a movie people actually went to see.

Even before Catwoman made her more bankable, Pfeiffer was under consideration for a new project being prepared by director Rob Reiner. His production company, Castle Rock Entertainment, had acquired the rights to a successful Broadway courtroom drama, *A Few Good Men*, about a young navy attorney, Daniel Kaffee, who must defend two marines accused of murder. Tom Cruise had agreed to play the attorney. Now Reiner was tossing around names for the female investigator. He was briefly intrigued with the possibility of Michelle Pfeiffer and Tom Cruise together in his movie. The rub was the lack of a romantic relationship between the two characters — and Reiner did not want to complicate the dramatic equation by adding one.

"We decided if you put two of the most beautiful people in the world together, the audience would be disappointed if there wasn't a love story," said casting director Jane Jenkins. Instead, Reiner read several up-and-coming young actresses for the part, including Julie Warner, who had appeared in *Doc Hollywood*, Penelope Ann Miller (*Other People's Money*), Elizabeth Perkins (*Big*), Linda Hamilton (*Terminator 2*), and Nancy Travis (*Internal Affairs*).

By the time Moore came to meet Reiner, she was seven and a half months pregnant and was only too aware that every actress in town had read for the role. For his part, Reiner was nervous about Moore. He had heard of her reputation for being difficult and demanding (film crews had dubbed her "Gimme" Moore). Still, when she auditioned with Tom Cruise, he could not help liking what he saw. "She had all the qualities I was looking for,"

Reiner said. "She projects intelligence, she *is* intelligent, she has strength and a sexuality."

Moore was still working on *A Few Good Men* when she heard about *Indecent Proposal*, the new film that director Adrian Lyne was preparing over at Paramount. The role called for her to play an irresistible object of desire, a happily married woman who, after some debate, can be had by a rich and attractive billionaire (Robert Redford) for $1 million.

Initially, Tom Cruise had appeared interested in playing the husband who goes along with the million-dollar adultery. His wife, the beautiful Australian actress Nicole Kidman, would become the stuff of a billionaire's dreams. Kidman was actually tested for the role. Then word came that Cruise would not appear in any movie that required him to sell his wife.[32] Lyne then tested the French actress Isabelle Adjani, the Canadian actress Lolita Davidovich, and Annabella Sciorra, who had appeared in *The Hand That Rocks the Cradle*. He tested Demi Moore on videotape, and her audition impressed him the most. "It was a scene where David and Diana are in bed talking about whether or not they would do this, and Demi had just had her baby, and she had a womanly quality that was nice to watch," he remembered.

Moore suddenly found herself in back-to-back hits. However, when she tried to go after her next movie, a romantic comedy titled *Sleepless in Seattle*, she found that no matter how hard she pushed and maneuvered, the door was closed. "The most 'out there' I've gone to get a film was for *Sleepless in Seattle*," she conceded. "Someone got me a copy of the script and I loved it. Whatever part of my fucked-up psychology it has to do with, I don't like to put myself out there like this, but I called the head of TriStar [Mike Medavoy] and said, 'I want to do this.' I don't like feeling that vulnerable. Sometimes roles I wanted have floated right by me, and I've thought: things that are meant to be are meant to be. Anyway, on *Sleepless in Seattle*, they were very nice, respectful, pleasant, all that kind of stuff they do, but obviously I got rejected."

The producers were not interested in Demi Moore. Instead, they were anxious for another actress who had captured the romantic imagination of the public more than anyone had done in years.

---

[32] Lyne also looked at Johnny Depp, who had appeared in *Edward Scissorhands*. Ultimately, however, he cast Woody Harrelson, who had appeared on the hit television series "Cheers."

# 20

# MOST *EXPENSIVE* PLAYER
### *The Julia Roberts phenomenon*

O N 5 JULY 1993, EIGHT DAYS AFTER HER SURPRISE WEDDING TO COUN-
try singer Lyle Lovett, Julia Roberts, the most popular actress in the
movies, slipped into a theater in AMC's Century City complex.
Accompanying the actress was her new husband, as well as another couple, and
a bodyguard who was part of a contingent of four from a Washington-based
security firm that watched her 24 hours a day. The day before, Roberts had
flown into Los Angeles from Washington, where she was shooting *The Pelican
Brief*. A thriller based on the bestselling novel by John Grisham concerning a
young law student who uncovers information about the assassinations of two
Supreme Court justices, *Pelican Brief* was in the midst of a 10-week location
shoot in the U.S. capital. This was Roberts' first movie in two years, but her
personal life had been providing endless fodder for the tabloid press. She canceled plans for one wedding days before it was to happen in June of 1991, and
now in June of 1993 had shocked everyone by marrying Lovett before it was
even generally known they were seeing each other.

As everyone seated themselves, a radio station that was piped into the
theater before the start of the movie was finishing a Lyle Lovett song. "And
that's Lyle Lovett singing to his pretty woman," announced the disc jockey. The
two newlyweds stared at each other in amazement, then broke into giggles.

Moments later, the main feature began. It was a love story titled
*Sleepless in Seattle*, and all through the early spring there had been encouraging
rumbles about it. If there was to be a surprise hit in the summer of 1993, it
might well be *Sleepless*, starring Tom Hanks and Meg Ryan. Actually, its success had been widely anticipated within TriStar, the movie's distributor, and
part of the cleverly orchestrated promotional campaign was to make it look as
though *Sleepless* was an underdog comedy and that its success was unexpected.

Even with this kind of calculation, though, the picture, since its 25 June opening, had done even better than TriStar thought it would. In its first weekend of release, *Sleepless* had outgrossed the considerably more hyped *Last Action Hero*, taking in $17 million. It was now on its way to making over $100 million.

Roberts and Lovett did not seem much concerned. For the first few minutes after the picture started, they kissed, and whispered, and giggled together, paying scant attention to what was on the screen. Finally someone a couple of rows behind called out, "Shhhh." The couple grew quiet and concentrated on the movie, even though little of it would have been any surprise to Julia Roberts. After all, she was supposed have been the star of *Sleepless in Seattle*.

Gary Foster, a 32-year-old producer, had found the original Jeff Arch script, and for a time it looked as though Meg Ryan and Dennis Quaid, who were romantically involved in real life, would do it. However, Foster had failed to get a director attached and so lost Ryan and Quaid to other projects. Then in January 1992, a director named Nick Castle was attached to it as a kind of consolation prize for stepping aside from *Hook* so that Steven Spielberg could do it. Nora Ephron, a former magazine writer and novelist who had written the screenplay for *When Harry Met Sally . . .* , was brought in to do a rewrite of *Sleepless*. By now Kim Basinger looked like a possibility to co-star with Dennis Quaid. However, Ephron's rewrite was so successful that, "We had actors coming out of the woodwork wanting to do it," Foster remembered, "Julia Roberts being one of them."

The script had come to Roberts early in 1992 via Ray Stark, the veteran producer of *Steel Magnolias*, the movie that proved to be the turning point in her career. Stark had an option on her services for one more movie. He sent her various scripts, all of which she rejected. This time, however, she responded favorably to the story of a widower in Seattle and a young woman in Baltimore who somehow manage to find one another and true love. By now, Nick Castle had left the project because he did not like Ephron's rewrite. Instead, Ephron herself became the director, and everything seemed in place for the project to go ahead with Julia Roberts in the lead. Then, abruptly in March, she changed her mind. She liked the script, but did not love it. There were reports that Roberts' new boyfriend, actor Jason Patric, had been influential in her decision not to do the movie.

Foster later professed to be just as happy that she did not do it. "Julia was too young," he said. Stark was not quite so sanguine. He was furious with the young actress and at one point threatened a lawsuit. But he never made anything more of it. In early 1992, Meg Ryan and Tom Hanks, who previously had appeared together in *Joe Versus the Volcano*, were supposed to co-star in a romantic comedy, *The Inns of New England*, written and directed by Lawrence Kasdan. But at the end of March, Kasdan decided the script was not working for him and canceled the movie altogether. That left Hanks and Ryan free. At the beginning of April, they were signed to co-star in *Sleepless in Seattle*.

Now, more than a year later, a new bride was curious to see what she had missed out on. After all, Meg Ryan was an actress who had had more than a passing effect on her own career. If not for Meg Ryan, it was doubtful Julia Roberts would be the most powerful and popular female star of the early '90s. She had become "the only actress in a male-dominated business," reported the *Los Angeles Times* in June of 1991, "who can be counted on to bring in audiences." It was because Meg Ryan stepped aside at just the right time that Julia Roberts became a star.

J ULIA ROBERTS WAS BORN IN SMYRNA, GEORGIA, SEEMINGLY A LONG WAY from Hollywood but, as it turned out, not all that far away at all. Her parents were familiar with show business, at least on a local level. They briefly ran a workshop for actors and writers in Atlanta in the 1960s, and her older brother Eric was an actor, best known as Dorothy Stratten's malevolent, manipulative boyfriend in *Star 80*, the 1983 movie biography of the *Playboy* Playmate's tragic life.

Roberts hurried away from Smyrna soon after high-school graduation in 1985, certain that if she did not escape, she would end up married and anonymous — and that was the last thing she wanted. She headed for New York, toward vague dreams of an acting career, and barely was settled in the city before she was spotted walking along Columbus Avenue. The next thing she knew, she had a manager, a man named Bob McGowan, and a speech coach, Sam Chwat, who helped modify her thick southern accent. What she did not have was acting lessons. She briefly attended some classes, then stopped going, feeling that whatever she had to offer as an actress was an instinctual thing.

The decision not to pursue classes may also have had something to do with *Blood Red*, a low-budget movie in which her brother was the star. Eric Roberts got her cast in it as his sister less than a year after she arrived in New York. Even so, McGowan was having trouble finding her an agent, and without one, it was almost impossible to get access to auditions. But then he found her a part in a mediocre rock 'n' roll comedy titled *Satisfaction* by telling the casting director his client could play a musical instrument. He hurriedly arranged for her to take a couple of lessons in how to play the drums. The ploy worked. *Satisfaction* gained Roberts access to the powerful William Morris agency, where she came under the protective wing of agent Elaine Goldsmith, who would orchestrate her astonishing success.

Through the William Morris agency, Roberts got roles in the TV series "Crime Story" as well as a Home Box Office movie, *Baja, Oklahoma*. There followed an opportunity to be part of the ensemble cast of another low-budget film, *Mystic Pizza*, about three young women working in a pizzeria in the small town of Mystic, Connecticut. One of the women, Jojo, was having trouble making a commitment to her fisherman boyfriend; another, Kat, was serious and on her way to Yale; Daisy, the third woman, was Kat's sister, hot and sexy, complete with a bad reputation.

When Roberts read the script, she believed she was up for the role of Jojo, a part requiring the qualities of earthiness she felt confident she could summon. She did not see herself as Daisy, described in the script as "the kind of girl men would kill for," so Roberts was amazed when she arrived for the audition to be asked to read for Daisy. The reading went well, but Daisy was supposed to be Portuguese, so the next day Roberts returned for a second reading, this time with her hair darkened. "If you touched it," she recalled, laughing, "your hands would be black."

Despite intense competition, she got the part. When *Mystic Pizza* was released in 1988, Roberts had been acting barely two years. Yet from the moment the movie opened, all eyes were on the voluptuous Daisy with "a rear end so melodramatic it dominated the film," wrote one critic, commenting on the portion of Roberts' anatomy most obvious to male filmgoers.

Roberts herself later conceded that she had gained weight to give her character needed voluptuousness, but in truth did not much resemble her screen persona. As Julia Roberts enjoyed the unexpected attention provided by

*Mystic Pizza*, another young actress was about to get a break. In April of 1987 it was announced that Meg Ryan was to portray Sally Field's daughter in the screen adaptation of Robert Harling's play, *Steel Magnolias*.

MEG RYAN, LIKE JULIA ROBERTS, HAD ALSO HAD SOMETHING OF A charmed existence as an actress. Raised in suburban Fairfield, Connecticut, Ryan attended the upscale public schools where her parents taught. They were divorced when Ryan was 15 years old. She attended New York University, vaguely planning to become a television journalist, with no thought of an acting career.

However, one day in 1980 her mother, who by this time was a casting agent, sent her off to an audition, hoping her daughter might earn a little extra money to help pay tuition fees. To Meg Ryan's astonishment, she won the part of Candice Bergen's daughter in George Cukor's *Rich and Famous* (1981). She was so green that she was only vaguely aware of who Cukor was, and initially mispronounced his name. "I had roughly ten lines," she recalled, "which I would repeat constantly each night with my prayers. There was an actor's strike, so it took five months for my scenes to be completed. When I went to Los Angeles to finish the film, I had never even been on an airplane. I was intimidated by everyone then. If you look at the film, you'll see that I was shaking in every scene."

Nonetheless, Ryan continued to act, becoming a regular on the TV soap opera "As the World Turns." For the next two years, she worked 14 hours a day. "I gained a love for acting," she said, "and a respect for it as a craft."

Three scenes as a navy pilot's wife in *Top Gun* in 1986, and suddenly she was everyone's movie girlfriend. In quick succession, Ryan showed up in *Armed and Dangerous, Innerspace, D.O.A., Promised Land,* and *The Presidio*, parts — with the exception of *Promised Land* — that required her to look pretty and be there to embrace the hero at the end of the picture. What eluded her was the kind of breakout role that turns a supporting actress into a box-office star.

By the time she accepted the role of Shelby, the doomed bride in *Steel Magnolias*, Ryan had been playing supporting parts nonstop for the better part of two years. *Steel Magnolias* was to be another supporting part. Then a new offer: the lead in a romantic comedy directed by Rob Reiner titled *When Harry Met Sally. . . .* She was to be the Sally of the movie's title, friend to Billy

Crystal's Harry. Once again she would be the girlfriend, but this time she did not have to wait for the hero to come home. It was the sort of part in a popular comedy that came along all too seldom for young actresses in the 1980s. Ryan exited *Magnolias* in favor of *Sally*.

Herbert Ross, the former dancer and choreographer who had agreed to direct *Steel Magnolias*, was upset when he heard the news. He viewed the loss of Ryan as a tremendous setback. "I desperately wanted Meg," he said. He looked at another actress, Winona Ryder, but deemed her too young. Julia Roberts' name came up via Sally Field's husband, Alan Greisman, who had been one of the producers of *Mystic Pizza*. According to Ross, there was not a great deal of enthusiasm for her. "There was a lot of resistance to casting her," Ross remembered. Ray Stark, the veteran producer of *Steel Magnolias*, asked the director to take a look at Roberts' performance in *Baja, Oklahoma*. Ross did not like what he saw. "She looked bad," he concluded, "and gave a bad performance."

Once again, as was usually the case when a substantial part was available in an industry full of eager young talent, there was a great deal of competition. Roberts had to read three times for the role of Shelby. Sally Field, for one, thought she stood out from the others. "Something about her makes you care for her, watch her," she said. "And it went far beyond her looks. The part did not call for a great beauty, which was fortunate because no one, including Julia, agreed with me that she was one."

Ross recalled that the issue of Roberts' looks was at the core of the resistance to her casting. He set make-up and hair people to work on her, transforming her into the poised, beautiful Shelby that was required. It was only then, Ross said, that the resistance to her being in the movie evaporated.

Once Ross had his youngest cast member looking the way he wanted, he proceeded to make life difficult for her during the filming. Observers have said that although Ross was endlessly diplomatic with other members of the ensemble cast, including Sally Field, Shirley MacLaine, Dolly Parton, and Daryl Hannah, he gave the newcomer no quarter. "Herbert has his ideas of action and result, and I have mine, and they did not always receive each other perfectly," Roberts later said.

Ross was more blunt. He felt she was not sufficiently trained, and maintained he was tough because he was trying to get a performance out of her. But at the end of filming, when Ross asked her if she was going back to

New York for more training, Roberts shrugged, "What for?"

Indeed. In the midst of one of the most potent female casts seen in movies during the '80s, Julia Roberts shone. *Steel Magnolias* in Ross's hands was generally panned as an over-produced tearjerker. Scant attention was paid to the other actresses. Everyone was too busy falling over themselves for the least trained, most criticized member of the cast. She was the only actress in the movie to win an Academy Award nomination for best supporting actress. The Julia Roberts phenomenon had begun. The ugly duckling was about to become a movie star.

C URIOUSLY, HOWEVER, THE ADVERSE REACTIONS SHE EXPERIENCED WITH *Steel Magnolias* continued. Roberts soon became interested in co-starring in a courtroom drama titled *Beyond a Reasonable Doubt*, but the film's financiers, Trans World Entertainment, rejected her and the proposed male co-star, a young actor named William Baldwin, who would go on to co-star in *Backdraft, Three of Hearts*, and *Sliver*. "They did not believe Julia Roberts could carry a film," recalled the film's producer, Phyllis Carlyle.

The Walt Disney studio had much the same attitude toward Julia Roberts as the backers of *Beyond a Reasonable Doubt*: Who is she, anyway? The studio had come into possession of a script called *Three Thousand*, about a Los Angeles prostitute paid three thousand dollars by a wealthy businessman to spend a week with him. The writer, J. F. Lawton, had written the script as a rather dark drama complete with an unhappy ending. When *Three Thousand* was at the independent production company, Vestron, one of the senior executives there, Steven Reuther, spoke to Roberts about the picture. But when he left the company, Reuther sold the project to Disney. Not only was the script not particularly liked, but at the studio, no one had seen either *Mystic Pizza* or *Steel Magnolias* and therefore had no idea who this Julia Roberts was. Once again, there was not much more than ambivalence where she was concerned.

Disney moved first to deal with the script, renovating it to fit into the kind of movie the studio had been most successful with — comedy. Roberts was stunned by this alteration of the movie's dramatic tone. She had been attracted to the dark tale of a hooker and her millionaire trick, now all was sweetness and light, a Cinderella story that was "hard to come around when you've fallen in love with this girl the way she was: it's hard to come around when suddenly you see her crack jokes and stuff."

Nonetheless, agent Elaine Goldsmith sensed this could be a huge break for her young client and kept after Disney to give Roberts a chance. Goldsmith also enlisted the help of Ray Stark, who arranged for Disney brass to have an advance look at *Steel Magnolias*, as well as Sally Field, who put in a good word with Michael Eisner, chairman and CEO of Walt Disney Productions. Roberts read for the role several times and was screentested, but still the studio held off making any decision until they had cast the part of the millionaire. Richard Gere turned it down early, and Sting, Al Pacino, and Sean Connery subsequently were approached. Finally, director Garry Marshall jumped on a plane and flew to New York to talk Gere into doing the movie. Disney waited until the moment before the option on her services lapsed before deciding to take a chance and cast Roberts in the movie that now was titled *Pretty Woman*.

Neither Gere nor Roberts was comfortable with making people laugh. It fell to Marshall, the veteran comedy writer and producer who cut his teeth on such television hits as "Laverne & Shirley" and "Happy Days," to act as guide. Roberts was particularly skittish, and once again her lack of formal training created problems. "We all went slowly, and Richard Gere was very helpful," Marshall said. "She had difficult scenes. She had to run the gamut of emotion from doing light comedy to almost being raped. I know it was hard for her . . . but she's a kind of a free spirit and very winsome."

When *Pretty Woman* opened late in March of 1990, Roberts was on location in North Carolina shooting *Sleeping with the Enemy*, a thriller Kim Basinger was originally supposed to do. But Basinger had dropped out in order to do *The Marrying Man*. "We thought we might be in trouble when Kim decided not to do it," recalled producer Leonard Goldberg. "*Steel Magnolias* was just out and Julia was an up-and-coming young actress. We were trading star power to work with a near unknown. Now of course, we look like geniuses."

Suddenly Roberts, at the age of 23, was in a Hollywood blockbuster that would go on to earn $170 million at the North American box office. Director Joseph Ruben, who later admitted to being a little bit in love with her, saw the actress's life change overnight. "Everything kind of tilted," he said. "When she walked down the street, strangers now called out her name.

At her hotel, people who did not know her called just to chat."

Despite tepid reviews, *Sleeping with the Enemy* was an immediate hit when it opened 8 February 1991, and no one had any doubt that it was due to Roberts' emerging popularity. A new box-office star was in town. What's more, she was female, and she could create $100 million hits, and she did not necessarily need a big name male co-star in order to do it. In the modern-day history of Hollywood, there had been almost no one like that. Thus Julia Roberts in less than two years had become the most in-demand young actress of her generation, a demand that was undamaged by her next movie, *Dying Young*, released in the summer of 1991. A soapy melodrama about a young woman who falls in love with a cancer victim, it turned out to be grim stuff for the summer movie audience. Still, because of Roberts' drawing power, it was widely expected to be a huge hit. It did all right, but such were the expectations that it was widely regarded as the first great failure of her career. Not that it made a lot of difference. "Julia," said publicist Nancy Seltzer, "is a phenomenon."

But even phenomena can be tripped up by their personal lives. After the release of *Dying Young*, the life of Julia Roberts was thrown into chaos. In June of 1991, she canceled her wedding to actor Kiefer Sutherland days before it was to take place, then ran away to Ireland with Sutherland's friend, actor Jason Patric. For a time, her participation in the role of Tinkerbell in Steven Spielberg's production of *Hook* was in doubt. Although he later denied that he had considered any other actress, it was widely rumored that both Michelle Pfeiffer and Meg Ryan were waiting in the wings in case Roberts decided not to play Tinkerbell. However, she reported for work in July. *Hook* appeared at Christmas of 1991, and it marked her last screen appearance for two years.

The longer she hesitated about committing to another movie, the more she found herself inundated with film offers. Now, instead of opportunities being opened for her, she made it possible for other actresses to improve their careers. Producer Sherry Lansing approached her first about starring in *Indecent Proposal*, and when she said no, Demi Moore was cast. She said no to *Sleepless in Seattle* and the role went to Meg Ryan. In October of 1992, she declined to play Tom Cruise's wife in *The Firm*, and newcomer Jeanne Tripplehorn, who had made her movie debut in *Basic Instinct*, inherited the part. Norman Jewison wanted her for a new romantic comedy tentatively titled *Him*. When she passed on it, the role went to Marisa Tomei, who already had benefited immensely from Geena Davis.

Roberts did agree to do *Shakespeare in Love*, a period romance about the great love of the bard's life. Sets were built in London, and director Edward Zwick prepared to start shooting in December of 1992. When Daniel Day-Lewis, who was to play Shakespeare, and with whom Roberts had a brief affair, abruptly dropped out, so did Julia. Suddenly, in October, despite the fact that Zwick was all set to go, there was no *Shakespeare in Love*.

By early 1993, concern about her inactivity began to surface. *US* magazine asked rhetorically, "Has Julia Roberts' Career Died Young?" while *Variety*, its tongue only partially in its cheek, listed her in its "Lost and Found" section. "It was smart of her to take time off because she was going from movie to movie without a break," said Joel Schumacher, who had directed her in *Flatliners* and *Dying Young*. "Now my advice to her is: Do Something."

But even as the media speculated and Hollywood gossiped, Roberts announced in February of 1993 that she was returning to work in two movies: *The Pelican Brief* and a romantic comedy titled *I Love Trouble*. Harrison Ford was touted as Roberts' co-star for the *Trouble* project, but it was Nick Nolte who was signed. The two would play competing reporters who are constantly trying to outdo one another. "I feel ready to blow the door open," said Roberts to *Variety* columnist Army Archerd in March of 1993. "I went with my instincts, waiting for something perfect, and what I've been looking for hasn't been around — until now."

*Pelican Brief* was intended as a highly commercial vehicle, carefully constructed to emphasize Roberts' strengths. Even before she was cast, it was not difficult to see Julia Roberts in the description of Darby Shaw, the heroine of John Grisham's bestselling novel. *Pelican Brief* was the kind of star-driven project that ordinarily was built up around male stars but almost never was constructed for women. The director was Alan Pakula, the same type of older, seasoned mentor who had guided Roberts in *Steel Magnolias* and *Pretty Woman*. She was surrounded by a first-rate cast that included Denzel Washington and Sam Shepard.

Even so, *The Pelican Brief* became a frightening example of what could happen to a young actress thrust so quickly into the upper reaches of superstardom. When the movie began shooting on location in New Orleans in May of

1993, it quickly became apparent that the shy young actress who needed patience and understanding to get her through *Pretty Woman* was now a megastar and demanded to be treated as such. The set was closed to journalists, and members of the crew had to wear special identification. A squad of four Washington-based security guards protected her 24 hours a day at a cost to Warner Bros., the studio distributing the film, said to be $50,000 a week. Although Roberts joked and flirted with the male crew members, she also displayed a hair-trigger temper and flew into obscenity-laced tirades when her schedule was changed — or if something was not going well. Once, when director Pakula asked her to do a third take of a scene — not unusual on a movie of the size and complexity of this one — she turned on her heel and stormed off the set.

By the time shooting of *Pelican Brief* had finished in September, Roberts appeared to have exhausted and frightened everyone. "It just doesn't have to be this tough," said one crew member, thinking back over Roberts' behavior. "No star has to be this mean."

On Monday 4 October 1993, Julia Roberts began work on the second of the two roles she had committed herself to, filming *I Love Trouble* on location in Wisconsin. Roberts and Nolte were to portray a pair of rival newspaper reporters trying to outwit each other for a story about poisoned milk while falling in love. But Roberts had no sooner started than she was again losing her temper on the set. After five days of this, the crew was called together and she appeared before them to apologize for the way she had been behaving.

In November, while production of *I Love Trouble* continued, it was announced that Roberts would star in *Mary Reilly*, a movie about the housekeeper who witnesses the transformation of Dr. Jekyll into Mr. Hyde, but falls for the good doctor anyway. For her services in the starring role, she would receive $10 million. At the age of 26, she had received the highest accolade obtainable by a movie star in Hollywood. She would be paid more money for one movie than any other actress in the history of motion pictures.

# EPILOGUE

AS I WOUND DOWN FROM THE RESEARCH AND WRITING OF THIS BOOK, I found myself often focusing on what movie stardom once was — and could never be again. In particular, I remembered an encounter with John Wayne, the most enduring of all movie stars produced by the sound era. We met in 1975 at his home in Newport Beach, just south of Los Angeles. The Duke had invited some journalists over for the evening to help celebrate the release of his new movie, a mediocre police thriller called *Brannigan*. He had already filmed (but not yet released) *Rooster Cogburn*, the follow-up to *True Grit*, the movie which had won him his only Academy Award in a career that spanned five decades.

He would make only one more movie, the elegiac *The Shootist*, before his death a scant four years later. That evening, though, he gave off no intimations of death. Rather, here was robust movie legend coming through sliding glass doors — virtually the entire history of American movies crowding into the room. Then 68, John Wayne had been making movies since 1928 when, still a student at the University of Southern California, he began doing bit parts for his friend and mentor, John Ford. He looked more like a prosperous Orange County Republican than he did the western hero he personified on the screen. His aversion to horses, except when he was sitting on one for a scene, was well known. He infinitely preferred the casual luxury of the guarded enclave in which he dwelt with his yacht, a converted minesweeper, moored a few steps from the rear of his house.

Drinks were poured. He insisted that I try his liquor of choice, Conmemorativa Tequila. Then, drink in hand, he ambled out onto the patio that overlooked the bay beyond. It was dusk and the last rays of sunlight were streaking violet across the sky behind the old frame pavilion outlined in lights across the bay. He had grown up in this area of California and as a kid had often gone dancing at that pavilion on Saturday nights. He smiled and tossed a beefy hand in the direction of the structure now beginning to glow in the deepening dusk. "I'll tell you something," he rumbled. "Some nights the only two things lit up around here are that pavilion — and the old Duke."

I have thought a lot about that night lately as I finish this book. Since then, I have met and talked to all sorts of stars, some of them with remarkable careers, but nothing has ever equaled the exhilaration of that evening with John Wayne. It practically goes without saying that movie stars are not what they used to be. The casting director Mike Fenton suggested elsewhere in these pages that today's superstars, the Schwarzeneggers and Stallones, the Tom Cruises and the Kevin Costners, lack the class of their predecessors. He is mostly right — regardless of the fact that today's stars possess power unknown to their forebears. Maybe that is part of the problem. Modern movie stardom has been stripped of its traditional iconography. Movie stars now seem all too human, less to do with giving form to our fantasies and dreams than with representing the corporate bottom line that preoccupies — and has always preoccupied — the movie business. Today's major stars are mini-conglomerates, and we know about the mechanics of their business in the same unromantic way stockholders know about General Motors. In the sometimes morbid process of uncovering, literally, everything about them, the essential mystery so necessary to the status of a screen icon has been lost. That is not to say there is not still a fascination — perhaps too much so. The preoccupation with stars' foibles and shortcomings often outstrips our enthusiasm for the movies in which they appear.

The public's fickleness, the constantly increasing thirst for the new, has taken its toll on the longevity that was once inherent in movie stardom. Clint Eastwood has been a star for 30 years, and so has Barbra Streisand. But that sort of endurance is probably a thing of the past. We may not have the patience for it any longer. The amazing thing is that, in this jaded age, stardom continues at all, that the people who pretend for a living remain so important to us. For all the revolutionary technological changes that have taken place since movies began to talk in 1927, we still want to sit together in the dark and watch people larger than ourselves perform the feats we otherwise dare summon only in our wildest imaginings.

Finally, it was time to leave John Wayne's house that evening. I was ushered toward the door, aware the moment was about to be lost, that John Wayne would return to the screen and I would be left to continue the ordinariness of a life. I abruptly turned to him, and blurted, "Would you mind if I gave you a hug?" He looked at me the way he squinted at Ward Bond in *The Searchers* when Bond suggested the Duke surrender his six-gun. "No," he said flatly. I felt as stupid as I had ever felt in my life. "I'll tell you what, though." He paused, and looked me up and down again. "I'll give you one."

And he did. And that is where this book ends. Not with who lost or won, who had the biggest grosses, or stood first at the box office, but where it should: with the memory of a hug from a movie star that I will carry through a lifetime.

# REFERENCE NOTES AND SOURCES

## Introduction

xii "He wasn't thinking straight..." Dick Clayton interview, 14 April 1993.

xii "When it came to choose..." Craig Modderno, *Los Angeles Times*, 4 January 1987.

xii "All you rock people, down at the Roxy..." *Inside Oscar*, Mason Wiley and Damien Bona (Ballantine Books, New York, 1993), 639.

## Chapter 1

18 George Jessel was asked in an interview ... from a 1980 television interview in the collection of Doug Galloway.

19 They sat down with Jessel in the summer of 1925 ... George Jessel, *So Help Me* (Random House, 1943), 76.

19 ... that he used a midget's birth certificate. Marcia Masters, *Los Angeles Times*, 4 November 1945.

20 "He didn't want his brain child touched..." Jessel, op. cit., 76.

20 "I'm glad you enjoyed my little play..." *Jolson: The Legend Comes to Life*, Herbert G. Goldman (Oxford University Press, 1988), 147.

20 Eddie Cantor had been responsible ... *The World I Lived In*, George Jessel with John Austin (Henry Regnery Company, Chicago, 1975), 17.

21 "Jolson was the icon..." Doug Galloway interview, 27 November 1992.

21 Even Jessel was willing to concede ... Steve Harvey, the *Los Angeles Times*, 26 May 1980.

22 Samson Raphaelson was a senior ... "The Jazz Singer," Audrey Kupferberg, *American Film Institute*, undated. Doug Galloway collection.

23 "Hell, I used to see those shows..." Goldman, op. cit., 146.

23 The Warner brothers brought him out to Hollywood ... Jessel with Austin, op. cit., 65.

24 Jessel later said he brokered the deal ... ibid., 64–5.

24 "My first look at the scenario..." ibid., 66.

25 Jessel was still angry when he went to visit Al Jolson ... ibid., 67.

25 Doris Vidor, the wife of Charles Vidor ... George Morris, *American Film Institute*, undated. Doug Galloway collection.

26 "berating what had been done to me..." Jessel with Austin, op. cit., 71.

26 "That was as true as..." ibid., 68.

26 The deal he secretly negotiated ... ibid.

27 "A cruel and intolerant man..." "You Ain't Heard Nothin' Yet," broadcast on the Arts and Entertainment network, 12 January 1992.

28 "Jessel suddenly confounded the wiseacres..." S. J. Perelman, *Holiday*, September 1952.

28 "Rather than be a star of a television show..." Maurice Zolowtow, the *Saturday Evening Post*, 17 October 1953.

29 "And he's still mad at me about *The Jazz Singer*..." Al Jolson, filmed at a Friar's Club roast in 1948, part of the Doug Galloway collection.

29 "The only actor he had any respect for..." Jessel TV interview in 1980, part of the Doug Galloway collection.

29 Earle Jolson ... said her late husband ... Earle Jolson, quoted by Doug Galloway.

30 That night Jolson and Earle were dining ... ibid.

30 "When I die..." ibid.

30 "A breeze from San Francisco Bay..." Eulogy For Al Jolson, delivered by George Jessel at Temple Israel, 26 October 1950.

## Chapter 2

31 In 1927 the movie industry in Hollywood ... *The Shattered Silents: How the Talkies Came to Stay*, Alexander Walker (William Morrow and Company, New York, 1979), 45.

31 Those rated as stars made $2,500 a week ... ibid., 45.

33 But in reviewing her first two sound films ... ibid., 49.

35 "I was in the last year of my contract..." *It Took Nine Tailors*, Adolphe Menjou (Samson, Low, Marston and Co., New York, 1950), 184–5.

37 Hedda Hopper reported that ... *Los Angeles Times*, 17 October 1941.

37 "The major studios such as MGM..." John Austin, the *Hollywood Citizen News*, 1 August 1970.

38 "They get you up before daylight..." *Each Man in His Time*, Raoul Walsh (Farrar, Straus and Giroux, New York, 1974), 301.

38 "...the hottest young man..." *Don't Say Yes Until I've Finished Talking: A Biography of Darryl F. Zanuck*, Mel Gussow (Doubleday, Garden City, New York, 1971), 68.

39 "Talent is like a precious stone..." *Long Live the King*, Lyn Tornabene (G.P. Putnam's Sons, New York, 1976), 127.

39 Everyone was afraid ... *Zanuck*, Leonard Moseley (Little, Brown and Co. Ltd, New York, 1984), 155.

40 "A very few times, we had visited him at his beach house..." *Child Star*, Shirley Temple Black (McGraw-Hill, New York, 1988), 199.

41 He said that Jack Robbins ... *The Wonderful World of Entertainment*, Hugh Fordin (Doubleday, Garden City, New York, 1975), 5.

42 "She looked more like Dorothy..." *The Making of the Wizard of Oz*, Aljean Harmetz (Alfred A. Knopf, New York, 1977), 111.

42 "A studio simply would not..." Interview with David Brown, 12 November 1992.

43 "Sure we have dimples in common..." Black, op. cit., 189.

43 "What can I say, Arthur..." Fordin, op. cit., 9.

43 "Instead of dancing down the Yellow Brick Road..." Black, op. cit., 198.

44 "peevish, greedy, spoiled brat..." ibid., 293.

45 "a shattering piece of symbolism..." ibid., 312.

46 Temple turned up where she should have been in the first place — at MGM ... Douglas W. Churchhill, the *New York Times*, 12 January 1941.

46 "The word was out..." Harmetz, op. cit., 48.

46 "Get out..." Black, op. cit., 319–20.

47 "She was too much trouble" Harmetz, op. cit., 116.

## Chapter 3

48 "A fantastic, arresting mask..." *George Raft*, Lewis Yablonsky (McGraw-Hill, New York, 1974), 146.

49 He was always an outsider ... George Raft, as told to Dean Jennings, *Saturday Evening Post*, 12 October 1957: "I know that many actors and executives considered me an alien, no matter what my pictures did at the box office. Perhaps the feeling was mutual."

49 Many times Raft would deny completely ... Lewis Yablonsky interview, 14 December 1991.

49 ... thought Raft the toughest guy ... *James Cagney: The Authorized Biography*, Doug Warren with James Cagney (St. Martin's Press, New York, 1983), 126.

49 "Nobody ever gave me anything..." Quoted from a Paramount studio biography, 1937.

50 "When they patted me on the back..." *The George Raft Files*, James Robert Parrish with Steve Whitney (Drake Publishers, New York, 1973), 158.

50 "The tango was his specialty..." ibid, 9.

51 He had seen Raft at a prizefight ... *Hawks on Hawks*, Joseph McBride (University of California Press, 1982), 48.

51 When he saw what Muni went through ... Yablonsky, op. cit., 67.

52 "I don't want to confine my work..." Raft biography at Paramount.

52 Goldwyn and director William Wyler ... Yablonsky, op. cit., 97–8.

54 Hal Wallis ... later said Raft was brought over ... *Starmaker, The Autobiography of Hal Wallis*, Hal Wallis with Charles Higham (Macmillan, New York, 1980), 47.

54 On 15 July 1939, Raft signed a long-term contract ... the George Raft personnel file, part of the Warner Bros. archives at the School of Cinema-Television, University of Southern California.

54 "George Raft tells me..." ibid.
54 "I was afraid the studio..." ibid.
55 "exactly the tough, low life type..." Wallis with Higham, op. cit., 48.
55 "...was just a little bit better than a bit..." *Inside Warner Bros. , 1935–1951*, Rudy Behlmer (Viking, New York, 1985), 132.
55 "...was a great part..." ibid., 132–3.
56 Jack Warner called Raoul Walsh to his office ... Walsh, op. cit., 306.
57 ... had a drunken John Huston ... *The Hustons*, Lawrence Grobel (Charles Scribner's Sons, New York, 1989), 210.
57 "How about Bogart..." Walsh, op. cit., 307.
57 "*High Sierra* marked a turning point..." Grobel, op. cit., 211.
57 "Bogey the Beefer..." Walsh, op. cit., 307.
58 "Just a drunken boy..." Grobel, op. cit., 192.
59 "Huston is a brilliant guy..." Yablonsky, op. cit., 139.
60 "As you know..." Behlmer, op. cit., 151.
61 "...who has adopted a leisurely suave form of delivery..." memo in *The Maltese Falcon* file, the Warner Archives, USC.
61 Bogart even contributed ... Grobel, op. cit., 222.
61 "There but for the grace of me..." Jimmy Fiedler, the *Los Angeles Times*, 16 October 1941.
61 "a dame who can only be trouble..." Yablonsky, op. cit., 149.
62 "It seems that for the past year..." Behlmer, op. cit., 156.
62 "an apple polisher..." *The Warner Bros.*, Michael Freedland (St. Martin's Press, New York, 1983), 101.
62 "A lot of people disliked him..." Warren with Cagney, op. cit., 124.
62 "Bogart has been typed through publicity..." letter to Martin Weiser in Warner Bros. Kansas City office. On file at the Margaret Herrick Library.
63 "Incidentally, he (Raft) hasn't done a picture here..." Behlmer, op. cit., 201.
65 "Tell it to me..." *Billy Wilder in Hollywood*, Maurice Zolotow (G.P. Putnam's Sons, New York, 1977), 117–19.
65 "He didn't dwell on the past..." Yablonsky interview.

**Chapter 4**

67 "...too big to go after..." Behlmer, op. cit., 21.
68 "Just because I did a fencing scene..." *The Life of Robert Donat*, Kenneth Baron (Methuen, London, 1985), 74.
68 "He is not in any way a comedian..." ibid., 77.
69 Judging writer Casey Robinson's work to be "poor" ... ibid., 78.
69 "What is a star..." ibid., 79.
69 "a stubborn young guy..." ibid.
69 Hal Wallis was now told ... Wallis with Higham, op. cit., 52.
71 "He had the guts..." *My Wicked, Wicked Ways*, Errol Flynn (G. P. Putnam's Sons, New York, 1959), 203.

71 "But as soon as he was on camera..." Wallis with Higham, op. cit., 52.
72 "To the Walter Mittys of the world..." Warner, op. cit., 232.
73 "Go ahead, bury yourself..." *Mother Goddamn — The Story of the Career of Bette Davis*, Whitney Stine (Hawthorn Books, New York, 1974), 56.
73 "I was heartbroken..." ibid., 57.
73 Then a call came from Darryl Zanuck ... *Fasten Your Seatbelts — The Passionate Life of Bette Davis*, Lawrence J. Quirk (William Morrow and Co. Inc, New York, 1990), 331.
74 "He never personally liked..." *I'd Love to Kiss You ... Conversations with Bette Davis*, Whitney Stine (Pocket Books, New York, 1990), 74.
75 "But it's in Technicolor..." Stine, op. cit. (*Mother*), 76.
75 "I'll bet it's a pip..." ibid., 76.
75 In late May of 1936, Kay Brown ... *Showman — The Life of David O. Selznick*, David Thomson (Alfred A. Knopf, New York, 1992), 212.
75 "...it would have been so simple..." *Memo From: David O. Selznick*, selected and edited by Rudy Behlmer (Viking Press, New York, 1972), 270.
76 Jack Warner offered more money ... Thomson, op. cit., 267.
76 "I was as perfect for Scarlett..." *The Lonely Life: An Autobiography*, Bette Davis (G. P. Putnam's Sons, New York, 1962), 214.
77 "...to me the only fly in the ointment..." Davis, ibid., 232.

**Chapter 5**

78 "*Gone With the Wind* is tremendous..." Thomson, op. cit., 213.
80 But Capra encountered trouble ... Tornabene, op. cit., 173.
81 "Shall I tell you the story..." Tornabene, ibid., 173.
81 "He didn't look like anyone else..." ibid., 174.
82 It was Irving Thalberg ... who thought of Gable ... ibid., 186.
82 "You've got the personality for Fletcher Christian..." *The Lion's Roar*, Bosley Crowther (E. P. Dutton and Co., New York, 1959), 231.
83 "People didn't just read that novel..." *MGM: When the Lion Roars*, Peter Hay, Turner Publishing Inc., Atlanta, 1991), 184.
83 So Gable badly needed the $100,000 ... *Selznick*, Bob Thomas (Doubleday and Co. Inc, Garden City, New York, 1970), 148.
84 "too unpleasant," she decided ... Thomson, 264.
85 She had sent Hepburn a copy of the typescript ... *Me — Stories of My Life*, Katharine Hepburn (Alfred A. Knopf, New York, 1991), 180.
85 "Don't read it, David..." ibid.
85 "I also felt that I would really be a disappointing choice..." ibid.
85 ... but he thought Scarlett much too unsympathetic, ibid.
85 "the day before..." ibid.

86 "The more I see of her..." Thomson, op. cit., 270.
86 "Her tests were funny..." ibid.
88 The director William Wyler had spent two years ... *William Wyler — The Authorized Biography*, (Axel Madsen, Thomas Y. Crowell Company, New York, 1973), 182.
88 "Vivien, I'll give you..." ibid., 185.
89 "a few quiet words..." *Confessions of an Actor*, Laurence Olivier (Simon and Schuster, New York, 1982), 107.
89 "I looked back at Vivien..." ibid., 108.
89 "She's the dark horse..." Selznick, op. cit., 180.
90 "They screwed constantly..." *Salad Days*, Douglas Fairbanks Jr. (Doubleday, New York, 1988), 344.
90 Powell would have been paid ... Selznick, op. cit., 262.
91 ... and partly because he had a passion for Joan Fontaine ... Thomson, op. cit., 305.
91 "Selznick looked in my mouth..." *Anne Baxter — A Bio-Bibliography*, Karen J. Fowler (Greenwood Press, New York, 1991), 9.
91 "She doesn't seem at all right..." Thomson, op. cit., 270.
92 "a talking magazine cover..." Thomson, op. cit., 308.
92 "We have tried to sell ourselves..." Selznick, op. cit., 270.
94 "drinking two quarts of whiskey..." Grobel, op. cit., 479.
94 "What surprised me..." *Gable's Women*, Jane Ellen Wayne (Prentice Hall, New York, 1987), 273.

**Chapter 6**

99 Jean Negulesco ... had seen a screen test of a young actor *Things I Did And Things I Think I Did — A Hollywood Memoir*, Jean Negulesco (Linden Press/Simon and Schuster, New York, 1984), 127.
99 "I was in *Candida*..." Marlon Brando screen test seen in *Here's Looking at You, Warner Bros. — The History of the Warner Bros. Studio*, 1991, a Robert Guenette production.
99 "He doesn't talk, he mumbles..." Negulesco, op. cit., 127.
100 "The only reason I'm here..." *Time*, 11 October 1954.
101 "I don't think Marlon can be explained..." Hedda Hopper, *Chicago Sunday Tribune*, 30 March 1952.
102 Sinatra was tested with a muscular young New York actor ... *His Way: The Unauthorized Biography of Frank Sinatra*, Kitty Kelly (Bantam Books, New York, 1986), 192.
103 "Eli Wallach made the best test of the three..." ibid.
103 Wallach himself was ambivalent ... ibid.
103 "Eli Wallach is a brilliant actor..." ibid., 193.
104 "There were no horses's heads involved..." *Fred Zinnemann — An Autobiography*, Fred Zinnemann (Charles Scribner's Sons, New York, 1992), 125.

104 "Frank had grown up in Hoboken..." *Elia Kazan — A Life* (Alfred A. Knopf, New York, 1988), 515.

105 "On first acquaintance..." *Lawrence of Arabia* souvenir program, Robert Bolt, 1962.

105 "I wouldn't have touched the original script..." *Spiegel — The Man Behind the Pictures*, Andrew Sinclair (Little, Brown and Co., Boston, 1987), 69.

105 "I'm going to kill that son of a bitch..." Kazan, op. cit., 514.

105 "I had a great deal of trouble with Budd..." Sinclair, op. cit., 69.

106 "I didn't want the son of a bitch..." Kazan, op. cit., 515.

106 One night in New York ... Sinclair, op. cit., 69.

107 "For me to tell you..." Kazan, op. cit., 516.

107 "If there was a better performance..." Kazan, op. cit., 516.

108 "I had made a picture..." Gregory Peck interview, 2 August 1982.

109 Charles Brackett suggested ... *Golden Boy — The Untold Story of William Holden*, Bob Thomas (St. Martin's Press, New York, 1983), 60.

109 "... lives in the past and refuses to believe..." Thomas, ibid.

111 Citron was appalled ... *Monty — A Biography of Montgomery Clift*, Robert LaGuardia (Arbor House, New York, 1977), 72.

111 "Bullshit!" he thundered ... Thomas, op. cit., 59.

111 "I agreed to do this picture..." ibid., 60.

113 There would be no more loanouts ... *Grace*, James Spada (Doubleday and Co., Garden City, New York, 1987), 87.

113 "I just had to be the country girl..." ibid.

113 "If I can't do this picture..." ibid.

114 "I wish you luck on the picture..." Thomas, op. cit., 111.

115 "Who would you like..." *Rock Hudson — His Story*, Rock Hudson and Sara Davidson (William Morrow and Co. Inc., New York, 1986), 92.

115 ... disliked the script's "interpretation..." *Burt Lancaster*, Minty Clinch (Stein and Day Publishers, New York, 1984), 149.

115 "We rejected the possibility of using him..." *Idol — Rock Hudson: The True Story of an American Film Hero*, Jerry Oppenheimer and Jack Vitek (Villard Books, New York, 1986), 52.

116 Joshua Logan was planning to direct *Sayonara* ... *Movie Stars, Real People, and Me*, Joshua Logan, (Delacorte Press, New York, 1978), 93.

116 "The worst mistake of my career..." Hudson and Davidson, op. cit., 104.

116 "It seemed to me..." *Rock Hudson — Friend of Mine*, Tom Clark with Dick Kleiner (Pharos Books, New York, 1989), 150.

**Chapter 7**

118 "Hey, you two queers..." James Dean, Paul Newman screen test seen in *Here's Looking At You*, Warner Bros.

119 "What determined the winner was his face..." *James Dean — the Mutant King*, David Dalton (Straight Arrow Books, San Francisco, 1974), 154.

119 "I wouldn't imagine..." ibid., 153.

119 "...was so adoring..." Kazan, op. cit., 538.

119 "Dean was never a friend of mine..." *The Dogs Bark — Public People and Private Places*, Truman Capote (Random House, New York, 1973), 338.

120 "I couldn't believe that was Jimmy next to me..." Dick Clayton interview.

120 "Jimmy was all set to do it..." ibid.

120 "It was quite a coup..." Robert Wise interview, 16 November 1992.

121 "Then we were up in the air..." ibid.

121 "I don't know you could say it saved his career..." ibid.

121 "*Silver Chalice* had knocked Paul out of the box..." Clayton interview.

122 Spiegel had one suggestion ... Sinclair, op. cit., 77.

123 Spiegel had Bogart in mind ... ibid., 77-8.

123 "Why should I go off to Ceylon..." ibid., 78.

124 "...rubbish, filled with elephant charges..." ibid.

125 "Lean, like Spiegel..." Robert Bolt, the *Lawrence of Arabia* souvenir program.

**Chapter 8**

126 The Hungarian-born producer Alexander Korda made the first serious effort ... *Lawrence of Arabia, The 30th Anniversary Pictorial History*, L. Robert Morris and Lawrence Raskin, (Anchor Books, New York, 1992), 13.

126 "Remember, this was not to be Lean's panoramic thing..." ibid., 27.

127 "It's all right, Mrs. Spiegel..." Sinclair, op. cit., 88–9.

127 "In a way they were very much alike..." Morris and Raskin, 33.

127 "There are so many actors knocking around..." ibid., 33.

127 "Psycho of Arabia..." Sinclair, 96.

128 "Lawrence will make a star..." Morris and Raskin, op. cit., 37.

129 Dressed in full costume, on elaborate sets . . . ibid., 38.

129 "It was a magnificent part..." Albert Finney interview, November 1991.

129 "On the screen, I saw this chap..." Morris and Raskin, op. cit., 40.

129 "No use shooting..." ibid.

130 ... and that provided Michael Caine, his understudy, with an unexpected break ... *Candidly Caine*, Elaine Gallagher (Robson Books, London, 1990), 29-30.

130 "It was the greatest time of my life..." Terence Stamp, *Hello!*, London, 1991.

130 "You're joking..." ibid.

132 "...one of those snotty, blue-blooded..." *What's It All About?* Michael Caine (Turtle Bay Books, New York, 1992), 154.

132 From the outset Wise was concerned ... Robert Wise interview.

132 "...but there was a little undercurrent..." ibid.

133 "So I flew to London..." ibid.

133 Now he would have to find another actor ... *Playboy*, July 1967: "And Christopher Plummer had a crack at Palmer before I did, but he turned it down for *The Sound of Music*."

134 Michael Caine was having dinner with Terence Stamp ... Caine, op. cit., 185.

134 "I suppose I underestimated the intelligence..." *Playboy*, July interview.

135 "Chris never quite made it..." Robert Wise interview.

135 "I actually spent three whole hours..." Caine, op. cit., 202.

136 "I had done it, hadn't I..." Kevin Thomas, *Los Angeles Times*, 6 August 1967.

136 "I reached page two of the script..." Caine, op. cit., 202.

136 "I had become a Cinderella-type figure..." ibid., 228.

136 Michael Caine first encountered Sean Connery ... ibid., 127.

136 "Sean was enormous..." ibid.

137 Saltzman left over his partner's determination ... *New York Times*, 1 January 1961.

138 ... became involved with the American-born producer Albert J. Broccoli ... *Rolling Stone*, August 23, 1979.

139 Broccoli remained skeptical ... *The Films of Sean Connery*, Lee Pfeiffer and Philip Lisa (Citadel Press, 1992), 14.

139 Connery later dismissed most of this ... Jonathan Mandell, *Sunday News*, 2 October, 1980:"The bit about my banging on the table and everything is absolute nonsense."

139 "The difference between him..." Pfeiffer and Lisa, op. cit., 14.

**Chapter 9**

141 One day Shaw telephoned Dick Clayton ... Dick Clayton interview.

141 Lean approached Peter O'Toole ... *David Lean*, Stephen M. Silverman (Harry N. Abrams, New York, 1989), 152.

142 "I don't think I can do it..." Clayton interview.

143 "That's the girl I want for Lara!" ... Robert Musel, *Weekend*, 17 July 1965.

143 "I'm going to be an actress..." *Newsweek*, 20 December 1965.

143 "She was not very good..." ibid.

143 "...showing her breasts and everything..." Brian Glanville, *Holiday*, September, 1966.

143 "One Saturday morning..." ibid.

145 "He was all a director could hope for..." Logan, op. cit., 269.

145 Robert Wise was also aware of Warren Beatty ... Robert Wise interview.

146 "Six feet one inch tall..." Robert Wise's *West Side Story* casting notes.

146 "It turned out it was a scene..." Wise interview.
146 "I thought he did a damned good job..." ibid.
147 "The only picture of mine I have liked..." Sue Chambers, the *Milwaukee Journal*, 5 May 1963.
147 ... one day over lunch in Paris ... *Gene Hackman*, Allan Hunter (W. H. Allen, London, 1987), 24.
147 "From the first day of shooting..." Thomas Thompson, *Atlantic Monthly*, 13 May 1968.
148 Originally, Beatty was not going to star ... Army Archerd, *Variety*, 21 June 1968: "It was my idea to direct it, have my sister play Bonnie, and have some guy play opposite her."
148 "I turned down Bonnie and Clyde..." Thomas Thompson, *Life*, 23 January 1970.
148 "This incredibly beautiful woman..." Jesse Kornbluth, *Vanity Fair*, August 1987.
149 "When Faye came in..." ibid.
149 "Warren dropped in to see me..." Hunter, op. cit., 26.
150 "Most of the people who don't like me..." Thompson, *Atlantic Monthly*.
150 "Let's put it this way..." ibid.
151 ... encountered problems over her contract with Otto Preminger ... *Time*, 19 January 1968.
151 ... and one night in November of 1973 ... Henry Sera interview, 5 August 1993.
152 "It's very hard to know who you are..." Jesse Kornbluth, *Vanity Fair*.
152 "That was a painful experience..." Hunter, op. cit., 211.

**Chapter 10**

153 Turman encountered an intriguing *New York Times* review ... Lawrence Turman interview, 30 October 1992.
153 "I read it and quickly concluded..." ibid.
154 "You do come away..." Craig Modderno interview, 26 January 1993.
155 "The direction really stood out..." Turman interview.
155 "One night I got back to my hotel..." ibid.
155 "Nobody thought it would make a movie..." ibid.
156 "We came from the same background..." Buck Henry interview, 14 September 1993.
157 "I think she is the most interesting..." Peter Bart, the *New York Times*, 1 January 1967.
158 "I was the graduate..." Tony Bill interview, 17 November 1993.
158 "He agreed to let me come in and audition..." *It Would Be So Nice If You Weren't Here — My Journey Through Show Business*, Charles Grodin (William Morrow and Co., New York, 1989), 148.
159 "You are our number one choice..." ibid., 148.
159 "Something had happened..." ibid., 150.
160 "I was told..." Tony Bill interview.

160 "fuck it..." Dustin Hoffman interview conducted by Craig Modderno, *The Graduate 25th Anniversary Special Limited Edition*, 1992.
161 "Every morning at three a.m...." Michael Williams, *Los Angeles Times*, 31 December 1967.
161 "I'm not supposed to be in movies..." Dustin Hoffman interview.
161 "He looked about three feet tall..." *Life*, 24 November 1967.
162 "I'd never ask a girl..." ibid.
162 "Him... ?" Eleanore Lester, *New York Times*, 3 December 1967.
162 "Here kid..." Dustin Hoffman interview.
163 "I woke you up..." *Los Angeles Times*, 12 December 1973.

**Chapter 11**

165 "What's gonna happen to us..." *My Husband My Friend*, Neile McQueen Toffel (Atheneum, New York, 1986), 171-2.
166 "...had been to the post too many times..." *Esquire*, October 1970.
166 "He was worried about Redford..." Thomas, *Los Angeles Times*, op. cit.
166 "I just didn't want to be there..." Luckinbill, op. cit.
167 "I saw a lot of kids..." Robert Wise interview.
167 "...because there's something sadder..." Aljean Harmetz, *New York Times*, 24 January 1971.
167 Paul Newman arrived for lunch ... Toffel, op. cit., 159.
168 "We had reason to believe..." David Brown interview.
168 He demanded top billing ... Toffel, op. cit., 175.
169 George Roy Hill was delighted ... Luckinbill, op. cit.
169 "Can you play Sundance..." *Entertainment World*, 4 March 1970.
169 "Nobody wanted Redford in the movie..." Luckinbill, op. cit.
169 "It's hard to recall..." David Brown interview.
170 "I remember thinking it was terrific..." Craig Modderno interview.
170 "I owe him..." Luckinbill, op. cit.
171 "Never before in our careers..." Richard Zanuck interview, November 1982.
172 Roman Polanski had been uninterested ... *Roman By Polanski*, Roman Polanski (William Morrow and Co., New York, 1984), 268: "For all his exceptional talent, Jack's faintly rakish and sinister appearance disqualified him from the role of an upstanding, clean-cut, conventionally handsome young actor."
172 Now here he was hanging around ... *The Joker's Wild — The Autobiography of Jack Nicholson*, John Parker (Anaya Publishers, London, 1991), 89.
173 "I was sure they had a hit..." *How I Made a Hundred Movies in Hollywood and Never Lost a Dime*, Roger Corman with Jim Jerome (Random House, New York, 1990), 157.

174 "Look, you can say a guy..." Ross Wetzsteon, the *Village Voice*, 30 May 1977.
175 "If the other guy is not Jack Nicholson..." Kenneth Turan, the *New York Times*, 1 October 1985.
175 "I could not go on playing 35-year-olds..." Parker, op. cit., 135.
176 "I was an idiot..." Kenneth Turan, op. cit.
176 "I'm not someone people come up to..." Joyce Haber, the *Los Angeles Times*, 19 March 1972.
176 Certainly he was the last person ... *Hurricane Billy — The Stormy Life and Films of William Friedkin*, Nat Segaloff (William Morrow and Co., New York, 1990), 112.
176 "A big, slobbering fat guy..." ibid.
176 "In the action stuff he was great..." Hunter, op. cit., 69.
176 "It was clear that..." Segaloff, op. cit., 112.
176 "You won't believe this..." Haber, op. cit.
178 "It seemed like a chance..." Hunter, op. cit., 72.
178 "I can't stand the guy up there..." Haber, op. cit.

**Chapter 12**

179 "Marlon was as dead..." Lawrence Grobel, *Movieline*, August 1993.
179 "He's an extraordinary, amazing actor..." Grobel, op. cit. (*Hustons*), 581.
180 ... Danny Thomas saying he wanted to play ... *Francis Ford Coppola*, Jean Paul Chaillett & Elizabeth Vincent (translated from the French by Denise Raab Jacobs), (St. Martin's Press, New York, 1984), 33.
180 Peter Bart ... suggested a 30-year-old filmmaker ... *Francis Ford Coppola*, Robert K. Johnson, (Twayne Publishers, Boston, 1977), 97.
181 "Bob ... they're going to throw you off..." Grobel, *Movieline*.
181 "...it was a popular sensational novel..." Johnson, op. cit., 97.
181 "What should I do..." ibid., 98.
181 "I must have interviewed..." ibid.
182 "As president of Paramount Pictures..." Chaillett & Vincent, op. cit., 34.
182 " ... who would inspire..." Johnson, op. cit., 99.
182 "Let's videotape it..." ibid., 100.
183 "It was fantastic..." ibid.
184 "He was the type..." Grobel, *Movieline*.
184 "Pacino's a self-destructive bastard..." Johnson, op. cit., 101.
184 "We didn't speak much..." Grobel, *Movieline*.
184 MGM filed a complaint ... *Hollywood Reporter*, 3 November 1971.
185 "I paid the lawyers..." Mark Sufrin, *Saga*, January 1975.
185 Carl Gottlieb was sitting at home ... Carl Gottlieb interview, 15 May 1993.
185 "*Moby Dick* meets *Enemy of the People*..." ibid.

186 "Close isn't close enough..." David Brown interview.
189 Robert De Niro moved from New York ... Robert Adams Sloan, *Los Angeles Herald Examiner*, 17 June 1975.
189 Simon's script ... was said to be based ... Judy Klemesrud, *Los Angeles Times*, 5 October 1975.
192 "studios would not finance a film about the war..." *Hearts of Darkness: A Filmmaker's Apocalypse*, 96-minute documentary, directed by Fax Bahr, George Hickenlooper, 1991.
192 In November of 1975,Coppola called Steve McQueen ... *Notes on the Making of Apocalypse Now*, Eleanor Coppola, Limelight Editions, New York, 1979), 11.
193 "Trust me," Coppola said to Pacino ... ibid., 13.
193 "The problem is not really actors like Steve McQueen..." Mary Murphy, *Los Angeles Times*, 9 February 1976.
194 He picked Harvey Keitel ... *Box Office*, 5 April 1976.
194 Coppola looked at a rough assemblage ... Coppola, op. cit., 34.
195 "We bit the bullet..." *Hearts of Darkness* documentary.
195 "His reaction was a mixture of shock and fury..." Joseph McBride, *Variety*, 19 April 1976.
195 "I wanted to make that movie..." *Interview*, August 1990.
196 ... and he agreed to play Willard ... *Variety*, 27 April 1976.
196 "It's like a great war..." *Hearts of Darkness* documentary.
196 "He was already heavy when I hired him..." ibid.

**Chapter 13**

198 "They thought I acted the part well..." Kevin Thomas, *Los Angeles Times*, 29 September 1976.
198 ... attracted the attention of casting director Lynn Stalmaster ... ibid.
198 "I don't think Stigwood would have..." *New York Times*, 11 December 1977.
198 "Baby ... you're going to be great..." Tom Burke, *Rolling Stone*, 15 June 1978.
200 "Everyone has a right to say..." Mikki Dorsey, *US*, 19 August 1980.
201 In pursuit of that sophistication ... *New York*, 6 November 1978.
201 "When I first read the script..." Ben Porter, *Moviegoer* (United Kingdom), November 1980.
202 Jerry Bruckheimer ... discovered on a Friday night ... Jerry Bruckheimer interview, 2 March 1993.
202 Robert Redford said it would take ... the *Los Angeles Times*, 15 January 1977.
202 "If we had cast a well-known star..." *Superman* production notes, 1978.
203 "He turned us down..." Bruckheimer interview.
203 Paul Schrader later said ... Fiona Lewis, *Los Angeles Times*, 15 April 1979.

203 "We sent Ed Limato..." Bruckheimer interview.
204 Director Taylor Hackford was after him ... *Continental Cablevision*, Craig Modderno, 1982.
204 "certainly one of the two or three best experiences..." David Rensin, *US*, 30 April 1990.

**Chapter 14**

208 ... Joan Singleton was a secretary ... Joan Singleton interview, 21 November 1991.
208 "You don't know anything about scripts..." ibid.
209 "I thought what if I..." *People*, 11 July 1988.
214 "He was the number one choice..." Pat H. Broeske, *Los Angeles Times*, 27 October 1985.
214 He was impressed by Marlon Brando's appearance ... Lawrence Linderman, *Playboy*, September 1978.
215 The way Stallone would describe it ... ibid.
216 The car Sylvester Stallone got ... ibid.
217 "The original Rambo was so bloodthirsty..." Broeske, op. cit.
217 "He gave us the character..." ibid.
220 "The focus they took..." Joan Singleton interview.
222 The genesis of *Beverly Hills Cop* ... Don Simpson interview, 2 March 1993.
222 "...the Baby Face Nelson of Anchorage..." Dale Pollack, *Los Angeles Times*, 18 November 1984.
223 "With all due respect to *Beverly Hills Cop*..." Mickey Rourke, Jerry Stahl, *Playboy*, February 1987.
224 "In the midst of this, 'Saturday Night Live'..." Don Simpson interview.
224 "This kid has instincts..." Bill Zebme, *Rolling Stone*, 24 August 1989.
225 "It was wild..." Eddie Murphy interview, December, 1989.
225 "All of a sudden, I'm hot..." ibid.
225 "*48 HRS.* is the most imitated movie..." David Rensin, *Playboy*, February 1990.
226 "It's interesting in terms of hindsight..." Don Simpson interview.
226 "Whoever's gonna give me the most lucrative deal..." Rensin, op. cit.

**Chapter 15**

227 In 1972, Mike Fenton ... Mike Fenton interview, 20 November 1992.
228 "It was the first time..." *Bantha Tracks* — Newsletter of the Official Star Wars Fan Club, 1980.
229 "Listen kid, let me tell you a story..." Roderick Mann, *Los Angeles Times*, 6 September 1981.
230 "I knew he was going to be a star..." *Vanity Fair*, August 1990.
230 "I was told they wanted me to do the part..." *Skywalking: the Life and Films of George Lucas*, Dale Pollack (Harmony Books, New York, 1983), 151–2.
231 ... he turned down *Butch and Sundance: the Early Days* ... Gregg Kilday, the *Los Angeles Times*, 14 December 1977.

231 On the day before Thanksgiving ... Mike Fenton interview.
232 "We wanted an unknown originally..." *Raiders of the Lost Ark* souvenir book, 1981.
233 "I got real melancholy..." Stu Schreiberg, *USA Weekend*, 22 November 1987.
233 "They knew where to find me..." Pollack, op. cit., 226.
234 ... thinking how nice it would be to some day work ... Michael J.Fox interview, 30 May 1985.
235 "What did we know..." Eric Stoltz interview, 7 March 1993.
235 "I made a very serious casting error..." Robert Zemeckis interview, 5 June 1985.
235 "It is such a fickle business..." Stoltz interview.
235 One night he went over to watch the taping of a new series ... Michael J. Fox interview.
236 "Maybe I'm a fool..." Jack Mathews, *Los Angeles Times*, 14 June 1985.

**Chapter 16**

238 Kevin Costner was confident ... Kevin Costner interview, 20 January 1987.
239 "If I make it big..." ibid.
239 "He never had a part in a major movie..." Ellen Stern, *GQ*, May 1987.
240 "Two years from now..." Costner interview.
240 "He was wearing a bomber jacket and air force shades..." *A Pound of Flesh — Perilous Tales of How to Produce Movies in Hollywood*, Art Linson (Grove Press, New York, 1993), 126.
241 "Kev, what's the matter..." Fred Schruers, *Rolling Stone*, 29 November 1990.
241 "He was worried..." Linson, op. cit., 127.
242 "You know I went to the movies..." Costner interview.
243 "She did not want to do the sex scenes..." Roald Rynning, *Empire*, January 1993.
243 "I'm surprised that people did not recognize..." ibid.
244 "Nobody trades people like ballplayers..." David Brown interview.
245 "Today, the desire to see the stars..." Mike Fenton interview.

**Chapter 17**

246 "I'll be back..." Arnold Schwarzenegger interview, 12 June 1993.
247 ... as he sat in his trailer ... Schwarzenegger interview, 20 March 1993.
248 What would always amaze ... Zak Penn interview, 17 August 1993.
248 "It's like if you plan a dinner party..." ibid.
249 "He wears this enormous fortune..." Nancy Griffin, *Premiere*, June 1993.
249 "the business of getting into business..." ibid.

250 "It had a wonderful first act..." Aljean Harmetz, *New York Times*, 30 May 1993.
250 "Having a kid" Griffin, op. cit.
250 "I thought he was a good guy..." Penn interview.
251 "Never change..." Benjamin Svetkey, *Entertainment Weekly*, 11 June 1992.
252 ... and Goldman was persuaded ... Harmetz, op. cit.
252 "Goldman gave Arnold a character to play..." ibid.
252 "This is a softer movie..." Schwarzenegger interview, March.
253 "My wife says I'm more relaxed..." ibid.
253 "When you have Arnold..." Griffin, op. cit.
254 Zak Penn and Adam Leff had been to the set ... Penn interview.
254 The first inkling that something was amiss ... Terry Pristin, *Los Angeles Times*, 30 June 1993.
255 "They did reshoots..." Svetkey, op. cit.
255 "Every movie I've ever done..." ibid.
255 Canton was said to be increasingly furious ... Alan Citron, *Los Angeles Times*, 18 June 1993.
257 "We feel great about the opening..." Bernard Weinraub, *New York Times*, Tuesday, 22 June 1993.

**Chapter 18**

261 ... the script by Jeff McGuire ... Bernard Weinraub, *New York Times*, Tuesday 20 July 1993.
262 "Far more than Stallone or Schwarzenegger..." David Halberstam, *Vanity Fair*, July 1993.
262 ... Kopelson did not have Ford in mind ... Arnold Kopelson interview, 3 June 1993.
263 Dissatisfied by the ease ... Patrick Pacheco, *New York Times*, 5 April 1992.
263 "Here's this guy..." ibid.
264 "Baldwin would later grumble..." Alex Witchel, *New York Times*, 20 May 1992.
265 "The day things fell apart..." Pacheco, op. cit.
265 "The deal dragged on and on..." Witchel, op. cit.
265 "With the movies..." ibid.
265 ... Kopelson still favored ... Kopelson interview.
266 Ford later claimed ... Halberstam, op. cit.
266 "Harrison Ford opens movies..." Kopelson interview.
266 "I discussed it with Al..." Martin Bregman interview, 4 September 1993.

**Chapter 19**

269 "She does a lot of flirting..." Kevin Sessums, *Vanity Fair*, April 1993.
271 ... according to the Screen Actors Guild ... Richard Corliss, *Time*, 18 February 1991.
271 "When I think of all the money..." *US*, November 1993.
271 "I want stardom..." Stephen Rebello, *Movieline*, February 1993.

271 "I've always had to fight for the movies..." *Premiere*, Fred Schruers, March 1991.
272 Orion acquired the project because Hackman ... *Variety*, 12 December 1988.
273 "Gene's decided he doesn't want to work..." Martin A. Grove, *Hollywood Reporter*, 15 January 1992.
273 "He always gets cold feet..." Liz Smith, *Los Angeles Times*, 7 July 1989.
274 "Most of my movies..." *Rolling Stone*, 3 September 1992.
274 "Michelle read it..." *Rolling Stone*, 21 March 1991.
274 A writer interviewing her ... Tracy Young, *Vogue*, February 1991.
275 "I just won an Academy Award..." Schruers, op. cit.
275 Hopkins, not particularly aware of the book ... *The Authorized Biography of Anthony Hopkins*, Quentin Falk (Interlink Books, New York, 1993), 172–3
276 ... was to cast Goldie Hawn as Thelma and Meryl Streep as Louise ... *People*, 26 February 1990.
277 "We weren't available right then..." Goldie Hawn interview, May 1992.
277 Tootsie was one of the first auditions ... *Premiere: Women In Hollywood*, special issue 1993.
277 "Fat chance..." *Playboy*, October 1989.
278 "In the interview I was very impressed..." Judith Michaelson, *Los Angeles Times*, 12 May 1991.
278 "Michelle obviously had read the script..." Michaelson, op. cit.
279 "We were serious..." ibid.
279 "She was the girl who almost always said no..." *The Club Rules: Power, Money, Sex, and Fear — How It Works in Hollywood*, Paul Rosenfield (Warner Books, New York, 1992), 179.
279 "How would Michelle do it?" ibid.
280 "That role really put Michelle out there..." Nancy Collins, *Vanity Fair*, October 1990.
280 "I can't remember a time..." Rosenfield, op. cit., 179.
280 "The shit was hitting the fan..." ibid., 183.
281 "I wouldn't fuck her..." ibid.
281 "People feel she's talented..." Collins, op. cit.
281 Penny Marshall saw the PBS documentary ... Martin A. Grove, *Hollywood Reporter*, 24 August 1992.
281 "That was my fatal error..." Elaine Dutka, *Los Angeles Times*, 9 June 1991.
282 "It was like being kicked in the stomach..." *Newsweek*, May, 1988.
282 Columbia became concerned ... Andrea King, *Hollywood Reporter*, 18 June 1991.
282 ... when the pop singer Madonna ... *Variety*, 7 June 1991.
283 "Debra was so wrong..." *Madonna Unauthorized*, Christopher Anderson, (Simon and Schuster, New York, 1991), 328.

283 "She's been prevented..." King, op. cit.
283 "It hurts when a project..." Tom Robbins, *Esquire*, February 1993.
284 "Here was this terrific, funny role..." Ryan Murphy, *Entertainment Weekly*, 19 March 1993.
285 "It was clearly evident from her first reading..." Paul Schiff interview, 17 November 1993.
285 ... that there was a scheduling conflict ... Anita M. Busch, *Variety*, 5 January 1993.
286 "I'm just grateful..." ibid.
286 "What struck me..." Rebello, op. cit.
287 "I kept saying..." ibid.
287 "We decided if you put two..." Peter Biskind, *Premiere*, January 1993.
287 "She had all the qualities..." ibid.
288 "It was a scene where David and Diana..." Adrian Lyne interview, 20 February 1993.
288 "The most 'out there' I've gone..." Rebello, op. cit.

**Chapter 20**

290 "We had actors coming out of the woodwork..." *Dramalogue*, 24–30 June 1993.
290 The script had come to Roberts ... *Variety*, 24 March 1992.
291 "Julia was too young..." *Dramalogue*, op. cit.
291 ... She was spotted walking along Columbus Avenue ... Elaine Dutka, *Los Angeles Times*, 9 June 1991.
292 "If you touched it..." James Kaplan, *Rolling Stone*, 12 January 1989.
292 "a rear end so dramatic..." Alan Richman, *GQ*, December 1989.
293 In April of 1987 it was announced ... *Variety*, 4 April 1989.
293 "I had roughly ten lines..." Craig Modderno, *Los Angeles Times*, 23 July 1987.
294 "I desperately wanted Meg..." Stephen Rebello, *Movieline*, July 1993.
294 "Something about her makes you care..." Dutka, op. cit.
294 "Herbert has his ideas..." Myra Forsberg, *New York Times*, 18 March 1990.
294 He felt she was not sufficiently trained ... Rebello, op. cit.
295 "They did not believe..." Dutka, op. cit.
295 "... hard to come around when you've fallen in love..." Forsberg, op. cit.
296 "She had difficult scenes..." ibid.
296 "We thought we might be in trouble..." *Time Out*, 10–17 April 1991.
296 "Everything kind of tilted..." Steve Pond, *Rolling Stone*, 9 August 1990.
297 ... it was widely rumored ... *Variety*, 17 July 1991.
298 "It was smart of her to take time off..." *US*, February 1992.

# INDEX

## PHOTOGRAPHY CREDITS

Page 64A–64H
  Courtesy of the Academy of Motion Picture Arts and Sciences, Los Angeles, Calif.

Page 160A (top)
  Courtesy of Cinematheque Ontario, Toronto, Ont.

Page 160A (bottom)–160G
  Courtesy of the Academy of Motion Picture Arts and Sciences, Los Angeles, Calif.

Page 160H
  Courtesy of *Marquee* magazine, Toronto, Ont.

Page 256A–256H
  Courtesy of *Marquee* magazine, Toronto, Ont.